Information Engineering for the Advanced Practitioner

WILEY SERIES IN
SOFTWARE ENGINEERING PRACTICE

Series Editors:

Patrick A.V. Hall, *The Open University UK*
Martyn A. Ould, *Praxis Systems plc, UK*
William E. Riddle, *Software Design & Analysis, Inc., USA*

Fletcher J. Buckley • Implementing Software Engineering
  Practices

John J. Marciniak and Donald J. Reifer
    • Software Acquisition Management

John S. Hares • SSADM for the Advanced Practitioner

Martyn A. Ould • Strategies for Software Engineering
    The Management of Risk and Quality

David P. Youll • Making Software Development Visible
    Effective Project Control

Charles P. Hollocker • Software Reviews and Audits
  Handbook

Robert Laurence Baber • Error-free Software
      Know-how and Know-why of Program
      Correctness

Charles R. Symons • Software Sizing and Estimating
      MkII FPA (Function Point Analysis)

John S. Hares • Information Engineering for the Advanced
  Practitioner

Information Engineering for the Advanced Practitioner

John S. Hares

Principal Consultant
SEMA Group UK Ltd

JOHN WILEY & SONS
Chichester · New York · Brisbane · Toronto · Singapore

Other Wiley Editorial Offices

John Wiley & Sons, Inc., 605 Third Avenue,
New York, NY 10158-0012, USA

Jacaranda Wiley Ltd, G.P.O. Box 859, Brisbane,
Queensland 4001, Australia

John Wiley & Sons (Canada) Ltd, 22 Worcester Road,
Rexdale, Ontario M9W 1L1, Canada

John Wiley & Sons (SEA) Pte Ltd, 37 Jalan Pemimpin #05-04,
Block B, Union Industrial Building, Singapore 2057

Library of Congress Cataloging-in-Publication Data:

Hares, John S.
    Information engineering for the advanced practitioner / John S.
Hares.
        p.   cm. — (Wiley series in software engineering practice)
    Includes index.
    ISBN 0 471 92810 0
    1. Electronic data processing—Structured techniques.   2. Computer
software—Development.   I. Title.   II. Series.
QA76.9.S84H37   1992
005.1—dc20   91-24276
                                                          CIP

A catalogue record for this book is available from the British Library.

Typeset in 10/12pt Palatino from author's disks by Text Processing Deptartment,
John Wiley & Sons Ltd, Chichester
Printed in Great Britain by Biddles Ltd, Guildford and King's Lynn

This book is dedicated to my sister Buff—by order!

CONTENTS

FOREWORD

With the possible exception of the Yourdon structured method, Information Engineering is the only non-governmentally backed structured method to have gained universal acceptance, and its dominance is increasing. Furthermore Information Engineering has a much wider scope than Yourdon. Indeed, it can be said with some conviction that it is the only "cradle to grave" structured method, covering information system strategy to system development. It has achieved the Midas touch in terms of market penetration and practitioner's respect on the basis of merit. Information Engineering has won its spurs, and deservedly so.

This book is designed for the experienced practitioner of the method. The reader will not learn Information Engineering from this book. It seeks to offer advice in two respects:

- on "tricks of the practitioner's trade" to take advantage of the strengths and overcome its weaknesses. Weaknesses are inevitable—there is no such thing as the perfect product;

- to show how Information Engineering can be used without change, only addition, for the data processing environments for which it was not initially designed. These environments are distributed, realtime, conversational, expert system and object oriented processing.

JOHN HARES
Ascot 1991

ACKNOWLEDGEMENTS

Few books are the work of only one person. Although the written material is the work of the author and relects his ideas and experiences, much valuable advice and assistance has been received from numerous colleagues and associates.

The author would like to thank James Martin and Associates (JMA) and Ernst & Young for freely giving all possible assistance in the preparation of this book, in particular the loan of manuals. On a personal level, my thanks go to Ian Macdonald, Technical Director of JMA, and to John Parkinson and my old room-mate Bob Philips, both of Ernst & Young, for their helpful comments on the draft material. Thanks are also extended to Mark Thomas of Ernst & Young for his valuable assistance regarding expert systems and the STAGES method. It is a pleasure to work with former colleagues.

I am also indebted to my colleague John Smart for his significant contribution to the chapter on object orientation, in particular for his advice on function name overloading, polymorphism and genericity. I am likewise grateful to Mike Banahan of The Instruction Set for the use of his material on object encapsulation.

Oracle Inc have kindly agreed to the use of SQL*FORMS for the illustration of an object oriented like man/machine interface. Learmonth & Burchett Management Systems Ltd have similarly allowed the use of parts of their structured method in such areas as dialogue design.

To all the above the author repeats his thanks.

1

INFORMATION ENGINEERING— ITS PAST, CURRENT AND FUTURE POSITION IN THE STRUCTURED DESIGN AND DEVELOPMENT METHODS INDUSTRY

1.1 THE BASIS AND PURPOSE OF THIS BOOK

This book is an assessment of the Information Engineering structured method and how it can be applied more effectively and more widely by experienced practitioners. The book:

- provides an independent and practical assessment of the strengths and weaknesses of Information Engineering;

- provides "pearls of practical wisdom" advice regarding "tricks of the practitioner's trade" that can be applied to the existing Information Engineering strategy, design and development techniques, procedures and standards;

- provides new and additional techniques where, in the author's opinion, Information Engineering requires enhancement;

- shows how Information Engineering can be used without change, only enhancement by addition, for new and additional data processing environments for which it is not currently targeted, namely the distributed, realtime, expert systems, object oriented and conversational environments;

- compares Information Engineering, where appropriate, to other competing structured methods;

- reviews its current and likely future position in the structured methods market place.

This book is therefore targeted towards:

- experienced practitioners of Information Engineering;

- those practitioners who wish to enhance the method so that it can be used to design application systems requiring distributed, realtime, expert system, object oriented or conversational processing.

The assessment is not yet another rewrite of Information Engineering. The reader will not learn the method from this book. It is assumed that the reader has not only a good theoretical understanding of the method, but up to a year of effective practical experience in applying the procedures, techniques and standards. No explanation of Information Engineering technical terms is provided. It is also assumed the reader has a reasonable understanding of database technology.

The book is targeted to the procedures and, in particular, the techniques for information systems strategy and the logical and physical design of computer systems. It does not address other associated aspects, such as project management, software package selection, contract negotiation and integration and quality management.

The book is the author's opinion of Information Engineering, its strengths and weaknesses, where and how it can be improved and how it can be extended to support additional data processing environments. Some may find the results controversial. All of the suggestions concerning enhancements to the existing techniques, additions of new techniques, "pearls of practical wisdom" in applying these techniques and in the application of the method in data processing environments for which it is not targeted are based on real world experiences. *None of this book is theory.* Each suggestion is supported by one or more examples. Almost all of the examples are themselves based on real world situations encountered by the author in applying information engineering based techniques. The examples have been "pasteurised" to protect client confidentiality. The pasteurisation has been achieved via a process of making the examples *generic to the industry being described*, substantial simplification of and modification to the real world functionality, the addition of extra but realistic functionality to the real world examples and, at times, alterations to the naming conventions used.

While this assessment of Information Engineering is based on the latest versions of the method as suppled by the vendors, the suggestions for the application of and enhancements to the method are appropriate to any future version. This is because the suggestions are generic to designing and developing any information system strategy and subsequent computer applications and, while they are described in the context of Information Engineering, are not specific to a particular version of the method.

There are two ways in which a product, such as a structured method, can be enhanced—by addition or by modification. If a structured method suffers from sins of omission and not from sins of commission, then enhancement by addition should be applied. The benefit of this is that nothing about the method need be unlearned, and the procedures, techniques and standards of the method are preserved. There is therefore no risk to the method in incorporating the enhancements. Only when there are sins of commission should there be enhancement by modification.

Information Engineering suffer from sins of omission and not commission. What is there is well thought out and thorough. Where this book makes suggestions for the enhancement of the method, the enhancements are those of addition. Nowhere is there any enhancement of modification. The readers of this book do not require to unlearn any aspect of Information Engineering.

There are a number of sources for Information Engineering. The two used for this book are the manuals written by James Martin & Associates (JMA) and by Ernst & Young (E & Y). Unfortunately there is no one legal design authority for Information Engineering, as there is for some other methods, in particular those that are from government agencies, such as the Central Computer and Telecommunication Agency for the SSADM method in Great Britain. It could be argued that James Martin, the man rather than the company that bears his name, is the de facto design authority, with the three volume book "Information Engineering" now in hardback from Prentice-Hall as the important reference point. But Mr Martin does not have executive powers to enforce a single standard. Rather one currently speaks of a method as being based on information engineering principles and techniques. This lack of a central authority with enforceable powers has enabled a number of companies to develop and market their own version of an information engineering based method. It will be seen that the versions have significant "variations on an information engineering theme."

The first and currently leading version (certainly as regards longevity and market penetration) is the Information Engineering Method (IEM) from JMA. Ernst & Young released their version of the method in early 1990 under the name Navigator System Series (hereafter called Navigator).

Both versions of Information Engineering are assessed as structured methods in their own right, that is without any consideration of the implications of the integration of the methods with their own CASE tools. The integration of IEM with its IEF CASE tool from Texas Instruments is total and one-for-one. It is noticeable that the IEM manuals make few concessions as regards manual documentation, presumably because it is assumed that the IEF encyclopedia will be used as the diagrammatic and documentary repository. This is in stark contrast with the open architecture approach adopted by Navigator. A tool guideline manual is provided as part of the manual set to demonstrate how a particular tool is used in Navigator. Navigator does not stipulate any one CASE tool. Ernst & Young has chosen the IEW/ADW CASE from Knowledgeware as the closest match to the ideal tool for Navigator, and the first release of the manuals has been written with IEW/ADW in mind. Guidelines for other tools are planned.

While it is virtually inconceivable that any data processing professional would apply Information Engineering without using a CASE tool to record the deliverables, it is entirely valid to assess the method, any method, on a standalone basis. The method drives the CASE tool and not the other way around. The CASE tool is a support tool and only a support tool. This book only considers the method of Information Engineering, it so happens in two versions.

1.2 THE DATA PROCESSING ENVIRONMENTS AND THEIR CONCEPTS, TECHNOLOGIES AND TECHNIQUES

Seven data processing environments can be identified. Two of the environments—centralised and realtime processing—have been long established and are well recognised and identified by widely used and understood terms. A further four—distributed, expert system, neural and object oriented—have been recognised only within the last decade, but will become established during the 1990s. The final environment, that of conversational processing, has been long established but is not often appreciated and seemingly little used in its initial form. It has been enhanced recently with new windowing technology and will, as represented in the new technology, become a standard as regards the man/machine interface. The environments are diagrammatically represented in figure 1.1.

Purists would say that there is a considerable degree of overlap in the scope of and technology used by the seven data processing environments and that any classification on these lines is therefore artificial. The purists are in part right, but any classification, particularly high level, is open to adverse comment. It will be seen that there is, in fact, no overlap between

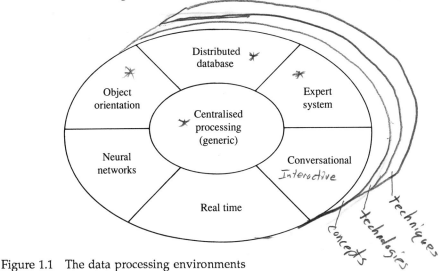

Figure 1.1   The data processing environments

the environments in either scope or technology, except for the one environment that is generic. All the other environments are unique.

It has also been suggested to the author that the word technology be used rather than environment. The author prefers to use environment, because there are underlying concepts that characterise the environments and the supporting technologies. The concepts drive the technologies, not the other way around. The environments are based on concepts and are supported by technologies and techniques. The physical hardware/software technologies are merely tools to do the job the environments seek to provide.

Centralised processing occurs where all data processing is to be executed on a single processor, with remote dumb terminals linked to the processor. The terminals are dumb in that they contain no data processing facilities. The terminals may be spread over a large geographical area, even at multiple sites.

The centralised environment is generic, with its technologies being used by the other data processing environments. The facilities such as the file handler, screen painter, query language and the report writer are all used by these other environments. All these environments contain batch and online processing. They function within a centralised environment. *They are, in fact, nothing more than centralised processing "plus a little bit".* This is because the vendors of the technology for these environments have followed a policy of *using the existing technology of centralised processing without change and adding additional software facilities on top.*

Distributed processing occurs where multiple processors support a set of multi-site application systems, each with a local database. The processors are widely distributed geographically, one to each site, and are linked dynamically, such that the applications and their databases function as a synchronised whole.

Much confusion exists as to the difference between realtime and online processing. The Yourdon method's definition of realtime best identifies the difference. Realtime is defined as "immediate output of current input". This means that, as an input message is received, it is immediately processed in a processor and the output from that process is immediately displayed.

For example, a radar aerial monitoring the movement of aircraft through the sky records the electrical signals received and passes the information to the processor, which then immediately displays the information on a visual display unit. The process may access a standard database to retrieve user data to ascertain, for example, the type of aircraft which matches the signal received. Much realtime data has a limited life-span, even as little as a few seconds. The radar system can discard the signal received after a few revolutions of the aerial if the task of the system is merely to monitor the flight movement of aircraft.

With online processing the output is not the result of immediate input. For example, an online request to display customer's orders may well have been stored in the database for some considerable time. Online processing produces immediate output, but not on the basis of immediate input. Using this realtime quotation for online processing would produce "immediate output of previous input".

Expert systems have the ability to store and access knowledge as well as data. This means that they can represent expertise regarding a particular application domain, for example how to service a car engine or diagnose an illness. Expert systems can therefore be relevant to different types of computer applications from those which have traditionally been developed. They are particularly suited to those applications that require expertise to solve problems. Traditionally data processing has been for those applications where dumb data is presented to users, for them as *homo sapiens* to interpret. Expert systems, by contrast, can offer advice as well as merely present data. They can therefore "assist" and "advise" in such expertise-based tasks as diagnosis, planning, design and interpretation.

Conversational processing is the least clear cut environment. It is an extension of online processing, where a user is requesting immediate response to database access requests. The difference is that the user is having a dialogue conversation with the processor at a terminal and hence requires to monitor previous iterations of the conversation. For example, a user may wish to terminate a conversation but record the state of the conversation, typically as represented by the data currently displayed at the terminal, at the point of the termination for subsequent recall. When the conversation is renewed at a later point in time, the user wishes to recall the state of the conversation, which may have been forgotten, by retrieving the relevant information from the last screen. The application program/system software therefore needs to recognise explicitly that the user requires continuous running iterations of online interactions with the application system, each iteration being represented by one or more screens. This is different from online processing, where the application program switches itself off between output and input screens and the data from the previous screen is lost.

The object oriented environment is a "modernised" version of centralised processing. Until recently all application systems were designed and developed on the basis that data and logic were kept separate—the data in the database and the logic in the application programs. It is now realised that this separation is illogical (after all, both data and logic are information) and inefficient (data has to be moved to the logic), with a raft of other inadequacies and inconsistencies. Object oriented technology has been developed in the database file handlers and application programming languages to bring both types of information together.

Given that object orientation is another form of centralised processing then why has it been treated as another data processing environment? The reason is that, of all the other environments, it is the one that is more than centralised processing plus a little bit. There are, as described in chapter 5, some differences in the technologies and design techniques for those parts that overlap centralised processing.

The neural network environment is not addressed in this book as the author does not have experience of it. It is the ability of computers to learn from the information they are processing. The environment is not considered further.

Each of the data processing environments is based on a set of concepts, technologies and techniques. The concepts are underlying principles that must be supported by the technical facilities of the data processing environment. The best way of describing a concept is by example. A concept for the distributed data processing environment is the concept of location, that data can be spread across multiple locations. The technologies for each environment require to provide a set of facilities that support the concept. There must be facilities that can find the data wherever it is located. The logical and physical design techniques have in turn been developed on the basis of the technologies and the concept. There is no point in having design techniques if there is not the technology to implement the designs and the techniques must include mechanisms to identify the location at which the data is to be located. There is therefore a cascading relationship. The concepts precede and are the basis of the technologies, which precede and are the basis of the techniques. *This relationship of concepts, technologies and techniques is rarely recognised—yet it is the basis of this book.*

The reason for the relationship dependency is easy to explain for the technologies to the techniques. Throughout the history of computing technologies have preceded techniques. The reason is simple. There is no purpose in developing a structured method containing a set of logical and physical design techniques if there is no physical technology to implement the logical design specification. There has been technology to support batch and online processing for the last three decades or more but structured methods with design techniques have only gained wide acceptance in the last 15 years. The time gap between technology and techniques is the same for the other environments. Object oriented technology has been available for the last 5 years, but the techniques are only now appearing.

The relationship of the technology to the concepts has not been addressed before and is more difficult to explain. The way this is done in this book is to explain the concepts and the supporting technologies and point out which concepts are not supported and what technology is therefore required.

The various concepts for each of the environments are described in the subsequent chapters, as are the technical facilities required. Suffice it to say that *if the technology has not been developed to support the concepts then the technology is unstable.* Chapter 5 shows that the technology to support the concepts underlying expert systems is fully and beautifully provided. The author believes that there is thus little improvement to be found in expert systems and that the technology will not change for the foreseeable future. This is in contrast to the technology for distributed databases. Neither of the two concepts are fully supported: for example there is no synchronisation of recovery for hardware across locations. Such technology is therefore unstable. There is much to do for distributed database technology.

What is true of the technology is true of the structured methods containing the logical and physical design techniques. Consider the Yourdon method. It is specifically targeted for realtime processing and explicitly recognises the concepts on which this data processing environment is based. The method was developed in its initial form by Ed Yourdon. The method has been further upgraded by others, such as Ward and Mellor. The author finds the method a delight to apply, with the techniques directly reflecting the concepts underlying realtime systems, and hence relating to each other most attractively and producing a set of excellent integrated deliverables.

The concepts for each of the data processing environments, the related technologies and the appropriate techniques are illustrated in figures 1.2–1.4.

Information Engineering provides design techniques solely for the centralised processing environment. It attempts to support distributed systems by recording the location of data and business requirements, but not only has no techniques to show the significance of the distribution but does not recognise the concepts of location transparency and update synchronisation that underlie distributed systems. Neither does the method

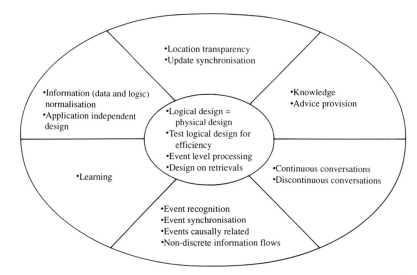

Figure 1.2   The data processing environment concepts

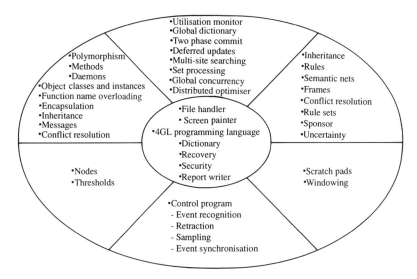

Figure 1.3   The data processing environment technologies

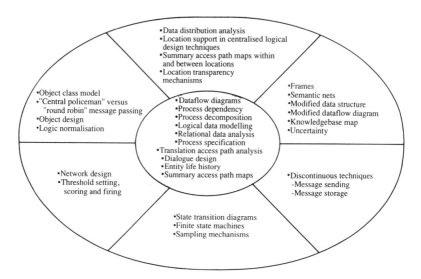

Figure 1.4   The data processing environment techniques

support the concepts appropriate to the other environments, such as event recognition and synchronisation for realtime, logic normalisation for object oriented design and processor interaction recall for conversational processing.

However, all is not lost for these other environments. It will be seen that the Information Engineering techniques, like the data processing environment it supports, are generic to all the data processing environments. *Information Engineering can therefore be used as the core component in these other environments.* The techniques specific to these other environments can be merged with or added to the Information Engineering techniques.

1.3 THE SCOPE OF INFORMATION ENGINEERING

Information Engineering is a structured method for the entire life cycle of computer system applications, i.e. from information system strategy planning to system implementation. Preceding the system strategy phase of the cycle is a business strategy study. This phase is outside the scope of Information Engineering, being strictly the task of senior and board level managers, who develop a business plan to support the overall mission of the company. No consideration of the information requirements of the business plan and the ultimate computer systems needed to support the information requirements is made at this level. This is only begun in the system/information strategy study. Information Engineering is concerned with everything regarding information from the business strategy stage onwards.

The full system life cycle has a number of widely accepted stages—information system strategy study, an optional information technology strategy study, an optional feasibility study, logical design, physical design, development/construction and transition/implementation. (Note that the term "logical design" and not "logical analysis" is used. The reason for this will become clear as the book is read.) Information Engineering supports all of these stages. Unlike some other leading design methods which do not contain strategy and development/implementation stages, Information Engineering cannot be regarded as being "headless" and "tailless".

Although not explicitly recognised in the manuals, Information Engineering is, in fact, focused. The method is currently targeted to batch and online processing in a centralised data processing environment and, notwithstanding the chapters on software packaging, is optimised for the application to be bespoke developed rather than implemented as a package solution.

As indicated, the centralised environment concepts and technologies for which information is targeted are generic. *As the technology of centralised processing is preserved so are the design techniques. Information Engineering is therefore also a generic method,* containing techniques and producing deliverables that are the basis for distributed, realtime, expert system, object oriented and conversational processing. *This is of crucial importance—one need unlearn nothing about Information Engineering when using the method in these new and additional environments.*

In contrast to the comprehensiveness of Information Engineering regarding the scope of the design and development techniques, the IEM (JMA) version of the method does not provide integrated advice or techniques for project management control, quality assurance and software packaging. This is surprising, as JMA have a separate project management method called PACE. There is additional guidance on quality assurance of the strategy/planning and design deliverables to be produced, although no criteria (a process must have one of three triggers—an external entity, time or a system condition, for example) as to what can be regarded as quality deliverables are defined. There is therefore no basis for quality measurement. Navigator integrates project management and software packaging in the structure of the phases and tasks of the method from the outset. It also integrates quality management (incorporating quality assurance and control) as a set of prevention and inspection activities, but again does not define the quality criteria for the deliverables. It has therefore legitimately been argued that Information Engineering is "measureless".

1.4 INFORMATION ENGINEERING STANDARDS

Any structured method can be divided into three sets of standards—structural, technical and documentary. Information Engineering based methods add a fourth, the organisational.

1.4.1 The structural standards

The structural standards are concerned with defining a sequence of stages/phases, each with constituent tasks to follow, techniques to apply and deliverables to produce. The actual application of Information Engineering by analysts/designers is undertaken at the task level.

There are seven stages within the IEM version of Information Engineering, all occurring in sequence, and are they illustrated in figure 1.5. There are four sequential phases in Navigator—Planning, Analysis, Design, Construction and Implementation. All these stages/phases of both versions are concerned with forward engineering, that is identifying the user requirements and then producing the logical and physical designs prior to subsequent development and implementation.

Navigator also recognises the approach through redevelopment engineering to generate "backwards" models of the structure of existing systems, to be integrated at the physical or the logical design level with the development of the required system. Navigator is unique in introducing this phase. The phase is called Evolution.

The first IEM stage is Information Strategy Planning (ISP). ISP is concerned with developing a set of plans/architectures for the design and development of future computer applications that support the business plans of the enterprise. Three architectures are planned—an information architecture, containing high level models of the data and functions of the enterprise and matrices that show their interactions, a business systems architecture showing the different types of probable major systems needed to support the information architecture, and a technical architecture showing the hardware, software and telecommunication environments needed to support the systems architecture. The information architecture is the basis of the input into the Business Area Analysis stage, the business systems architecture is the basis of the input into the Business Systems Design stage, and the technical architecture is the basis of the input into the Technical Design stage.

Following ISP the Business Area Analysis (BAA) stage is concerned with identifying in detail the data (in the form of entity types) and function requirements (in the form of processes) of selected business areas identified

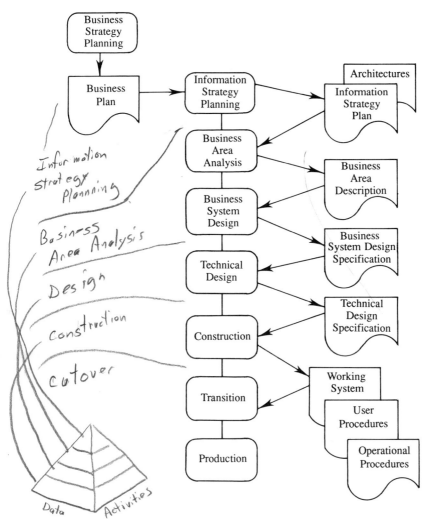

Figure 1.5   Stages and deliverables of Information Engineering

in ISP and ascertaining their interactions (in the form of matrices). It is only concerned with specifying *what* is required in the business areas. The current systems are used as a means of confirming the business area model. At the end of this stage a prioritised and resourced sequence of business areas, each a logically related set of business functions, is defined, with each business area forming the basis of a number of design areas. Each design area becomes the subject of a separate BSD design and development project.

BAA is the major investigation stage, often requiring the bulk of the project work.

The Business System Design (BSD) stage has three prime tasks, the first of which is converting the "what is required" defined in the BAA phase into the "*how* it is to be achieved" (entity types into record types, processes into procedures) for each business system. A generic physical design is produced, that is a design that takes into account constraints that are generic to all computer systems, such as whether a business requirement should be batch or online, but not constraints specific to a particular hardware/software environment, such as the query optimiser facilities of relational file handler X and whether the Y screen painting and programming facilities are integrated or separate. The final task is to design the man/machine interface, with the menu screens for the selection of the business requirements and the transaction screens for the display of the business requirement information.

The Technical Design (TD) stage takes the BSD generic design for a business system and converts it into a refined and codeable physical design specification that meets data storage and response time performance objectives for the chosen hardware/software environment. Each business system is decomposed into a number of design areas, each with a number of implementation areas. TD prepares the data and program design for one or more Construction and Transition implementation projects.

The Construction stage builds the computer systems for a defined implementation area for the business areas and business systems identified and specified in the earlier stages. Databases are established, programs are written and tested and hardware (processors, peripherals and telecommunication lines) is installed.

The Transition stage is the phased replacement of existing system(s) with the new system(s) developed in the previous stage. It is governed by the transition plan, which includes a work plan and resourcing estimates.

The final stage, Production, is not supported by a manual detailing tasks to do and techniques to apply.

Navigator has only four phases, within which there are a number of stages that can occur in sequence or parallel. The Planning phase is similar to the IEM Planning stage but with minor differences. The phase constructs an Enterprise Business Model that delineates the business functions, information needs and organisation to support the strategic business plans and corporate objectives. Statements of principles about information systems are identified and there is more emphasis on the analysis of the current systems. The IS principles, the current information systems assessment and the enterprise model are then used as the basis of the future systems architectures and application master project plans.

There are four architectures within the Enterprise Information Architecture (EIA)—applications, data, technology and management/organisation.

The Analysis phase concentrates on the data and applications components of the planning architecture. It formally identifies business requirements for a business area identified in the Planning phase, performs a "build or buy" analysis and produces a conceptual system design of the proposed business solution for a business area. The conceptual design is logical in that hardware/software issues, be they generic to all application design and development software or specific to particular products, are not considered. The major input into the Analysis phase is the EIA. If there has not been a Planning phase Navigator indicates in the "Definition Route" the essential precursors required for Analysis. The major output is the conceptual system design for an application as detailed in the Business Area Information Model (BAIM). It is a more detailed subset view of the EIA model. Technology and organisational requirements are documented. A business area can contain multiple applications.

In the Design phase the logical conceptual design for an application is progressively translated into a physical design. It is initially developed into a business system design (BSD) and then into a Technical System Design (TSD) to produce a complete specification of the application, including the user interface. The user interface can be prototyped. The BSD takes physical constraints that are generic and universal to all computer systems into account, such as deciding which transactions are online and which are batch. The BSD is then converted into a TSD in that it is designed within the constraints specific to the hardware/software environment on which it will run. The major input is the BAIM. The major output is the BSD and TSD designs, with the appropriate data conversion, test and IS infrastructure designs.

In practice the BSD and TSD phases are iterative, with the BSD phase being "how the users would like the system" and the TSD detailing a list of "can't do items" because of implementation constraints. The two are iteratively compared.

The Construction and Implementation phase builds and tests a working application(s) from the physical specification produced in the Design phase. A full range of procedure manuals are produced and the hardware, software and telecommunications facilities are set up. The phase ends with an evolution plan for the application.

Navigator has introduced the facility of the route map. The routes are designed to cater for different types of projects, such as small projects, projects for which there has been no Planning phase and those requiring fast, time limited development. The map points the user to which parts of the method to use.

1.4.2 The technical standards

In parallel with the stages Information Engineering uses a set of analysis and design techniques. The base techniques and their interrelationships are illustrated in figure 1.6.

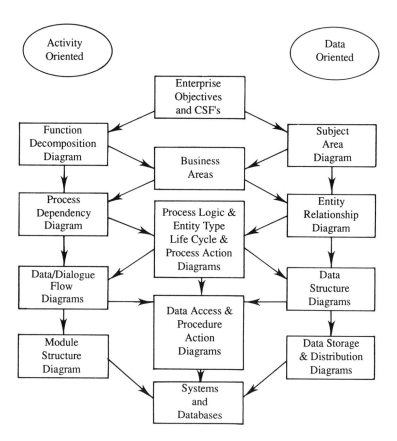

Figure 1.6   Information Engineering techniques

A technique is not necessarily specific to a particular stage. A number of techniques are applied in several stages. This occurs where the deliverable(s) from the technique can be progressively decomposed into more detail as one progresses through the stages. The prime examples of this are the entity relationship data modelling, process decomposition and process dependency techniques of the strategy and analysis stages. The action diagramming technique can also be applied throughout much of Information Engineering, with the analysis logical "what is required" code in the process action diagrams being progressively converted into the physical generic "how it is to be achieved" program design language code in the procedure action diagrams and from there into the physical source code in the application programs.

Other techniques are more specific in the deliverable(s) produced and are to be found applied in only one stage of the method. Entity life cycle analysis is undertaken only in the analysis stage and the man/machine interface is only addressed by the dialogue design and visual layout design techniques in the design stage.

The logical design techniques used by Information Engineering are:

- *Entity relationship modelling*
  This technique builds an entity relationship diagram (ERD) logical data model that supports the business objectives of the company in general terms and of application systems that are developed in particular. The data objects are at the entity or entity sub-type level. The ERD model is primarily built from the definition of the business requirements, particularly from the data retrieval business requirements, but is verified for correctness by the normalisation of the data attributes defined in each entity. In IEM the ERD is constructed in the BAA stage. It is preceded by a subject area model constructed in the ISP stage. This data model is at a higher level of data abstraction with the data objects at the subject area level. The technique is applied in the corresponding Navigator Planning and Analysis phases.

- *Relational data analysis*
  This technique takes the data attributes required by a system and applies a set of rules to reorganise the attributes into the relations/entities to which they sensibly belong. For example, the attributes customer name and customer address belong to the relation customer and order delivery address and delivery date belong to the relation order. The technique is applied in the Navigator Analysis phase and in the IEM BAA stage.

- *Process decomposition*
  The business processes in an enterprise are identified at various levels of abstraction. Within IEM the technique is applied in both the ISP and BAA stages. In the ISP stage the technique identifies and decomposes the processes from the highest level business areas to the function level. In the BAA stage the decomposition is to the process and elementary process levels. Within Navigator the technique is applied in the Planning and Analysis phases.

  Although not stated in the Information Engineering manuals the technique only considers the data maintenance and not the data retrieval business requirements. Look at all the examples of process decompositions in the Information Engineering manuals and all the processes are to do with processes that update the database. Data retrieval business requirements are intrinsically at the event level. They cannot be at the function and business area levels and are therefore not susceptible to the same degree of decomposition.

- *Process dependency*
This technique identifies the sequence in which processes occur. The technique is applied in the IEM ISP and BAA stages. The technique is not applied in Navigator.

Just as there are different level of processes in the process decomposition diagrams, so there are in the process dependency diagrams. For each level of process decomposition diagram there can be a comparable level of process dependency diagram. Again, like the process decomposition diagrams the process dependency diagrams are concerned only with processes that update the database. Data retrieval business requirements are intrinsically standalone and are not in any sequence with other data retrieval business requirements. Only data maintenance business requirements need to be sequenced. The process "Create customer" must occur before the process "Receive order".

- *Dataflow diagrams*
Dataflow diagrams incorporate all of what is supported in the process decomposition diagrams, but are also able to show additional information. This additional information is the flow of data around the enterprise, that is between processes and the users of the system(s). The storage of the data is also illustrated. Like the above two techniques concerned with processes, dataflow diagrams only represent, or should only represent, the data maintenance processes. Data only "flows" from state A to state B because it has changed its state by being updated. Dataflow diagrams are drawn in the IEM BSD stage and the Navigator Planning and Analysis phases.

Given that both versions of Information Engineering contain the process decomposition technique it is not surprising that dataflow diagramming is not accorded the same importance as in other structured methods, such as SSADM. Navigator recommends the technique to be applied selectively, to identify the "top" level processes and the bottom elementary processes. What about the middle level of process decomposition? IEM constructs the dataflow diagrams from the process/procedure dependency diagrams. Dataflow diagramming does not seem to be a technique in its own right. And neither Navigator nor IEM show how the technique provides design information that the process decomposition and process dependency diagramming techniques do not. The added value of the technique is not explained.

- *Process logic/data usage/data navigation/access path analysis*
Notwithstanding the various titles, the technique undertakes data access path analysis against the ERD model for chosen transactions/business requirements. Unique among all structured methods the author is familiar with, and much to be recommended, Information Engineering also produces summary access figures of all the transactions. The technique is applied in the IEM BAA and BSD stages and the Navigator Design phase.

- *Involvement analysis*
This is nothing more than recording the type of access against an entity ascertained from the data navigation technique in a matrix of entity by event—entity A is created by event 1, ... The matrices can be used to relate other pairs of dimensions, such as goals versus functions.

- *Entity life cycle analysis*
This technique records the sequence, iteration and selection order in which events update an entity in the ERD model. It is applied in the IEM BAA stage and the Navigator Analysis phase.

- *Action diagrams (process and procedure)*
This is the basis by which the logic of processes identified by the above techniques is documented. A list of operation commands and syntax is defined as a program design language and is used to record the logic. A set of diagramming symbols re-expresses pictographically the types of commands being used. The basic symbols represent the classic process logic constructs of sequence, selection, iteration and branching and the record-at-a-time access logic constructs of read, write, update and delete. The action diagrams are produced in the IEM BAA and BSD stages and the Navigator Analysis and Design phases. In the analysis stage the action diagrams are specified against the process and elementary processes and detail *what* is required of a business requirement. In the design stage the action diagrams are specified against the procedures and procedure steps and detail the logic of *how* it is to be achieved.

- *Information view analysis*
Each process receives input data and produces output data and, while being executed uses database data. This technique records the four types of data views—import, export, entity action and local. The technique is applied in the IEM BAA stage. It seems to be the same as the Navigator entity model view.

- *Data views*
  This technique applies only to Navigator. It is concerned with constructing data interfaces with online and batch procedures. It seems to be similar to entity model views—see below.

- *User view analysis*
  This technique is a pictographic means of representing the relationships between data items. The relationships are the same as those identified when normalising data with the relational data analysis technique. It is officially applied only against the data in the current systems. The technique is applied in the IEM BAA stage. There is no Navigator equivalent technique.

- *Entity model view (Navigator)/Canonical synthesis (IEM)*
  EMVs are graced with the title of technique. The best way to illustrate what an EMV is is to describe what it is. An EMV is the part of the ERD that is used by a process—thus only the entities and attributes accessed by the process are detailed. One can produce the enterprise level ERD by merely combining all the EMVs. The nearest physical equivalent is a Codasyl subschema for an application program.

  The rationale for the EMV is that it is more natural to ask a user about his/her view of the business with which he/she is concerned than with showing the whole ERD logical data model.

  The relational view is not the same as an EMV as it is defined at the user not the process level.

  The "technique" is applied in the Navigator Planning, Analysis and Design phases.

  In IEM all the user views are aggregated to produce an ERD model of the current systems. The technique is applied in the BAA stage.

- *Dialogue flow diagramming/Online conversation design*
  The sequence in which the transaction screens for a procedure or procedure step are represented in this technique. The associated screen processing logic is recorded in the normal procedure/procedure step documentation. The IEM manual makes one small reference to menu screens and Navigator makes no distinction. The menu screens front-end the transaction screens and are the means by which users select the business requirement they wish to trigger and for which the transaction screens are displayed.

  The technique is applied in the Navigator Design phase and the IEM BSD stage.

- *Visual layout design*
  The facilities that are provided for screen design by the database products/teleprocessing monitors are described, as well as a set of

practical tips that should be followed in screen design. The technique is applied in the IEM BSD stage and the Navigator Design phase.

- *Prototyping*
  This facility for designing and developing the data and processes of a computer system is addressed in Navigator. The technical facilities for prototyping, such as the relational file handler, query language and screen painter, are detailed, as is the scope for which the technique can be applied, namely from the Analysis through to the Construction and Implementation phases. Navigator envisages the technique being progressively applied to all the application business data and processes—indeed, prototyping is seen as an alternative to the application of the logical and physical design techniques.

- *Preliminary data design*
  The business area ERD model is converted in the IEM BSD stage into a database design conformant with the data structuring and data access rules of the database file handler to be used for the developed system. Rules are only provided in the IEM version of Information Engineering for the DL/1 file handler and a generic relational database file handler. In Navigator the technique follows logical database design—see below.

- *Database design*
  The preliminary data design of the business area is upgraded in the IEM TD stage to a refined design for an implementation area. The full range of the database file handler facilities are used to optimise data storage and transaction response times. The refined design is implementable and will hopefully meet the transaction response time and data storage objectives. The perceived data structure (the application program view of the database data) is also identified.

  Within Navigator there are two stages to the design of a database. Both are applied in the Design phase. The first design is a "logical" Business System Design (BSD) database of the ERD logical data model, that is a design that takes into account the physical constraints applicable to the type of database file handler being used. Three types are identified: relational, Codasyl/network and hierarchical. The "logical" design is then converted into a physical Technical System Design (TSD) that is based on the specific constraints of the file handler product of the file handler type used for the database.

- *Application program design*
  Advice is provided as to how to convert the procedure and procedure action step action diagrams into application programs and their constituent modules in the form of program structure charts.

- *Performance assessment*
  For each implementation area design the database and accessing transactions are measured to assess their ability to meet storage and response time performance objectives. Where the objectives are not met the database and/or the transactions are modified. The technique is applied in the IEM TD stage and the Navigator Design phase.

In addition to the above set of techniques Information Engineering also provides a set of guidelines/statements of good practice that provide support to the techniques. These guidelines will add value to and enhance the quality of the deliverables produced by the techniques.

- *Interviewing*
  Information Engineering rightly stresses the importance of the interviewing process to establish the user requirements for future and developing computer systems. The interviewing task is therefore carried out in the main investigative stages of Information Engineering, namely the strategy and analysis stages. Advice is provided as to the types of users to be interviewed at each stage, the type of information to be ascertained from them and the means of recording the results.

- *Completeness checking*
  Completeness checking is applied at the end of the analysis and design stages. Its task is to ensure that the business area and business systems models are complete (no processes/procedures have been omitted and there is supporting data) and watertight (all the data is inserted, updated and deleted). The various components of the model are correlated.
  Information Engineering produces probably more matrices that relate any two design objects together than any other structured method the author is familiar with (some 8 methods). Matrices are not design deliverables, but can and are used by Information Engineering to verify that the information recorded in the design deliverables properly cross-refer and correlate to each other, for example that an entity is accessed by processes/procedures that insert, update and delete it. The main type of matrices used in completeness checking are the involvement matrices.

- *Correctness checking/quality*
  Correctness checking confirms the designs created in the analysis and design stages.
  In the Information Engineering analysis stage advice is provided as to how the various deliverables produced by the design techniques should be vetted. For example, the ERD model can be validated by normalising the data items and practical tips are described as to what to look out for

when checking the process dependency diagrams. Each step in the stages and phases have defined quality criteria that must be satisfied.

Correctness checking in the design stage is the nearest that Information Engineering comes to defining a walkthrough procedure/quality assurance function. Advice as to the members of the walkthrough teams and their responsibilities is provided.

- *Cluster analysis*
  Cluster analysis is applied in the IEM BAA stage. The processes that access the same entities are grouped/clustered together. The extent of the relationships of the entities to the processes that maintain them is established by some numerical formula. The greater the relationship value the greater cohesion of the processes. This cohesion can be the basis of identifying business systems to be developed in the next BSD stage of the method.

- *Analysis of problems*
  This is a mechanism in the IEM BAA stage and Navigator Analysis phase for identifying the problems of the current system(s) and tracing their relationship back to the causes in a cause and effect diagram.

1.5 INFORMATION ENGINEERING EVOLUTION AND MARKET PLACE POSITION

The evolution of structured design methods has followed a set of distinct patterns. The streams of evolution are illustrated in figure 1.7. There have been two noticeable and highly successful evolutions, each from a single product into a subsequent stream of products. These two streams are classified by the author as the BIS and James Martin streams. Both have become the basis of a set of subsequent methods, all of which are designed for batch and online processing in a centralised environment. Both streams have seen the development of a structured method that is now established among the market leaders.

BIS is a large software house and consultancy based in the United Kingdom, which developed in the mid 1970s a structured method now called MODUS. Two ex-BIS consultants, Roger Learmonth and Rainer Burchett, set up their own company, Learmonth and Burchett Management Systems (LBMS), and developed an enhanced version of MODUS. The method was eventually called LSDM. Prior to its "baptism" LSDM was chosen by the Central Computing and Telecommunication Agency (CCTA) as the basis for producing the United Kingdom government's standard design method. The method is the Structured System Analysis and Design Method (SSADM). The CCTA is a UK government body and is the design

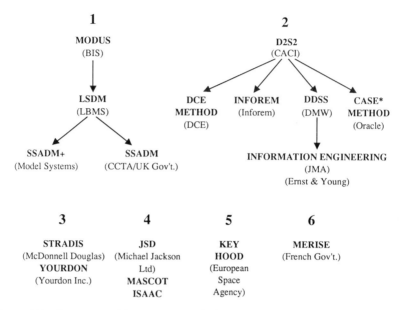

Figure 1.7   Current position—structured design methods

authority for SSADM. SSADM is not an information system or application system development method—it contains, for example, no techniques on critical success factors or program specification. Three senior consultants from LBMS (John Hall, Alan Cooke and Keith Robinson), created a company called Model Systems and developed a structured design and development method, initially called SMDM but now called SSADM+. The "+" indicates the development aspect of the method, which includes techniques and procedures for application programming (in this case based on the ideas of Michael Jackson).

There is a very close "blood" relationship between these methods. If you know one method, then, as far as the procedural standards are concerned, you will have no difficulty in knowing and applying the other methods. There are inevitably differences between the methods, but they are of degree and not of scale. SSADM+ is fully compliant with SSADM. LSDM is not fully compliant, with increasing divergence in techniques and terms. The different diagramming standards for entity life histories and dialogue design are but two examples. All the methods contain the design techniques of data modelling, dataflow diagramming, relational data analysis, entity life histories, dialogue design, process specification, database design and tuning and program specification.

The other major stream is the James Martin stream. The starting point was a publication called "Information Engineering" by James Martin and Clive Finkelstein. This was published as a Savant Research Report in 1981. Subsequently, Finkelstein developed his own version of Information Engineering from his base in Australia, owing little or nothing to the JMA/E & Y school. Similar information engineering based work was being undertaken at CACI, which developed a method called Development of Data Sharing Systems (D2S2), with significant design input from Ian Palmer and Ian Macdonald. Design input to the method was also received from an ex-ICL team of Chris Ellis, David Gradwell and Richard Barker.

CACI is a United States information systems consultancy company, with offices in the United Kingdom and continental Europe, and had the rights to market the ORACLE database product. The ORACLE team left CACI, set up on their own as Oracle Corporation UK Ltd, and used the D2S2 method as the basis for developing the Oracle Development Method, now called CASE*METHOD. A CACI director (Tony Carter) left to create a company, with others, called Doll Martin Worldwide and developed the DDSS method. The similarity of the DDSS title with D2S2 indicates the "blood relationship" of the two methods. Doll Martin World evolved into James Martin Associates and the DDSS method correspondingly evolved into a method which JMA entitled "Information Engineering Method" (information engineering is a term coined by James Martin). IEM is integrated with the IEF (Information Engineering Facility) CASE software support tool from Texas Instruments. The IEM structure was specified by 1982 and in 1983 Texas Instruments funded its development. At the same time James Martin had an active dialogue with DDI (= Database Inc = Knowledgeware). DDI were pursuing a similar methodology philosophy at that time and were in turn working with researchers at the University of Michigan.

At the same time as the above events (early 1980s), James Martin collaborated with the international firm of management consultants Arthur Young (now Ernst & Young) and the software development company Knowledgeware to produce yet another information engineering based method. The definitive method was released in 1990 and is called the Navigator System Series, hereafter called Navigator. There are signs that the information engineering dictionary/encyclopedia support in the Knowledgeware CASE tool IEW/ADW will become a standard, as it is possible that IBM will base their planned Repository for recording logical design specifications in part or in whole on it.

A senior manager from CACI (Keith Greystoke) created, again with others, the Database Consultants Europe consultancy company, which developed and markets the DCE method. Yet other staff hived off from CACI to market the INFOREM company and method. Both of these methods are only loosely part of the information engineering scenario, as the techniques and procedures of both methods are noticeably different from the information engineering base. This could, perhaps, be because of personal influences in the creation of the methods. For example, Rosemary Rock-Evans has played a major role (perhaps *the* major role) in the development of the DCE method. In the European context both methods are small time players. The Inforem company has been bought up by Computer Sciences. The move towards a few small and internationally widely used methods puts these two methods under pressure and one wonders as to their long term survival.

Taken together, these approaches can all be viewed as variants of a generic information engineering method. Although these methods have a common "blood" ancestry, there is a wider degree of variation between these methods than the methods in the SSADM branch. The absence of a design authority for information engineering has not encouraged a common standard. This must be regarded as a deficiency.

The third stream is those methods that have evolved in the United States to play a significant role in Europe. The first is STRADIS (Structured Analysis, Design and Implementation of Information Systems), which is marketed by McDonnell Douglas. STRADIS has an ancient history in structured method terms, evolving from the ideas of early researchers, such as De Marco, Constantine and the husband and wife team of Gane and Sarson. It is designed for batch and online processing in a centralised environment. Yet another early researcher was Ed Yourdon, who developed the Yourdon structured method, this time targeted towards realtime processing.

Of the methods so far described, the two that have gained the most widespread acceptance in the United States are Information Engineering and Yourdon.

Another stream is those methods that have evolved independently of each other in the United Kingdom. The JSD method is a design evolution of the structured programming method JSP from Michael Jackson and is also targeted for realtime processing. In early 1990 Michael Jackson Systems Ltd was taken over by and merged into LBMS. LBMS do not intend to use the JSP programming standards in LSDM, which will continue, like SSADM, to exclude the systems development stage. LBMS plan to release a method incorporating JSP principles called Systems Engineering, specifically for systems development, construction and testing, presumably based on the JSP principles.

MASCOT (Modular Approach to Software Construction, Operation and Test) was developed to satisfy a particular requirement of the United Kingdom's Ministry of Defence for realtime processing. Its essential facilities originated at the Royal Signals and Radar Establishment during the period

1971–1975 from the work undertaken by Ken Jackson and Hugo Simpson. MASCOT uses a much upgraded dataflow diagramming technique.

The ISAAC method evolved in Sweden and is primarily targeted towards process design. It does not yet seem to have penetrated the private sector market very successfully other than in Sweden and, for some reason, in Holland where it has been teamed with SDM.

The two methods in the fifth stream are the KEY method, designed and developed by Dr Basil Barnett, and the HOOD (Hierarchical Object Oriented Design) method developed for the European Space Agency. HOOD resulted from merging Matra's experience on Abstract Machines and Cisi-Ingénérie's experience on Object Oriented Design. The reason why these methods have been mentioned is not because they are successful or widely used, although HOOD shows signs of becoming established, but because they reflect an emphasis on new design techniques for the object oriented environment. All existing methods are based on traditional approaches to computer systems design, namely that data and logic are separate, the data in the database and the logic in the application programs. The move towards combining data and logic is being spearheaded by object oriented design. Many leading industry thinkers consider that object oriented design is the next "leap forward" in the 1990s, in the same way as relational technology was in the 1980s. Object oriented design is considered in chapter 5.

The above consideration of structured methods may give the impression that the only real centres of evolutionary thought and development are the United States and the United Kingdom. This is not the case. Structured methods have also evolved in the continent of Europe. Trends there have, however, been different. Due to the federal system of government in Germany there is no national standard method. DAFNE, KEIN and SDM are de facto national standard methods in Italy, Spain and Holland. Although there has been no French governmental involvement two methods have become established as national standards—RACINES has been designed for information system strategy planning and MERISE has been designed for batch and online processing in a centralised environment. Many would regard MERISE as the French equivalent of SSADM.

The author believes that the future of information engineering based methods to be extremely bright. The author believes that two streams of structured method evolution will triumph over all the others. The two streams are Information Engineering and the proposed Euromethod. Part of the reason for the strong showing of information engineering based methods is the strength of the method in its own right, but another major reason is that IBM has "anointed" the information engineering approach in the probable choice of the information engineering based Knowledgeware CASE tool as the basis of their future repository. It says much for Information Engineering that it is the only privately developed structured method, with the possible exception of the Yourdon method, to provide a major challenge to the government sponsored methods and is, in the author's opinion, the only private method that will sustain that position.

The precise shape and contents of Euromethod are still to be ascertained, but, given the strengths of the national structured methods already in place and widespread use the combining of the national standards in some way should produce a formidable result. The rumours the author has heard is that Euromethod is likely to be a set of standards as regards the content and quality of the deliverables, but not to be a definitive set of techniques by which the deliverables are to be produced. This reflects:

- that there are a number of techniques for producing a design deliverable. For example, in realtime processing one of the requirements is to synchronise asynchronous events. This can be modelled by such techniques as Petri nets, state transition diagrams and finite state machines. There is also a variety of techniques for data modelling, the most widely used being entity modelling and Chen diagramming.

- there is much finance and skill invested in the existing national structured methods. Adopting the rumoured approach will preserve that investment.

It is likely that the other stream methods will survive as second division players, and then only if they tag along with the two leading streams by being compliant to their standards. The battleground is laid out.

2

STRENGTHS AND WEAKNESSES

2.1 THE BASIS OF EVALUATION

Like all structured design methods, Information Engineering does not get "ten out of ten", even for the data processing environment to which it is targeted. The perfect method still does not exist. The strengths and weaknesses of Information Engineering are of two kinds—conceptual and systematic.

Although the design of a computer system is based on a combination of systematic skills, as represented in applying the design techniques, and flair, as represented in the balancing act of trying to reconcile often mutually conflicting aspects of design (flexibility versus performance, for example), it is also based on a set of underlying concepts. Some of the concepts are generic to all seven data processing environments and some are specific to a single environment. The concept of "logical design = physical design" is generic, while the concept of event level processing is specific to batch and online systems, the concept of location specific to distributed systems and the concept of event synchronisation specific to realtime systems, to mention but a few. *Unless the techniques and procedures of a structured design method recognise and reflect these underlying concepts the resultant logical and physical design deliverables will lack an inherent soundness, elegance and rigour.*

Information Engineering is therefore assessed as to its support for these generic concepts and to the concepts specific to the environment for which it was developed, namely centralised batch and online processing. The concepts and techniques appropriate to the other environments for which Information Engineering can be enhanced are addressed in chapters 4 and 5.

Only occasionally will an attempt be made in this chapter to advise as to how to rectify the deficiencies or take advantage of the strengths of Information Engineering. This will be done where the advice can be easily and briefly be described, but without sacrificing detail. The vast bulk of the advice will be presented in chapters 3 to 5.

2.2 DESIGN CONCEPTS FOR INFORMATION ENGINEERING

Some concepts are universally recognised by any student of structured design and development methods and are therefore not addressed—for example the concept that the logical design is the basis of the physical design, a concept explicitly recognised and fully supported by Information Engineering.

2.2.1 Generic concepts

There are certain design concepts that are generic to all data processing environments. They are:

2.2.1.1 Logical = physical

Analysts/designers need to be aware of a fundamental change in the emphasis of designing and developing computer systems. In the past, and all too often currently, systems are designed and developed only at the physical level appropriate to a hardware/software environment by analysts who believe they understand the user requirements because a consultation process has occurred. A design specification is produced and is then manually "handcrafted" into a physical design and coded.

This "seat of the pants" approach is perfectly plausible because it has worked successfully. The trouble is it is outmoded and has produced too many failures. The adoption of structured design techniques to produce a logical design specification independent of hardware/software constraints as the basis of a subsequent physical design is a considerable improvement on the previous approach. It does not, however, go far enough.

The author believes that a statement of truth regarding computer systems design can be made and that this statement, provided a modern file handler, programming language and teleprocessing monitor software are used, will, with one exception, become a law. Modern software does not suffer the design constraints found in early generation products. The statement is *the greater the variation of the physical design from the logical design the greater the inefficiency of the developed system.* This statement can be converted into "logical design = physical design".

This statement is true from the strategic down to individual lines of application program code and for all data processing environments. Examples of the validity of this statement are based on live case studies.

A port authority illustrates the strategic truth in figure 2.1a. The situation is that a downstream container port, built after the Second World War, currently undertakes some 80% share of the business and the upstream port dating from medieval times some 15% share. The head office generates some 5% share. Because of historical factors the allocation of computer resources across these two ports considerably mismatches the volume of business, with the share being some 15% for the container port and 80% for the medieval port. The physical allocation of resources therefore mismatches the logical demand for resources.

The inefficiency that inevitably results is, inter alia, unnecessarily high data communication costs. The container port is constantly issuing remote data access calls to retrieve information about its business from the database at the medieval port, located some 60 kilometres away. Although only some 5% of all business of the container port was with the medieval port logically the computer system was designed physically as if some 75% of the business was with the medieval port. From being an overwhelmingly centralised business the computer system was implemented as being overwhelmingly distributed, with very heavy access to remote data that should have been local—and remote I/O on a wide area network telecommunication line can be up to 100 times more expensive in processor overheads than local I/O to a disk pack!

Early database file handler types, particularly first generation hierarchical and hybrid types, such as IMS from IBM and TOTAL from Cincom Systems, provide numerous examples of inefficiency down to the lines of application code necessary to access the data, because they are unable to support the logical design data requirements on a one-for-one basis in the physical design. One example suffices. The inefficiency is illustrated in figure 2.1b. The figure shows a logical data model that is four levels of hierarchy deep. TOTAL is only able to support a single depth of data hierarchy and therefore requires the physical design technique to squeeze the logically deep hierarchy into a shallow physical network. As one squeezes the vertical logical data structure so one elongates the horizontal physical data structure. Thus, in order to support the logical data model TOTAL requires to create link record types A/B, B/C, C/D and D/E as illustrated.

These record types are solely in the physical design as link records between record types A–E. They contain no user data, support no business requirement and have no meaning to the user. For all accesses to the logical data model that require to access more than one record type it is necessary

(a) Uneven allocation of business and computer resources within port

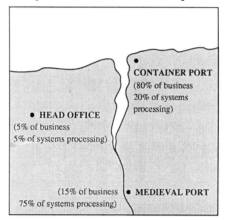

(b) Physical design not equal to logical design

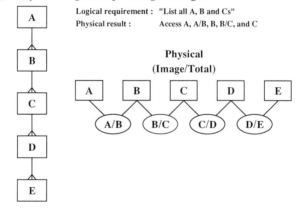

Figure 2.1   Mismatch of logical and physical resources

to access one of the link records. For example, if the business requirement is "For a specified A retrieve all related Bs", it will be necessary at the physical level to access record type A, then to access record type A/B (whatever that is, thinks the user) and then access record type B. The link records not only add extra data maintenance costs whenever a record type A–E is inserted, but also add to data retrieval overheads. There is inefficiency in extra data storage, extra disk I/O to modify and retrieve the link record types, extra database access commands/lines of code in the application programs to access the link record types and higher user learning curves for data that has no meaning.

The author can hear cries of disagreement with the above law. The argument of using data redundancy to increase performance has often been put forward in discussion with many reputable database administrators (DBAs). Even DBAs of modern relational file handlers have argued that it is often worthwhile to store redundant data (derived or duplicated) in non third normal form to increase performance. But consider this. The holding of redundant data in a table to which it doesn't rightly belong (for example, the order delivery date of the latest order received as redundant data inside the customer table) creates "storage anomalies". Figure 2.2 illustrates a number of such anomalies. Here a table is in first normal form. Strictly speaking there should be three third normal form tables—project, person and a link table showing the time that a person has spent on a project.

FNF Relation - Project/Person						
Project Code	Person No.	Name	Grade	Salary Scale	Date Joined	Alloc Time
ABC001	2146	JONES	A1	3	1.11.86	36
ABC001	3145	SMITH	A2	3	2.10.87	36
ABC001	6126	BLACK	B1	9	3.10.87	17
ABC001	1214	BROWN	A2	3	4.10.87	17
ABC001	8191	GREEN	A1	3	1.11.87	12
XYZ002	6142	JACKS	A2	3	1.11.87	5
XYZ002	3169	WHITE	B2	10	2.11.87	5
XYZ002	6145	DEAN	B3	10	14.11.87	3

Figure 2.2   Storage anomalies

By producing a physical design from a table in first rather than third normal form the following inefficiencies occur:

- One cannot insert a person until that person has been allocated to a project.

- Deleting a project also wipes out all associated person data.

- If grade A1 is switched to salary scale 4 it would be necessary to read the entire table and make multiple amendments where only one should be necessary.

The ability to support a logical design on a one-for-one basis in a physical design has effectively only been possible with the advent of second generation Codasyl file handlers, such as IDMS, and even more so with third generation relational file handlers. Such file handlers have no data structure and virtually no data access limitations. The entities and relationships between entities in a logical data model would convert directly into tables and indexes in a relational design. The extra disk I/O and data access commands to support the link record types and storage anomalies would not be incurred. Efficiency would inherently be increased.

A comment has been made to the author that this law does not distinguish between a first cut physical design and a tuned/optimised physical design. The reason for this is that it is not necessary. If the law is followed there is no need for a first cut design to be followed by an optimised design—the physical design is automatically the optimised design. Where the law has been applied it has never been necessary to optimise the physical design.

The one area that the author has found that this law does not apply is with distributed systems. The problem is the cost of sending data messages between sites across wide area network (WAN) telecommunication lines. The cost of accessing a local disk is, depending on the type of file handler and data access call, on average some 5000 path length instructions (PLI) to a single table row in a typical IBM 370 type mainframe processor. The cost of sending a data message across a WAN can, again depending on the network design, be up to 500,000 PLI. This is a difference in PLI costs of a factor of up to 100. It is clearly extremely expensive to send data messages across a WAN network.

The problem of telecommunication costs in a distributed system is further compounded in that, when conducting database concurrency control and updates across multiple sites the updates must be synchronised. The concurrency control mechanism of multi-phase locking involves two remote I/O message pairs between the triggering and the remote sites. The alternative mechanism of transaction timestamping also involves multi-site intercommunication to co-ordinate the timestamps. WAN costs are yet further increased.

As will be described in chapter 4 it may therefore be necessary to break this law of logical design = physical design. Design "tricks of the trade" to "bend" the physical design from the logical requirements may be necessary in order to get any chance of reasonable performance. Examples of how to achieve this using enhancements to the Information Engineering techniques will be described.

Note: the current data access limitations suffered by relational file handlers are mainly concerned with access from the master table to its dependent table row occurrences. Typical access restrictions include being unable to support directly the following kinds of business requirements:

- "For a specified customer list the most recent order". The user and the computer system do not know which is the latest order. With a Codasyl type file handler the detail member record types, in this case the orders, could be stored in receipt date time order and a simple read reverse data access call from the master customer record type to the order record type could be issued. The Codasyl file handler would merely access the last order for the specified customer in the member chain of orders by following the prior direct address pointer contained in the customer record type pointing to the order record type.

- "For a specified customer display the last six orders". The Codasyl file handler type would merely require to issue the read reverse call type six times. The first read reverse would follow the prior pointer from the customer record type to the last order for the specified customer in the member chain of orders. The next five read reverse calls would follow the prior pointer in the order record type and access the member chain backwards.

SQL version 2 includes such Codasyl-like facilities, so to be able to read the detail table rows from a master table in a forward and backward direction. This is via the cursor control facility. Come back Codasyl, all is forgiven!

2.2.1.2 Test logical design for efficiency

This second concept is a corollary of the first. It is based on the simple premise that, given the logical design is the physical design, it makes sense to ensure that the logical design is efficient. The first two concepts combine to produce the conclusion that there should be no need to undertake physical design and optimisation! Much of the design phase could be eliminated.

This is a somewhat radical suggestion in theory but proven in practice. On two major projects all the "pearls of practical wisdom" detailed in chapter 3 to get over the deficiencies of Information Engineering, including testing for logical efficiency, were applied to the techniques for producing the logical design specification. The logical design specification was then used as the direct basis of database and program coding. Using the existing code generation facilities in the CASE tool for these projects the "improved" logical data model (improved because of the "pearls of wisdom") definition in the tool encyclopedia was converted into the SQL data definition language constructs of Create Table and Create Index, with the data attribute definitions becoming the table columns. The action diagrams were handcoded (the application program code generators were just appearing and were at that time regarded with some suspicion), but on a direct translation basis. No physical design was undertaken and no database or program optimisation of any kind was required.

The implications of the law logical = physical are far reaching. Firstly, it is the basis on which code generators work. A syntactically complete logical design specification is produced, a button is pressed and the physical code appropriate to the target hardware/software environment is generated. The problem is that none of the structured methods which are now widely used to produce a logical design specification explicitly recognise this law. They noticeably still produce logical design deliverables which are, in many cases, not complete, *and certainly only ensure that the logical design works* in that it can support the user business requirements, *rather than ensure the logical design works well.*

Given that the logical design should be the direct basis of the physical design it is incumbent to ensure that the logical design is efficient—if it is not then the physical design will *a priori* be inefficient and require optimisation. Currently none of the structured design methods incorporate techniques of ensuring the logical design specifications they produce are efficient. It is not surprising that the experience of those who have used code generators has been disappointing, often with extremely poor transaction response times. In some cases the disappointment has been such that some well known companies have abandoned automatic code generation.

It may be that the inefficiencies are the result of poor code generation facilities. It may also be that the structured design method used does not recognise this law and therefore does not produce efficient logical designs. The sooner the structured methods recognise and practice this law the better. At least then the code generators can be judged on their merits.

2.2.1.3 *Business requirements = events*

A computer system responds to triggers. Triggers can be "fired" in a number of ways. A user can pose a query (Display all customers with red hair) or make an input of data (Insert a customer with red hair). The computer system can also be programmed to fire triggers automatically. For example, the passage of time beyond a certain point requires an output (List month end accounting statistics); a certain condition occurs and the user requires to be informed or some action taken (Stock levels are below a certain threshold, therefore create a re-stocking order). A trigger is fired only because there is a business need to do something. This business need is a business requirement. Each triggering of a business requirement is an event—"do something": display customer, list statistics, re-order stock.

2.2.1.4 Event level processing

This concept is the corollary of the previous concept. A computer system contains application programs that execute logic for a given task to "do something". The application logic is justified, written and executed because there is a business requirement. Business requirements are ultimately re-expressed as physical application programs. Given that business requirements are identified, defined and undertaken at the event level, application programs themselves should also be designed, developed and executed at the event level. Most structured design methods do not explicitly recognise (Yourdon does) that all non realtime processing is at the event level. Certainly the event can be decomposed into sub-processes, as we shall see, but the processing itself is event fired. This simple rule is also in line with the concept of logical = physical.

Events are easy to identify, as they are objective triggers and occur at logically distinct times. The event "create customer" is identifiable and each occurrence of the event is distinct. A user could insert a customer record into a database at, say, 11 o'clock and another at, say, 10 minutes past 11 or .... Event decomposition into sub-processes, by contrast, is a subjective skill. In line with the concept of logical = physical the author uses a "trick of the trade" and decomposes a business requirement event into its constituent problems-to-solve (an elementary process to Information Engineering). Problems-to-solve are more difficult to identify, partly because they all occur at the same point in time as the event and partly because a problem-to-solve can also be, in its own right, an event. Consider the former problem. Problems-to-solve for the event create customer can be to check the customer's input documentation, check the customer's identification and check the customer's credit worthiness. These problem-to-solve tasks must all be executed whenever the create customer event occurs.

Depending on the physical solution adopted the problems-to-solve may take, particularly if computer controlled, less than a minute to complete or may each be several minutes apart if manually undertaken. Nevertheless they all logically occur together with an event. An example of the latter problem could be that the problem-to-solve check customer's credit worthiness could itself be a standalone separate event.

Unlike events, which are distinct and separate in time, problems-to-solve within an event are causally related. This is because they all occur at the same point in time. Problem-to-solve one in an event causes problem-to-solve two to occur causes problem-to-solve *n* to occur *et seq*. For example, validate the customer input document triggers check the customer ID triggers check credit-worthiness.

Following the concept of logical = physical the logical event level business requirements produce physical application programs and the problems-to-solve produce application program modules.

Given the nature of events in batch and online processing, application programs should not, repeat not, talk to each other. Modules yes, programs no. As Yourdon correctly states "programs are schedulable, modules are callable". The scheduling is either ad hoc for online or regular for batch programs. The calling is of modules calling each other as appropriate *within* an application program.

2.2.1.5 *The separation of the logical design from the physical design*

Logical design is concerned with applying a set of techniques to produce a specification of the proposed application system that pays no attention to the constraints of the target hardware/software environment on which the application will run. Physical design is concerned with taking the logical design specification and, using a different set of techniques, "re- expressing" it (not redesigning it given the concept of logical = physical) so that it can run on the target environment. Each set of techniques needs to be applied in one or more stages of the method, stages that are wholly concerned with either logical or physical design, i.e. the logical design techniques in the logical design stages and the physical design techniques in the physical design stages. Unfortunately, as we shall see, some structured methods have intermingled the logical and physical design techniques in a single stage, such that the stage is neither "fish nor fowl", neither logical nor physical design.

A structured method should not intermingle logical design techniques with physical design techniques within the stage of the method. A design stage of the method is either wholly part of logical design or wholly part of physical design. The author would look with suspicion on a method that included within the same stage design techniques that are clearly logical, such as dataflow diagramming, and design techniques that are clearly physical, such as the preliminary design of a DL/1 database.

This seems simple enough. However the world is not so clear cut. It will be seen in the practical case studies used to demonstrate "tricks of the practitioner's trade" that when undertaking logical design it is occasionally necessary to take into account certain physical aspects of computing. The author has found that it is sensible, and indeed most useful, *to take those physical aspects that are generic to computing as permissible considerations when undertaking logical design.* After all the logical design is a generic design appropriate to any hardware/software environment, so why not use generic technology?

Such generic aspects could include, using file handler data storage and access facilities as an example, that direct access to a record occurrence could be by a randomiser or an index. These two facilities are generic to file handlers in general, not specific file handlers. Another generic file handler facility the author is constantly using in logical design is the blocking factor when requiring to access *n* record occurrences. All file handlers transmit record occurrences between disk and processor main memory a page/block at a time. It is necessary to know how many record occurrences/table rows there are in a page/block in order to ascertain whether a scan of an entity in the ERD model is efficient or not. It has been found that when undertaking transaction access path analysis the above generic but very physical facilities are very relevant to logical design. Several examples of using this generic physical technology in logical design are given in chapter 3.

What is not permissible is to consider the physical facilities that are specific to the hardware/software on which the application will run. It is not correct, for example, to take into account when building an ERD data model that the resultant database will be DL/1 and therefore build hierarchically structured ERD models, or, when undertaking transaction access path analysis, to alter the chosen path against the ERD because DL/1 does not necessarily provide an efficient or complete access path as, for example, when accessing directly on a non root segment/record type.

2.2.2 Specific concepts

There are additional concepts specific to batch and online processing in a centralised data processing environment and hence of particular relevance to Information Engineering. They are:

2.2.2.1 Events are standalone

Business requirements/events do not impact on, are distinct from and occur at different times from each other. Such events are not causally related. Event A does not cause event B does not cause C ....

This is particularly the case for data retrieval events. Consider two such events—one to "Display all orders for a specified salesman" and the other to "List the profit and loss by month for the last financial year for a specified account". The first business requirement event could have been triggered at 11 o'clock and the second at twelve o'clock or vice versa or 10 minutes apart or .... Intrinsically data retrieval events are random, standalone and not causally related.

Data maintenance events are similar but require to be sequenced. Consider the events "Accept customer application" and "Receive customer order". They are also random, standalone and not causally related. Accept customer application could occur on 1st January and receive customer order could occur on 2nd January or 31st March or not at all. Accept customer application does not trigger receive customer order. They are however sequenced in that it would make no sense for the event receive customer order to occur before accept customer application.

2.2.2.2 Problems-to-solve are event based and causally related

A business requirement event can be composed of many problems-to-solve, i.e. specific tasks to be done whenever the event occurs. Assume an event "Receive customer order". It is composed of a number of problems-to-solve that must be undertaken before the order can be received—the customer's credit must be checked against the price of the product on order, if the credit is OK then the availability of the product in stock is ascertained, if there is sufficient stock then the stock is allocated and the order quantity decremented, ... All these problems-to-solve are undertaken together at the same time as the event itself is triggered, and in a specific and causally related order, with problem-to-solve one triggering problem-to-solve two triggering problem-to-solve three *et seq*. They are causally related because the cause of all but the first problem-to-solve being triggered is the completion of the preceding problem-to-solve.

2.2.2.3 Database design is based on total data structure and total data access

Figure 2.3 illustrates the basic components of logical and physical design and their relationships. They are relevant to all the data processing environments. In Information Engineering terms the data structure equates to an entity relationship diagram, data access equates to process action/data navigation diagrams and process logic equates to the process action diagrams. Data structure must be accomplished before data access can be undertaken and data access must be accomplished before data process can be undertaken. Data cannot be processed (the constructs of sequence, selection, iteration and branching) until it has been accessed (the record-at-a-time constructs of read, write, update and delete and the set constructs of select, union, intersect, difference and divide). Equally data cannot be accessed until a data structure has been built. Intrinsically, therefore, those structured design methods that are data oriented are more soundly based than those methods that are process oriented. Information Engineering is a data oriented method.

Logical	Physical
Data Structure ⎫ Data Access ⎬ Data Process ⎭	Data Base/File Design Program Design
Message Access	Dialogue Design

Figure 2.3   Logical to physical components

At the physical level a database design must be accomplished before program design can be undertaken, for the same reasons as at the logical level.

The data structure and data access components are the building blocks of database design. Any database designer will tell you that he/she must take these two elements into account when producing the design, the data structure being the static component and the data access being the dynamic component.

This concept is based on the principle of the database. A database is defined as "a single common pool of data which is structured to model the natural data, their relationships and usage which exist in an enterprise". There are two significant points. The database is composed of data that is structured and accessed and, perhaps more importantly, it is a "single common pool" of data "in an enterprise". *Therefore a database is designed for the system as a whole—the total data structure and the total data access.* The database is not designed for individual transactions.

2.2.2.4   *Design the database on data retrieval business requirements*

This is probably the most difficult concept to accept. When users, possibly excepting senior managers, are describing their existing computer systems and new business requirements they are, perhaps unwittingly, mostly talking in terms of data maintenance business requirements. "We have customers who place orders with us for products, for which we allocate stock, make despatches and raise invoices against which we receive payments". In this brief statement the user has identified six data maintenance business requirements—create customer, receive orders, allocate stock, make despatches, raise invoices and receive payment—and at least seven entities—customers, orders, products, stocks, despatches, invoices and payments. A dataflow diagram can be constructed from these business requirements and an entity relationship model can be constructed from the entities and their relationships.

In fact the only reason why this information is recorded is that the enterprise can now control and improve its operations. However, it can only do this if the information can be retrieved. "How many orders are outstanding for customer X?"; "Is the stock level too low for product Y?"; "How many invoices are overdue for payment?". Having retrieved this information action can now be undertaken. *It is the data retrieval business requirements that actually drive the data maintenance business requirements, because it is the retrievals that decide what data is required in the database.* One does not put data into a computer system for the fun of it. One puts it in so as to retrieve it subsequently. Furthermore only when the information is retrieved and presented in a valid form and timely manner to the appropriate user(s) and manager(s) can a computer system be justified.

Clearly, the data maintenance business requirements must be part of the overall system design. The concept of database says so. As business requirements they will ultimately produce database update application programs. As business requirements they generate accesses to the entity model and are therefore part of the overall database design. However, the final entity model should be based on data retrieval and only the data retrieval business requirements.

2.2.2.5 *Business requirements should be CSF and inhibitor based*

Computer systems are developed to support a company's business objectives as defined in the business strategy. These objectives need to be measured so as to ascertain the company's success or otherwise. A widely accepted approach used in most information system strategy methods is John Rockart's critical success factors (CSFs). Rockart analyses the business objectives and for each identifies their CSFs—those critical measurements which, if satisfied, indicate a company's good health. A CSF could be "The proportion of the market our company has captured in the last month for our products/services". Another could be "Has the minimum % of the customer satisfaction been achieved and is the % rising?"

The CSFs are the internal measure of a company's success—the factor that makes life difficult for the company's competitors. But what about the opposite of CSFs, the inhibiting factors that make life difficult for a company—the external inhibitors, namely competitors, and the internal inhibitors, namely bottlenecks? They also need to be identified and recorded in like manner. An external inhibitor could be "The number, quality and price of our competitor(s) product(s)/service(s)". An internal inhibitor could be "The areas of the production process causing holdups".

As defined above, the CSFs and the inhibitors seem innocuous enough—the managers receive reports on their desks detailing the market share by volume and value obtained by their own and competitor companies products/services with explanations as to why their share is going up or down or whatever. That, on the face of it, is the end of it. Not so: behind these usually few and seemingly simple requests for management information is a great mass of supporting raw data. For the two CSFs identified above the information requirements are enormous—the products and services provided by the company and competitor companies, information about their quality and price, the size, type and geographical spread of the market for the product/service, any significant and total orders received this month by the company and competitors by region and type of customer, and the number of customer complaints.... Each CSF and inhibitor can thus describe a substantial part of the database data.

There is yet more to CSFs and inhibitors than voracious information needs. Each level of management requires to identify their CSFs and inhibitors and all management reports are about the measurement and causal explanation of the success or failure to meet an objective(s) as re-expressed in the CSFs and inhibitors. *All management data retrieval business requirements should therefore be reports that are CSF and inhibitor based.* The only business requirements that need not be so based are those for the day-to-day operational running of the company. Yet even these business requirements have their ultimate origins in business objectives and their associated CSFs and inhibitors.

The information to support the management and operational data retrieval business requirements has to be put into the database. Data cannot be retrieved unless it has been previously inserted into the database. This, of course, is only achieved through data maintenance business requirements. It therefore follows that CSFs and inhibitors also form the ultimate source of both types of business requirement. All CSFs and inhibitors thus form the source of a corporation's database, are data retrieval business requirements in their own right, the fathers of other more detailed data retrieval business requirements and hence of all the data maintenance business requirements.

CSFs and inhibitors are an excellent mechanism for tracing company strategy to its implementation.

All information in computer systems should be CSF and inhibitor based.

2.2.2.6 Achieve balance in the emphasis of the techniques

The basic logical and physical components of a computer system illustrated in figure 2.3 can be broken down further. For example, the data access and data process components are actually in two parts—to the message queue for screen dialogue design and to the database for normal data processing in the action diagrams. The relationship of the various Information Engineering design techniques to the more detailed breakdown is illustrated in figure 2.4.

Components	Techniques
• Logical	
- Data Structure	ERD, RDA.
- Data Access (database)	Process logic (data usage/data navigate)
- Data Process	DFD, action diagrams, function decomp, process dependency, etc,
- Message Access	Dialogue flow
• Physical	Data structure design, performance
- Database	assessment
- Programs	Software structure design, program & module design

Figure 2.4   Information Engineering techniques to system components

The point of this concept is that each of these components requires to be specified and designed to an equal degree of thoroughness in both the logical and physical stages of computer systems design. To do this requires techniques of comparable sophistication for each component. Suspicions would be raised if the manual describing a structured design method contained, for example, 250 pages describing techniques for data structure, 10 pages describing techniques for data access and 250 pages describing techniques for data processing.

2.3 INFORMATION ENGINEERING STRENGTHS

The Information Engineering strengths are formidable. They fall into two broad classifications—general and systematic—with the systematic being further broken down into three categories—the conceptual, the structural and the technical.

When assessing the strengths and weaknesses of Information Engineering it has often proved difficult to "pigeon hole" a facility or a technique definitely into a strength or weakness category. For example, the use of semantic descriptions in the ERD technique is a strength, but the use of the facility is not as good as it could be. This part is a weakness. The approach adopted has been to pigeon hole a facility or technique on the basis of the balance of strengths and weaknesses.

2.3.1 The general strengths

The general strengths are those that are applicable to all stages of the method. For Information Engineering they can be summed up as near completeness and thoroughness in the strategy and design techniques. Both assets are related.

The completeness relates to the fact that the method:

2.3.1.1 *is not "headless" or "tailless"*

Information Engineering has a front-end stage concerned with information systems strategy planning with a sequence of logical and physical design stages preceding the back-end stages concerned with application systems development and implementation. Information Engineering is not just a design method.

The thoroughness relates to various factors:

2.3.1.2 *the standards are consistent*

The documentary standards for the deliverables, whether they be diagrams or written documents, are consistent. A process decomposition diagram, a process dependency diagram, or an action diagram is recognisable wherever it is produced, be it in the strategy, analysis and design stages. Indeed a diagramming symbol has the same meaning even when used on different diagram types. For example, the crows foot sign representing the one-to-many cardinality of one object's relationship to another is used in the ERD data model and the process dependency diagrams. The meaning of the symbol, wherever it is used, is preserved. This consistency significantly reduces the learning curve.

2.3.1.3 *the standards are integrated*

The structural, technical and documentary standards are an integrated set, each reinforcing and therefore adding value to the other. While the standards are interrelated their relationships differ. The structural standards define the procedural sequence of tasks in which the techniques and documentary standards should be applied. The technical and documentary standards are more closely related in that they are symbiotic to each other. Some documents, such as the matrices, provide a supporting role to the diagrammatic deliverables from the ERD, process decomposition, process dependency, dataflow diagram, entity life cycle, dialogue design and layout design techniques. Other documents, such as action diagrams, are deliverables in their own right for the non-diagrammatic techniques.

2.3.1.4 *there is "bureaucratic rigour"*

When giving presentations on Information Engineering the author has often been asked to comment on the "bureaucratic nightmare" of the method. The chief complaint is that the method is regarded as being ponderous to apply. Three aspects are constantly raised:

- Why can't the planning stage be optional when certain applications "blindingly obviously" require to be computerised to enable a company to function, some obvious examples being invoicing and payroll? It is argued, with some reason, that such housekeeping type applications have nothing to do with strategy.

- Why is it necessary to analyse the current system(s) before embarking on the logical and physical design of the planned systems?

- The method produces vast quantities of deliverables.

The author has little or no sympathy with any of these criticisms.

One of the main reasons why many computer systems have not provided the benefits anticipated is that all too often they have been developed on a standalone basis and not as part of co-ordinated information system and technology strategy plans supporting a well thought out business plan. The absence of such a plan has been identified in a number of studies as the single most important reason behind much of the disappointment in many of the existing computer systems. This was the prime finding of the Kobler Unit of the Department of Computing at Imperial College in London in their report "Does information technology slow you down?" The report identified that "Investing in IT on a piecemeal basis.... is no guarantee for business success and in fact can slow a company down and hamper its profit performance". It was concluded that a strategy plan for the development of computer systems that supports the business objectives was one of the few factors that correlated to success in information technology.

All applications, of whatever type, be they management reporting, operational or housekeeping, must all be developed and function within the business and resultant information systems strategies. Granted that companies need housekeeping systems, irrespective of whether there is an information systems strategy or not, nevertheless the priority for developing all computer systems for a company can only be established within the framework of an IS strategy. The housekeeping applications must wait their turn along with all the other applications.

Regarding the analysis of the current systems, information engineering does not require that this must be done before undertaking the design of the required systems in the analysis stage. It advises that the current systems be analysed solely as a means of confirming the business area model. As explained in detail in section 2.4.1.3 the author believes that this limited attention to the current systems is inadequate.

The author is a firm believer in making sure that the current system is well documented. The rationale behind the analysis of the current systems is that it provides:

- a firm basis for understanding the current system(s) strengths and weaknesses prior to defining the requirements of the proposed new system. Only by formally identifying the current weaknesses can it be certain that they are properly catered for in the new system. Furthermore the real worth of a new system can only be established if it can be compared against the system it is replacing. This can best be achieved if both are properly specified and documented, preferably to the same standard.

- a clarification of the user's perceptions of his/her problems and requirements.

- a possible springboard for future systems development. It could be that the current system is to be extended or upgraded rather than superseded.

It is essential, not just good practice, to have the current system properly documented. What happens if the new system turns out to be a disaster and the current system has to be resurrected—and there is no record of its capabilities?

Those who criticise Information Engineering for producing vast quantities of deliverables possibly forget that any thorough specification of a computer system, logical or physical, will produce voluminous deliverables. *Given the move towards producing a logical design specification that is the source of direct code generation the specification must be syntactically complete down to the last dot and comma in order to be generatable.* The more the specification is complete logically the less work there should be physically. The production of a logical design is not of itself the means of reducing the work effort or deliverable output.

2.3.1.5 the incorporation of project management guidelines

Both versions of Information Engineering contain guidelines for the conduct and management of computer projects, IEM as a separate manual under a different title/name of PACE and Navigator as a manual in the Navigator set of manuals. This book is not addressing project management and will therefore not consider the topic further.

The stages of Information Engineering can be conventionally divided into three types of "projects". The projects types are based on differing skills requirements.

The strategy stage is one such project type, with the skills appropriate to understanding broad issues of business and information systems strategy, setting priorities, the identification of business systems requiring development and the preparing of information technology plans, all done without going into too much detail about the information that will ultimately become application systems. The "art" of interviewing is also a necessary skill. The strategy project is applied across the company.

The next project type is concerned with producing the logical design for an application. This is done in the analysis and to some degree in the business design stage. The skills for producing a logical design do not require the knowledge of and expertise in the "bits and bytes" of the physical technology of database and application programming, but, given the move towards code generation from the logical design, do require the detailed application of the logical design techniques and the creation of the logical design deliverables to the last "dot and comma" appropriate to physical technology. Interviewing skills are still needed.

The final project type is the physical design and development/implementation of the logical design specification. The skills required are physical technology skills and are traditionally divided into database and application programming.

The boundaries between the strategic, logical and physical projects are not hard and fast. Very experienced persons may have a complete set of techniques (i.e. non-technology) skills spanning both strategy and logical design, and others having a complete set of design skills, spanning both the logical techniques and physical technology. Indeed the widespread use of CASE tools and their use as the logical design specification encyclopedia from which physical code can be generated is making the boundary between the logical and physical design stages increasingly imprecise.

These project types and their different skills means that it will probably be necessary to have a different manager and team members for each project type, but with the flexibility to enable persons to span the "project" boundaries where their skills portfolio is sufficiently wide. Indeed, it is necessary to ensure that for each project type there is at least one project team member who has the skills appropriate to the next project type, so as to ensure continuity in the team for the project stage.

The point of this section is that, because of the different levels of perception and attendant skills for the different stages in the project life cycle, from the broad strategy progressively to the more detailed implementation, it is necessary to have a permanent body sitting above the "hurly burly" of the responsibilities of the various project stage managers. This body is the projects board (sometimes called the steering committee), which is established the moment an application area and the constituent applications that need to be developed are identified from the information system strategy study. It is the responsibility of the board to establish the business and technical direction in which the applications should go. The board therefore contains senior company business and technical directors. It must also contain senior users of the application being developed, so as to ensure the specific application is what the users want. The directors are permanent members of the projects board, whereas the senior user(s) is a member for the duration of the application(s) being developed.

The board as such is not part of project management, and is, regrettably, not recognised in the Navigator project management guidelines, but must be part of the wider management structure, given the crucial role that information technology now plays in the running of company affairs.

2.3.2 The systematic strengths

The systematic Information Engineering strengths are those that relate to particular aspects or techniques of the method. They fall into three categories—the conceptual, the structural and the technical. The concepts relate to those defined at the beginning of this chapter, the structure is the procedural stages, steps and tasks of the method and the techniques are those used by the method for information systems strategy planning and application system design and development.

2.3.2.1 The conceptual strengths

Information Engineering supports more concepts than any of the structured methods the author has used. It is therefore a method founded on sound principles. *The benefit is that the techniques that produce physical design deliverables will require much less tuning when running operationally than those produced by other methods the author has used.* The benefit is significant. The concepts supported are:

1 *Logical = physical*   Information Engineering as defined in IEM is the most impressive structured method the author has used in its ability to

support this important concept, both on the data and the process side. The IEM manual explicitly states that "the database design will follow the ... structure of the business data (the ERD model) as closely as practical.... Only as a last resort is the (database) data structure altered to meet otherwise unattainable performance standards." "The preliminary data(base) structure ... is as similar as possible to the original entity relationship (ERD) model, differing only to conform to the structuring rules of the selected database management system." These statements are merely different ways of saying, certainly as regards data, the logical design = the physical design.

The method also goes a long way to supporting the concept on the process side—"the logic of the ... action diagrams can readily be transformed into executable code." Explicit enough. The method also explicitly encourages a one-for-one mapping of processes and elementary processes into procedures and procedure steps and procedures and procedure steps into application programs and program modules. Notwithstanding the author's dislike of procedures and their "half way house" position between a logical process and a physical application program the principle is established of a direct linear trace from the logical design to the physical implementation as far as the physical technology allows.

Navigator is weaker in supporting this important concept. There is no explicit reference to the need for a one-for-one trace of the logical design to the physical design. There is, unfortunately, no reference in the sections describing database design that the design should be altered from the logical data model "only as a last resort" when performance is not met. It is there, nevertheless, but has to be gleaned from the manuals. For example, the elementary processes become procedures which in turn become application programs.

The position of Ernst & Young is that IEM has it "easy" when it comes to supporting this concept. The only physical target that IEM has to support is DB2/CICS/COBOL2. Navigator cannot be so restrictive— it needs to support other relational and pre-relational environments, such as Oracle and IMS. Hence the logical–physical transformation has to be generalised, with the ERD logical data model requiring to be denormalised to some degree. The author believes this argument to be unnecessary if the logical design specification is efficient. How to ensure this is addressed in chapter 3.

There is a clear understanding in Information Engineering that the logical data structure, data access and data process component parts of a computer system can be specified to a sufficient degree of precision using modern design techniques that they can be the basis of physical design and development. *Note the word basis, not the word source.* "Business Systems Design is based ... on the description of the business area developed by a

Business Area project". "Technical Design is based ... on the design of a business system developed by a Business System Design project".

It is a pity that none of these IEM comments are clear and unambiguous statements of a direct *one-for-one* physical code generation through translation from the logical design specification. By implication further "handcrafting" of the logical design into a physical design will be required.

2   *Database design is based on total data structure and total data access*   This concept is an extension of logical = physical. As stated in the description of this concept in section 2.2.2.3 a database system is based on the total of these two components and therefore designed not for individual transactions but for the application as a whole. If the database supports all applications then the database must be designed for the enterprise as a whole. Databases should not be designed and even less tuned for individual transactions (a controversial statement). People who tune the database design to satisfy the performance of individual critical transactions perhaps fail to realise that a database is like a bowl of spaghetti—pull a spaghetti strand out at one side of the plate and you disturb the other side. A transaction equates to a spaghetti strand. Optimise the database here for a transaction and you degrade it there for another transaction. You never get something for nothing.

Until recently all leading structured methods, including Information Engineering, have not produced summary data access information against the logical data model. Database designers have therefore not been able to see the advantages of ascertaining total data access in the logical design specification. *Information Engineering is the first structured method, as far as the author is aware, that makes any significant attempt to provide summary data access information.*

One administrative but not insignificant point is that these two crucial inputs to database design are combined on one (or at most five) sheets of paper. Secondly, and most importantly, *a balanced database design can now be produced.* It is balanced because it is based on a total data access map drawn on a total data structure diagram that, being combined, automatically and simultaneously *takes these two basic components of database design (see figure 2.3) into account in due proportion to their significance to each other.*

Because total data access is included in the database design no one transaction is favoured, no one transaction is excluded. Each transaction is automatically given its appropriate significance in the total design, based on its proportion of access to each entity. If one transaction incurs 50% of the database accesses logically, this will be directly reflected in the physical design. Transactions are therefore automatically given their due significance in the overall application performance. *Balanced designs are a priori efficient.*

This is proved in section 3.1.4. Wherever and whenever the author has applied this concept application/enterprise databases have never required re-tuning.

Where performance in the balanced design was below the objectives set it was because of the nature of the application. Where this occurs nothing can be done, so long as the business remains unchanged.

Figure 2.5 illustrates the relevant portion of a logical data model the author produced for an airfreight company. The purpose of the application was to record the rates charged to customers for the shipment of goods by air across the world. The application was developed and implemented at the time of high inflation in the United Kingdom in the late 1970s and early 1980s. The rates were therefore under constant change. In total some 80,000 rates were added per year. Each rate was mandatorily related to 12 master entities. This was the widest network data structure the author has ever seen. Thus, whenever a rate was inserted the referential integrity constraints demanded that each of the 12 master entities to the rate were checked to ascertain their presence in the database.

This referential integrity access inevitably generated extremely high disk I/O, because each master entity was spread around like "grass seed" on disk, with the rate being able to be clustered in the same page/block on disk to only one of the master entities. The clients had installed IBM's high performance DL/1 database management system and yet were suffering from disastrous response times on many transactions, particularly on inserts of rates. The fact that DL/1 only supports implicitly a hierarchical data structure and a single breadth of network data structure was, given the broad network, immaterial to the overall problem. Any file handler would have faced such referential integrity performance problems.

The purpose of the study was to find the cause of the problem. All traditional approaches to database tuning had been tried. No logical data model had been produced. Once a model had been constructed and the breadth of the data structure finally understood it became readily apparent that the file handler was not the problem. It was the nature of the business. The airfreight company had no option but to purchase a much larger computer.

The point of this example is that the solution to the problem was not found by expensive physical transaction performance monitoring and tuning as advised by the Information Engineering performance assessment technique but by a quick exercise to build an ERD model and review it. It so happened that the cause of the problem was found in the total data structure component of database design rather than in the total data access component. A budget of some three man-months work of physical database tuning had been planned by the client. The solution to the problem was found logically in two days.

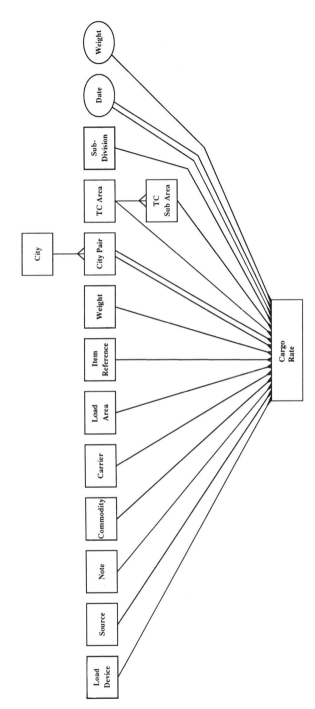

Figure 2.5   A "bad news" data model

A perfect example of how total data access on total data structure, i.e. summary access path maps on the ERD model, can provide many physical answers occurred at an insurance company. The company was using a relational file handler that was providing appalling performance on response times. The ERD model contained some 60–70 entities. The model was not particularly significant—there were no deep hierarchies and, most importantly, no broad networks. The total data structure was therefore not the problem. It was not until the various summary access path maps were produced that the problem was spotted and a solution was devised. 85% of all the data accesses were to six entities and of these accesses 80% were data maintenance. The six entities contained the bulk of the application data with many thousands of entity occurrences.

The file handler was ORACLE, an excellent product in the round but flawed for this particular application. ORACLE up to version 5 locks data at the entity/table level. The six tables were continuously in a state of being X locked (the exclusive lock preventing any other access until lock release) in their entirety, even though only a few table rows at a time were actually being modified. There was inevitably a permanent queue of transactions waiting to access these tables. The other problem, minor by comparison, was a slow processor. Whenever the transactions could be processed the queue backlog cleared only slowly. There was thus a mutually self-reinforcing "traffic jam". The solution was simple—adopt ORACLE version 6 with the teleprocessing sub-system and lock the tables at the row level.

The point of this example is that, in contrast to the airfreight example, the total data access component of logical design as mapped against the total data structure component was the crucial element in ascertaining the reason behind the physical performance problems. Again it was the logical design of total data structure and total data access that found the problem and provided the answer, not the performance assessment technique.

Both the IEM and Navigator versions of Information Engineering recognise the concept in full as regards data structure by producing an ERD model for an application, a set of applications or for the entire enterprise. IEM and Navigator also recognise the need to summarise the data accesses to the ERD model by producing summary access matrices, showing the volume of accesses to and between each entity. *This is the single most significant feature that distinguishes Information Engineering from all other structured methods.* For reasons described earlier it is a major enhancement.

However, while the matrices are a substantial improvement in that they are an explicit recognition of the need for summary data access information, they are not a good medium for illustrating summary accesses. Summary data access is a many dimensional aspect of database design—the entities being accessed, the type of access if the entity is an entry point to the ERD for a business requirement, the volume of accesses, the direction of

accesses between entities, whether the accesses are for data maintenance or data retrieval or. . . .
Matrices

- are not easy to interpret. While they are diagrammatic they are not pictographic. Matrices can represent access volumes between entities in number form but do not illustrate access volumes between entities as directional flows. Both access numbers and directional flow are needed by a database administrator;

- more seriously do not contain/show all the access information that needs to be recorded. They cannot show, for example, the types of entry point access (direct, logical sequential or physical sequential) to an entity and the split of the entry accesses by type of entry point access (i.e. 70% of the accesses are direct), or whether the accesses between entities are in a forward or backward direction or. . . .

- The data accesses are in actuality against the data model. Why not draw them as such?

The two basic features of database design that the database administrator requires are total data structure and total data access. Summary access path maps provide all of the above requirements—all on a single sheet of paper—and are much easier to interpret. Unless all the information necessary for summary data access is ascertained, presented and interpreted the full benefit of accepting this concept will not be obtained.

3 Business requirements should be CSF and inhibitor based CSFs, the indicators of a company's success in achieving company or departmental objectives, and their opposites, namely those aspects of business life that externally and internally inhibit the achievement of the objectives, are management data retrieval business requirements and the basis for all subsequently identified data maintenance and more detailed data retrieval business requirements.

One of the great strengths of Information Engineering is that it includes a stage for information systems strategy planning. The IEM ISP stage explicitly requires the analyst to identify the CSFs, inhibitors and objectives of each organisation unit, along with their performance measures. Indeed IEM includes a suggested questionnaire with specific questions regarding the issues for business objectives and their likely CSFs and inhibitors. Navigator explicitly demands that CSFs are considered when designing application systems—"focusing on CSFs when designing systems" is emphasised in the Monograph series manual. There is a specific chapter in the techniques manual on executive information needs analysis. It also explicitly requires external CSFs to be identified, and is therefore outwards looking, presumably in relation to the company's competitors. Information Engineering therefore fully supports this concept. This is a major strength.

One point, perhaps niggardly, is that both IEM and Navigator could be more specific in their support for this concept by stating explicitly that data retrieval business requirements for management must be CSF and inhibitor based. This is not done and has to be gleaned by implication by the intelligent reader of the manuals. It would also be useful to state the need to create a trace of each data retrieval and data maintenance business requirement back to a CSF or inhibitor as a quality assurance exercise.

It is a pity that Navigator does not identify inhibitors.

4 Achieve balance in the emphasis of the techniques   This concept has been added as a result of the author's experiences with other structured methods, where balance has very definitely not been achieved, particularly in the design techniques. The major logical and physical components of a computer system are illustrated in figure 2.3. Some widely used methods in the United Kingdom and elsewhere, including SSADM, STRADIS and LSDM, are substantially unbalanced regarding the description and application of the design techniques for these components, particularly data access. The significance of this can perhaps be appreciated when it is realised that, with version three of the UK government design method SSADM, for every 15 pages in the manuals devoted to describing the techniques for data structure and 10 pages for data process only 1 page details the techniques for data access, and even here there are no examples and explanation provided. Yet data access is the component that produces the greatest inefficiency and overhead in a computer system and is the most tuneable.

In Information Engineering the three logical components are specified in full in the analysis stage. There are design techniques to cover the data structure, data access and data process components—and the techniques are detailed with no major elements missing. Unfortunately Navigator as defined in the Development Techniques Manual is not well balanced, although better than SSADM. The sections on the backgrounds to the techniques, such as attribute and business transaction identification, have been ignored. The page ratio split from the logical design techniques is 48 for data structure, 6 for data access and 52 for data process. The IEM version is better endowed with the page ratio split being 96, 15 and 66. *There is little doubt that data access is the weakest part of Information Engineering* and it was a close run thing as to whether to include this section within section 2.4.2.

There are, of course, design techniques to cover the physical component parts of a computer system and both methods achieve a balanced, although, as we shall see, not complete, description of database and program design.

Imbalance in the description of the strategy and design techniques in a structured method will produced unbalanced, and therefore suspect, deliverables. Imbalance against data access is particularly severe.

5 Business requirements = events and event level processing   Both of these concepts are, as near as makes no odds, implicitly supported in IEM and are explicitly supported in Navigator.

In both IEM and Navigator two types of business activity are identified—functions and processes. A function is described as a group of business activities supporting an aspect of the business. Examples given of functions are purchasing and distribution. The use of a gerund and a noun as a descriptive title is a useful way of indicating that the function is above the event level. A process is described as a defined business activity which is executed to process some data input to produce some data output. Typical processes could be receive customer order and allocate stock. The verb noun "do something" title to the process indicates very clearly it is at the event level.

Without explicitly stating it is clear from the descriptions, title names and examples in the manuals that processes are business requirement/events within a function and a function is a logically related group of events. The BAA of IEM stage therefore fully supports this important concept with event level processes. As we shall see the picture is less clear with Navigator.

The processes are further decomposed into elementary processes. An elementary process is described in IEM as "the smallest unit of activity of meaning to a user". The use of the user as the unit of measurement is most unfortunate, as different users may, and probably will, have different understandings of a "unit of activity". Nevertheless, it is a business activity, such as checking the customer's credit-worthiness within the process of receiving a customer's order. It is also the lowest level of process decomposition. Again the IEM manual all but explicitly states that an elementary process is a problem-to-solve within an event level process.

How this matches the definition in Navigator that "an elementary process includes all the processing within a business area needed to respond to an event" is not quite clear. Navigator states that an event usually invokes just one elementary process, with the exception being where the business area has to respond in a number of different ways. This means that Navigator does not seem to recognise the concept of problems-to-solve process, that an event can itself be composed of further sub-processes. This is explicitly confirmed when it is stated that an event cannot be broken down into its constituent parts, as it is "atomic".

This surely cannot be correct. An event is not the lowest level of decomposition. Endless examples exist where an event has multiple lower level problem-to-solve elementary processes. Two examples of this are given in section 3.2.1. Examples of this are given in the IEM analysis manual with the event level process Take Order being composed of the sub-processes Receive Order, Allocate Stock and Check Customer Credit. As described in section 3.2.1 these sub- processes can also be events in their own right.

The response from Ernst & Young to the above is that Navigator is only interested in events as stimuli for system responses, and as such, the presence of an event triggers a process. For Navigator, Receive Order is the elementary process. A process decomposition was supplied and is shown in figure 2.6. It shows that the elementary process, such as Receive Customer Order, is at the event level and that further decomposition of processes to the problem-to-solve level, such as Check Credit, is allowed beyond the event level. This is not in line with the manuals. Thus Navigator supports event level processing; it happens to call them elementary processes. What is the name for the problem-to-solve processes?

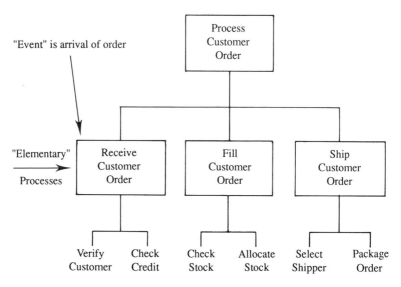

Figure 2.6   Elementary processes

It is clear that overall the analysis stage of Information Engineering exactly matches these two concepts.

Fortunately IEM continues the good effect in the BSD stage. The BAA processes which describe what is required of the events are converted into procedures which detail the logic of how the event is to be achieved. A procedure is defined as "a method by which one or more elementary processes can be carried out". As just described an elementary process is the smallest unit of business activity—that is, a problem-to-solve within an event level process. The IEM manual states that the relationship of an elementary process to a procedure can be one-to-one, one-to-n or n-to-one. The manual is saying that an event can have one or more problems-to-solve, which can themselves also relate to more than one event. The naming of the procedure examples with a "do something" title—prepare invoice, check registration—certainly suggests that they are at the event level. A small point, but if it is necessary to have a technique for process to procedure mapping then obviously the relationship between the two is not one-to-one.

There is also great clarity with the definition of a procedure step. A procedure step is a subdivision of work within a procedure—a discrete activity. It sounds very much that a procedure step is an elementary process—a problem-to-solve.

It would be nice to think that a procedure maps directly to a process and be therefore pitched at the event level and the procedure step maps directly to an elementary process and be therefore pitched at the problem-to-solve level. Wherever the author has used Information Engineering there has always been a one-for-one match.

If, as stated, the procedure specifies the "how it is to be achieved" logic of the process's "what is required" description of the business require-ment why not state that there is a simple one-to-one relationship between processes and procedures and elementary processes and procedure steps? IEM is all but there. Why not make it explicit?

IEM further continues the good work in the TD stage of the method. Ideally a procedure maps directly to an application program and a procedure step maps to a program module. If this was always followed then IEM would be directly in line with the concept of the logical design = physical design. While following this ideal as much as possible IEM quite legitimately also details a number of technical reasons as to why this one-for-one mapping may not be possible in the actual physical design of application programs.

The author finds process decomposition within Navigator very difficult to follow—what is the top level process and the lowest level process and at what levels are they pitched? The essential objects in the Navigator process model are shown in figure 2.7. The author is still confused. Firstly, there is no indication of the levels of the decomposed processes. Further, assuming that the elementary processes are at the event level, then a process is at the event level, and assuming that the application becomes the application program (n-to-n with business transactions, n-to-1 with elementary process) then an application program is pitched at higher than the event level.

Of all the structured methods the author has used, Information Engineering comes closest to supporting these two important concepts.

The process object model

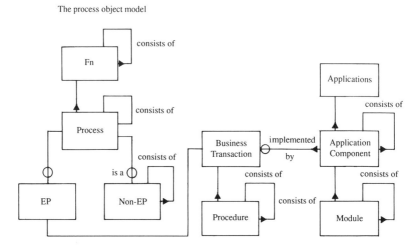

Figure 2.7   Navigator process model

Certainly the method all but explicitly defines processes and elementary processes at the event and problem-to-solve levels, certainly does not discourage a direct mapping of processes to procedures and elementary processes to procedure steps, and explicitly encourages a one-for-one mapping of procedures to programs and procedure steps to program modules. It is therefore possible to show a perfect correlation of the logical events and problems-to-solve to the physical programs and program modules.

2.3.2.2 *The structural strengths*

The structural strengths are:

1   *The "cascading waterfall" sequence of stages, steps and tasks*   All structured methods supporting a single data processing environment have adopted this top down "start at the high level and decompose to progressively greater levels of detail" approach. In Information Engineering there is an implied and classical threefold division of the stages into strategy (ISP), logical design (BAA and ?BSD) and physical design (?BSD and subsequent stages). Although not discussed in the manuals a feasibility study can be

inserted as an optional front-end stage to logical design. The merits of the cascading approach is that it:

- enables the strategy and design techniques to be applied in an orderly sequence, so that the output deliverables of one technique can be used, if appropriate, as input by another technique;

- provides a firm set of procedural guidelines for the inexperienced practitioner to follow;

- provides a definitive set of points for the quality assurance function to be practised against known deliverables;

- provides boundaries between what are widely accepted as different skills groups—strategy planning, logical design and physical design. It is therefore easier to delineate task responsibilities to different peoples across the skill groups.

2 *The progressive construction of the major deliverables*   Information Engineering starts by identifying the high level data and processes that are required to support a company's business strategy, and from this identifies and prioritises business systems that can be developed to provide the necessary information. From this initial skeleton there is a progressive infilling of data and decomposition of processes as the logical design techniques are applied. Navigator calls this the "divide and conquer" approach.

Three of the techniques have a continuous thread from the strategy stage through to the completion of the logical design—the ERD model, process decomposition and process dependency. The deliverables of these techniques are produced in skeleton form in the ISP strategy stage and finally completed in detail in the BAA stage. There is thus a continuity in these deliverables from the beginning of strategy planning to the end of logical design. This continuity provides both a quality assurance trace and a trace back to the initial business justification the deliverable is supporting.

3 *The separation of the Construction and Transition stages*   Many structured methods incorporate the Construction and Transition stages together as a single stage, on the basis that the design and development of a computer system should simultaneously include the consideration of conversion/transition from the existing system(s) to the new system. This has been an entirely reasonable position until recently. The advent of code generators and the hoped for acceptance of the concept of logical design = physical design, with the resultant ability to use the logical design specification as the source of direct code generation for the new system, requires that the issue of transition only be considered after the code is

generated, because the logical design specification quite rightly should not consider transition. Generate the code and then use it to support transition. Information Engineering is in line with this requirement.

4 Fastpath   IEM states that a fastpath approach to application system design can be adopted in two ways:

• selective system development.
  This takes a system identified at the end of the BAA stage as offering exceptional returns on investment and clears its path for immediate development.

• rapid application development (RAD).
  RAD uses only the RAD techniques and focuses on the delivery of systems as quickly as possible. It is dependent on the availability of integrated CASE tools, such as IEF, not only as an aid to rapid and easier recording of the logical and physical deliverables, but also to enforce standards and quality. All project work must be completed within a limited and fixed timespan, typically some 13 weeks.
  RAD achieves its claimed improvements through a different approach and by-passing some of the techniques so as to "shorten" the application of the full method. The philosophy is "just in time and just enough". The approaches include timeboxing management of the project tasks, such as the discussion on a topic, extensive prototyping and use of the latest facilities for fast application design and development with an integrated CASE tool used by skilled experts. The permanent assistance of the user is essential.

The author has found that it is possible to take short cuts on large projects using a "fastpath" approach. Conditions in the real world may make the full application of all the Information Engineering stages and techniques impractical and unnecessary. A new system is suddenly identified as an urgently required business necessity. It cannot wait for its formal inclusion into an information system strategy. Instead of following the full structure and applying all of the techniques of the method why not adopt a "fastpath" approach and apply the Information Engineering techniques directly in the sequence of data structure, data access and data process once, rather than iteratively in a series of stages.

The author has often used a fastpath approach to applying the Information Engineering techniques. For reasons explained in section 2.4.1 the procedure action diagrams have been omitted, the process action diagrams have been upgraded to specify the how logic of the events/business requirements (easy to do given they use the same command syntax as the procedures), the dataflow diagrams have been merged with the process decomposition diagrams (the dataflow diagrams record process decomposition as well as data flow), the dialogue and layout designs have been integrated as a single task and the entity life cycle technique has been merged with the process dependency diagrams (the ELCs show process dependency). Given the importance of data access, the data navigation technique is included as a separate task before undertaking the process action diagrams. A new document to describe the what about business requirements/events of the event level processes has been introduced.

5 The analysis of organisational responsibility The RAEW (responsibility, authority, expertise, work) technique identifies who is responsible for what business in a company's organisation. At face value this might appear outside the task of an information systems strategy study. Such a strategy study is concerned with information, not with organisation. The organisation of a corporation is the responsibility of management and is therefore one of the results of a business strategy study. The structure of the organisation units is the result of commercial responsibility for supporting the business strategy. However commercial responsibility also needs information in order to function. RAEW therefore identifies the responsibility of organisational units for business functions and hence of the information in an application system. The difference is subtle but important—RAEW is about information not commercial responsibility. The commercial responsibility is obtained from the business strategy, which in turn leads to information responsibility. Information Engineering is quite right to include the technique within the strategy stage.

2.3.2.3 The technical strengths

The technical strengths are divided into those techniques concerned with information systems strategy and those concerned with application systems design. *Strategy is concerned with identification and prioritisation and design is concerned with converting the identified and prioritised into a set of working system(s).*

THE STRATEGY TECHNIQUES

The strengths of the strategy techniques are:

1 Classical divisions The IEM strategy components follow classical breakdowns. Classical divisions have the merit of being widely accepted.

They are usually widely accepted because they are valid. The breakdowns are:

- a division of the information to be ascertained into three architectures—an information architecture containing both data and functions, a systems architecture and a technology architecture;

- the division of the business systems into the categories of strategy, planning and analysis, monitoring and control and transaction is also classic. Each type of system category has its own characteristics, for example, the transaction type systems requiring high transaction volumes and fast response times with usually short access paths to the data, whereas the strategy type systems have browsing type queries with long access paths to the data.

For each of these categories there are differing technology requirements. Again, for example, the transaction category requires a high performance teleprocessing monitor and database file handler; the strategic category requires a flexible and easy to use query language with an extensive array of powerful built-in functions for massaging large volumes of retrieved data with a single macro. It would be helpful if the Information Engineering manuals could specify the technology requirements of each of the system categories.

A point of detail. The author would modify the planning and analysis category to be planning, interpretation, design and diagnosis. These types of applications all require knowledge and expertise and are therefore suitable to being supported by expert system technology.

The principles in the technology architecture diagram in figure 2.8 are most attractive—three technology usage levels with their different underlying processor types, four information technology areas with their different technical facilities and all tied together as a set of conceptual networks, one for each information area across the usage levels. The technology usage levels are again classical—the three divisions of a central mainframe type processor, a set of local, typically departmental, processors and a further set of single point processors, such as PC/PS computers or intelligent robots/instruments. The four information technology areas with their conceptual networks are based on their roles and the different types of database, teleprocessing and telecommunication facilities required. The transactional network is essentially online processing; the factory automation network is found only with manufacturing companies with intelligent instruments and process control processors; and the professional automation (typically decision support, CAD/CAM and personal computing) and the messaging networks (office mail and diarying)

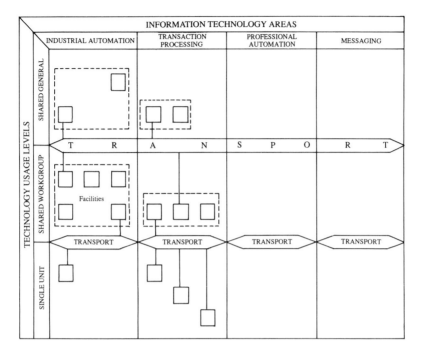

Figure 2.8   Technical architecture diagram

come under the generic title of office automation. The author is not familiar with telecommunications and therefore can pass no comment on the viability of the classification. Certainly the technology architecture diagram is the best schematic layout the author has seen and has found most useful in practice.

A point of detail about the diagram. The single unit processors are connectible to the central processor only via the local processors. This may not be the case in reality. There is nothing to prevent single point processors being connected to a central processor.

2   Integration of the strategy and design deliverables   The integration of the three strategy architectures with each other and the subsequent design stages is impressive. This is shown in figure 2.9 a and b for IEM and Navigator. It is possible to show and validate the architecture's inter-relationships and thereby add value to each other's information. For example, at a detail level the IEM business systems architecture diagram requires the function architecture as a major input. More generally the

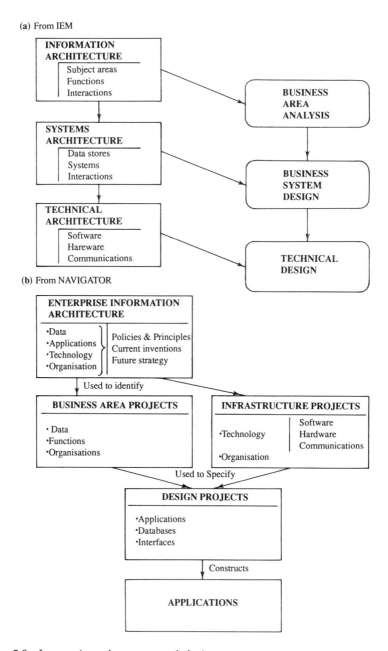

Figure 2.9   Integration of strategy and design

information architecture is the basis of the BAA stage, the systems architecture the basis of the BSD stage and the technology architecture the basis of the TD stage.

There is, however, a concern. The author believes that there should be a clear boundary between the end of strategy and the beginning of logical design and between logical design and physical design. The information and systems architectures are the basis of identifying future application systems that need to be developed, and from this for each application there should be logical design to be followed by physical design. This is not the case, with the "logical" design techniques within the BSD stage including very physical aspects of computer systems. The data stores in the very logical design technique of dataflow diagramming are based on the design constraints of the target file handler. The author would much prefer the information and system architectures to feed directly into the clearly logical design BAA stage. The author's dislike of the BSD stage is discussed in section 2.4.2.2.

There is also the beneficial use of techniques in the ISP stage (entity modelling, process decomposition, process dependency and dataflow diagramming) that produce deliverables that can be further used in the subsequent BAA and BSD stages of the method. This provides an easy mechanism by which the design deliverables can be traced back to their strategic justification.

THE DESIGN TECHNIQUES

The strengths of the design techniques are:

1 *Entity relationship diagramming (ERD)*   This technique is comprehensive in the information that is recorded about data for centralised data processing.

The author has heard it said that the ERD model has more information than the current database technology can support. File handlers are not able to document and even less make use of the semantic descriptions and annotated conditions of the relationships between entities and cannot support exclusive and inclusive relationships, so there is no need to record this information. Technically this is becoming less and less true, with the ability to record exclusivity and inclusivity as database rules ("fired"— another buzzword—when specified business conditions occur on entity access) and triggers (fired automatically whenever the entity is accessed). New data access languages (and this does not include SQL) are now able to make use of relationship semantics. This will be discussed in chapter 5. The argument is rejected.

Navigator defines the facility of attribute cardinality—that an attribute can have multiple values for a given occurrence of an entity. Strictly speaking this is not legal as it breaks the relational rule of first normal form, but there are occasions where it is useful to be "sinful". Typically this is where the repetition is fixed, for example the months of the year. The method also introduces something the value of which the author is doubtful—maximum per value—the maximum number of attributes that can have the same value across all occurrences of the entity. What does it mean? Why is it useful?

Navigator also explicitly states that entity sub-types "inherit" the attributes/properties of the master entity. This is the first "traditional" structured method to identify this facility, although there is no explanation of what it means and how it should be used. It is important to realise that the current non object oriented file handlers are not able to support property inheritance between entities/objects. The significance of property inheritance is discussed in chapter 5.

2 Process decomposition   This technique is complete for the purpose for which it was designed—to decompose progressively high level business area processes, which senior managers can relate to, down through several levels of decomposition to the lowest level elementary processes, which those concerned with the operational running of the company can relate to. The levels of function, event and elementary process decomposition in IEM are more precisely defined than in Navigator, which merely identifies functions at the "highest level", various lower levels of discrete and distinct processes to the lowest level of the elementary process. Advice that "functional decomposition ... is a process of breaking functions or processes into smaller, more detailed parts ... is continued until the product is at sufficient detail to meet its predetermined objective" is not very helpful. Apart from the elementary processes, no advice or example as to the pitching of the intermediate level processes is given.

The author can suggest no improvements to the advice offered in the IEM manuals, which are amplified with examples in section 3.2.1. The author would also refer the reader to section 2.4.2.3 for the reasons for his dislike of the technique.

3 Process dependency   The comments made for process decomposition are also appropriate to process dependency. The technique is not used by Navigator.

4 Process logic/data navigation/data usage   This part of logical design is better covered in Information Engineering than any other structured method the author has used, particularly in that the individual transaction access paths are used to produce summary access information. This is a major strength and is why it has been included as a strength. Summary data access information is the basis of a balanced and hence efficient database design. However, the strength is purely relative, with the method still significantly short of what is required.

A few suggestions for improvement are:

- Apply the technique at the process/procedure/event level rather than at the elementary process/procedure step/problem-to-solve level.

  The database is accessed only because there is a business requirement requiring data. Business requirements are events. We know this from the description of the third concept. An event can have 1-to-n problems-to-solve. IEM pitches processes and procedures at the event and elementary process and procedure steps at the problem-to-solve level. Data navigation in the BAA stage is undertaken at the elementary process level as process logic diagrams and at the procedure level in the BSD stage as data access diagrams. There is therefore inconsistency between the problem-to- solve data navigation in the BAA stage and the event level data navigation in the BSD stage.

  The author believes Navigator is inconsistent in its application of the technique. The technique is applied against elementary processes/procedures, online or batch procedures, data views and application or database. Surely the technique should only be undertaken once for each business requirement against the logical data model and once for each application program against the database? Why apply the technique more times than is necessary? The production of the summary access statistics is also applied only against the online transactions. What happens if most of the accesses are batch?

  Ernst & Young's response to the above paragraph is that the various access models "represent different levels of abstraction in the modelling process" and as such are not inconsistent. The question is why do you need different levels of abstraction. If Information Engineering supported object oriented design techniques then this would be understandable (see chapter 5). Surely the only level of abstraction needed is the event level access to the ERD model, so as to ascertain the access logic component of the event.

  The approach used by the author is to undertake transaction access path at the event/business level and record the data accesses for each problem-to-solve/elementary process as normal in the sequence of elementary process execution in the process dependency. The boundary of each elementary process is marked with a line across the business requirement access path document.

Neither version of Information Engineering illustrates how to represent the summary accesses to the ERD logical data model and, most importantly, how to interpret the results to produce a balanced database design. What is the point of having summary data access information if it is not used physical design? Both the illustration and interpretation of the summary accesses should be included.

- Produce summary access path maps showing the total accesses against the ERD data model and interpret the results to produce a balanced database design.

The title of the technique as process logic in the IEM BAA stage is very misleading, for it has nothing to do with data process, only data access. Process logic is to do with massaging data once it has been accessed from the database. The massaging constructs are sequence (move A to B), selection (if...then...else...), iteration (do while or do until) and branch (go to). Access logic is to do with inserting, updating and deleting data in the database, using either record-at-a-time or set access constructs. The record-at-a- time constructs are read, write, update and delete. The set constructs are select, union, intersect, difference and, very rarely, divide. The process logic technique is only concerned with the access constructs. The technique title is a misnomer.

- Record the access volumes to the entities in the ERD model for each business requirement accessing the model. This is advised by Navigator, but not by IEM. It is essential information. Without the access volumes it is impossible to ascertain with certainty that the ERD model is efficient. It could be that the model creates very long data retrieval access paths, which could be much shortened by the insertion of a low data mainte- nance cost entity. If there are multiple access path options which one is the shorter path and via which entry point entity? Solutions to these kinds of problem can only be provided with transaction access path volumes.

The access volumes are as important to a database designer as the actual access path.

Ascertaining that the ERD the model supports the business requirement is only half the problem. It is also necessary to ensure that the model supports the business requirements efficiently. The tragedy is that this is not done by any structured method, including Information Engineering. Techniques as to how this can be done are described in chapter 3.

The data items/attributes to be accessed for program processing purposes are identified in the separate technique of information views analysis/entity model view. Perhaps the author is being pedantic, but why not record this information with the transaction access path as the path is being mapped? That is where the information required is identified.

- Identify the entry point type for each business requirement. Navigator talks about entry points but does not define the different types. The entry point types can be direct to a specific table row, logical sequential to *n* table rows in the sequence of some key or physical sequential to *n* table rows where the order of access does not matter. The type of entry point required affects the database design. For example, if the entry point access to an entity is always direct a randomiser facility is probably the best choice; if it is logical sequential then index support is necessary.

All of these aspects and others appropriate to comprehensive transaction access path analysis are addressed in chapter 3.

The IEM BAA stage manual makes some strange comments: do not spend too long on a process logic diagram; only use the diagrams to check that the ERD model can support the business requirement! Data access is the area of greatest overhead in database performance and transaction access path analysis is the technique to ensure that the ERD model not only supports the business requirements but supports them well. Both IEM and Navigator also state that the access paths of simple processes which only use one or two entity types should be considered. How can one produce summary access path maps (the need for which is identified and described in chapters 3 and 4) if some transactions are not access mapped against the ERD model? It may well be these transactions run the most frequently. Significant summary access information could well be missing.

The author very definitely spends as much time as is necessary with transaction access path analysis for each business requirement.

The significance of transaction access path maps is still not recognised in the IEM BSD stage "the (data access) map ... is not a formal deliverable of BSD, but an intermediate aid to understanding a procedure". This means that at the end of the logical design specification (assuming that BSD is the final stage of logical design, which is uncertain for reasons explained in section 2.4.2.2) transaction access paths have not been given their due significance as one of the three logical components of a computer system—data structure, data access and data process. They should be on a par with the ERD model and the action diagrams.

Indeed IEM further compounds the problem by only formally drawing data access diagrams for each procedure against the preliminary data structure. This data structure is not a logical data model, as is the ERD model, but a structure that "conforms to the rules of the data handling software to be used". It is all but a preliminary database design. That means that formal transaction access path analysis is not undertaken at the logical level! This is a serious omission, because it guarantees that the ERD model is not tested as to whether it is efficient and that the logical summary data access path maps so crucial to a balanced database design are not produced.

Fortunately the principles of data access against the preliminary data structure can be used directly against the ERD model. All that is required is to move the skill from the BSD stage to the BAA stage.

There is one further problem the author has with the IEM BSD manual describing the summarisation of data access. The BSD stage produces a preliminary data structure from the ERD model and maps the data access diagrams against it. Given the physical aspects of the preliminary data structure it seems strange that it is the logical ERD model that is then used as the basis of recording the summary data access usage. The author approves of recording the summary data access against a logical data model, but why leave it until the BSD stage? Why not include the creation of logical summary data access/usage models in the BAA stage?

Notwithstanding these adverse comments on transaction access path analysis this crucial aspect of the logical design is, in the author's opinion, still covered more comprehensively in Information Engineering than in any other leading structured method, some of them of long standing.

5 Information view analysis   The feature that is attractive about these views is that they are generic to all the techniques that identify updates to the ERD model—process dependency, entity life cycle analysis and process logic/data navigation maps. One only needs to define the views once. Other methods, such as SSADM and LSDM, require different documents to record the data being processed on the dataflow diagrams, layout diagrams and the transaction access paths. It is a matter of style.

Given the importance of transaction access path analysis the author very much insists on recording the data items/attributes required when applying the transaction access path technique, and not ascertaining the data via another technique. The approach adopted by Information Engineering is better suited to software support in a CASE tool, which can automatically allocate the data items in an information view to a transaction access path or any of the other techniques that access or use data.

6 Process/procedure action diagrams   This is a technique where Information Engineering can feel pleased with itself. It has proved to be much more difficult to get data processing professionals to agree on the recording of logic than on the recording of data, yet the merits of action diagrams are recognised to be such that they are now a competitive technique to the other major standard for recording logic, namely Jackson structured programming. The parallel use of symbols with a program development language to represent logic pictographically has proved a powerful element in its success.

A particularly attractive feature provided by both IEM and Navigator is the definition of a command language with appropriate syntax for the writing of logic in the action diagrams. If this facility is not provided then there is no basis for application program code generation from the logical design specification. It also greatly reduces the risk that different analysts/designers/programmers may not be not able to understand this component of the logical design specification when it is passed to them. Structured methods which do not provide a command language for the recording of logic permit *n* project teams working on the design of *n* application systems to produce *n* different results with n sets of heads being scratched. The author can suggest no improvement.

7 Distribution analysis   It is recorded as a strength because Information Engineering is one of the few structured methods that makes any attempt at supporting the distribution of processes and data by recording the location at which they are triggered and stored.

However, it should be pointed out that Information Engineering, having identified that certain processes and data can be triggered and stored at multiple locations, makes a wholly inadequate attempt at ascertaining the significance of the distribution in the logical design and pays no attention to distribution in the physical design. Techniques to do this are described in chapter 4. Neither is the technology of distributed database described. This is a major oversight as the distributed design techniques are based on the technology.

8 Analysis of problems   An excellent IEM technique exists for analysing the deficiencies/problems of the current system. The cause and effect deliverable is more usually appropriate to management solution than the design of a computer system. However, it is crucial that the problems identified in the cause/effect diagrams are explicitly solved by management and, if appropriate, be incorporated in the design of the new system.

9 Relational data analysis   The strength of the technique is that it is applied up to third normal form, which many regard as the "standard" degree of the normalisation of data into relations/entities. In recent years it has been proposed that higher powers of data normalisation are required, the higher powers going up to sixth normal form (6NF).

The first three steps of normalisation as defined by Dr Codd are widely understood and accepted. Unfortunately there is disagreement as to what the higher powers are. This disagreement is reflected in that IEM, Navigator and the author have different definitions of the additional normalisation steps. IEM includes the identification of entity sub-types in the definition of 4NF. To the author 6NF identifies entity sub-types. Navigator does not include the normalisation step for entity sub-types, be it 4NF or 6NF.

From a practical point of view the first three normalisation steps used by IEM and Navigator are adequate in most application cases. The three additional normalisation steps are described in chapter 3. Assuming 6NF is concerned with entity sub-types then 4NF and 5NF are quite frankly, of more academic than practical relevance given current file handler technology. Some relational file handlers, such as DATACOM/DB, can now support entity sub-types in the database schema definition, although the entity sub-types are still stored as separate tables. It has been quite rightly pointed out to the author that SQL, the facility for defining data access to a relational file handler, does not support entity sub- types, so the benefit of the DATACOM/DB facilities is of doubtful value. Object oriented file handlers are more capable by being able to support property inheritance, the entity/table sub-type inheriting the properties of the super-type entity/table.

10   Visual layout design/online conversational design   Visual layout design is not so much a technique within IEM as advice as to the facilities that are available for screen design, such as the display properties, the program function and access keys and headers and footers. Many structured methods do not detail this information. The beginner to online design is left to find out this information from the technical manuals of the appropriate teleprocessing monitor/screen painter. The author would have saved much time and expense if this information had been available when he first designed screens.

Navigator makes a distinction between the way that a user and a system developer has an online conversation with the computer. The former is represented by a conversational network diagram and the latter by a conversational hierarchy diagram. Both are produced for each online conversation. This is the first time the author has come across this distinction and its purpose is not clear. The third deliverable produced is a dialogue action diagram.

11   Prototyping   This is explicitly addressed in Navigator. This is a positive because the more modern database products include excellent facilities for quickly developing part of a proposed system to see how it works and performs from the designer's and developer's viewpoint and what it looks like from the user's viewpoint.

Navigator believes that prototyping can be applied as an "almost universal" design and development approach from the analysis through design through construction and implementation phases. Navigator clearly has high hopes of what can be achieved. It correctly identifies the limitations—that prototyping does not address security, integrity and error recovery and that it is invariably applied to a limited set of the application's functionality. The author does not see why the technique cannot be used for performance testing, something that Navigator does not advocate.

Navigator talks about evolutionary prototyping—the continuous and iterative application of the prototyping tools "to define a highly limited scope of functionality and carry through with a full operational implementation of that limited functionality. The limited but operational system may be incrementally enhanced by repeating the prototyping process for successive, 'adjacent' sets of functionality". It is clear that, provided that the proper tools are available (these are specified), Navigator sees prototyping as a substantial alternative to applying the techniques of logical and physical design. The aspects of security, etc., that are not addressed in prototyping need to be added to the prototyped operational system by "conventional development means".

The positive side about Navigator's view of prototyping is that much advice as to what can be prototyped is given. What is missing is what prototyping cannot provide. This is discussed in section 2.4.2.3.

12 Database design and performance assessment This task is rightly separated into two parts in both versions of Information Engineering—an initial database design that is structurally legal according to the file handler being used but without any performance considerations, followed by a tuning exercise by timing transactions against the design where performance objectives are not being met.

In IEM a preliminary database design is produced in the BSD stage. The BSD manual identifies a set of basic design principles for database design, followed by a set of rules for converting the ERD model into a first cut DL/1 and a relational design. The basic design rules will produce database designs that are legal and will work. The preliminary design is then tuned to a refined design using the performance assessment technique in the TD stage.

Navigator has introduced the technique of logical database design. This technique has been included as a strength because there are substantially more positives than negatives.

The technique produces logical data structures and access paths that conform to the physical constraints of the target DBMS type. To grace the technique as being "logical" when the constraints of the file handler type are the basis of the design seems a bit incongruous, a point recognised by the method. The technique has the advantage in that it is designed to produce a database design that is generic to the type of DBMS being used (that is, the relational, Codasyl and hierarchical types) but not specific to a particular product within the DBMS type, such as the relational ORACLE and INGRES products. Navigator recognises that file handlers within a DBMS type have a set of generic facilities (Codasyl file handlers use direct address pointers whereas relational file handlers use symbolic pointers but does not extend the commonality across DBMS types. This is regrettable. Information Engineering based methods still do not recognise the concept of a universal file handler, universal in that all file handlers, of whatever types, have certain generic facilities, such as flat records, indexes, attributes and page blocking of records. Nevertheless, credit is due to Navigator for recognising the concept of generic file handler facilities, which can then be tuned according to the specific file handler used. The basis of a universally based initial database design is there.

The new released SSADM version 4 has formally introduced the concept of the universal file handler and therefore likewise supports the concept of logical database design, but takes the concept beyond the DBMS type to the universal DBMS/file handler. Facilities that are generic to all file handlers are detailed, for subsequent modification of the database design for the file handler used for implementation. It would be a positive development if Navigator progressed to the next stage and adopted a universal logical database design in a similar manner.

Navigator identifies the facilities generic to the different file handler types and their significance in database design. The author is glad to see that the importance of working cardinality ratios (what Navigator calls the relative average cardinality) is recognised (the ratio between master and detail tables rows when a relationship exists) when ascertaining transaction access to the database. As far as the author is aware Navigator is the only structured method to identify explicitly the working cardinality ratio rather than the more usual average cardinality ratio and to encourage its use in database design and transaction performance assessment. It is crucial to any reasonable transaction performance when not accessing via a unique key to a table (access all customers with red hair who have outstanding orders for brown coloured parts) or when there are multiple choices as to the entry point to the database (access all stores items for a specified depot and product).

Unfortunately Navigator does not explain the reason why the working cardinality ratio is so important, particularly for relational file handlers. Relational file handlers use two types of query optimisers. Query optimisers ascertain the optimum access path between the tables of data in response to a data access call. The two types are rule and statistically based.

The rule based optimisers are the simpler, and use the way in which the query is posed as the basis of ascertaining the access to the data tables. The trouble with this approach is that the user may pose a query that is sensible as far as he/she is concerned but is hopeless as regards efficient access to the database. ORACLE currently uses a rule based query optimiser with the last search argument being used as the basis of the entry to the database where there is a multiple choice option. The query is "Select * where A.a

= "whatever" and B = "whatever" and access all related C's". Given the database design represented logically in figure 2.10 it would be much more efficient to access the database on the table A than on table B, but the search argument for B is specified last. ORACLE will therefore access the database via table B.

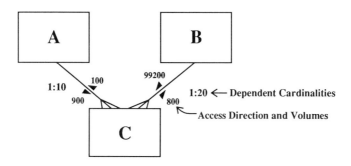

Figure 2.10   Table clustering

The statistical query optimisers use a count of the ratio between the master tables rows and the related detail tables rows as the basis of ascertaining the optimum access path between the data tables. The statistical count almost always used is the working cardinality ratio. Using the same example in figure 2.10 the ratio statistic of the cardinality between tables A/C are narrower than between B/C. Access to the database will therefore be via table A. DB2 and INGRES use the working cardinality.

A set of 12 logical design steps are advised, along with detailed explanations of what they involve. Any experienced database designer would recognise that the advice is good. There is a general concern, however, that the initial steps to produce the logical database design are all about data structure and none of them take into account the volume of data access to the database. The step "define access paths" is only about identifying the relationships between tables, such that access between tables can be achieved. The actual transaction accesses between the tables are not considered. Half of the criteria that go into an initial database design are therefore ignored. Navigator, like all other structured methods, including IEM, still does not recognise the concept of database—total data structure and total data access. Only after the data structure component has been produced is the design reviewed as part of database optimisation to take into account the data access component. The two should go together *simultaneously* so as to ensure a balanced and efficient database design. This is addressed in chapter 3.

The logical design is then converted into a physical database design by adding data access facilities, such as indexes, pointers and randomisers, data storage facilities, such as physical or logical sequential, and other facilities, such as buffering, logging and recovery. The physical facilities are considered within the constraints of the file handler product being used. If, for example, the product is ORACLE then a constraint will be that there is no randomiser. The Navigator design techniques manual is very detailed in providing some excellent design tips for database when it is necessary to do more than merely convert the ERD model on a one-for-one basis into the database design.

What is surprising and disappointing is that Navigator does not provide any advice as to how to use the summary data access information which is produced. The importance of this is explained in sections 3.1.3 and 3.1.4. Advice is provided on total data structure but still not on total data access.

IEM, by contrast, supports both of the concepts of total data structure and total data access pertinent to a balanced and efficient database design. The IEM manual explicitly states that the physical design should be one-for-one with the ERD model as far as possible. This is in line with the concept of logical design = physical design. *Furthermore IEM is the only method, as far as the author is aware, that uses summary data access information in database design.* The method therefore goes a long way to producing a database design in line with the concept of designing the database on total data structure and total data access. As explained in section 2.3.2.1 such databases are balanced and *a priori* efficient. It is unfortunate that the advice on interpreting the summary data access is not very detailed, being limited in the technical design manual to choosing those transactions with the highest execution frequency. Not very helpful! Nevertheless, in this important aspect IEM is the market leader.

Thus it is clear that Information Engineering in large measure does not make use of a great opportunity to be substantially ahead of its competitor methods in this crucial area of system performance. It is such a pity, as wherever the author has produced database designs that do take data structure and data access into account performance tuning has never been necessary.

The Information Engineering summary access information is primarily presented in the form of load matrices but it can be presented as a summary access path map(s). The author prefers the summary access path maps as they are better able to show all the data access information on data structure on one or at most five sheet(s) of paper. They are also easier to interpret. It is a matter of style.

The matrices shown in the IEM manual have a number of deficiencies:

- The matrix showing the number of entry point accesses does not show the type of entry point access—is it direct to one occurrence of a table row, logical sequential to a number of table rows in the sequence of some key, or is it physical sequential to a number of table rows in no order of sequence? The type of access and the proportion of the accesses of a particular type to a table are important factors in choosing the facilities to be used for entry access to a database and the storage of data in the database.

- The matrix showing the accesses between tables does not show whether the accesses are in a forward or backward direction against a key sequence or are to the first or last table row in the chain of detail table rows when accessing from the master table.

Summary access paths maps do not suffer these deficiencies. Examples of how to interpret summary access information for database design as shown in summary access path maps and specifically how to ascertain the best type of entry point access is given in section 3.1.3.

Notwithstanding these deficiencies the load matrices are an enormous improvement on other structured design methods, which provide no such summary access information. Information Engineering is to be commended.

The performance assessment technique that Information Engineering uses for transaction response times is particularly impressive. Four approaches to assessment are suggested. The only one of interest to the author is the analytical approach, that of measuring transaction response times by "paper" calculations. The basic calculation is to use the path length machine instructions (PLI) for each database and control software action, multiply the figure by the number of times the action is triggered and divide the result by the speed of the processor. This provides the processor time. Add the disk I/O time to the processor time. There is a reasonable assumption that the control software actions are triggered as a result of the database record being accessed/actioned. Information Engineering estimates this overhead as some 20% on the processor. No mention is made of the disk I/O overhead incurred. The final overhead to include is the telecommunication line times. This total overhead is calculated for each transaction/business requirement in what are called record action lists.

The author is not aware of any other structured method that attempts to measure transaction response times analytically. The other method the author is most familiar with—SSADM—undertakes equally detailed analytical measurements but only attempts to measure transaction resource utilisation time, that is the sum of the processor and the disk I/O time.

Resource utilisation time is within the domain of responsibility of the database administrator. The control software wait time is usually within the domain of the systems programmer and the telecommunication line overhead within the domain of the telecommunication specialists.

Response time is nothing more than resource utilisation time plus:

- the various wait times that inevitably occur in a multi-programming environment as control and application program software is paged in and out of the processor main memory. Wait time is estimated/calculated with a queueing algorithm or just by adding an additional overhead percentage;

- the telecommunication line times to transmit the data between remote sites and terminals.

The author suggests a few minor points for enhancing the record action list:

- Separate the disk I/Os into those that are caused by access to the database, access to the log file and access to the indexes. These I/Os can be calculated analytically very accurately as it is known when the accesses are triggered. The accesses to these data management facilities are each invoked at different points in a transaction execution and should therefore be monitored separately;

- Add a separate processor I/O overhead for the disk I/O incurred by the virtual paging of the application and control software. The I/O resulting from the paging of software cannot be calculated as the paging of the blocks of code is random as far as the designer is concerned. The 20% extra overhead suggested by Information Engineering for the processor is as good estimate as any the author has seen and is in line with other figures provided to him. The highest percentage has been 30%;

- Calculate the extra number of logical I/Os incurred in accessing a table row in a page/block if the index pointer does not include the block offset position of the table row in the block. This usually occurs where the index only points to the block and not to the table row. An example of this is given in figure 3.18 for the IBM VSAM keyed sequential data set. The number of extra logical I/Os is half the number of table rows per block. Multiply the logical I/Os by the PLI figure and add the result to the processor overhead.

13 Program design   There is a direct relationship from the procedures and procedure steps to the application programs and program modules. Given that it is possible to trace a procedure directly back to a process there is thus an explicit recognition of the concept of logical design = physical design as regards logic. Program design is therefore a minor task, as it has already been done in logical design. The Information Engineering approach is therefore to be recommended. The procedure and procedure step action diagram logic merely has to be upgraded with such facilities as action blocks and dialogue and layout actions to become logic in the application program and supporting module(s).

Understandably and quite correctly Information Engineering also lists the design facilities that may require the ideal one-for-one conversion to be broken.

The technique of program design is based on the traditional program structure chart of a hierarchy of dependent modules in an application program, with the controlling module at the top pointing to a set of sub-controlling modules, pointing in turn to "worker" modules at the bottom. The basis of the structure chart is the traditional transform and transaction centred approach to identifying and relating application program modules together. The author has concerns over this approach, which are discussed in section 2.4.2.3.

There is an explicit statement that the record action list used in the performance assessment technique for database and transaction tuning must be produced when specifying a program. This is thus a positive requirement that the logic in the application program is based on tuned access to the database.

Both versions of Information Engineering use their own formal commands and syntax for the specification of logic in the action diagrams. This is much to be encouraged. With the close integration of both versions of the method with their own CASE tool (IEF for IEM and IEW/ADW for Navigator) from which physical code can be produced, it is to be hoped that the advantage of having a formal command language for the logical process specification as the basis of physical application program code generation will be recognised.

A feature appealing to the author is that Navigator provides a detailed explanation of good module coupling (interdependence between modules), cohesion (the extent to which actions in one module relate to another module) and factoring (separating functionality in a module into another module). The objective is to have low coupling, high cohesion and high factoring. A long list of features to look for is given and is the most comprehensive the author has seen.

The significant points made are that the only coupling (the level of interdependence) between modules is the interface specification and the statement of function to perform the connection. Modules cannot be totally independent of each other, otherwise there would be no system, but the ripple effect of modules impacting each other when changes are made is minimised by the interface being the only connection. Detailed and excellent advice as to how to achieve low module coupling and what kind of coupling should be used is provided as well as how to maximise cohesion between the modules.

The basic message for coupling in order of desirability is to use data coupling (the fewer the data items used the better) with the data containing no control information, merely data values, in preference to control coupling, where a module requires to report back to its controller module the outcome of its actions, in preference to external, content and pathological coupling, where one module refers to the inside of another module, either obtaining data within the second module, branching to a point inside the second module or modifying the way the second module operates.

The basic message for cohesion is that high cohesion leads to low coupling Thus the optimum cohesion is where all actions performed by a module relate to the completion of one problem-to-solve (one activity as defined in the Navigator manual). There are 7 levels of cohesion, the lowest level being coincidental cohesion, the actions performed by a module being totally unrelated.

Navigator is also to be lauded with the extremely detailed description, although unfortunately without example, of the basis on which modules are identified. Modules are initially identified from the procedures, their transform and transaction centred basis established and the transaction recognition, input, transform and output "processing blocks" established, and the modules then factored into more focused processing, for example the input modules being factored into a read and an edit module.

There is one extraordinary statement in the Navigator Development Techniques manual that surely must not be true. It is stated that the procedure specification action diagrams should detail only *what* is to be done. By implication the preceding process specification action diagrams should also specify what is to be done. What this means is that the specification of the *how* logic for the processing of business requirements in the logical design cannot be made. If this is the case how can the logical design specification of processing be used as the basis of application program code generation, which is one of the benefits of producing a detailed logical design specification? If the concept that the logical design is the basis of the physical design is accepted then it is imperative that code for all parts of the application can be developed from the logical design. One can generate the data definition language code from the ERD logical model, so why not the access and process logic from the logical processes/procedures?

The authors of Navigator have graciously admitted that this is an error that got through the final production checks. It is being corrected.

Information Engineering is a particularly impressive structured method in database and program design.

14 Statements of good practice This is particularly the case with Navigator, which provides "pearls of wisdom" on a wide variety of logical and physical design, such as report design, screen design, the conduct of prototyping and various aspects of planning, user training, back-up, recovery and disaster planning, data conversion and security. It also provides a series of monographs on such topics as quality, software package integration, rapid systems development and project management.

2.4 INFORMATION ENGINEERING WEAKNESSES

Like the strengths, the weaknesses of Information Engineering fall into two broad classifications—general and systematic—with the specific being further broken down into three categories—the conceptual, the structural and the technical.

2.4.1 The general weaknesses

The general weaknesses are those that cannot be "pigeon holed" into one of the specific categories. They are applicable to all the stages of Information Engineering. They are discussed in the following sections.

2.4.1.1 *The absence of quality points and criteria (IEM only)*

This is a most surprising deficiency of IEM, given the large amount of strategic and logical and physical design deliverables that are produced. At a minimum there should be explicit quality assurance points at the end of each stage, so that the deliverables produced are signed off before being input into the next stage of the method.

There should also be a quality assurance point when the list of user business requirements is finally completed. After all, this list is the basis of all subsequent logical and physical design work and should formally be signed off by the users. This is not identified in the method. And incidentally which document is used to record the user's business requirements, both data retrieval and data maintenance? Once it is signed off all subsequent changes requested by the users should be subject to change control procedures.

It would be helpful if advice were provided as to the structure and skill level of the quality assurance team. A practice that is followed by the author following his experiences with the PRINCE project management method is for the QA team to be composed of three assurance co-ordinators. The user assurance co-ordinator ensures that the business requirements are fully identified and supported; the technical assurance co-ordinator ensures that the quality of the deliverables satisfies the necessary standards; and the business assurance co-ordinator ensures that the business objectives of the company are being met. Clearly as the project types change from strategy to analysis to design to development to implementation the skills of the QA team also change. There are thus usually three QA teams: a strategy team, a logical design team and a physical design/development/implementation team.

The advice offered by IEM on ascertaining the correctness of the logical design in the BAA and BSD stages is an attempt at defining a quality assurance function, with the team members and their responsibilities detailed. Nevertheless, there is still much that is missing—what to look for when assessing the deliverables; what work and deliverables can legitimately be omitted and under what conditions; what level of detail is required and to what level of rigour must the QA be carried out....

JMA provide a separate document that details the deliverables to be produced from each stage of the method and the supporting quality approval activities. While the document is useful it does not define the quality criteria that show whether a deliverable is up to standard or not. It is a QA activities, not a QA criteria, document.

Navigator includes a comprehensive set of quality assurance guidance, both as regards the tasks that need to be undertaken, when they should be undertaken and by whom and, most importantly, the quality assurance criteria for each deliverable to be produced. The IEM documents should do the same.

Most of the quality criteria set by Navigator are more about what to do than what to test. For the enterprise data modelling technique the first criterion is "Confirm with the appropriate level of business user that the model adequately represents data requirements". This should be defined as something on the lines of "Ascertain that each data subject entity is identified in a business requirement and has...".

2.4.1.2 An excess of enthusiasm

Notwithstanding the need for thoroughness (where Information Engineering is excellent) and completeness (where Information Engineering has some weaknesses) Information Engineering does perhaps suffer from an "excess of enthusiasm" in places. The author has found that in practice certain deliverables can be ignored:

- Many of the involvement/association matrices.
  The matrices show the relationship between any two objects. Information Engineering based methods seem to have a propensity to produce large numbers of such matrices. The author counted some 11 in the ISP stage of IEM and then gave up counting any further. Navigator has over 50 possible association matrices in the planning phase alone!

  Many of the matrices have little practical value and many in fact end up as "dead end" deliverables. They are produced because the method advises it but, once produced, are not used. The distribution factor to business system datastore, the business system to location and the datastore to location matrices are some examples of this wastage. Indeed the datastore to location matrix is pointless as one decides data distribution across location at the entity level, not the datastore level. Matrices of everything to everything are not very helpful.

  Navigator states that the matrices are to be used as an analytical tool to supplement a technique. All the techniques are drawn as two dimensional deliverables and therefore are all amenable to matrix support. Many of the techniques, such as process decomposition, are sufficiently rigourous not to require this support. Others, such as entity type life cycle, benefit from matrix support. The entity/update event cross reference matrix is a good way of ascertaining that an entity at least has a birth (insert) and death (delete) event in its life. It would be beneficial if Information Engineering were to state where technique support should be provided. All that Navigator states is that the use of matrices "should only be considered when the resulting properties add value to the analysis being performed". Not very helpful. Other structured methods, such as LSDM, have made no use of matrices and still function perfectly well.

  The only involvement/association matrix of practical use as far as the author is concerned is the business function/entity matrix. This matrix has proved useful for cluster analysis for the identification and definition of the scope of design areas for future systems development planning.

- The procedures
  As explained in section 2.4.2.2 procedures are neither "fish nor fowl", neither logical nor physical. They have proved to be a superfluous task. One can quite happily go straight from the logical event level processes and constituent problem-to-solve elementary processes to physical programs and program modules. Many other successful structured methods, such as SSADM, LSDM, Yourdon and STRADIS, do this and the concept of logical design = physical design requires it.

- Wastage/excessive overlap in the techniques.
A structured method is composed of many techniques, each of which produces one or more deliverables. The ideal is that the deliverables do not overlap in the information they contain, but that they relate to each other like pieces in a jigsaw puzzle.
Information Engineering provides a mixed message here. The ideal described above is found in a number of the Information Engineering techniques. Consider the techniques of ERD, data navigation, dialogue design, layout design, program design and database design. There is no overlap and therefore no wastage, each supporting a different aspect of the logical and physical design specification. Yet the techniques all reinforce each other's information, the data navigation diagrams, for example, validating that the ERD supports the business requirements.
Contrast this with:

- the techniques of function decomposition and dataflow diagramming. Both techniques are concerned with progressively decomposing high level business area processes down through functions and processes to the elementary processes. Dataflow diagrams also show the storage of data in datastores and the flow of the data between the processes, datastores and external entities. The important point is that the dataflow diagrams contain all the information contained in process decomposition diagrams, namely the decomposition of processes. Why use the process decomposition technique? Nothing is gained from it.

- the process dependency diagrams and the entity life cycle (ELC) diagrams. Both techniques record the sequence in which events/business requirements that update the database should occur. The ELCs also show the iteration and optionality of processes and the state variable/classifying attribute that re-expresses the sequence of update events in numeric form. Again the important point is that the process dependency diagrams contain no information that is not also contained in the ELCs. Why use the process dependency technique? Nothing is gained from it.

- the relational data analysis (RDA) technique and the user views and canonical synthesis. RDA is all about establishing the relationship between the data items through a set of data normalisation rules and grouping them into relations/entities. User views are also all about establishing the relationships between data items, in this case pictorially, by following a set of guidelines which are very similar to the normalisation rules. Canonical synthesis groups the user views into entities. Given that RDA is applied the author has never found user views and canonical synthesis add value to the logical design specification. They contain no new information.

2.4.1.3 The failure to use the current systems as the springboard for future systems development

It is noticeable when reading the IEM ISP manual that the chapter on the analysis of the current system(s) merely produces the following deliverables—a description of the existing data stores and the current systems, a dataflow diagram (to what level of process decomposition is not specified), a number of matrices and a description of how well the current business is supported/what problem areas exist. This is hardly a full and proper logical design specification of the current system(s). Missing is an ERD model and the lists of the business requirements and the problems of the current system. While it is quite reasonable to limit the detail in a strategy study (it has rightly been said that "detail is death in strategy") the finalising of the detail of the current system logical specification should be completed as the first task in the next stage.

Unfortunately the BAA stage does not do this either. The only reference to the current system is the task dependency diagram, which shows that the analysis of the current systems so far undertaken is used only as a one of the inputs to confirming the business area model of the new required systems. Yet it is almost always the case that the current systems are the business, if not the technical, springboard for future systems. The business of a corporation is usually very stable (particularly the data element) and if the current system is logically specified then much of the groundwork of the logical specification of the new required system has already been undertaken—the additional business requirements and corrections to the current deficiencies merely need to be incorporated. Equally many corporations cannot afford to abandon their investments in their existing systems and therefore occasionally make the new system an enhancement of the old.

Navigator recognises the importance of assessing the strengths and weaknesses of the current systems. "This information is critical in the development of an applications architecture that supports the future goals and objectives of the enterprise". Time and money could be wasted replacing perfectly adequate applications. Unfortunately Navigator only undertakes a fact finding exercise about the user's and IS department's perceptions of the current systems rather than a detailed logical design, from which the perceptions could be confirmed. The only logical design technique applied is process decomposition. Neither method is impressive in this important area.

Many other structured methods, such as SSADM and LSDM, create a detailed logical design specification of the existing systems (an ERD model, dataflow diagrams to three levels of process decomposition if necessary, a list of problem areas, descriptions of the lowest level processes from the dataflow diagrams, a business requirements list and optionally relational data analysis) and then upgrade it to support the information needs of the new business environment.

It is not merely good practice that the existing systems are fully documented. Only by comparing like with like—existing system(s) specification against new system(s) specification—can the full capability and benefit of the new system(s) be fully appreciated.

2.4.1.4 The absence of a document to record the user's business requirements

Information Engineering contains techniques to identify the user's data maintenance business requirements to the event level, such as the process dependency diagrams. But nowhere is reference made as to where to record the resultant business requirements. The method also does not make explicit the absolute necessity to identify and define the data retrieval business requirements. This is all the more surprising for, as explained in concept 9, it is the data retrieval business requirements that are the basis of all subsequent design. Again no document to record these business requirements is mentioned.

2.4.1.5 Too many "dead end" deliverables

Figure 2.11 shows the correct and incorrect relationships between the deliverables produced in a structured method. The ideal is that a number of working documents and design deliverables are initially produced, each covering a different aspect of the strategy, design or development process. The working documents can then be used with other documents to upgrade and rationalise the existing design deliverables. As the design process continues progressively fewer design deliverables remain.

In terms of Information Engineering the final logical design specification deliverables should be the ERD model with the by-products of the entity descriptions and their volumes and cardinalities, the procedure (? process) action diagrams and the dialogue and layout designs. The ERD model is the data structure component of the logical design, the action diagrams are the data access and data process component and the dialogue and layout designs are the man/machine component. The working documents include the process decomposition and dependency diagrams and the entity life cycle diagrams. The information they contain is used to enrich the design deliverables. For example the state variable/classifying attribute from the entity life cycle analysis technique is input into the procedure action diagrams to be tested for correctness for a given update event. These

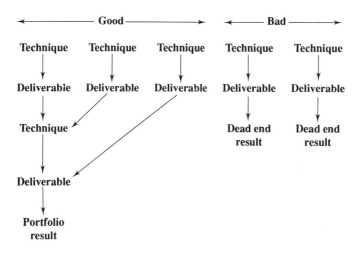

Figure 2.11   Good vs bad deliverables relationship

working documents add value to the design deliverables but eventually, having served their purpose, die a natural death in a history file of some sort.

What should not occur is "dead end" working documents and design deliverables that serve no purpose once they are produced. To say the documents contain information in their own right is not adequate. The whole purpose of a structured method is that the many individual components (techniques which produce documents and deliverables) play a supporting role to each other and therefore add value to the overall whole.

Unfortunately Information Engineering contains rather a number of such dead ends:

- the large number of matrices for which no advice is given as to their subsequent usefulness—see section 2.4.1.2;

- the entity life cycle diagrams which cannot then be used in the logic of the action diagrams to ensure that events that update the database occur in the correct sequence because no advice is provided as to how to specify and use the classifying attribute values;

- the various procedure documents/deliverables that are neither " logical fish nor physical fowl";

- the dataflow diagrams that play a not quite sure what role and certainly are of no subsequent benefit;

- the data structure diagrams in Navigator which contain no information that cannot be gleaned from the ERD model and the supporting documentation describing the entities and constituent attributes, and the other means of data input/output, such as screens and data views.

2.4.1.6 Inadequate use of the techniques as information gatherers

The criticism relates to Navigator. In reading the phase manuals the author was struck by the hundreds of pages containing words to the effect "gather the following information, ascertain their associations (over 30 were identified) and then have a review". What was not mentioned is that the logical techniques are like "hoovers" in gathering the information. What should be advised is that the application of the techniques should of itself be adequate. A project the author is advising on has explicitly banned writing up interview notes following interviews with the users. As the users talk so the ERD and process models are drawn and the supporting documentation, such as the attributes and entity volumes, are filled in. There is no wastage of effort, and the users can see the system being dynamically created before their eyes. Credibility is very high.

2.4.2 The systematic weaknesses

2.4.2.1 The conceptual weaknesses

Information Engineering is found wanting against many of the concepts detailed in section 2.2, specifically:

1 *Test the logical design for efficiency*   Of all the concepts this is the one where Information Engineering is most seriously flawed. The concept is totally ignored.

Information Engineering certainly and obviously recognises the concept that the logical design is the basis of the physical design. The information strategy deliverables are used as the skeleton onto which the logical design specification is built, which is then converted into a physical design. The method is based on this obvious, and hence unnecessary to state, concept.

Information Engineering makes no reference to the concept in the ERD data modelling and data navigation techniques, the prime techniques for this task. As will be detailed in chapter 3, there are easy to understand and apply techniques to test the logical design for efficiency. They are easy to understand and apply because they are enhancements to existing Information Engineering techniques.

The area where the greatest testing for logical design efficiency should be is in transaction access path analysis against the ERD model. Logical data accesses to the ERD model convert to logical and physical I/O accesses in the implemented computer system. Database I/O is of two kinds. Logical I/O occurs when the requisite data to be accessed by an application program is located in the processor main memory buffer pool. The data is then copied into the program working memory when a data access call is issued. Physical I/O occurs when the requisite data is not in the buffer pool and must be accessed and retrieved from disk, when the buffer pool is full and some data must be written to disk to empty it or when there is a COMMIT call (either an explicit call in the application program or implicit call at the end of application program processing) and data is flushed out to disk. (Chapter 4 describing distributed database shows that there are two other types of I/O to database I/O.)

I/Os are expensive in machine path length instructions (PLI). Assume an IBM mainframe processor environment. The author has PLI performance figures from a number of database vendors. A logical I/O is on average some 1500 PLI. A physical I/O for a single record occurrence/table row with no referential integrity constraints or pointer linkages is some 4000 PLI. If the processor speed is 5500 machine/path length instructions per second the access to a disk would require one second of processor time. Access logic is therefore a resource-hungry process in processor terms. Physical I/O is also slow, as it occurs at the mechanical speed of the disk driver, whereas logical I/O is at the electronic speed of the processor. The disparity between the mechanical and the electronic speed is continuing to increase. Typical disk I/O times have declined from some 35 milliseconds to less than 25 milliseconds. This almost 50% improvement in physical I/O times has been vastly outpaced by the enormous increase in processor speeds, from millions of instructions per second to over 50 million instructions per second and growing.

In contrast to access logic, process logic is relatively cheap in PLI and, because it is executed in processor main memory, functions at electronic speed. Advice the author has received from a number of independent sources and database vendors is that, again on average, the PLI process logic overhead between data access calls in an application program is on average some 500 PLI for 3GL and 700 PLI for a 4GL programming language. Programs that do not have to massage data prior to or after input or output to a terminal or database can ignore process logic overhead.

The important point is that access logic is much more expensive than process logic. Fortunately, if the application is well understood and fully and correctly specified, the number and type of logical accesses to the data, given known assumptions about the application—this online business requirement is executed 100 times a day and a customer has on average

1000 orders outstanding—can be measured very accurately. Using "tricks of the practitioner's trade" to be described in chapter 3 to the technique of transaction access path analysis it is possible to ascertain for each business requirement:

- if a business requirement has multiple entry point possibilities to the ERD data model, which is the best entry point;

- if a business requirement has multiple access path options, which is the best option;

- where, when and how to modify the ERD or transaction if either is inefficient;

- when to "cheat" and incorporate derived or redundant unnormalised data in the ERD.

All this will keep data access overheads to a minimum.

Unfortunately the standard Information Engineering data access techniques of process logic analysis (in the analysis stage) and data usage definition (in the business design stage) do not support any of these tests to ascertain if the ERD model or business requirement data accesses are efficient.

Given the failure to test for logical efficiency it is not surprising that the author has found in many consulting assignments that much database optimisation/tuning using the performance assessment technique has been needed. Many man hours of unnecessary effort could have been saved if Information Engineering supported this concept.

2 Events are standalone and problems-to-solve are causally related   The two concepts are nowhere explicitly explained in the Information Engineering manuals and neither is it shown in any of the design techniques for data processing, such as process decomposition and process dependency. The only technique that can diagrammatically represent these two concepts is dataflow diagramming. DFDs can show the standalone nature of event level processes by having data stores separate processes, as shown in figure 3.22. Such processes must be separated in time and therefore standalone. The simultaneous and hence causal relationship between problem-to-solve processes can be represented by dataflows between processes, as shown in figure 3.23, where process 4.1.1.1 triggers 4.1.1.2 *et seq.* All the problem-to-solve processes for the event "choose container crane" occur at the same time as the event. Unfortunately, DFDs in Information Engineering do not play a significant role in logical design.

However, as described in section 2.3.2.1, Information Engineering very much makes amends in its definition and description of processes and elementary processes. Although not explicitly stated processes are, based on the examples given, clearly pitched at the event level and elementary processes at the problem-to-solve level. It is also possible to trace a direct relationship of the logical processes and elementary processes to the physical application programs and program modules via procedures and procedure steps. The program modules obviously execute whenever programs execute. It follows that elementary processes in a process must also occur simultaneously whenever the process is triggered by an event/business requirement. The causal relationship between modules in application programs is established in modules calling modules. This is shown as hierarchically structured program structure charts, with modules directly related to modules. This is in line with Yourdon's statement that modules are callable, programs are schedulable.

Working backwards from the application programs it can be established that Information Engineering implicitly supports the two concepts. It would be better if the dataflow diagramming technique played a larger role in the method as a replacement for the process decomposition and process dependency techniques and an explicit statement of the need to support these two concepts in the logical design were made.

3   The separation of the logical design from the physical design   One of the most serious failings of Information Engineering is that there is not a clear boundary between logical and physical design. With many structured methods one is in logical design in one stage and paying no attention to hardware/software constraints of the target environment on which the system is to be implemented, and then in the next stage deep into physical design, with close attention to the specific constraints of the target hardware/software. The boundary between logical and physical is explicit, precise and distinct.

Information Engineering fails in this regard in the IEM BSD stage, which includes:

- design techniques that are clearly logical (dataflow diagramming). Yet IEM unbelievably states that identification of the datastores depends on the target database file handler!;

- design techniques that are clearly appropriate only to specific hardware/software (preliminary file handler design, such as for DL/1);

- deliverables that are neither "fish nor fowl", neither fully logical nor fully physical. Consider the procedures. Logical processes identified in the earlier analysis stage are converted into procedures in the business system design stage, which in turn are converted into physical application programs in the technical design stage. In reality there are only logical processes and subsequent physical programs. What are these "halfway house" procedures?

Information Engineering states that the process action diagrams specify the *what* is required of a business requirement and the procedure action diagrams specify the *how* it is to be achieved, the how containing the precision from which physical code can be generated. Yet both the what processes and the how procedures use a common command language in a common structured format in action diagrams. Yet a what explanation of a business requirement only requires a general free-form description and therefore does not require a formal command language to be structured in action diagrams. If the procedures are the correct place for specifying the how logic then what is the purpose of the processes? If both the processes and the procedures specify logic then one of them should go. Alternatively the specification of the processes should be relaxed and allowed to be free form. This is, in the author's opinion, the thing to do, as it is necessary to record the business in simple "easy for the user to understand" what terms. If the logical processes are not used for this then another deliverable is required.

The failure to provide a clear cut separation of the logical design from the physical design is a serious deficiency in Information Engineering. When the concepts of logical design = physical design and test for logical efficiency are finally accepted, such that the logical design can be the source of an efficient directly coded physical solution, then the production of these neither "fish nor fowl" BSD deliverables will be seen as the hindrance they are.

4   *Design the database on data retrieval business requirements*   This is nowhere addressed by either version of Information Engineering. The data maintenance business requirements do not add any new information in the ERD model that has not already been identified as required by the data retrieval business requirements. They do not enrich the model, or indeed the company's business. It was argued in sections 2.2.2.4 and 2.2.2.5 that the retrieval business requirements drive the data maintenance business requirements. The data maintenance business requirements are a necessary evil. Data is only in the ERD model, and hence in the database, because there is a need to retrieve it—only then does the data have value.

It should be noted that *ad hoc* retrievals cannot specifically be catered for in the database design process. The best that can be done is to ensure that the ERD model, and hence the database, supports all conceivable data retrieval needs.

The data accesses of the data maintenance business requirements are not forgotten in database design because they are included in the summary access path maps. The design of the database will therefore automatically give due weight to the data maintenance accesses. However, the initial structure of the design is based on the data retrieval accesses. The reader will find in chapter 3 that the ERD model is also tested for logical efficiency against the data retrieval accesses. The efficient ERD becomes the initial database.

2.4.2.2 The structural weaknesses

1 The neither "fish nor fowl" IEM BSD stage There is no need to apply the neither "logically fish nor physically fowl" BSD stage, with its confusing inclusion of design techniques that are clearly logical, such as dataflow diagrams, dialogue and layout design and the creation of summary data access/usage against the ERD model, and clearly physical, such as preliminary database design. Why is it not possible to include in the clearly logical BAA stage of the method, with its major logical design deliverables of the ERD model, process decomposition and dependency diagrams and process/elementary action diagrams, the also logical dataflow diagrams and dialogue and layout design deliverables of the BSD stage and from there go directly to the clearly physical TD stage and include in it the also physical preliminary physical database design? The BSD stage would then be eliminated. This would be in line with the concept of a clear separation of logical design from physical design.

Navigator does not face this problem, with the logical design techniques being in the analysis phase and the preliminary and detailed physical design techniques being in the design phase. It has already been argued that the boundary between the logical and physical is at times difficult to identify, with the technical facilities that are generic to all computing, such as pages and indexed access, being included in the logical side of the "equation". The conceptual system design produced in the analysis phase is therefore logical.

2 Waterfall versus ring approach The cascading "waterfall" approach to applying the strategy and design techniques in a fixed sequence of stages and tasks is a policy followed by all the leading design methods. James Martin refers to a "stepwise refinement", which is a more cyclical concept than a waterfall. This is fine so long as the method is being applied to only one data processing environment. It breaks down when multiple data processing environments require to be supported in an application.

While preserving this waterfall approach, change is under way with the "ring" structure application of the design techniques. This is illustrated in figure 1.4. There is a set of core mandatory techniques that are generic to all data processing environments. These generic techniques are in fact those appropriate to centralised batch and online processing, as this environment is itself generic. Given the generic nature of the centralised data processing environment, it is to this environment that the waterfall approach will continue to be applied. Subsidiary to the core component are techniques to be applied to the other data processing environments, such as realtime and distributed database, each with their specific design techniques. The techniques are applied at the corresponding stage of the design process, for example the summary access paths are drawn in a distributed system parallel with those for a centralised system.

Designers of applications that span data processing environments should "cherry pick" the appropriate satellite specific technique(s) on an as required basis while continuing to "cascade" use the core generic techniques.

2.4.2.3 The technical weaknesses

Like the strengths of Information Engineering the weaknesses are considered from two viewpoints—the techniques for information systems strategy planning and the techniques for application systems logical and physical design.

1   *The information strategy planning techniques should be outward as well as inward looking*   Information Engineering fails in this regard. The techniques used in the IEM ISP stage include the identification of the business mission, CSFs and inhibitors and the setting of objectives and goals, which are then used as the basis of the company's information needs. Navigator also identifies the above, excluding the inhibitors. All good stuff and no complaint. But it is, in fact, information that is about how the company itself should and does operate—that is the company on a standalone basis. In the opinion of the author, both versions of Information Engineering tend to be inward looking, although this is disputed by the vendors.

But what about the outside world? Companies do not operate in a business vacuum. The strategic planning method (formerly called LEAP) from LBMS very much considers the information that is required to record the outside pressures on a company. It does this by considering three additional aspects, viz:

• The five main competitive forces identified by Michael Porter and which have become universally accepted as a valid interpretation of the outside business forces making life difficult for a company. The competitive forces are new entrants, supplier, customer and substitution, all four influencing the final force of rivalry. Porter's excellent books "Competitive Advantage" and "Competitive Strategy" fully describe these forces. The basic information technology questions to be answered by these forces is whether any proposed new computer system(s) raises the cost of entry associated with competing with the company, whether it alters the balance of buying power between the company and its suppliers, whether it alters the balance of selling power between the company and its customers, whether it stops or makes it very difficult for the customer to drop the product/service in favour of a competitor's and whether the new system improves the company's position against its rivals? Much information requires to be stored to answer these fundamental questions—the various prices and bulk buying deals from suppliers, customers buying habits and expenditure profiles, ... The forces are therefore the basis of the critical success factors and inhibitors.

- All the information needed for management to know what kind of market sector the product/service is or should be in. Porter has also identified four competitive strategies—high or low cost, differentiated or focused. A high/low cost producer strategy puts the emphasis on competing by offering a product/service at a high/low cost. A Rolls Royce car versus a Beetle, for example. A differentiation strategy puts the emphasis on showing that a product/service is different from the competition. Singapore Airlines differentiate themselves from other airlines by their Singapore girls. A focus/niche strategy takes one or both of the first two strategies but with the product/service targeted to a specific narrow sector of the market. For example James Martin and Associates have focused on the information technology structured methods and CASE tool market. The reader can decide as to whether JMA is low or high cost and differentiated.

- The competitive advantage now and in the future of a product/service and how information technology can help on both fronts. This is identified by using the "Portfolio" technique developed by the Boston Consultancy Group. The technique categorises whether a product/service is a "wild cat" (long term potential), "star" (high revenue now and in the future), "cash cow" (high revenue now) or "dead dog" (no/little revenue now), and whether it is worthwhile prolonging the commercial life of a dead dog by investing in it to make it a cash cow and likewise making a cash cow a star. Much information requires to be stored to answer the questions.

Strategic planning requires that the information needed to measure these competing forces, ascertain the state of a product/service and the necessary investment profile and the market sector being tapped be included in information strategy planning as part of the corporate information needs. The method is then able to ascertain the information that a company needs to know to answer the two great business issues—who and what are making life difficult for the company (competitive force) and how a company can make life difficult for its competitors (competitive strategy and portfolio)— and the measures of its own successes and failures.

The nearest to outwards looking is Navigator, which states that the CSFs should include external issues beyond the control of the executive. This is not quite the same thing as defining CSFs against the competitors.

2   The absence of a cost base to the prioritisation of business systems development
The IEM prioritisation of the business systems into a sequence for development is based on a set of weightings of such factors as objectives, goals, CSFs and "usefulness" of the information in supporting a business function, all cross multiplied to provide a compound result, the business systems with the highest score being first in the development queue.

While all of this is valid it loses sight of the fact that all computer systems are developed for one purpose only—to increase a company's financial bottom line. Surely the financial viability of a proposed business system is a crucial aspect in the choice as to whether to proceed with its development? Information Engineering pays inadequate attention to whether a business system adds to a company's financial strength and identifying which business system adds the most value. The chapter on cost/benefit analysis in the IEM BAA stage is the traditional approach, but the chapter details what requires to be done and not how to do it. For example, there is no advice as to how to measure the intangible benefits of a computer system. There are also many aspects of financial measurement that should be included in cost/benefit analysis which are ignored. There is no measurement of the cost of the risk of the investment and the value of offsetting the risk with flexibility.

The chapter also does not identify the raft of modern costing techniques now available for measuring the value and benefit of investing in information technology. This book is not about measuring the success or otherwise in investing in information technology and therefore will not describe the costing techniques in detail. A brief description is all that can be made. The techniques are of two kinds—those that are for the strategic identification of the projects likely to yield the best financial return and those for measuring the potential and actual success of a project.

The major strategic techniques are:

- Strategic Value Analysis. SVA was developed by R. M. Curtice of Arthur D. Little and is detailed in "Strategic Value Analysis"Prentice Hall, 1985. The technique identifies, decomposes and prioritises the business objectives. The ability of the information technology facilities to support the objectives is then assessed for the lowest event level processes. The priorities and abilities are multiplied together and related to the cost of the facilities. The result is a "pound bang for a capability buck". The project with the biggest bang per buck is a candidate for development.

- Critical Success Factors. CSFs is very similar to SVA.

- Value Chain Analysis. In simple terms this technique ascertains the degree to which a computer system enables a product/service to have a higher selling price against the cost of production at each stage of its manufacture. The price/cost difference is multiplied by the number of times the product/service is sold and if the result is more than the cost of the proposed computer system then the project is a candidate for selection.

The above techniques are not mutually exclusive and can very easily incorporate each others facilities to mutual advantage, but that is another book.

The major project techniques are:

- Ascertaining the Correct Discount Rate. This is not so much a technique as a series of factors and good financial practices that need to be taken into account when calculating the discount rate. The calculation of the discount rate is a many faceted skill. The purpose of the discount rate is to take account of the fact that the investment life of a project can last over a number of years and therefore incurs inflation, which must be offset. It also incurs a risk and therefore demands a higher financial return. Non-discounted cash flow techniques are now very discredited.

- Decision tree analysis. This technique has evolved from work done by J. Magee and is described in "How to Use Decision Trees in Capital Investment", Harvard Business Review, Sept 1964. It is designed to measure the added value of a project when measures are taken to minimise the risk of a project not succeeding. The cost and benefits of investing in flexibility to offset risk given certain conditions are measured. There are other techniques for measuring risk, such as Monte Carlo simulation and Contingent Claims Analysis.

- Multiple Attribute Decision model. The technique is described by C. Berliner and J. A. Brimson in "Cost Management for Today's Advanced Manufacturing", Harvard Business Press 1988, pp 189–196. This uses a scoring (a measure of usefulness), weighting (a measure of importance) and risk (the probability of success) approach to all the benefits, tangible and intangible. The three components are multiplied together to obtain a ranking. Those benefits with the highest ranking should be invested in.

- The quantification approach. This is probably the ultimate in measuring the financial return to be obtained from the intangible benefits of a computer system. A series of steps are followed from identifying the intangible and making the intangible measurable, quantifiable and costable. The last two components are multiplied to give a value.

There are a number of other techniques establishing themselves as a means of assessing the value of investing in information technology, such as Paul Strassman's return on management and B. Ives' customer resource life cycle.

The issue of cost justifying an investment in information technology is a major subject and is addressed in a book being written by the author of this book in conjunction with a former colleague for release in 1992.

3 The absence of an information technology strategy   Information Engineering is only concerned with information systems strategy planning, that is with identifying the long term information requirements of a corporation and planning the development of business systems to support the information requirements. No advice is provided as to the techniques for choosing the most suitable hardware or software to support the information system strategy. An information technology strategy study should therefore follow an information systems strategy study, particularly for a green-field site or where major investment decisions are pending.

There are two techniques to follow when undertaking an information technology strategy study:

- Create a detailed template of the technical facilities required of the hardware and software. The author has tended to break the template into the processor and its peripherals, such as the disk and tape drives, the telecommunication facilities and the database and control software. The template must be very detailed and precisely defined, so as to leave no ambiguity. This is particularly important when going out to tender. In order to appreciate the degree of detail required the author has created a template for database software of more than 500 facilities that should be supported. The template is continually expanding.

- The template produces a result that assumes the world is flat—all the facilities listed in the template are given an equal weighting, everything is equal. The real world is not so kind. Certain facilities will be more important than others. For example, if the systems to be implemented are only required at one location then the facilities for distributed database are of small or no consequence and should be given a low weighting. The template therefore needs to be put in the context of the company's technical requirements. The weighting mechanism is a widely used approach for this. It is also advisable to prepare an Evaluation Plan based on the above to evaluate the responses of the vendors of the technology against the template.

The information technology architecture diagram used by IEM should not be confused with an information technology strategy. The diagram only records the layout of a hardware/software architecture once the information technology strategy has been decided. It is not a technique for identifying the facilities of and ascertaining the requirements for information technology.

The author is not aware of any structured method that provides techniques for conducting an information technology strategy study.

THE DESIGN TECHNIQUES

There is a general weakness. Both versions of Information Engineering refer to the need to identify the location of business activity, but neither makes any attempt to show how location can be built into the logical and physical design techniques. Navigator devotes less than one page to the subject in the Development Techniques manual. The page makes no reference to any techniques.

1 The ERD model   While the technique is given high marks, points of improvement can nevertheless be made. They are:

- Build the ERD model based on the data retrieval business requirements only. This is in line with the ninth concept described earlier, where the reasons for the data retrievals being the driving force behind the data requirements of an application are explained. Data maintenance business requirements do not identify any new entities and relationships and should therefore be ignored. They serve no data modelling role. The trouble is that when one is talking to the usual user they are talking only in terms of data maintenance—"We receive orders, allocate stock and ship the goods...." It is only senior management which, without prompting, talks in data retrieval terms—"I want to know how much profit was made last month."

- Validate the ERD against the data retrieval business requirements to ensure that it can not only support them, but also does it efficiently. The need for this and how it should be done is not identified in the Information Engineering manuals. The way this can be done is described in section 3.1.1.

- The diagramming conventions for the drawing of the ERD model suffer from an excess of enthusiasm. The cardinality of the detail to master relationship between entities is always 1-to-1 and from master to detail 1-to-n (where n can be 0, in rare cases a fixed 1 or any value greater than 1). The drawing of a bar symbol across the relationship line to indicate a cardinality of 1 from detail to master and the crows foot symbol representing the cardinality of many from master to detail is not necessary, provided the detail entity is drawn below the master entity. The symbols add nothing to the information implicit in the model. They do not enrich the model.

  The necessity for the crows foot is, in fact, an explicit recognition of poor diagramming practice. In over a decade of drawing entity models the author has never found it difficult to position the detail entity below the master. There is also the benefit that the model is much easier to interpret. One can quickly appreciate which entity is the master and which is the detail just by looking at the model rather than following a potentially labyrinthine maze of relationships to ascertain via the crows foot which entity is the master and which entity is the detail. It is also much easier to ascertain the impact of the model on database performance, broad networks being bad news on disk I/O. It can readily be appreciated that the entity model in figure 2.5 will create performance problems, with heavy referential integrity overheads.

- Introduce operational entities. Operational entities occur where a data retrieval business requirement requires to access an entity on other than the prime or relationship key. Assume there is a requirement to retrieve all customers with red hair. The prime key of customer is customer number. It would therefore, as the model stands, necessitate a scan of the entity table to ascertain customers with red hair. It would be a better approach to create an operational entity of colour of hair as an entry point to customer and access directly on colour with a value of red and from there access the requisite customers. The use of operational entities is a common practice in a number of other widely used structured methods.

  Draw the entities which serve as operational entry points with a different symbol—they will be implemented as indexes in the database design rather than as tables/record types of data.

- The ERD model does not record all the semantic information about the relationships between data. Semantics is a "buzzword" meaning nothing more than the description of meaning. Semantics is becoming increasingly important to post relational file handlers, particularly as used in expert systems and object oriented databases. This trend and its supporting design techniques and physical technology are discussed in chapter 5. The semantics of data occur at two levels—inter-entity and inter-attribute. Information Engineering supports inter-entity semantics in the ERD model. The relationships are given a descriptive title appropriate to the purpose of the relationship. Customers "place" orders, which are "received from" customers.

  It is the inter-attribute relationship that is not given a semantic description. An example is given in figure 2.12. This facility is known as the triple facility, with a relationship between the subject, which equates to a prime key of a table of information, and the property, which is a non-key attribute of the table. There could be a semantic relationship description between the subject key and all the attribute properties of the table. The example illustrates two such semantic descriptions—that an employee "earns" a salary and an employee "lives" at an address. "Employee" is the subject, "earns" is the relationship and "salary" is the property.

- **The triple facility**

Subject	**Relationship**	**Property**
Table	Description	Attribute
Key		

  e.g.

TABLE	SUBJECT	RELATIONSHIP	PROPERTY	TYPE	LENGTH (key)
Employee	Employee No (key)			CN	10
		Earns Lives at	Salary Address	N X	7, 2 50

Figure 2.12   Inter-attribute semantics

- Another issue. For a technique to be valid it must be applicable under all conditions. A situation should not occur where a technique is fine if it is applied on Monday but falls apart on Tuesday. Such a situation occurs in the ERD model when trying to represent the exclusivity of relationships between master and detail entities. Information Engineering shows relationship exclusivity by drawing an arc between those relationships that are exclusive. Consider figure 2.13. Exclusivity certainly works in simple scenarios. When entity C in figure 2.13(a) is inserted it can relate either to entity A or entity B. It is a pity that Information Engineering does not state that there could be conditions to this exclusivity, for example that if entity A is inserted on Tuesday then the relationship is not exclusive, but when inserted on any other day it is exclusive. But consider the compound situation in figure 2.13(b). One can easily envisage a situation where when entity G is inserted it is exclusively related to entity C or D or E (exclusivity arc 1); E or F (2); B or C or D (3); A or B (4); ..., depending on certain conditions appropriate to the application. The simplicity and ease of interpretation of the ERD model is lost. In none of these exclusive relationships has any conditionality to the exclusivity that may be present been specified. The use of exclusivity arcs is not a component of the ERD modelling technique that is watertight.

  Given that exclusivity has to be supported through process logic it should be supported in the action diagrams. When the action diagrams are converted into the physical design, if the file handler supports the specification of trigger rules in the database schema then that is where the exclusivity conditions can be specified. If the file handler does not support triggers then the exclusivity conditions must be coded in the application programs.

- Navigator identifies that relationships between entities can be one-to-one, but unfortunately does not offer advice as to how to handle them. "Combining them" is not very helpful. This is addressed in chapter 3.

2 The paucity of ERD model and data navigation data statistics   The ERD model requires by-product information about the entity volumes, lives and cardinality ratio statistics. The need for this in logical design is not discussed in detail in the IEM BAA stage. Cardinality, for example, is only described in general terms as one-to-n occurrences of master to detail entities. The different types of cardinalities that a database designer requires to know are not considered. Entity volumes and lives are not discussed at all. These statistics are also not considered in the BSD stage. The volumes of entities is only discussed in the TD stage as a general requirement when calculating disk space requirements.

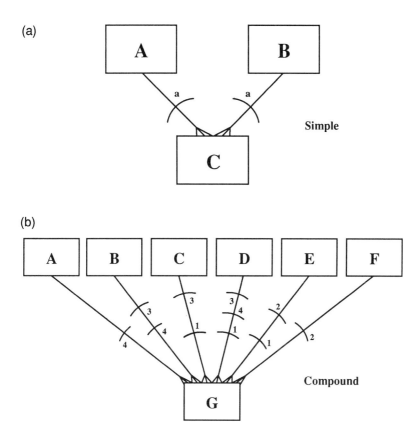

Figure 2.13 Exclusivity

The cardinality statistics that are required are minimum, maximum, average and working average. Assume that the customer entity has 100 occurrences in the application and the order entity has 1000 occurrences. The minimum cardinality is zero as a customer may have placed no orders; the average cardinality is 10 orders; the maximum value established in discussion with users is that a number of customers can have up to 150 orders. The cardinality that is not addressed in most structured design methods, including IEM but, uniquely as far as the author is aware excluding Navigator, is working average. The working average is the average that actually exists when a customer has placed orders. For example, assume that 50% of customers have no orders and the remaining customers have, more or less, an equal amount of business. The working average would therefore be 20. If it is known that certain customers have fairly high volumes of orders then these can be explicitly identified in the documentation. For example, it is known that all customers located in Birmingham have on average 20% more orders than customers located elsewhere. When it comes to undertaking transaction access path analysis if it is known that the vast bulk of accesses are to those customers that place orders, which seems not unreasonable, then clearly the working average is the value to go for. If the customer is based in Birmingham then the number of orders for that customer is 24.

Given the thoroughness of the ERD technique the tardy IEM description of the need for this crucial statistical information about the data is surprising. The statistics are as important for logical design as they are for physical design. The entity volumes and cardinality ratios are crucial information for the data navigation technique. Without this information the technique cannot be applied properly and certainly it could not be established whether the ERD model or transaction access path is efficient.

3 The failure to have three distinct data modelling techniques   Information Engineering has one technique to produce the application/enterprise logical data model—entity relational diagram (ERD) modelling. This technique begins its life cycle in the strategy stage of the method by identifying the data subject areas and their relationships to build a subject area data model. The subject areas are then decomposed in the strategy and analysis stages into their constituent entities/entity sub-types and the relationships between them and the attributes and domains within each entity defined. Having built the ERD model it is then "confirmed" by checking the correctness of the allocation of the attributes to the entities by applying the technique of data normalisation/relational data analysis (RDA). RDA is applied against the ERD. This would be a perfectly valid approach, were it not for frailties of "homo sapiens".

Other structured methods, such as SSADM (until version 4, which has heavily modified the approach) and LSDM, deliberately have three separate and distinct data modelling techniques. The reason for this is that each technique has different strengths and weaknesses. Where entity modelling is strong is different from where relational data analysis is strong. Entity modelling builds a logical data model based on data retrieval business requirements, works largely at the entity level, and with skilled designers and knowledgeable users is quick and easy to build. RDA, by contrast, builds the data model based on the mechanistic grouping of the raw data items into relations by the application of the data normalisation rules. *Crucially, however, both techniques provide different perspectives to the data (entity modelling being top down and based on business requirements and RDA being bottom up and based on data) and thereby may produce different results, even for the same application.* This may sound surprising but it has very often occurred.

In one application for a railway company the users were quite explicit in defining a thing called a train. A train entity was correspondingly identified in the ERD data model. However, when RDA was applied it was found there was no such thing as a train. What was identified were such things as engines, coaches and guards vans that were joined together for the purposes of undertaking a journey. Another example for a major international oil company—the users kept on talking about oil wells. Analysis of the data identified no such thing. What there was was a derrick (they were exploration wells), a hole in the ground into which were inserted conduit pipes, which can branch out and hopefully hit oil and gas accumulations. Together all of these things formed the concept of an oil well. Yet again in an insurance application the users spoke about brokers and underwriters. Relational analysis of the data items identified that they did not exist. There were account holders, and a holder could be simultaneously a holder for broking accounts and a holder for quite separate underwriting accounts.

These examples are but a few of the wide variations between the data model results that can be ascertained from these two data modelling techniques. Information Engineering would be enhanced if it kept entity modelling and relational data analysis as distinct separate techniques, to be applied at different points in the method procedures, preferably by different designers. The danger of the Information Engineering approach of keeping the two data modelling techniques together, with RDA being used to "confirm" the ERD is that the designers would not be human if they did not view the data items in the entities in the context of the ERD, particularly if they were responsible for building the ERD in the first place. There is also the danger, which the author has often encountered, that building the model from the business requirements lacks the rigour of the relational approach and that issues of the business appropriate to the application data model can be "argued to death" and still no solution is found. The insurance data model based on the business requirements was abandoned in frustration and left "pending" until the relational data model clarified the situation.

Keep the two techniques separate and apply them at different points in the method by different designers. This assists the independent application of the techniques. It adds an extra element of rigour. The author listened to a lecturer on Information Engineering describe the data modelling techniques of methods like SSADM and LSDM as "awesome". It was said with respect.

4 Process decomposition When one is undertaking process decomposition one is taking a high level process and breaking it down to the next level of detail. IEM clearly identifies three level of decomposition, from the function level to the process event level to the elementary process/problem- to-solve level. What one is not doing is decomposing from a given level to the same level, for example from a function level to a function level. Yet this is what IEM and Navigator permit. The process Take Order may be decomposed into the processes Receive Order and Allocate Stock. The process Take Order is at the "do something" event level *as are the other two*, the event Allocate Stock occurring in time after the event Receive Order. This is not decomposition into lower levels of detail. All the processes are at the event level.

Navigator is much less precise in the advice offered for this technique. The top level process is for the whole business area. The aim is to decompose the top level process into the lowest level elementary processes, that is "all processing ... to respond to an event". "Elementary processes are the lowest level of a functional decomposition diagram". No attention to the decomposition of an event into any problem-to-solve processes is undertaken! Given the concept of logical design = physical design events become application programs and problem-to-solve within the event become the modules, then Navigator contains no logical design technique for the identification of application program modules! The deficiencies of this are discussed in paragraph 17 in this section. No realistic advice is offered as to the number of process levels required in between. Advice such as "decompose the single business area process ... in a way which is easiest for the users to understand" is not very helpful.

The comment from Ernst & Young on this was that the logical design equates to the physical design, because the "physical design requires constraints that are not represented in the designabstraction derived from the logical models. Events are not processes. Navigator identifies application programs on the basis of business transactions, not essential (replacing the term elementary in new versions of the method) processes, because essential processes are not 1–1 with business transaction in all cases". This is where the author parts company with the designers of Navigator. Events are processes and are the direct basis of application programs.

The processes can represent events/business requirements to which the system must make a response. Navigator only recognises two types of events—those that are triggered by an external entity and those triggered by the passage of time. While this is perfectly valid, it is not enough. There is a third type of trigger, a system condition. For example, there could be a trigger that when the stock level in a warehouse reaches a minimum quantity an order to purchase some more of the product is automatically to be raised. No advice about these event types is provided, such that an important part of a business could be missed. This is not a minor issue.

This third type of trigger is recognised by a number of other widely used structured methods, such as SSADM.

Of the three event types, time and condition events are triggered automatically.

5   *Process dependency*   The author fails to understand the benefit of this technique. It shows the sequence in which event level processes that update the database occur. The technique has no purpose for processes higher than the event level, for the simple reason that the higher level process can contain many event level processes and which event is to be used to identify the dependency?

The sequencing of update events is also and perhaps better supported by the entity life cycle technique, which has been specifically designed for the sequencing of update events. The technique is also based on sequencing the events per entity, and is therefore better able to be the basis of identifying an entity state variable value to be contained in the entity for a given event and which can be tested in an application program to ensure the events occur in the correct order. And at least the entity life cycle technique can provide a logical design deliverable, the state variable. There is no such benefit from the process dependency diagrams.

The technique is not used in Navigator.

6   *Entity type life cycle analysis*   This technique is seriously flawed, both as regards its use and the quality of its deliverable.

The technique is used in such a manner that it is bound to be one of the "dead ends" of Information Engineering. The purpose as defined in Navigator, and matched in IEM, is "to associate the data and process models ..., to ensure and confirm that the data and process models are complete in supporting one and the other". Nowhere is it stated that the ELCs are to be used as a technique producing a logical design deliverable. ELCs are only to be a means of reconciliation between the deliverables of other techniques. It does not say much for these other techniques that they require cross correlation of their own deliverables with the assistance of another technique!

The technique is only able to record that entity lives have a sequence of update events (insert, modify and delete), that the updates can iterate and be optional, that an entity can only have one life and hence state at any one time. How this latter point relates to the rule in IEM that states that an entity type can have multiple life cycles, presumably simultaneously, is not explained, and no advice is given as to how the entity state variable/classifying attribute is to be defined and used. Without the state variable the technique has no practical value for application systems implementation.

In the real world the life of an entity can be much more complicated. An entity can have multiple lives simultaneously. A person can have a life as a married individual, as a sportsperson, as an employee, as a..., all occurring simultaneously, in parallel and independently of each other. The sequence of some modify events may not be predictable between the time the entity is inserted and deleted. A person can change his/her address at any time. It may also be necessary to "jump" the normal sequence of events in a time forward or backward direction through what is called a quit. A time forward jump could be a person taking early retirement. A time backward jump occurred on a application the author analysed issuing public documents on demand. Before release to the public each document was vetted for accuracy and quality of printing. If it failed the document reverted back to a previous state in its life to be ready for reprinting. The ELC technique provides no facilities to support these and other complexities.

The IEM manual compounds the problem by making a series of extraordinary statements about ELCs:

- That processes that do not update the entity but only retrieve it can also be drawn on the ELC—if space permits! To what purpose and where in the life of the entity the retrieve event should be recorded is not advised. The inclusion of non update events in an entity life cycle diagram shows a misunderstanding of the purpose of the technique. Retrieval events have no mandatory sequence. And what happens if space does not permit?

- Only draw ELCs for the major entities in the ERD model and for entities with complex lives (Navigator also makes this statement)! On what basis is a major entity and a complex life decided? And what about the minor entities?

- It is rarely worth drawing up ELCs as formal design deliverables! Why then have the technique if the deliverable has little practical value?

- It is rarely worth having the ELCs reviewed by the users responsible for validating the logical design specification!

Navigator also makes some strange comments. Entity sub-types have their own lives, yet their life cycle should only be drawn if the life is "significantly different" from that of the super-type! What does significantly different mean?

It is clear that IEM and Navigator do not understand the full requirements of this technique. Yet it is the only technique in Information Engineering specifically designed to ensure that events that update the database occur in the correct sequence. Without such a technique there is no guarantee that the database will correctly reflect the state of the world it is representing. This is not a minor issue! *The failure to have a proper technique to ensure a*

valid sequence of database maintenance events and to pay due attention to the requirement is one of the major failings of Information Engineering.
There is planned to be an upgrade to the technique in version 1.1 of Navigator.

7 User view analysis While impressed by the thoroughness of the technique the data analysis diagram is nothing more than a pictographic representation of relational data analysis. The same results can be achieved through RDA. There is a 100% duplication of effort. And if user views are so useful why only produce the views for the current system?

8 Canonical synthesis Given the comments on user view analysis the worth of this technique, which merely aggregates the user views into an ERD model, in providing new information to the logical design specification is very doubtful.

9 Dataflow diagrams There are number of significant concerns over the way DFDs are drawn and used:

- It is stated in the IEM manuals that DFDs indicate how one procedure depends on another! Navigator also states that a procedure dependency diagram is similar to a DFD. DFDs fundamentally cannot represent process/procedure dependency when the process is at the event or higher level of decomposition! *The reason for this is that DFDs do not represent time between procedure/processes (it matters not which) that are separated by data stores.* There is nothing to say that the procedure retrieving data from a data store is triggered after the procedure putting data into a data store. The procedure retrieving data from a data store can be accessing different entity occurrences in the data store than the procedure putting data in the data store. The only dependency between processes is at the problem-to-solve level, where the processes are connected by dataflows.

- Navigator states that the elementary process is the lowest level of process decomposition and, certainly on the basis of the examples given, that an elementary process is effectively synonymous with an event. This latter point is disputed by the designers of Navigator. Yet it will be shown in chapter 3 that event level processes can be further decomposed to problem-to-solve processes!

- It is not certain whether the DFDs are contributing to the logical or physical design specification. All other structured methods the author has applied use DFDs as a logical design technique. The methods include SSADM, LSDM, STRADIS and Yourdon. The technique is applied in IEM in the BSD stage, during which the logical processes identified in the previous BAA stage are converted into procedures, which are a sort of "half way house" conversion to application programs. The statement that the identification of datastores in the DFDs depends on the target database file handler is certainly a strange mixture of the logical (data stores) and physical (file handlers)!

- The IEM advice for procedure decomposition in reverse for the grouping of the lowest level procedures into sub-systems and then into business systems is somewhat dubious. For example, where a procedure level DFD is drawn over several pages each page is a "candidate" sub-system. What happens if one person diagrams in small type and places the procedures close together and another person draws them in large and separates the procedures widely?

- No advice is provided that DFDs should record only data maintenance business requirements. Data changes its state and "flows" from one state to another only because an update has occurred. Data retrieval business requirements do not cause data to flow and should therefore not be included on DFDs. A DFD can very rapidly become cluttered up with a large number of data retrievals that serve no purpose.

10   Dialogue flow diagramming   This technique is concerned with the online processing man/machine interface. There are two distinct parts of this interface—the menu selection screens and the transaction screens for a business requirement.

The menu screens are solely concerned with enabling the user to select a business requirement option. They front-end the transaction screens and are related to each other as a sequential hierarchical cascade of screens from the main menu screen. Menu screens do not require procedure support. The only logic in menu screens is the "if...then...else" implicit in the selection of the options on the screens. The software for the menu screens is separate from the transaction screens, being a separate menu program, which can be generated automatically by the menu definition software if the database product provides the facility.

Once the business requirement has been chosen then a set of transaction screens is presented containing information relevant to the chosen business requirement. The transaction screens are concerned with the man/machine dialogue interface for the business requirement and are related to each other in sequence, selection and iteration, either singly or as a group of screens. The software for the transaction screens is hand-written application program code.

Transaction screens require both access and process logic, but the logic is not concerned with the business requirement and database processing, only with the man/machine interface. The access logic is to the message queue to retrieve data from an input screen and send data to an output screen. The process logic checks the input screen data for accuracy and validity and formats the data for the output screen. Screen handling procedures need to be defined to support this screen processing logic.

IEM makes a clear distinction between database processing and transaction screen processing when describing the dialogue flow diagramming technique. "A dialogue procedure consists of one or more screen interactions and associated processing logic." The technique is therefore pitched correctly.

The main concerns that the author has with this technique is the:

- poor diagrammatic representation of some of the facilities that the man/machine interface requires. The manual talks about using program function keys for issuing dialogue commands but does not indicate how this can be shown on the dialogue flow diagram;

- absence of specifying the conditions when control is transferred to other screens;

- absence of any information as to where in the dialogue flow the user requires to make decisions, for example whether to proceed with the dialogue;

- one-to-one relationship of a transaction screen and a procedure or procedure step. This rule is defined in the IEM manual. Recall that a procedure is at the event level and the procedure step is at the problem-to-solve level. The statement therefore means that an event or problem-to-solve can only have one screen associated with it. Surely that is not the real world! The event might have so much information that it will not physically fit on a single screen. The author can remember many business requirements/events requiring many screens to display all the relevant information.

Navigator has a similar technique called online conversation design. The author does not find the technique impressive because:

- there is no distinction between menu and transaction screens;

- the conversational network diagram for the transaction screens does not show the full information about the dialogue, that is the user decision points that may have to be made before the next screen is processed, the attributes being input, displayed and output to and from the screen, the conditional branching in the selection and iteration of which screen may be required next and the processing of the screen attributes that may be necessary before and after database access. The conversational hierarchy diagram contains some of this information—conditional logic for the next screen to display—but still does not show the attributes input to and output from the screens.

- the use of action diagrams for specifying screen processing is understandable given its standard role in Information Engineering based methods, but the resultant use of three deliverables to provide not all the information necessary for online dialogue design where one can suffice is not impressive;

- there is not a clear distinction between screen and database processing in the hierarchy diagrams. This is particularly severe in that there is a move towards co-operative processing with front-end intelligent processors able to support the functions associated with screen processing, such as editing the attributes entered on a screen for a data maintenance business requirement and screen formatting, and a back-end processor specifically for database access. Both tasks are defined in the conversational hierarchy diagram. Database processing has nothing to do with online conversational design.

- while the method talks about the different screen facilities now available—scrolling, windowing and intelligent screens—the technique does not identify how the online dialogue is to cater for them;

- there is no diagramming convention to represent global function and program keys that can be used in online dialogues, the function keys being used for systems purposes, such as display the next screen, and the program keys being used for application purposes, such as display the bonus of the salesman being interrogated.

These are serious flaws because they do not reflect clear thinking about the boundary between what is online and what is database processing.

The Navigator designers "are moving away from enforced hierarchies of action (top-down menus) and towards user centred design based on common tasks". This is entirely welcome and has been adopted by other structured methods, such as SSADM version 4.

Neither IEM nor Navigator provides advice as to what level the menu screens should be pitched at. It is increasingly being recognised that the top level menu screen should be pitched at the user role level. The latest version 4 of SSADM now follows this practice. There is one menu screen hierarchy for each user role. For example there could be a menu hierarchy for the storekeeper, for the store manager and for the goods despatcher, if that is the way the goods store/depot is run. A single user could have more than one role—the store manager may also be a storekeeper and therefore be able to use the two menu selection routines, one for the storekeeper and one for the store manager.

11 Visual layout design The advice offered on screen design is oriented to traditional 3270 type screens. Modern screen design now takes into account the X-Windows facilities of pop-up and overlay screens and pull-down menus, facilities that are appropriate to conversational processing.

12 Information views There are two kinds of data views—the program view and the user view.

The program view is a feature of the program languages, usually 3GL, that access the first generation hierarchical (e.g. IMS) and hybrid (e.g. TOTAL) type database file handlers and the second generation Codasyl (e.g. IDMS) database file handlers. The usual technical term for first generation program views is program specification block and for second generation program views is subschema. Information Engineering quite rightly identifies and defines program views in the perceived data structure.

The user view facility has become available with the advent of relational file handlers. The user view is the same as the program view, in that it defines the data items and the conditions under which they can be accessed, but in this case the view is at the user not the program level. The user view is related to a user(s) who can then use the view facility to access the database data as defined in the view. Information Engineering unfortunately does not identify user views.

13 Data views The technique is described in Navigator. The author is not able to see the purpose or usefulness of the technique. Its purpose is to describe data interfaces for online and batch procedures. The technique seems to construct a subset of the enterprise ERD model from one or at most two entities, but may be "supplemented with other data." Why only up to two entities are involved is not explained. What purpose the data views have in an implemented system is not explained.

14 Entity model view There is nothing wrong with this technique in that it identifies the view a process/application program has of the data in the ERD model/database and any other data it may require to function. It should be stated that the technique has no practical relevance if the implemented system is to be relational. Relational systems do not use application program views of data. The only view used is the user view as defined in the view facility. This restricts the user, not the application program, access to the data.

There is also a wastage aspect about entity model views. The technique models the data to be accessed by a process/application program. So does the technique of transaction path analysis/data navigation. Entity model views are therefore not relevant to many current systems and can be eliminated from the method by a replacement technique without loss of quality or completeness in the logical design specification. Other structured methods, such as SSADM, do not bother with the technique.

15 Action diagrams The author has already indicated the excellence of this technique. The only concern is a comment made in the Navigator manuals. When does analysis end and design begin in the development of the elementary processes for which the logic has been specified in the action diagrams? "The guideline is that at the end of the analysis phase the solution must be sufficiently stable to be able to estimate the design costs within 15% with an 85% level of confidence and the construction and implementation costs within 20% with a 75% level of confidence." What on earth does this mean? Surely the end of analysis is when the logical specification is complete, with all the deliverables finished and quality assured by users and technical specialists.

16 Prototyping This is addressed in Navigator. The concern is not that it should be regarded as a positive development, which it is provided the proper tools are available and used in a proper manner, but that Navigator only advises the good points about prototyping and does not identify any shortcomings. Prototyping cannot provide a total answer to systems design and development. The prototyping shortcomings are:

- it cannot be a substitute for the application of the logical and physical design techniques and the production of their deliverables. Furthermore, prototyping tools, by their nature, can only produce physical design deliverables for the simple reason that the tools function in a hardware/software environment. They can produce:
  — a database schema;
  — the table definitions of the attributes;
  — the menu and transaction screen formats and their dialogue sequence;
  — the data access logic implicit in the selection of menu options;
  — the process logic for the business requirements that require to massage the data prior to output.

This is fine for computer technicians but, apart from the man/machine interface of menu and transaction screens, totally unsuited to untrained users. One of the major reasons for the move towards the use of techniques of logical design is that the methods produce deliverables that are logical and mostly diagrammatic and therefore, by and large, understandable by the users. This means that prototyping only has limited practical use for the user for the full specification of the system.

Another problem is that prototyping cannot represent all the design information contained in the logical design deliverables. The deliverables that cannot be supported are:

- the dataflow diagrams/process dependency diagrams/process hierarchy diagrams. Prototyping cannot represent the decomposition of processes or the relationship of processes to each other. These diagrams are most useful tools for increasing the user's understanding of the system as well as being, if used properly, a logical design deliverable;

- the entity life cycles. Prototyping cannot represent the sequence, selection and iteration, the grouping of iterations and selections, the abnormal quitting from the usual sequencing of events and the state variable used to re-express the sequence etc. in which the data maintenance events for a particular entity occur;

- the physical deliverables needing to be "re-engineered" back into their logical form. This re-engineering of a physical deliverable back into its logical form is now a major science in its own right, and is particularly useful for logically re-expressing a current implemented physical system, many of which were developed many years ago without the aid of a structured method and therefore were not specified in logical form. The database schema, for example, needs to be converted into a logical data model and the menu and transaction screens to be converted into menu and transaction screen structure charts. Users in the future will not be able to review the system specification as detailed in the physical deliverables of a prototyping tool unless it is represented in a logical manner.

17 Database design The IEM manuals provide comprehensive advice on the design of a DL/1 database and adequate generic advice on the design of a relational database, but no advice is provided on the design of hybrid (e.g. TOTAL) and Codasyl (e.g. IDMS) databases. To be frank the author is not too upset, as it is most unlikely that these two products types, excellent in their time, will be bought or used for new applications. The move is away from such pointer chain database file handlers to the symbolic pointer relational database file handlers.

The IEM BSD manual details some database design principles in preliminary database design. The principles are basic and many of the finer generic points of database design are not mentioned—when and how to use the different types of entry points to a database, table clustering and logical sequential versus physical sequential data storage facilities for relational file handlers are but three. The manual also ignores the specific design rules of other widely used database file handlers, such as ADABAS, with its non-relational and limited facilities for supporting repeating groups and fields within a table.

Information Engineering does not advise on is to how to ensure the two components that go into database design—total data structure and total data access—are assessed in due proportion to their significance in the initial first cut attempt at database design. This is most strange, given that the method goes further than any other in ascertaining the summary data accesses to the ERD model. The two design deliverables—the ERD total data structure and the summary access path maps—are required to be used together as complementary components of database design if the concept of database—total data structure and data access—is to be supported.

Consider figure 2.10. Should table C be clustered on disk via table A or table B in order to reduce physical disk I/O (logical I/O to the buffer pool cannot be reduced because data has to be accessed)? Some structured methods the author has used state that a detail table should be clustered on disk next to the master table to which it has the fewest dependent occurrences. Table C should therefore be clustered via table A and not via table B. But this rule takes no account of data access. What if the summary access path map showed that the number of access between tables A to C were 1000 per day and between B to C were 100,000 per day as illustrated? Clustering C to A as recommended would save, assuming all dependent occurrences of C were in the same page/block as A (this can be easily calculated), 1000 physical I/Os but at the cost of 100,000 physical I/Os between B and C. Table C's rows would be spread around on disk like "grass seed" as far as table B is concerned. If table C was clustered via table B instead, because it is much the busiest access path, then, again assuming all dependent C's are clustered on the same page as the master B, 100,000 physical I/Os would be saved, at a cost of 1000 physical I/Os between A and C—a hundredfold improvement in performance based on taking total data access into account. It is only when data access to the master entities are more or less equal that the database set cardinalities should be considered.

The failure to take data access into account in this manner in the data structuring rules means that extra work may subsequently be required in the performance assessment technique. Why not take data access into account on these lines earlier in logical database design rather than later in physical design? It is easier to accomplish and potentially would save considerable transaction tuning in the much more difficult and laborious task of database tuning.

Having undertaken transaction timings using the performance assessment technique Information Engineering does not show how to interpret the result—is it the transaction, the processor or the database at fault?

The logical database design technique in Navigator, described in section 2.3.2.3, suffers from some problems. The negatives are:

- why is it necessary to partition the logical database design "into areas for which diagrams will be created if the number of relations are too large to fit in one diagram?" Since when has database design been influenced by the size of a diagram?

- derived attributes in the data tables. No advice as to when to use a derived data attribute is given. This is addressed in chapter 3.

Much of the advice is given without explaining how a design decision is made and on what evidence. For example "Add ... access path (foreign keys) to simplify navigation and access path loading". But on what basis is an access path to be regarded as being overloaded and data navigation to be simplified? Another example—"Denormalise data structures". When and why and to what extent—should one go back to second normal form or first normal form?

18 Program design   The weaknesses here relate to Navigator, which uses the technique of "transform centred" and "transaction centred" design to construct program module structure charts. The transform centred approach works on the basis of a beginning input process, a middle transform process and an ending output process. The transaction centred approach works on the basis that the input record is checked as to its type (record type A, B or C, for example), and the appropriate transform centred processing of record type is then invoked. There are a number of concerns about this approach to program design:

- The transaction centred approach is fine for batch processing where many record types are input in a single batch of records, but of little use in online processing.

- The transform centred approach is more appropriate to data maintenance processing where a record contents is edited for correctness, followed by database processing, followed by the formatting and presenting of the output. It is over simplistic, assuming a nice self-contained front end, a nice self-contained middle bit and a nice self contained back end piece of processing. The real world of writing access and process logic for a business requirement can be much more complicated. The blocks of code are more usually split into the problems-to-solve for the business requirement/event, with each in turn broken down further into pieces of code typically for message receiving from a screen, most probably some database access and data massaging and finally message formatting and passing out to the screen, this then iterating several times as control is passed to the next problem-to-solve in the event.
  It is also not well suited to the undoubted move towards object oriented processing that will inevitably occur during the 1990s. The transform based approach is based on the valid concept of event level processing. All computer systems are based on this basic premise, which remains valid no matter what approach to logic design is used. However, it is

the way that the blocks of code are structured that causes the problem. The object based approach is that the blocks of application code are "allocated/normalised" to their appropriate objects/entities in the same manner as the data. The use of hierarchical structures of code with each block of code allocated to a problem-to-solve is abandoned. The basic problem is that problems-to-solve can relate to many entities/objects. It is replaced by a main procedure of co-ordinating code sending messages to the objects (there is still a master controlling procedure) *broadly in the sequence in which the objects would be accessed as if they were tables of data* to invoke the relevant object based code to access the relevant data in the object. Middle level controlling modules have no relevance.

The main procedure also contains the logic that is not normalisable to the "natural" data objects, typically regarding the screen handling processing. The main procedure thus has many of the features of the traditional transform based approach but the hierarchical structure of blocks of code as in program structure charts resulting from the transform based approach is gone.

The object oriented approach is discussed in detail in chapter 5.
At the more detailed level there is a further concern:

• The technique for identifying application program modules from the procedures and applying a set of conversion rules is extremely suspect. The author is not concerned about the direct conversion from a procedure to a module—this is in line with the one-for-one conversion of the logical design into the physical design—but in the rules for the further identification of more modules containing more focused processing. The advice is that the procedure be classified as to whether it is transform or transaction centred and that the constituent "processing blocks" that recognise transactions and transform input into output be identified become the basic application program modules, which can then be further factored into smaller modules. The input modules could be factored into the read and edit modules, for example. However, no definition by example of what the "processing" blocks are is given. The identification of the blocks is therefore hit and miss, try it and see, use your intelligence and experience, preferably in reverse order.

Surely the processing blocks are the problem-to-solve processes that are the constituent processes within the event level business requirements. If one follows the concept of logical design = physical design the events become the application programs and the problems-to-solve become the application program modules. The identification of events and their problem-to-solve processes is discussed in section 3.2.1.

The problem with Navigator is that process/procedure decomposition technique does not "allow" decomposition beyond the event level, the lowest level being the elementary process. Therefore the process/procedure decomposition technique on which the transaction/transform centred "approach" to application program design is based cannot identify the problem-to-solve modules. Within Navigator it is necessary to have an additional step beyond process/procedure decomposition to identify application program modules. Advice is provided as to what is a module—"a collection of program statements that possess the characteristics of a black box—a set of inputs, a transform and a set of outputs". There is no technique for the identification of the modules. There is much about the what and nothing about the how.

19 No batch program design Information Engineering effectively ignore this important subject.

Nowhere in the IEM BSD, TD or C & T manuals could the author find any advice as to how to design batch programs. Notwithstanding the fact that batch programs are a necessary evil on some processors, notably IBM and ICL, the failure to provide such advice for this still major component of many application systems is a serious omission.

Navigator identifies batch procedures. The main reason for batch procedures is "to economise on data handling". Thus procedures handling common data and frequency and timing (i.e. daily, weekly) are batched together. And a somewhat extraordinary situation of standalone batch procedures can exist. But apart from providing advice as to how to identify potential batches no technique of batch procedure/program design is provided. The advice is once again all about what to do, not how to do it. A technique describes the how, not the what.

3

"PEARLS OF PRACTICAL WISDOM"

Chapters 3 to 5 provide advice as to how Information Engineering can be applied:

- more effectively for the data processing environment to which it is targeted;

- more widely in data processing environments for which it is not targeted.

All the advice is based on practical experiences and is correspondingly supported by real world or representative examples from case studies on which the author has worked.

For the new technology trends of knowledge based expert systems and object oriented systems the practical experience is still patchy. The policy followed for this book is that where there is an absence of practical experience, so that worked examples based on real life cannot be described, advice on the application of Information Engineering is explicitly caveated in that it is based on the author's knowledge rather experience.

This chapter describes "pearls of practical wisdom" the author has learnt over a decade of applying a number of structured methods and found useful and practical in the specific application of Information Engineering. The pearls have found re-expression as "tricks of the practitioner's trade" that ensure that the concepts identified and described in chapter 2 are fully met when producing the logical design deliverables. The tricks have been tried and tested and have not been found wanting. They are proven. All the examples of the tricks are based on real world experiences. None of this chapter is theory.

The tricks are generic to information systems strategy planning and logical and physical design and not specific to any method or data processing environment. Given the purpose of this book they are considered in the context of Information Engineering. The tricks fall into two categories—conceptual and systematic.

All the conceptual tricks reflect the generic concepts that logical design = physical design and test the logical design for efficiency. The tricks are:

- ensuring the entity relationship diagram (ERD) model is efficient;

- ensuring the transaction access paths are efficient;

- producing and interpreting summary access path maps;

- ensuring a balanced database design.

The systematic tricks are:

- ensuring that process decomposition is consistent and sensible;

- ensuring that the process decomposition/dataflow diagram processes are used correctly in application program design;

- appreciating the different kinds of keys to an entity; building a composite ERD model;

- taking relational data analysis to sixth normal form;

- ensuring that events that update the database occur in the correct sequence;

- integrating the different aspects of the man/machine interface;

- applying additional points of detail in the application of the design techniques.

In assessing the Information Engineering strengths it became apparent that the method is better at supporting more of the "tricks of the trade" than any other method the author is familiar with. There was a danger that this chapter would look a bit "thin". Information Engineering already supports some of the tricks that are included, such as summary access path statistics. The reason that these tricks have been addressed in this chapter is either because they are not supported in full (no advice on how to interpret the summary access path statistics) or that "smart reading " of the manuals is required to extract information not defined explicitly (the logical design is the physical design).

3.1 CONCEPTUAL TRICKS

3.1.1 Testing for logical design efficiency

The testing of the logical design for efficiency is a crucial concept that Information Engineering, along with all other leading structured design methods, pays no attention to. Given the concept that logical design = physical design, a concept that Information Engineering overwhelmingly if implicitly supports, and the inexorable move towards using the logical design as the source for code generation, it is incumbent to make sure that the logical design is efficient. At least the physical design has a chance of being efficient from the start and may not need any subsequent optimisation at all.

The two aspects that need to be tested are the ERD model and the transactions that access it. The testing, however, is not equal for all the transactions. There is a substantial difference in the nature of transactions that update the ERD model and those that retrieve data from it. The data maintenance transactions overwhelmingly have short access paths, mostly to only one entity occurrence (create customer, change order quantity, delete stock). There is not much testing for efficiency to be done there. By contrast many of the data retrieval transactions have much longer access paths (display orders for customers where ... and products where ... and invoices where ...). As will be seen it is against the data retrieval transactions that the ERD model most needs to be tested for efficiency. All the case study examples are for data retrieval transactions. Never once has the author found it appropriate to test data maintenance transactions against the ERD model.

Any inefficiency in the ERD model and the logical transaction accesses to the model can be ascertained during the process of data navigation/transaction access path analysis. (The use of the term transaction here is a logical transaction, not a physical transaction. A logical transaction is the same as a business requirement. A physical transaction occurs in an application program and is a logical unit work (LUW). A LUW is a unit of database and program recovery and is defined in the program between a BEGIN and a COMMIT statement. Any database modifications made between these two points is flushed from the buffer pool to the log file and possibly to the database when the COMMIT is reached.)

Testing the ERD model and transactions is undertaken together because it is difficult to separate them in practice. If a transaction is found to be extremely inefficient against the ERD model it could be either the transaction or the ERD model that is at fault. The "tricks" in this section show how logical inefficiency can be ascertained and how the ERD model and transaction can be optimised.

The following aspects of efficiency are considered:

- business requirements with multiple entry points;
- balancing data retrieval versus data maintenance overheads;
- data redundancy;
- key sequence;
- minimising entry points.

3.1.1.1 Business requirements with multiple entry points

The issue of logical access path efficiency occurs where a business requirement has multiple entry points. A typical example in figure 3.1 occurred in an application system for a local authority. Store items were held in stock and the policy followed was that whenever a store item was issued an order was immediately placed to re-stock the store, so as to maintain a constant stock level. Thus, whenever an issue was raised, money to pay for the order was involved, such that an issue related to an account. Analysis of the ERD model had shown that for an account there was on average 1000 issues and for a store item 70 issues, with 10 issues matching an account and store item.

The business requirement was "For a specified account and store item list all issues". The entry point options were on the specified account or store item. Entry on the account generated 1000 accesses to all its issues, 10 of which related to the specified store item. There were therefore 10 further accesses to the store item in order to obtain the description of the item. The total logical accesses when accessing via the account entry point was therefore 1011. The reverse access path via the store item generated only 81 accesses. Thus access via account produced an access path more than 12 times less efficient logically than access via store item.

The author concedes that a physical design could negate the above conclusions. However, the author works on the principal that, as a rough rule-of-thumb, one logical access against the data model will produce on average one physical I/O access to disk. A quick estimate of the number of physical I/Os a typical relational file handler would incur against figure 3.1 would be one physical I/O to access the index pointing to the account, which would generate a further physical I/O to access the appropriate account table row. Assuming there is an index on the issues table by account number and the bulk of the index is in main memory the number of index accesses to issues would be, say, 10 physical I/Os. 10 index pages at the bottom level of the index contain 1000 pointers to the 1000 issue table rows relating to the specified account. The issue table rows, assuming they

Multiple Entry Points - i.e. Multiple access path options

Requirement is:

"For a specified account & stores item list all issues"

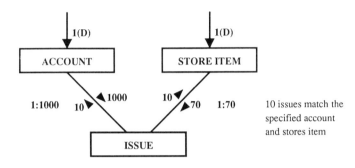

Access via stores item =   81 accesses ⎱ both produce
Access via account   = 1011 accesses ⎰ same output

Conclusion

Access via account is 12 times less efficient than via stores item.

Figure 3.1   Logical access path efficiency: 1

are stored in entry sequenced order (the most usual mechanism used by relational file handlers) would generate a further 1000 physical I/Os, as the issues relating to the account would more than likely be spread around like "grass seed" on disk. Direct access to the 10 occurrences of the specified stores item relating to the accessed issues would generate one physical I/O via the index and 10 further physical I/Os to the stores item table rows. The total number of physical I/Os is therefore 1022. This compares to the 1011 logical accesses to the data model. The assumption of one-to-one logical access to physical I/O is therefore not unreasonable.

The only occasion in practice where the basis of direct conversion from logical to physical has ever been significantly awry was where a very small database (some 8 megabytes) was pulled in its entirety into processor main memory. This virtually eliminated the physical I/O overhead on the processor, which was only incurred on the initial load of the database tables, but in no way affected the logical I/O to the buffer pool—data has to be accessed. In all other cases there has been a remarkable similarity of the physical I/Os to a balanced database design taking into account total data structure and total data access overhead and the number of logical accesses to the ERD model.

Where the disparity between the accesses between two entry points is as great as in the example then the logical conclusion—access via store item rather than via account—is valid at the physical level. One does not need the database optimisation techniques to tell you this!

3.1.1.2 Balancing data retrieval versus data maintenance overheads

This situation occurs when the logical data model appears to be inefficient at supporting a business requirement and potentially requires improvement by modification. The questions are—how to ascertain if the ERD model is inefficient and will modification result in improvement?

Both examples in this section relate to clients in the third world. The author's terms of reference were to minimise any unnecessary complexity in application programming.

The first example in figure 3.2 shows the situation where the ERD model was inefficient but the proposed modifications proved to be the reverse of an improvement. The application was a personnel system, with the database containing some 10,000 persons. The business requirement was "List all persons who are 55 years of age" and ran twice a year. The users requesting this requirement were the pension support staff. People retire at the age of 60 and the staff required to know the pension cash flow requirements in some 5 years time. There was no requirement to list the persons in person number order. The entry point access type was therefore physical sequential.

The first access path chosen was to scan the person entity to ascertain who was 55 years of age. Each scan generated 10,000 accesses. The client company was, however, composed of young people, so that out of 10,000 accesses only 5 persons were retrieved—a hit rate of 1 in 2,000. Even with a large blocking factor it was clear that this was a very inefficient access path. The installation used IBM hardware and it was known that the largest block size could go up to the full track on a disk, which would equal some 20K. However, it was also known that the person entity contained many attributes and would require some 600 bytes of data. (Notice here that the boundary between logical and physical is extremely imprecise. Physical considerations that are generic to all hardware and software requirements can quite legitimately be considered as part of the logical design process. After all one is producing a logical design specification that will be physically implemented. What is not permissible at the logical level is to include product specific hardware/software considerations. This at times is difficult to achieve if one knows the target physical environment.)

It was crystal clear that the initial logical access path was going to be inefficient, whatever the target physical environment. The ERD model was therefore modified with an operational entity of age above person. The

Data Retrieval vs. Data Maintenance Overheads (1)

Requirement is:

"List all persons who are 55 years of age" (2 x year)

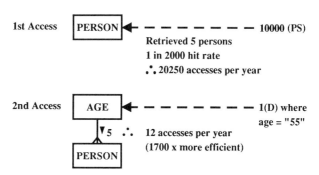

1st Access PERSON ◄─ ─ ─ ─ ─ ─ ─ ─ 10000 (PS)
Retrieved 5 persons
1 in 2000 hit rate
∴ 20250 accesses per year

2nd Access AGE ◄─ ─ ─ ─ ─ ─ ─ ─ 1(D) where
age = "55"
▼5 ∴ 12 accesses per year
PERSON (1700 x more efficient)

BUT Costs of person/age maintenance = 10000 x 250 per year
2.5 million access per year

Conclusion

Data maintenance costs of 2nd access 123 > than data retrieval benefits

∴ adopt 1st access

Figure 3.2   Logical access path efficiency: 2

access path was now extremely efficient, with direct access on age where age = "55", which in turn related to the 5 persons of that age. The total logical accesses via age was therefore 6 as opposed to 10,125 accesses via person—a data retrieval improvement by a factor of more than 1700!

However this improvement was more apparent than real. Nobody has the secret of eternal youth. We all have birthdays. Assuming 250 working days per year, the need to keep people's ages up to date and the resultant requirement to scan the person entity each working day to ascertain who has a birthday, the cost of maintaining the second access path was found to be 2.5 million logical accesses per year. The data maintenance access costs on the second access path were therefore 123 times greater than the data retrieval benefits!

It was therefore clear that the first access path was the one to choose, even though it was not very efficient.

Many people have pointed out that a simple alternative solution would be to write the application program to test for date of birth. However, this would have involved the users or the application programmers in some mathematics. Given the terms of reference it was not followed.

The second example is the reverse of the first—that is, where the ERD model was inefficient and the proposed modification proved to be a substantial improvement. The example is based on the same personnel system. It is illustrated in figure 3.3. The business requirement was run once a month and analysis had shown that a person changed his/her job seat twice a year and their section once every two years. Given that the business requirement wanted to list the staff movements during the last two years then the cardinalities between person and person/job seat for this trans-action is 4 (note the concept of transaction cardinalities introduced. As far as the author is aware the Navigator version of Information Engineering is the only structured method that supports transaction cardinalities). Person/job seat was stored in time order.

Assuming that the dependent person job/seat is related to person in time order then the access path and the number of accesses was as illustrated. The entry point type on person is logical sequential, as it was necessary

Data Retrieval vs. Data Maintenance Overheads (2)

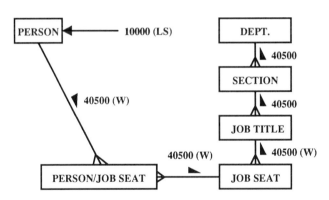

W = Wasted access

The Requirement is:

- "List all staff departmental movements during the last two years detailing dept & section information." (1 x month)

- Person changed job seat 2 x year & section once every 2 years.

- Total access 212500 per transaction. Wasted access = 121500

Figure 3.3   Logical access path efficiency: 3

to list the persons in person number order. The total accesses for each running of the transaction was 212,500 logical accesses. Given that the only entities holding data of relevance to the business requirement were person, section and department the accesses to person job/seat, job seat and job title were totally wasted—a total of 121,500 accesses. Assuming on average that one logical access generates one physical disk I/O (as indicated earlier a not unreasonable assumption) and that each physical I/O is some 30 milliseconds then about one hour of dedicated I/O time would be wasted per transaction execution. The ERD model was therefore inefficient for this transaction.

The relationship between a person and a section was relatively stable—to be precise 4 times more stable than between a person and a job seat—and would therefore have low data maintenance overheads. A link data group between person and section was therefore created—see figure 3.4. The transaction set cardinalities between person and person/section, given the time span of the business requirement, was unity so that the total data retrieval accesses was now 40,500, a reduction of some 172,000 accesses. This was a saving of some 86 minutes of dedicated disk I/O time, of which only one quarter—the accesses to the person/section link entity—were wasted. The data maintenance costs of this new data group was found to be only 843 accesses per month, i.e. some 204 times less than the savings on data retrieval. It was clear that, unlike the first example, the ERD model required to be modified.

As with the multiple entry points example the logical conclusions based on the above clear cut evidence would be valid in any physical design.

3.1.1.3 Data redundancy

The example as to when it is profitable to introduce redundant data into a logical data model is based on figures 3.5 and 3.6. Redundant data can either be derived data as a result of a computation or a duplicate copy of data stored elsewhere in the database. The client was an oil company. The oil wells were exploration wells, so that tests, injections, flow rates and hours off per day were constantly monitored, often at one second intervals. This information was required to be stored for many months in order to obtain a pattern. The set cardinalities between conduit and test, flow rates, injections and to a lesser degree hours off per day were therefore enormous—over 1,000,000 for example.

The data retrieval business requirements were typically of the kind "Display the average flow rates for a specified well for the last month" or "Display the average down time for a specified conduit for a specified week". The number of accesses to the detail entities to conduit were far too high, particularly for online transactions. It was clear, even at this

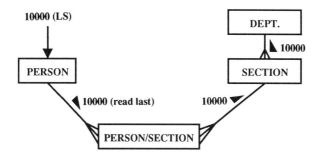

With this Access Path:

- Data retrieval accesses = 40000 therefore save 172000 accesses per transaction

- Data Maintenance accesses = 843 accesses per month

Conclusion

- Data maintenance costs on Person/Section 204 times < data retrieval benefits

- ∴ Adopt this access path

Figure 3.4 Logical access path efficiency: 4

logical design stage, that the physical transactions would fail the response time objectives. The solution was to introduce a weekly summary entity as a detail of conduit. The summary data group would hold summarised statistical data of each of its detail data groups. Most data retrieval transactions now finished at weekly summary and were highly efficient.

Clearly there was a data maintenance cost involved. It was ascertained that the extra data maintenance costs were high at the logical level but low at the physical level. This example also illustrates that the boundary between logical and physical design is often blurred. The reason why the physical cost of inserting weekly summary on to the ERD model was low was that the data structure is a hierarchy and weekly summary could therefore be clustered in the same page/block as its conduit, which was the usual entry point entity. The set cardinalities between conduit and weekly summary was a fixed 52 (i.e. one year of historical information) so that with a large block/page size a conduit and all its associated weekly summaries could fit in one block/page. The weekly summary entity could convert into a physical table of data, with each row requiring some 30 bytes of packed decimal data storage. 52 rows would therefore fit easily within a 2K

Data Redundancy (1)

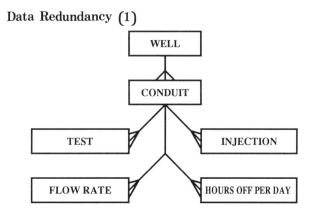

Constant Need to Know Such Things as:

- Average flow rates per week/month
- Average conduit down time per week/month

Very wide cardinality of conduit to detail entities, therefore expensive to provide answer

Figure 3.5   Logical access path efficiency: 5

block/page, even including the master conduit table row to which weekly summary was related.

It was clear that the proposed logical design would be physically efficient. Accessing weekly summary would generate one logical I/O access to the buffer pool for every insertion of test, flow rate, injection and hours off per day and therefore appear to be expensive. Crucially, however, physically no extra disk I/O would be involved whatsoever. As explained in section 2.4.2.1 physical disk I/O is slow and expensive and requires to be kept to an absolute minimum. The transaction would therefore be physically efficient. The redundant data was therefore highly profitable.

If the logical data structure had been a broad network with weekly summary relating to many master entities then clearly the logical conclusion would have been entirely different, because every insert of weekly summary would incur heavy disk I/O maintaining the referential relationships to the master entities. Weekly summary could only be clustered via one of its master entities. All the other master entities would have incurred disk I/O.

3.1.1.4 Key sequence

This trick is illustrated in figure 3.7. The client was a holiday travel company and the requirement, inter alia, was to monitor the locations at which

Data Redundancy (2)

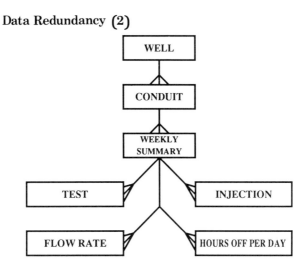

Created a Weekly Summary:

● High data maintenance logical accesses but low
  physical cost:
  - Conduit not an entry point entity
  - Hierarchical data structure, therefore can cluster
    Weekly Summary via Conduit
  - Have to access through Weekly Summary anyway
    to insert dependent data groups.

Figure 3.6   Logical access path efficiency: 6

persons had taken their holidays. Analysis had shown that a person takes
on average 3 holidays a year and that a location has about 1000 holidays a
year. It was necessary to hold 20 years of holiday history. The set cardinality
between person and holiday was therefore 60 and between location and
holiday was 20,000. A typical business requirement that was frequently
triggered was "For a specified person display all holidays taken during
the last 2 years". Assuming that the holiday entity is unsequenced then
the access would be to enter on person and to read all 60 holidays for
that person to ascertain which occurred during the last two years. If the
relationship between person and holiday was sequenced on the keys of
date of holiday and person number then reading reverse from the specified
person to the holiday entity would require only 6 accesses.
   It was clear that sequencing holiday by time in relation to person would
provide major physical design optimisation benefits, irrespective of whether

Key Sequence

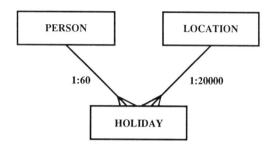

Business Requirement:

"For a specified person list all holidays taken in the last two years"
(With key sequence read reverse for 6 records)
(Without key sequence read all 60 records)

Figure 3.7   Logical access path efficiency: 7

the file handler was first generation hierarchical, second generation Codasyl
or third generation relational. Sequencing the relationship by time improved
the retrieval access efficiency by a factor of 10. There was also no data
maintenance overhead, as the holidays were entered in time sequence
anyway.

Clearly if other business requirements want to access holiday via
person on another search key the date sequence of holiday would not be
appropriate. The search key most frequently used requires to be the chosen
sequence key of an entity. The choice of key sequence is, of course, the
usual design balancing act.

3.1.2 Producing summary access path maps

The need for summary access path maps is based on the concept of database. As explained in section 2.2.2.3 a database should be designed for the
enterprise as a whole and is based on 2 of the 3 major components of a
logical design specification, namely data structure and data access. Given
that the database is for the whole enterprise then it is necessary to ascertain
total data structure and total access.

Many of the leading structured design methods acknowledge the concept
of database as regards data structure, in that they produce an ERD model
for the total system, but not as regards data access. Information Engineering
certainly produces a total data structure for the enterprise as a whole in the

form of the ERD model and also produces a total data access in the form of load matrices showing total accesses per entity. Information Engineering therefore goes further than any other structured method in supporting the concept of database. Unfortunately no advice as to how to interpret the summary accesses as part of database design is provided. Statements that "The frequency of data usage may influence the data structure" with no amplification is not much use. Much more attention is paid to describing the accesses of individual transactions in the process logic/data navigation technique, but a database is not designed for particular transactions—tuned yes but designed no—but for all transactions.

As detailed in section 2.3.2.3 the data access matrices do not show all the summary access information that the summary access path maps drawn against the ERD model can contain. The maps are an exact picture of the accesses to the ERD model and can be easily interpreted in database design terms. By designing a database on the basis of total data structure and total data access the author believes that the design *a priori* will be balanced and that a balanced database design is inherently efficient. "Tricks" to support this concept are discussed in this and the next two sections.

The mechanism for producing summary access path maps is to add up the access paths of each individual transaction. Five different summary access path maps are required:

- *Overall system.* This is the total data accesses for all the applications at an enterprise and is the access component of a balanced database design.

- *Online transactions.* This map shows those portions of the ERD model that require high performance.

- *Batch transactions.* This is the least critical map and has not proved of value in practice.

- *Data retrieval transactions.* This map shows the total retrieval accesses against the ERD model.

- *Data maintenance transactions.* This map shows the total modification and referential integrity accesses against the ERD model.

These two last summary maps are essential for distributed database design and are discussed in chapter **4**.

The sum of the batch and online and the data retrieval and data maintenance transaction summary access path maps each equal the overall system summary map.

Consideration of the summary access path maps is in two parts—how to produce them and how to interpret them.

The production of the summary maps is a slow and repetitive but vital task. The steps are as follows:

1 *Decide a time span.* The author tends to use a time span of one month. Any time span is acceptable. On a highly volatile online system the author has used a time span of one day.

2 *Obtain the transaction volume and frequency.* The frequency of a transaction could be, for example, daily or weekly. The volume is the number of times the transaction runs per frequency, for example 500 times per day.

3 *Assuming a one month time span:*
If the frequency is daily multiply each transaction access to an entity by 21 (working days) or 30 (calender days) as appropriate.
If the frequency is weekly multiply each transaction access by 4.2.
If the frequency is monthly multiply each transaction access by 1.
If the frequency is quarterly divide each transaction access by 3.
etc.

4 *Multiply access volumes to each entity in each transaction access path by the result of 3.*

5 *Draw the monthly access volumes on the ERD model for each transaction.*

6 *Do the above for each transaction.*

7 *Combine all the accesses to produce the total summary access path map.*

A walked through example of the above is given in figures 3.8 to 3.12. The time span assumed is one month.

Once the summary maps have been produced the database administrator has the two components that go into database design—total data structure and total data access—on a single sheet of paper. Contrast this with the current situation with most structured methods. The database administrator will have an ERD model and a whole set of transaction access path maps, one for each business requirement. If there is a grand total of 200 data maintenance and data retrieval business requirements then the database administrator will have 201 sheets of paper, 1 of which shows total data structure (the ERD model) and 200 of which show individual transaction access paths. In order to get an overall "feel" of the total accesses the database administrator will have to read and absorb the information from 200 individual transactions— a virtually impossible task.

The Information Engineering manuals describe the basics of producing summary access statistics in load matrices, but the advice is not comprehensive. The IEM manual only requires that summary statistics be prepared for batch and online transactions and the total system, with no mention of the need for data maintenance and data retrieval transactions.

Data structure against which summary access path map will be built

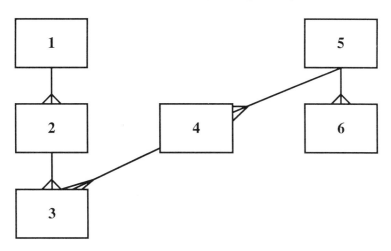

Figure 3.8   Summary access path maps: 1

The way the statistics can be decomposed into more detail, the different types of entry point access, for example, are also not described and neither is a worked example provided. The above worked examples represent the minimum the author would expect and, indeed, requires.

3.1.3 Interpreting the summary access path maps

Figures 3.13 to 3.17 illustrate 5 representative summary access path maps for an enterprise. They require to be interpreted in order to achieve a balanced database design, balanced in the sense that the design takes total data structure and total data access into due account.

The interpretation is as for a typical relational file handler. Starting with figure 3.13:

1 Each entity becomes a table.
2 Each relationship between master entity and detail entity becomes an index.
The key of the index is the key of the master entity and the index points to the detail entity.
3 Each entity not at the bottom of the ERD model (i.e. an entity with detail entities) requires an index on its prime key.
This to ensure efficient support for referential integrity.
4 Decide entry point types.
Entity A is accessed only directly. It is a highly stable data group (see figure 3.16) with the few data maintenance accesses being updates rather

SYSTEM: ANY

(1 x day)

FUNCTION NO: 123   FUNCTION NAME: EXAMPLE 1

Data Group	Acc. Type	Read Type	Acc. Via	No. Acc.	Data Items	Conditions and Comments
1	R	D	-	1		
2	R	P	1	10		Read entire set forward
3	R	P	2	10		Read last
4	R	C	3	10		

Access Type

I = insert   D = delete
M = modify   L+ = add to optional link path
R = read   L = remove from optional link path

Read Path

D = direct
PS = physical sequential
LS = logical sequential
C = via child
P = via parent

EXAMPLE 1

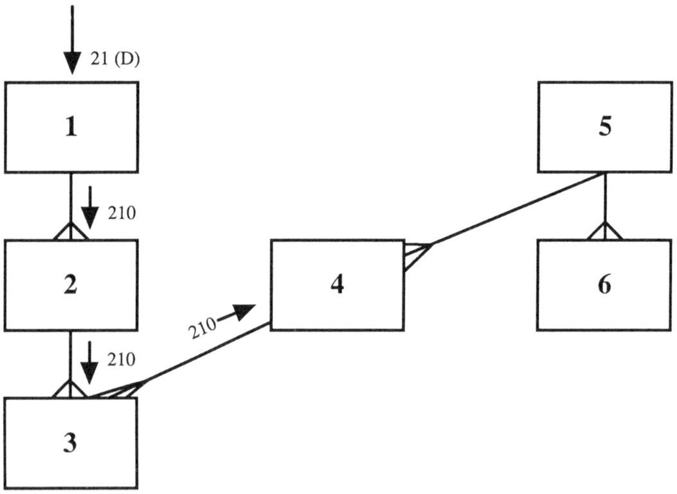

Figure 3.9   Summary access path maps: 2

than inserts and deletes (for the sake of brevity the summary maps do not show a breakdown of the type of data access, but can easily be detailed to do so). The message from the summary maps is to choose a randomised direct entry point access mechanism. Indexed access would be more expensive in disk I/O and processor overhead because it requires to be accessed and

SYSTEM: ANY

(150 x month)

FUNCTION NO: 321		FUNCTION NAME: EXAMPLE 2				
Data Group	Acc. Type	Read Type	Acc. Via	No. Acc.	Data Items	Conditions and Comments
5	R	D	-	1		
6	R	P	5	3		Read reverse last three occurrences
4	R	P	5	10		Read last
3	R	C	4	100		Read entire set
2	R	C	3	100		

Access Type

I = insert   D = delete
M = modify   L+ = add to optional link path
R = read   L = remove from optional link path

EXAMPLES 1 & 2

Read Path

D = direct
PS = physical sequential
LS = logical sequential
C = via child
P = via parent

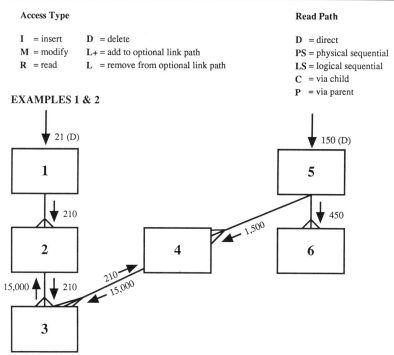

Figure 3.10   Summary access path maps: 3

maintained. If the file handler does not support randomised access an index would be required to provide direct access entry. The disadvantage that randomisers incur, that they do not provide logical sequential access unless a specific type of algorithm is used and the randomised key values are in a known continuous ascending or ascending sequence, is not a concern here as there is no requirement to access on entity A in logical sequential order.

SYSTEM: ANY

(1 x week)

FUNCTION NO: 456					FUNCTION NAME: EXAMPLE 3	
Data Group	Acc. Type	Read Type	Acc. Via	No. Acc.	Data Items	Conditions and Comments
1	R	D	-	1		
2	R	P	1	10		Read entire set backwards
3	R	P	2	10		Read last

Access Type

I = insert   D = delete
M = modify   L+ = add to optional link path
R = read   L = remove from optional link path

Read Path

D = direct
PS = physical sequential
LS = logical sequential
C = via child
P = via parent

EXAMPLES 1 + 2 + 3

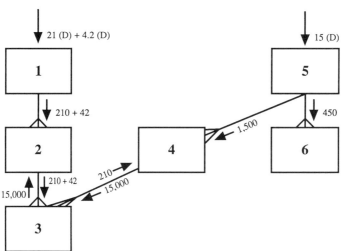

Figure 3.11   Summary access path maps: 4

There are no entry points on entity B so cluster entity B via entity A on disk. The data group volumes and set cardinalities document shows that the working average set ratio is low—let's say 10—and that 50% of entity A have detail entity B. The entire cluster of entity A and its related entity Bs will therefore fit on one page/block, such that the 100 logical accesses between entity A and entity B will not generate any physical I/Os in the implemented system. Clustering here would be very advantageous.

System Summary Access Path Map

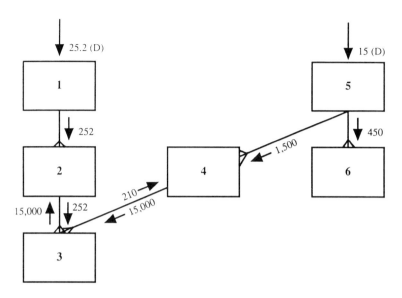

Figure 3.12   Summary access path maps: 5

Entity C is a problem as regards what entry point mechanism to choose. 90% of all entry point accesses are direct, so that randomised access initially looks a good choice. However the remaining 10% of entry point accesses require logical sequential retrieval. If the accesses were batch then an extract and sort routine would be acceptable and randomised entry point access still a good choice, in order to avoid the cost of maintaining and accessing via an index. However, referral to figure 3.14 shows that the logical sequential entry point access is online, so high performance is required. Dynamic online sorts, particularly with large volumes of data, are bad news and should be avoided wherever possible. It is clear that entry point access on entity C needs to be via an index.

Entities M and N appear not to require any entry point access. This is not the case. They require either randomised or indexed access (preferably randomised as all the entity accesses are direct) to support access from entity G.

5 Cluster the non entry point entities.

Entities E and F are not entry point data groups, so cluster them via a master entity. In this case there is only one master entity, so cluster them via entity D. 100 accesses between E and F are last, i.e. for a given E access its last occurrence of F where the sequence of F is known, and 200 accesses are read reverse from the last occurrence of F. Given that relational file handlers do

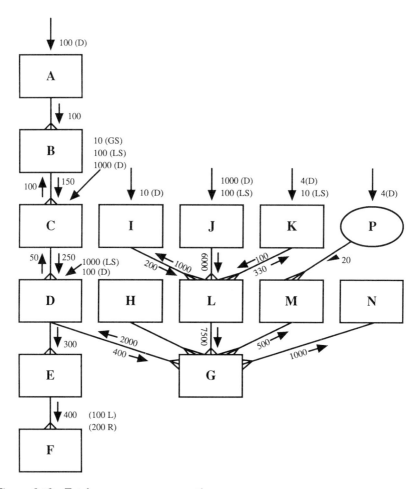

Figure 3.13   Total summary access path map

not support pointer chain technology, a scan and sort routine for these transactions requiring last and first access will be necessary, followed by access to the desired entities. If the key sequence on which the last and reverse access is different from that of the foreign key relationship key between E and F then access to F can be optimised with an index on the last and reverse key(s). For example, if the last and reverse key is date and date is not part of the foreign key in F to E then index F on date.

Entity D is the opposite of entity C. 90% of the entry point accesses are logical sequential, the data maintenance overheads are low—see figure 3.16—and the access is entirely online—see figure 3.14. Indexed rather than randomised entry point access is therefore required. In addition it

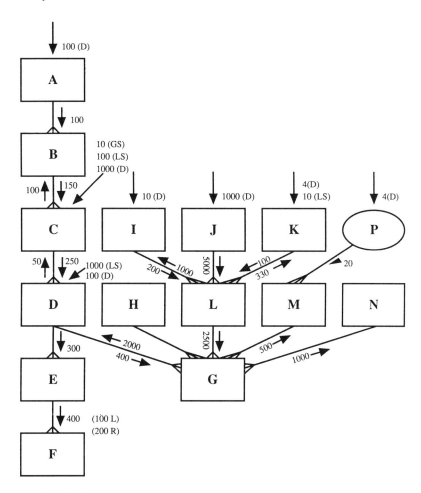

Figure 3.14   Online summary access path map

would be worth while, based on the above evidence, to store the data on disk in logical sequential order as a "key sequenced data set".

Cluster entity G via entity L and entity L via entity J. Both entities relate to multiple master entities, so to which master should they be clustered? The total summary access path map provides the answer. Entity G is accessed more than 3 times more frequently via entity L than via any other master entity and entity L in turn is accessed 5 times more frequently via entity J than via any other master entity. Clustering as advised above would therefore have the maximum benefit as regards reducing physical I/O on access between these three entities.

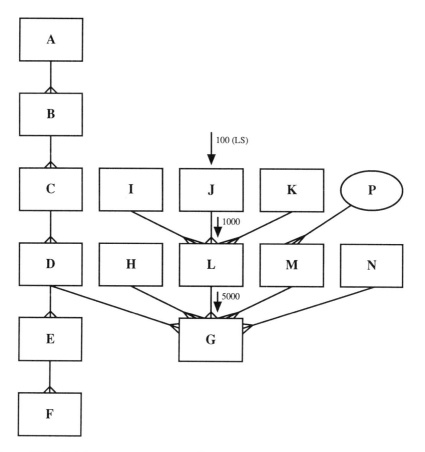

Figure 3.15   Batch summary access path map

A KSDS has one possible and one definite advantage. First the prime index on the key data item on which the file is now sequenced is much smaller (by a factor of the number of record occurrences per page/block) than the secondary indexes or any indexes if the file is not key sequenced. For example, if 10 record occurrences could fit per page/block then the prime index would be 10 times smaller than the secondary indexes. This is because an index on the key sequence data item only requires one pointer per page/block—see figure 3.18. The example here is the VSAM KSDS file handler from IBM. A control interval equals a page/block. The control area is all the control intervals in a cylinder on the disk. It illustrates that the lowest sequence pointers in the index point to the last table row in a control interval block and that there is only one pointer per control interval, not per table row.

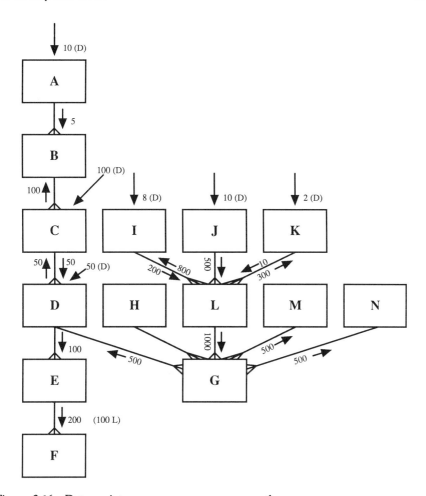

Figure 3.16   Data maintenance summary access path map

By contrast, all secondary indexes and indexes on non-key sequenced files require one pointer per table row occurrence. The key sequence index is therefore smaller and more likely to be held in the processor main memory buffer pool and thereby reduce disk I/Os.

But care needs to be taken. The strategy of one pointer per page/block has a significant disadvantage—the block offset position of each table row in the page/block is not given. The file handler therefore has to read on average half the rows per block to find the desired row. Logical I/O to the buffer pool is thereby substantially increased. If the blocking factor is 20 the logical I/O overhead on the processor would be increased by a factor of 10!

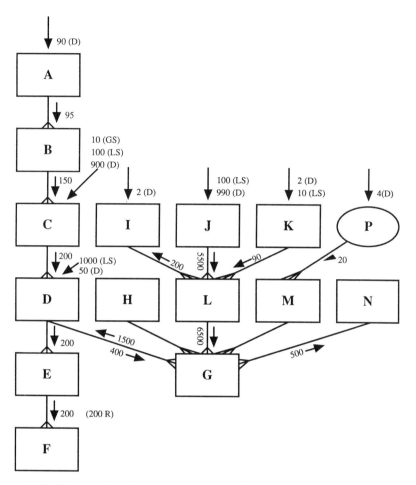

Figure 3.17   Data retrieval summary access path map

The second and undoubted advantage is that, by storing the table rows in logical/key sequenced order, 10 key sequenced accesses to 10 records stored in key sequence would generate only one physical I/O. The main disadvantage of key sequence data storage is on record insertion. If the block into which the table row requires to be inserted in order to maintain key sequence is full then overflow of some kind, such as block splitting, is required. However, figure 3.16 shows the data maintenance accesses per month to entity D are low, and of these 70%, let's say, are updates. Block splitting through insertion is therefore low risk. Make entity D a KSDS.
6 *Delete non accessed entities.*
Delete entity H from the database. It is never accessed.

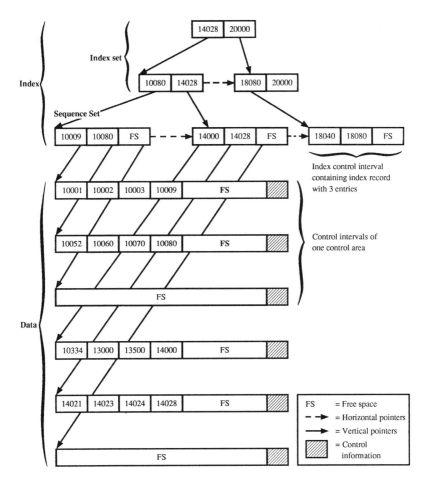

* VSAM is an IBM trademark

Figure 3.18 Index structure for a VSAM key-sequenced file. (Reproduced by permission of IBM Corporation from *DOS VS Access Method Services User Manual*)

7 Make P an operational entities index.
Entity P becomes an index.

3.1.4 Producing a balanced database design

This trick reflects the concept that the database design is based on total data structure and total data access. While Information Engineering produces a total data structure ERD model and total data access matrices the method does not guarantee to produce a balanced database design because the matrices do not show all the necessary summary access information as represented in the summary access path maps. For example they cannot show direction of data access flow. They are also not as easy to interpret—they are not very pictographic, to say the least. Information Engineering therefore is liable to produce a tuned design—tuned for the transactions that happen to be selected for optimisation. There is also a further problem: the data structure component of database design is at the enterprise level whereas the data access component is mainly at the transaction level. An Information Engineering database design may not therefore match the definition of database as detailed in section 2.2.2.3.

By accepting the concepts of logical design = physical design, testing the logical design for efficiency and producing and interpreting the summary access path maps as detailed in section 3.1.3, the basis of balanced database and program designs that are inherently efficient can be easily achieved.

Information Engineering implicitly accepts the first concept and produces the deliverable for the third concept but fails to provide advice as to how to take advantage of the information contained. It is this failure that prevents Information Engineering from ensuring that the database and program designs are balanced and *a priori* efficient. Once that advice is provided then much of the need for subsequent database and program optimisation will be eliminated. Much man effort could be saved.

Two Information Engineering design techniques need to be enhanced to take total data access into account as well as total data structure. The first technique is preliminary data structure design. The technique is applied in the BSD stage to produce a preliminary database design based on the data structuring and data access rules of the appropriate database file handler. The enhancement is the inclusion of advice as to how to interpret the summary access path maps in database design terms. The advice is detailed in the previous section. A balanced and efficient database design would be the result.

Notwithstanding that the author believes physical database optimisation should not be necessary if a balanced database design is produced the real world is likely to require some physical optimisation. No file handler currently gets "ten out of ten" so that compromises to and a certain amount of "tweaking" of the design for certain types of transaction access may be required. Of course, given the concept of logical design = physical design the fewer the better. Database optimisation is the task of the second technique, namely performance assessment. The technique itself is excellent in all respects but one. It fails to indicate which transactions need to be tested against the database to ascertain if it meets performance objectives regarding data storage and transaction response times. There are 500 business requirements in the application and hence 500 transactions. Which ones should the database be tested against?

The conventional wisdom offered by a number of structured methods is to select those transactions that:

- require fast response times;
- occur at the highest interactive peaks;
- occur in high volumes;
- run for a long time.

All good stuff. But what if the following occurs? The database is as drawn in figure 3.19, with the vast bulk of the data accesses occurring in only a small part of the database. This would be difficult to spot within the load matrices, which merely give access statistics. Summary access path maps against the ERD model give a good visual impact. From the summary maps in figure 3.19 it is clear that the small part of the database requires the greatest optimisation. Yet it so happens that the "flashy" transactions selected for testing are to be found in the 20% area. There is no guarantee that the transactions selected on the basis of the above criteria will always fall within the small 80% area. Probably yes, but certainly no. *It is only by having summary access path maps as described earlier that the part of the database requiring greatest optimisation can be properly ascertained.*

The Database

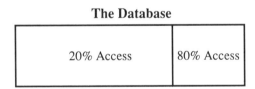

Figure 3.19   Database access distribution

By having summary access path maps the transactions to be selected for timing can be chosen on the basis that they access those parts of the database that have the greatest accesses and therefore require, without question, the greatest design optimisation.

By using the ERD model and summary access path maps as the basis of choosing where the design optimisation technique will be applied the inherent efficiency of a balanced database will be reinforced. The mechanism by which the technique should be enhanced is the interpretation of the summary access path maps as detailed in section 3.1.3.

3.2 SYSTEMATIC TRICKS

3.2.1 Ensuring process decomposition is consistent and sensible

This is a notoriously difficult task to achieve, primarily because so much of it is subjective. The Information Engineering manuals provide advice that is mostly implicit in the examples they give of a function or an elementary process or whatever. The use of naming conventions is most useful, as will be seen shortly, but no statement as to why is given. It is very much left to the intelligence of the reader of the manuals to glean the expertise.

The processes in the process decomposition and dataflow diagrams can be drawn at multiple levels of detail appropriate to the user specifying their requirements. This is one of the great strengths of these two techniques. They can be pitched at whatever level is appropriate. The author has found it appropriate to decompose the processes to four levels of decomposition—business area, business activities/functions, events and problems-to-solve.

Information Engineering uses two techniques that are designed to support the decomposition of processes—process decomposition and dataflow diagramming. Unfortunately there is some confusion in the two versions of the method considered in this book in dataflow diagramming. The IEM version does not identify the need to decompose DFD processes. Certainly no diagramming conventions to support decomposition is provided. (With IEM the DFD processes are identified from the procedures in the procedure dependency diagrams. These procedures in turn have evolved from the processes identified from process decomposition undertaken earlier in the BAA stage. Furthermore, as far as the author is aware IEM is unique in suggesting a reverse exercise to "recompose" (author's quotation marks) the procedures into groups of procedures/subsystems for presentational purposes.) By contrast the Navigator version does identify the possibility of DFD processes at the context and elementary process level, excluding problems-to-solve! What happens if an event level process has many problems-to solve?

The problem with process decomposition is that the identification of business areas, functions and problems-to-solve is subjective and therefore open to interpretation. A hypothetical but realistic port authority is used as an example to illustrate the four levels of decomposition. The decomposition is illustrated as dataflow diagrams (DFDs). They could just as easily be drawn as process decomposition diagrams (PDDs).

The island port company has 6 major business areas as detailed in figure 3.20. These business area processes very often match the high level management structure of the enterprise, but it is not necessary for this to be so. Indeed, it is extremely important that the decomposition is undertaken "logically", that is to say without consideration of any physical constraints, such as management organisational structure. Any match between the

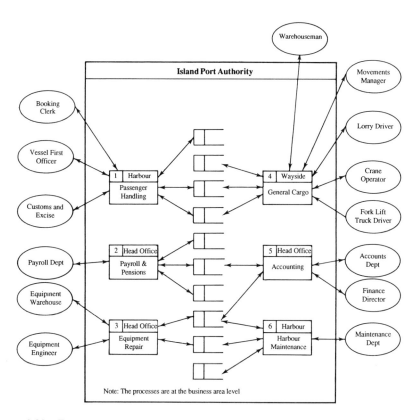

Figure 3.20   Dataflow diagram: level 1

organisational structure and the decomposed processes is because the management structure is also "logically" organised to reflect the natural breakdown of the company's business operations.

The cargo handling business area is decomposed into a set of four functions—see figure 3.21. Business area and function processes are higher than the event level processes. A trick to identify processes that are higher than events is to entitle the processes using either a gerund ending with an "ing" suffix for the title (for example accounting and passenger handling) or a double noun for the title (for example general cargo, harbour maintenance). The boundary between business areas and functions is not precise. Using a paraphrase of the official definition of a function in IEM a function is a group of business activities which together support one aspect of the company's business. What is an aspect? If one takes the function of cargo loading then, as illustrated in figure 3.22, there are 6 events, all of which are "sensibly" associated with the function in that they are concerned with the aspect of loading cargo onto a vessel. One could

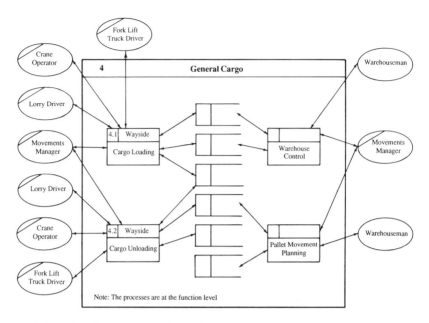

Figure 3.21   Dataflow diagram: level 2

follow this argument further and say that a business area is nothing more than a sensibly related group of functions. For example, the functions in figure 3.21 are obviously associated with the business area of general cargo.

Event level processes are much easier to identify, as they are objective triggers to which the computer must make a response. A naming convention trick that the author uses to identify event level processes is to give them a "do something" title. In figure 3.22 the processes are so named— Load Pallet, Allocate Crane, Move Pallet (to Crane). This style of naming convention is also appropriate to problem-to-solve processes, as illustrated in figure 3.23. This is because problem-to-solve processes can, depending on circumstances, also be events. In the example the problem-to-solve Advise Movements Manager so happens to be a problem-to-solve within the event of choosing/allocating a fork lift truck. In another business context it could well be a standalone event apropos anything to which the Warehousman, the Fork Lift Truck driver and the Movements Manager require to be advised on.

The advice on naming conventions for processes is provided in the Information Engineering manuals as a general statement, but does not explicitly relate the different types of names to above and below the event level boundary.

Decomposing processes on the lines described above has a number of advantages:

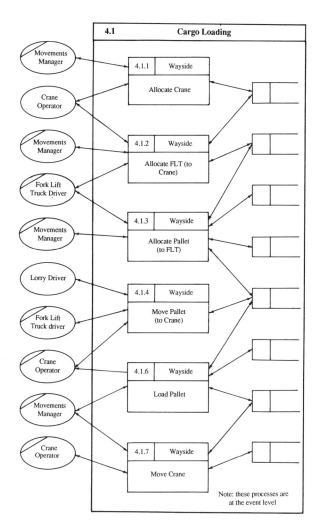

Figure 3.22   Dataflow diagram: level 3

- It automatically pitches the processes at the two highest levels of decomposition to a level that is readily appreciated by the senior user/manager. The naming conventions of using gerunds and double nouns to describe the processes also facilitates an understanding that the processes are higher than events. The processes on the level 1 DFD/PDD is a deliverable that can be presented to and understood by the users of the major business areas in an enterprise, namely the senior managers. The functional processes at level 2 are logically grouped within business

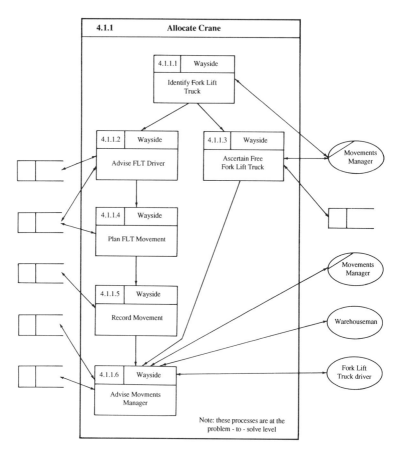

Figure 3.23   Dataflow diagram: level 4

area and are processes that typically reflect middle management. The port company had a middle manager responsible for warehouse control at the main port and the organisation of all pallet movements within each of the ports, and a middle manager responsible for cargo loading and unloading within each of the ports. Notwithstanding that the business areas and functions are subjective groupings of business requirements/events for users/senior managers to understand the processes identified are logical to the business and not the management structure. It so happened that the port management was "logically" structured.

- It explicitly recognises that events are triggers on the computer system by using the "do something" naming convention. The fact that events in batch and online processing are standalone is explicitly reflected in that the processes in the DFDs are separated by datastores. Process A does not trigger process B. This ability to "time" separate processes is a facility in DFDs not provided in process decomposition or process dependency diagrams.

- The DFDs are able to recognise explicitly that problem-to-solve processes in an event are causally related and occur logically at the same point in time as the event by linking the processes by dataflows. Process A triggers process B. It also recognises that problems-to-solve can also be events by naming them with a "do something" title.

- The processes at the two lowest levels can be used directly as the one-for-one basis for identifying application programs and their constituent modules. Given the concepts logical design = physical design, business requirements are events, event level processing, events are standalone and problems-to-solve are causally related it is natural that the events become programs and the problems-to-solve become modules. It also has the advantage of recognising that in centralised processing application programs should not talk to each other. It confirms Yourdon's statement that "application programs are schedulable, modules are callable".

3.2.2 Group the man/machine interface to best advantage

There needs to be a clear distinction between the menu selection and transactions screens. The dialogue flow technique in Information Engineering does not do this. The author has found the dialogue design technique from the LSDM structured method to be the best currently available and uses their material as the basis of the examples.

In LSDM the menu selection component is called the "Invocation Dialogue Structure" (IDS) and the transaction screen component is called the "Transaction Dialogue Structure" (TDS). Different diagrammatic and documentary support for each of the screen types is provided, such that their different role in defining the man/machine interface can be clearly ascertained.

Using the LSDM notation a representative menu screen structure chart is illustrated in figure 3.24. The main menu contains four options, sales menu, sales invoice menu, marketing menu and a exit option. If the sales menu option is chosen the sales menu screen will display five options, four of which are for choosing a business requirement. The business requirement options are salesman bonus, area sales, product sales and customer sales. The final option, of course, is the exit. Once a business requirement is chosen the user implicitly exits the IDS and enters the TDS appropriate to the business requirement selected. The TDS for the salesman's bonus is illustrated in figure 3.25. The first screen displayed is screen 1 requesting the input of a salesman's number in order to trigger the query. The response

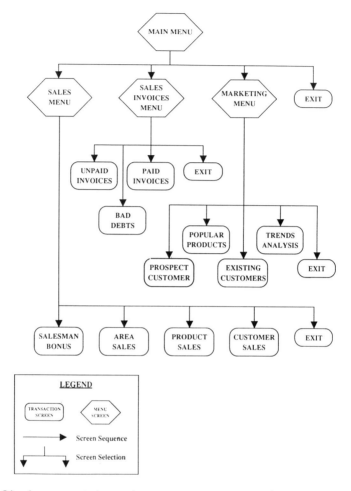

Figure 3.24   A representative main menu screen structure chart

would be input screen 2 for the entry of salesman's data. Depending on whether conditions 1 or 2 were appropriate screens 4 or 3 would be displayed. For screen 3 depending on the value of condition 3 the next screen displayed would be either screen 5 or screen 6.

The author has found that the business requirements which a user triggers in the menu selection process are not specific to individual users but to user types and that these user types overwhelmingly reflect the decomposition of the processes in the dataflow diagrams and process decomposition diagrams.

If the process decomposition is as advised in section 3.2.1 then there is a direct match between the user type and the process decomposition. Using

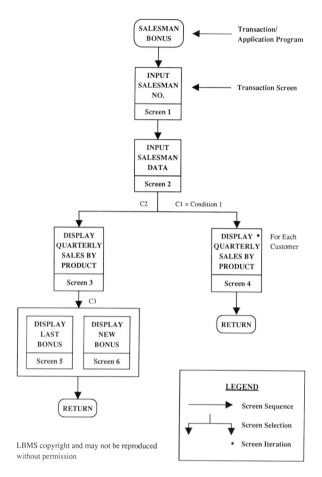

Figure 3.25   A representative transaction screen dialogue structure chart

the port authority as an example user types could be the finance director, personnel director, crane operator, fork lift truck driver, warehousman and harbour maintenance engineer. The finance director in the accounts department would be concerned with the business functions in the accounting business area, the fork lift truck driver would be concerned with the functions in the general cargo handling area and the equipment engineer would be concerned with the functions in the equipment repair business area. Therefore when a particular user type logs on to the menu selection routines the top level menu has already been implicitly selected.

The crane operator is also concerned with general cargo, so that the top level menu screen for data maintenance would also show the two business areas as options. The first menu displayed, and hence the top level main menu in the hierarchical cascade of menu selection screens, is the list of business functions appropriate to the user type. For example, if the crane operator user type logged on then the functions appropriate to the general cargo business area as shown in the next level of process decomposition could be displayed, namely the functions of Cargo Loading and Unloading—see figure 3.21. The warehousman is only concerned with warehouse control and pallet movement planning and the fork lift truck driver is only concerned with cargo loading and unloading. If the crane operator chooses the cargo loading option the next level menu option displays the options of the events appropriate to cargo loading for the crane operator, that is load pallet. *The policy followed is that only those events, functions and business areas appropriate to a user type would be displayed.*

The processes so far identified are those concerned with maintaining the database. The front-end to the main menu would enquire as to whether the user wished to undertake data maintenance or data retrieval. The retrieval business requirements would reflect the type of user in the same way as the data maintenance business requirements, such that the finance director would enquire on accounting matters and the equipment engineer would enquire on matters relating to equipment repair.

The top level boundary set per user type for the menu selection design is therefore at the function process level identified in the level 2 process decompositions. A higher level menu is not required as the business areas are implicit in the user type, unless, of course, the user is responsible for two or more business areas. The options detailed in each level of the menu selection option decomposition matches exactly the process decomposition levels, with the "scope" of the user's data maintenance and data retrieval requests being progressively focused within the process decomposition.

3.2.3 Appreciating the different keys in an entity

There are four different keys used in data modelling. Information Engineering does not recognise all of them. The keys are:

- Simple key
  This is a single data item key used to identify an entity occurrence. An example is customer number to identify each occurrence of the customer entity. Each customer number value is unique.
  This type of key is recognised by Information Engineering.

- Compound key
  This is a multi-part key used to identify an entity occurrence, but with each item of the unique in its own right. Assume three entities—product, depot and stock. The stock entity records the amount of stock of a particular product in a particular depot and acts as the link record on

a many-to-many relationship between product and depot. The simple keys of product and depot are product code and depot number. The compound key of stock is product code and depot number. The key is multi-part with each item a unique value in its own right. Each element of a compound key is also a foreign key. Multi-part keys are recognised by Information Engineering, being sometimes called compound keys, but they are also called composite keys.

• Composite key
  This is a multi-part key used to identify an entity occurrence, but where each item of the key is not unique in its own right. A higher qualifying key item is required to make the key unique. Assume four entities— customer, order, order line and product. Simple keys identify customer, product and order. A multi-part key is used for the order line entity— order number and order line number. One might think that order line number is adequate to identify the order line entity. Such is usually not the case. Most orders contain many order lines, which are usually numbered in a sequence of 1 to n as required. Thus, all the order lines for all the orders have the same sequence number values. Order line number is therefore not unique and requires some higher qualifier. This qualifier is order number.

  There is now a multi-part key, but to show that it is not a compound key (order line number is not unique in its own right) the usual convention followed is to place ( ) round the composite items of the key. The higher qualifying key (order number) becomes a foreign key.

  Composite keys are only significant in logical data modelling. Once the higher qualifying key item has been identified then the composite key is treated as a normal single key item. As such it can be part of a compound key. Composite keys have no specific significance in physical design.

  Information Engineering does not recognise composite keys.

• Foreign Key
  If a non-key data item in entity A is also the key of another entity B the non-key item is a foreign key. An example could be in the order line entity with a foreign key of product code. Information Engineering recognises foreign keys.

A full understanding of these keys and their roles is essential to correct data modelling, as is described in the next section.

3.2.4 Building a composite ERD model

Although not explicitly recognised by Information Engineering as separate techniques there are in fact two very different ways to build a logical data model—from the data retrieval business requirements and from analysing the raw data items. The first technique is usually called entity modelling and the second relational data analysis (sometimes third normal form analysis).

Building an entity model from the business requirements can be undertaken very quickly once the business requirements have been identified. This speed is because entity modelling works at the entity level and not at the data item level. For reasons explained in concept nine only the data retrieval business requirements should be used for entity modelling. A quick exercise illustrates the point. Assume the following business requirements:

- "For a specified customer display all the orders and order lines for products priced at more than £10 stocked at a specified depot".

- "Display all discounted customers with red hair".

- "List all overdue invoices for a specified sales territory".

- "Display all order lines where no invoice has been received".

The resultant ERD logical data model from the above is illustrated in figure 3.26. Bearing in mind that this book is for the experienced practitioner the relationship of the ERD model to the business requirements is overwhelmingly obvious and will not be explained, apart from the entities status and discount. These entities are operational entities, not data entities. They are there for operational reasons. There is a business need to access invoice and customer on other than their prime keys of invoice number and customer code. One can do this by scanning the entity, but this would probably be very inefficient. There are 10,000 customers, of whom only 1% are discounted, and some 100,000 order lines, of which only some 5% do not have related invoices. It would be more efficient to create operational entities as entry points to the ERD model. The discounted operational entity points to the appropriate customers and the status operational entity reflects the status of invoices, some of which may be overdue.

One can rapidly verify that the ERD can support the business requirements by walking them through the model. For business requirement two enter on operational entity discounted and from there access customer. The model can support this business requirement. That is all that has been ascertained. What has not been ascertained is that the model supports these business requirements efficiently—that is the task of another technique, as described in section 3.1.1.

The other approach to data modelling is to apply the technique of relational data analysis to the raw data items in the application. The data items can be ascertained from a variety of sources. The author uses the data definitions of the information views of the dataflows in the dataflow and

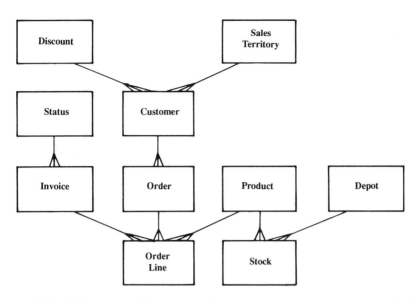

Figure 3.26 ERD model. The relationship semantics have been omitted. The notation has followed the Navigator standard

process dependency diagrams—other practitioners obtain the data from the report and screen designs and file definitions. So long as all the data about the application is obtained the actual source is a secondary issue.

The normalisation rules of relational data analysis are applied to the data items. At a minimum the rules up to third normal form should be applied. It is recommended in the next section to progress up to sixth normal form. The technique of data normalisation will not be described—there are numerous reference books on this. At the end of applying the technique a set of fully normalised relations/entities is obtained.

Unfortunately this is often as far as many methods go, including Information Engineering. Both versions of Information Engineering considered in this book identify the need to do relational analysis, but only as a means to check the validity of the ERD model, not as a separate technique to build a separate data model. A number of further steps should be undertaken.

These further steps are based on the SSADM/LSDM methods.

Having decomposed the data from the source material the third normal form relations require to be optimised—that is, all those relations with common keys to be combined. The data contained on the various source material can be normalised to relations with common keys and common non-key data items. The danger of optimisation is that the relations can revert back to second normal form. The rules of normalisation need to be applied once again.

In order to be sure that the relations are truly in third normal form the "TNF" tests need to be applied. The tests are:

- "For a given value of the key is there only one possible value for each of the associated non-key data items?"
- "Is each data item directly dependent on the entire key?"

To be in third normal form the answer to both these questions must be yes. The relations are now ready to be used as the basis for building a relational logical data model. SSADM/LSDM provide a set of rules for this task. Assume the case study in figures 3.27 to 3.32. The relations and their attributes are defined in figure 3.27. The data structuring rules are:

- Rule 1 TNF relations become entities/relations. All the relations in figure 3.27 become entities—see figure 3.28.

Invoice	*Sales Territory*	*Product*
Invoice No	Sales Territory No	Product No
Date	Sales Territory	Description
Invoice Total		Weight
		Standard Price
		*Product class
		Total Stock

Invoice Line	*Customer*	*Customer/Territory*
(Invoice No	Customer No	Sales Territory No
Invoice Line No)	*Brick No	Customer No
*Product No	*Sales territory No	
Quantity	Discount Code	
Price	Credit Limit	
	Delivery Insurance	

Stock	*Brick*	*Discount*
Product No	Brick No	Product No
Depot Code	Depot Code	Discount Code
Depot Stock		Discount Price
Depot Location Code		
Ordered YTD		

Product Class
Product Class Code
Invoice Code

Figure 3.27 Optimised relations

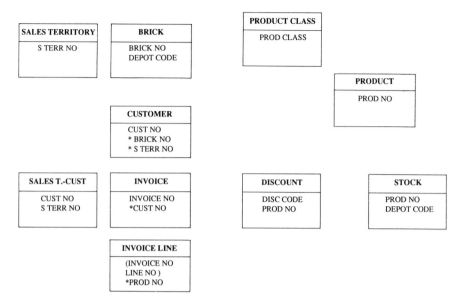

Figure 3.28   TNF relations become entities

- Rule 2 Composite keys contain foreign keys. If the entire primary key of a relation is a composite, mark the higher qualifying element(s) as a foreign key. Do not treat this type of relation as a compound key relation as in rules 3 and 4.

  The relation with a composite key is Invoice Line. The higher qualifying key to the Invoice Line is Invoice Number, which becomes a foreign key— see figure 3.29.

- Rule 3 All masters of compound keys must be present. Check that each element of every compound key occurs as a simple or composite key of another relation. If an element is part of a compound key, but is not the sole key of another relation then:

  — create a new relation with the element as its key;
  — make this new relation a master of each relation which has the element as part of its compound key;
  — if the element is not a date, mark it as a foreign key in all other relations where it appears as a non-key data item.

  The relations with compound keys are Discount, Sales Territory/ Customer and Stock. The Discount Code and Depot elements of the compound keys do not have sole key relations, which must there- fore be created, and the attributes Depot Code, Sales Territory number

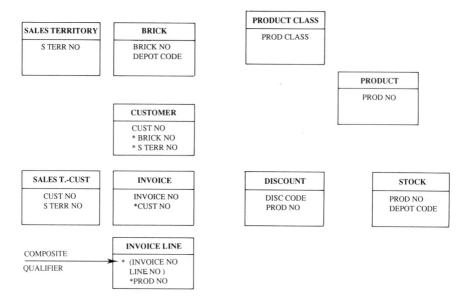

Figure 3.29   Composite keys contain foreign keys

and Discount Code in the Brick and Customer relations are marked as foreign keys—see figure 3.30.

- Rule 4 Compound key relations become details. Make compound key relations the details of those relations that have either a single or multiple elements of the compound as the total key. Allocate each element only once.

    The compound key relations Discount, Sales Territory/Customer and Stock become details—see figure 3.31.

- Rule 5 Foreign keys indicate masters. Make the relation with a foreign key the detail of the relation that has that key as its total prime key.

    The relations with the foreign keys now become detail entities, that is Customer, Brick, Invoice and Invoice Line—see figure 2.32.

One has now constructed two logical data models—an entity model and a relational model, both for a common business application. As detailed in section 2.4.2.3 these two logical data models may well be different. The remaining task is therefore to reconcile the two data models. The mechanism here is a set of steps to undertake, but in contrast to building the relational data model, they are not of the prescriptive rule based approach. A considerable amount of subjective compromise may be required. Start by taking the points of agreement in the two data models regarding the entities/relations and relationships and use them to build the base

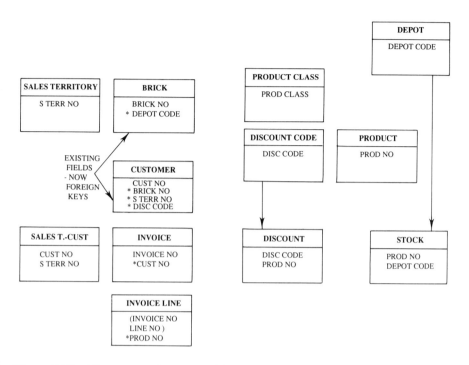

Figure 3.30   All masters of compound keys must be present

composite ERD model. Then review the TNF relations that were created from rule 3 when building the relational data model. Depending on the circumstances, discard them, make them operational masters or include them as entities if further data can be envisaged. Of the remaining steps it is a case of referring to the list of business requirements to resolve any differences between the two models. This latter point is significant—given that the logical design specification defines a business the composite ERD is more likely to be "oriented" to the entity data model rather than the relational data model.

When the composite ERD model has been finally completed it must be validated that it supports the data retrieval business requirements as described above and tested for logical efficiency as described in section 3.1.1.

3.2.5 Taking relational data analysis to sixth normal form

Currently the two versions of Information Engineering differ in the degree to which relational data analysis is undertaken. IEM identifies a

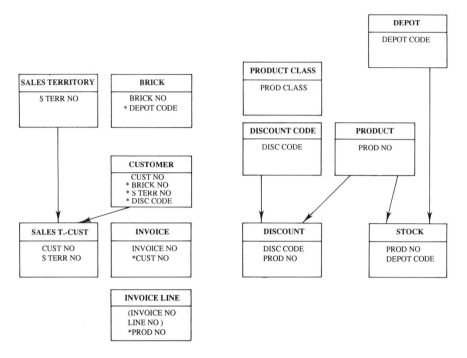

Figure 3.31   Compound key relations become details

four stage process to fourth normal form and Navigator goes to third normal form while recognising that higher orders of normalisation can be achieved—Boyce/Codd normal form and fourth normal form. Yet further differences exist. IEM's fourth normal form is not the same as Navigator's fourth normal form. IEM's identifies entity sub-types, while Navigator's is something the author has never come across before—an associative entity which is at the many end of more than two optional one-to-many relationships.

While the first three normalisation rules of relational data analysis are universally accepted there is still considerable disagreement as to the higher orders of normalisation, as the two versions of Information Engineering show. Further confusion arises when the author states that his understanding of the higher orders of normalisation are different from IEM's and Navigator's. Described below is the latest position as currently understood.

Both versions of Information Engineering decompose raw data items into third normal form relations. For the last decade this has been widely accepted as the ultimate in data normalisation/data decomposition. It was believed that relations in third normal form have no further hidden

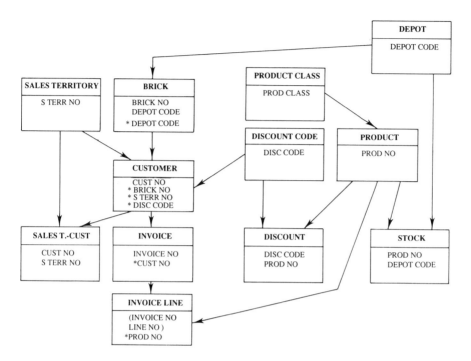

Figure 3.32   Foreign keys indicate masters

relationships—the non-key data items are dependent only upon the entire prime key of the relation and there are no relationships between the non-key items.

Within the last few years it is being increasingly argued that there are further stages of data decomposition, three more to be precise. The full six normalisation rules are:

• first normal form (1NF)... test for repeating groups;

• second normal form (2NF)... test for inter-key dependence;

• third normal form (3NF)... test for inter-data dependence;

• fourth normal form (4NF)... test for multi-valued dependences on multi-key key only relations;

• fifth normal form (5NF)... test for derived information;

• sixth normal form (6NF)... test for conditional dependence.

The rules of fourth to sixth normal form, and another situation of data normalisation called Boyce/Codd normal form, are described in C. Dates' book "An Introduction to Database Systems" Volume 1. They will not be repeated and described here. Only sixth normal form is considered, as the facility of entity sub-typing will play an increasingly important part in object oriented systems, as we shall see in chapter 5.

Sixth normal form (6NF) is concerned with entity sub-types. The rule is to test whether certain data attributes in a relation are dependent on the prime key based on certain conditions, conditions set by the application. A simple example illustrates the point. A vehicle relation is composed of vehicle number, wing span, sail area and weight. This relation is in third normal form because it satisfies the two tests for normalisation. However it is obvious that wing span relates to vehicle of type aircraft and sail area relates to vehicle of type sailing boat. The relation needs to be split into two sub-types within vehicle—of aircraft with the attributes of vehicle number and wing span and of sailing boat with the attributes of vehicle number and sail area. The vehicle relation would contain the attributes of vehicle number and weight and be the super-type relation to the aircraft and sailing boat entity sub-types.

A complete hierarchy of entity sub-types can be obtained. Consider customer in figure 3.33. It contains generic attributes relevant to all customers, such as name and address. It also contains attributes relevant only to non-credit-worthy customers—debt amount, litigation mechanism—and attributes relevant only to credit-worthy customers— amount loaned, repayment period, loan type. The entity sub-types credit-worthy customer could simultaneously be an entity super-type as well as an entity sub-type. Credit worthy loans could be secured—description of security, security value—and unsecured—insurance cover amount, insurance monthly premium. There is no potential limit to the degree of entity sub-type decomposition.

An entity sub-type can relate to more than one super-type. The loan type attribute in the entity sub-type credit customer acts as a foreign key to the entity super-type loan type. Thus the entity sub-type credit customer has two super-types, customer and loan type. A complete hierarchical and network data structure of entity sub-types and super-types can therefore exist.

A little trick the author uses. Never apply relational data analysis to the output data flows from an application. They are nothing more that the input data flows plus a process. No data is lost and the amount of data to be analysed can be reduced by up to half.

3.2.6 Combining entities

There are occasions when there is a one-to one relationship between entities. The suggestion has been made by Information Engineering that one solution

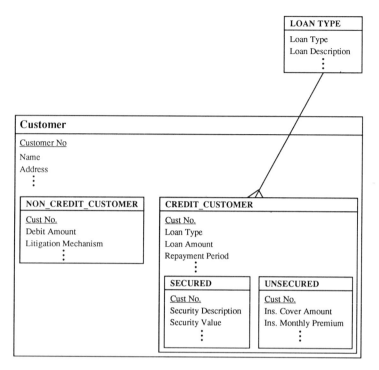

Figure 3.33   Sixth normal form/entity sub-types

to this is to combine the entities, but no advice as to when and when not to do this is given.

Assume a one-to-one relationship between the entities Member of Parliament (MP) and Constituency. They could be combined into a single entity. Whenever this is possible a number of questions need to be asked:

- What should the name of the combined entity be? Whichever name is chosen from the two source entities the name not selected will be lost as will the role of the previously named entity. It should be borne in mind that the two entitles play different roles and that an MP is not a Constituency.

   Assume that the key of the MP entity is MP Code and the key of the Constituency entity is Constituency No. Which of these two keys should be used for the combined entity?

- Has flexibility been lost by combining the entities? The answer is invariably yes. What if one subsequently requires to keep a history of the MPs in a constituency? The implemented model would not enable this to be supported. The real world situation, of course, is that over time there is a many-to-many relationship between these two entities.

The principle followed by the author is never to combine one-to-one relationship entities. Where a one-to-one relationship is initially established it is always the case that only the present state of affairs is required to be recorded. At any point in time there is only one MP to one Constituency. The author always asks "What if you require to record the history about the entities?" Invariably one entity is more stable than the other, the MPs being more frequently changed than the Constituency, so that a Constituency can have many MPs. The question, however, is not enough. Having established that one entity is more dynamic than the other, it is also necessary to establish whether the entity occurrences can change in relation to each other over time. The standard question to establish this is, using the above example, "Can an MP relate to more than one Constituency over time and can one Constituency have more than one MP over time?" The answer is, of course, yes to both questions and a many-to-many relationship is established.

3.2.7 Entity life histories

This technique is concerned with identifying and recording the sequence in which events that update an entity occur. It fulfils the same role as the entity life cycle analysis technique of Information Engineering, but, as will be seen, does not suffer any of the deficiencies. The technique is from the SSADM method.

Consider figure 3.34. To record the full complexities that can occur in the life of an entity ELHs requires to provide the following facilities:

• sequence: the events that update an entity can occur in an orderly sequence, one after another.

• iteration: an update event can occur many times during the entity's life. An account entity can be updated many times by a record monies event.

• selection: there can be a group of update events of which only one can occur at any one point in time—one of the group must be chosen. A person entity has a group of events called buying. A person could have multiple buy events options—buy house, buy car, buy holiday or buy nothing. The terms of the application are that these events are mutually exclusive and hence optional.

• parallel lives: an entity can have multiple lives simultaneously such that not all events affecting an entity will occur in strict sequence—if they did, there would be no need for the ELH technique. A person could have a life as a business professional and a simultaneous life as a married person and.... All are occurring asynchronously to each other. The parallel life

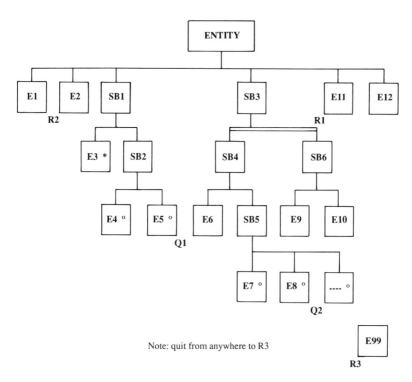

Figure 3.34   Entity life history structure: 1

can occur at any point between the creation and deletion of the entity, but usually occurs at a particular and identifiable point in the entity life.

- unpredictable events: certain events can occur at any point between the creation and the deletion of the entity in a totally unorderable manner.

- quits and resumes: there can be a change in the prescribed sequence of events. The person dies, potentially anywhere between the insert and delete events in the person entity's life. The entity life resumes, in this application, at the delete event.

- state indicators: for each entity there is state indicator, to which is allocated a predecessor and successor value appropriate to each event that affects the entity. Each entity life requires its own set of state indicator. An entity can therefore have multiple state indicators, one for each life. The state indicator is an additional attribute stored in an entity, and is used to re-express the ELH structure in numeric form. The state of an entity as regards its life can be tested by reading the event predecessor value held in the state indicator. If it is correct for the event updating the entity then the update proceeds and the state value is changed to the event successor value. If the value is wrong the update is rejected. Thus the state indicator can be used to ensure that events that update the entity occur in the correct sequence. The logic for testing the state indicator(s) should be specified in the action diagrams.

The diagramming notation and ELH structure is illustrated in figure 3.34.

• The box at the top of the structure is the entity and the boxes at the bottom are the events. If the events need to be grouped (a number of events iterate as a group, for example) or there is an option or iteration within the sequence then a structure box is drawn. The boxes SB1, SB2, SB*n* in figure 3.34 are such structure boxes.

• A sequence of events is left to right—event 1 occurs before event 2.... Event 1 is an insert event, events 2 to 11 are update events and event 12 is a delete event.

• A selection of events is illustrated with events E7 and E8. They are optional to each other—only one can occur. The optionality is indicated by the small circle in the top right of the event box. There can also be a null event with selection. This occurs when the option is not taken up. The null event is indicated by the horizontal bar. Thus events E7 or E8 or no event could occur.

• An iteration of events is illustrated with event E3, which repeats *n* times (*n* can be 0) during the life of the entity. The repetition is indicated by the * in the top right of the event box.

• Sequence, selection and repetition events can be grouped and used within each other. For example event E3 occurs before events E4 and E5. E3 iterates and only when the iteration is complete can E4 or E5 occur. These three events are grouped within the structure box SB1.

• Quits and resumes are also illustrated in figure 3.34. When event E5 occurs quit (Q1) from E5 and jump to resume (R1) at event E11 and when event E8 occurs quit (Q2) to resume (R2) at event E2. The "jump" can be in a forwards or backwards direction in time—Q1 to R1 being a forward direction in time and Q2 to R2 being a backward direction in time.

• There are also occasions where the time that a quit situation arises is totally unpredictable—the death of a person being a classical example. This quit situation can occur anywhere after the insert event and before the delete event. This is the purpose of the quit R3. Quit R3 can be anywhere in the life of the entity. It is not shown, as it would be detailed for each of the update events and clutter up the ELH. When it occurs jump to event E99, E99 being the actions to be taken, in this case following a person's death. There can be a full ELH structure to deal with E99. E99 is known as an "off the structure" box.

• After events E4 or E5 a parallel life occurs. The structure box SB4 is for the normal life events continuing. While events E6 and E7 or E8 are occurring events E9 and E10 can also occur in sequence.

A complete ELH with state indicators is illustrated in figure 3.35. The state indicators are stored as an attribute in the entity and are updated with the successor state value for the event that has occurred. The entity life is as follows. The entity is inserted into the database by event E1 and the state indicator is set to 1. The "normal" entity life sequence is an iteration of event E2. On the first iteration the predecessor state indicator value is 1, to be set to 2, on the subsequent iterations the predecessor value being, of course, 2. Event E2 is followed by event E3, which sets the state indicator value to 3. Events E4 and E5 follow and are optional. Both have a predecessor state indicator value of 3, as they occur after event E3. If event E4 occurs then quit to R1 at event E9. Event E8 occurs after event E5 and changes the state indicator value to 6. E8 also sets the parallel life state indicator to blank. Event E9 occurs after events E8 or event E4 (because of quit 1) so there are two predecessor state indicator values, value 4 from event E4 and value 6 from event E8. The delete event E10 obviously sets the state indicator value to blank.

The events of the parallel life of the entity are occurring at the same time as the events of the normal life of the entity, but only between events E1 and E8. Since the parallel events are occurring asynchronously and totally independently of the normal life they do not affect the state of the normal life. The state indicators monitoring the normal life are therefore unaffected and are not modified. The predecessor values of the normal life state indicators are still tested as per normal, but are not modified, as indicated by the * successor indicator value. Within the parallel life, however, the events require to be monitored in the usual manner. Event E7 occurs in sequence after event E6. The parallel life state indicators are identified by being bracketed. When event E8 occurs the parallel life state indicator needs to be set to blank to indicate the parallel life has completed.

The purpose of the state indicator is that the logic for the event can test the state value for the event and if the value of the predecessor state is not correct for the event then to issue an error message.

The SSADM/LSDM ELHs do not support entity sub-types. Yet entity sub-types are real nonetheless and have occurred in many applications the author has worked on. Research work being undertaken by many universities and relational database vendors is almost all pointing towards supporting entity sub-types in a logical data model as standalone entities with an enhanced SQL schema data definition language syntax.

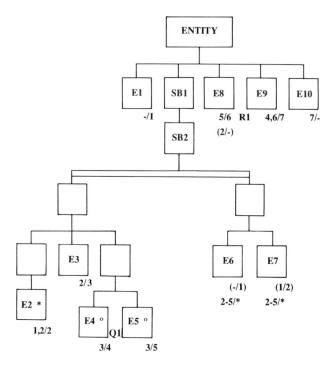

Figure 3.35   Entity life history structure: 2

Currently most relational file handlers do not support entity sub-types.
Entity sub-types are treated as separate tables and linked *explicitly* in the
SQL *data manipulation language* constructs using table joins. What is needed
is to link the entities *implicitly* in the schema definition in the dictionary
as defined in the SQL *data definition language*. Dr Codd has proposed an
extended relational RM/T model. RM/T includes, inter alia, support for
entity sub-types. When describing the RM/T model in volume 2 of his book
referred earlier, Date proposed an enhanced SQL data definition language
to support entity sub-types and super-type relationships.

An example of an enhanced SQL data definition language syntax as
proposed by Date to support figure 3.32 is detailed below:

```
Create Table Customer
Create Table Non_Credit_Customer Sub_Type Customer
Create Table Credit_Customer Sub_Type Customer, Loan_Type
Create Table Secured Sub_Type Credit_Customer
```

Thus at the physical level table sub-types are still stored asseparate tables
of data, but will eventually be supported implicitly by schema definition
rather than by explicit data access calls.

The important point for ELHs is that entity sub-types and their relationships to entity super-types can still be treated as normal standalone entities. As far as the author is concerned the technique does not require modification to support entity sub-types.

ELHs can also be used to support referential integrity between entities. To be frank the author has never used ELHs in this regard. For example, on the delete of a customer entity the author has never drawn a customer ELH to ensure that the customer's orders have previously been deleted. Standard referential integrity constraints for inserts (always check the foreign key value in the detail entity is matched by a master entity prime key value), updates (...) and deletes (...) are specified in the action diagrams and explicitly coded in the application programs. ELH state indicators do not enrich the referential integrity specification mechanism.

Enhancements to the SQL data definition language in version 2 have been made to support referential integrity constraints through database triggers. The formal version 2 syntax has not yet been finalised by the ANSI committee, but several database vendors, such as Cincom for SUPRA and Computer Corporation of America for DATACOM/DB, have already created their own syntax.

For example, when an order is inserted or a foreign key is modified on an existing order a referential integrity constraint is that a customer table row appropriate to the foreign key value of customer number in the order table being inserted/modified must also exist. The constraint will be defined in DATACOM/DB as:

```
Create Table Order
Column
Foreign Key (Customer_No ) Reference Customer.Customer_No
```

Equally when deleting a customer a constraint check should be made that no related order exists. The SQL syntax is:

```
Create Table Customer
Column
References Order on Delete Check (search condition)
```

Given the ease with which referential integrity constraints can be specified logically in the action diagrams and physically in the schema data definition language the "hassle" of drawing ELHs to reflect the potentially large number of referential integrity constraints possible (how do you handle the n exclusive relationship constraints that can occur on a broad network data structure as in figure 2.5?) is not worth it.

The entity life cycle technique used by Information Engineering cannot support parallel lives, quits and resumes, "out of structure" events and event groups.

3.2.8 Batch program design

This is not discussed in the IEM manual and yet it is a significant part of many current systems, and, given the continued use of processors that support batch processing, in particular IBM processors, will remain so for many future application systems.

The author has found the best technique for designing batch programs to be that used in the SSADM version 3 structured method. To use the technique it is necessary to have adopted the entity life history (ELH) technique described in section 3.2.7. The description of the batch program design technique is based on the SSADM manuals, but rephrased to be compatible to information engineering terms.

Batch programs are more difficult to design than online programs because of the need to group and sequence a number of programs together within a time frame. The sequence of tasks to be followed is:

1 Define basic flows and dependencies   This is the major task of the technique. The procedure action diagrams (the author would prefer process action diagrams for reasons explained in section 2.4.2.2) which update the database and are to be run as batch programs are first allocated to functions. This is not difficult as the functions have already been identified in the process/procedure decomposition diagrams. A sequence map is then created of all events in the functions in the order in which they must occur—hence the need for the ELHs. A separate sequence map is drawn for each batch function. The maps are then grouped by time-frame, for example for the daily batch run; for the weekly batch run, into a master sequence map. The time-frame sequence map identifies the sequence in which all the batch update programs run.

A worked example shows the elegance of the technique. Assume the three ELHs in figure 3.36. The functions are as detailed in figure 3.37, along with the event level processes/procedures that occur within the function. All the functions occur on a weekly basis. Beneath each event on the ELHs is the number of the function to which the event belongs. It can be seen that function three occurs before function four, which in turn occurs before function two. These three functions must run in the sequence identified as all three affect an entity, in this case person and posting. Function one only has to run before function two as it affects a different entity—it has nothing to do with functions three and four. The master weekly sequence map is functions three, four, two and one, two. Each function becomes an application program. The resulting sequence of batch programs is detailed in figure 3.38. Each entity becomes a file. It is assumed that the input transaction files do not need to be sorted.

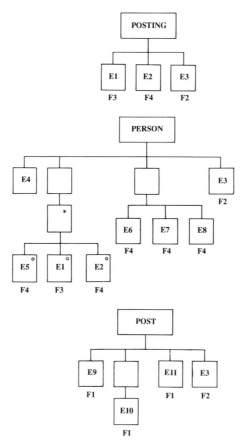

Figure 3.36   Batch program design: 1

Function No	Description	Events
1	Doing This	E9
		E10
		E11
2	Doing That*D3	
3	Doing Other	E1
		E4
4	Doing Something	E5
		E2
		E6
		E7
		E8

Figure 3.37   Batch program design: 2

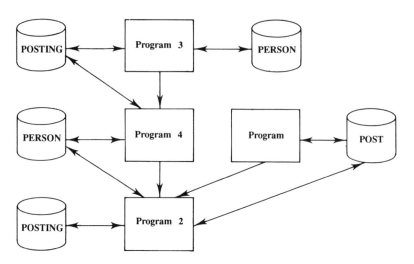

Figure 3.38   Program run chart

The remaining tasks will be familiar to the experienced practitioner.

2 Deal with input transaction files   Each batch program will require data from the database or a transaction file or both. The transaction files can be identified from the temporary data stores in the data flow diagrams. What a pity Information Engineering pays so little attention to this most useful technique! The logic for processing the transaction file(s) or database needs to be added to the action diagrams.

3 Specify the transaction files   This is nothing more than defining the record type and data content as well as the data storage medium.

4 Consider the transaction sequence within each program   This task ascertains whether it is necessary to sort the transaction files. Bearing in mind that a batch run can be processing many transaction types, each potentially updating a different table on the database, it may be necessary to sort the transaction file to get the record types in the correct file sequence. The sequence of transaction processing can be obtained from the entity life histories.

5 Deal with program output   The output from a program could be going to any one of an output transaction file for other programs or to other application or spooling systems.

6 Deal with non-database processing   This type of processing is typically concerned with such tasks as input data editing and transaction file reformatting.

7 Batch enquiries   No explanation is required.

The author finds the technique, particularly the defining basic flows and dependencies, a most elegant solution, because it is prescriptively based on a technique the author already admires. There is one problem. The batch programs are at the function level and not the event level. This is not in line with the event level processing concept. No hassle! Use the technique as described but do not group the programs by function.

3.2.9 Additional points of detail

This section addresses each of the Information Engineering design techniques and identifies points of improvement that can be made.

3.2.9.1 Entity relationship modelling

The entity model should only be built on the data retrieval business requirements. The reasons for this are discussed in section 2.2.2.4 and are based on the concept of design on data retrieval business requirements.

Always position the master entities above the detail entities—customer above orders. Aim for consistency in the logical data models with this diagramming approach. One can quickly perceive the degree to which a logical data model is composed of deep hierarchies or broad networks. The significance of this is that hierarchical data structures are cheaper to maintain and access in a database because of table clustering on disk (if the file handler supports clustering) and the fact that there is only one relationship between entities requiring referential integrity support, as compared with broad network data structures, where only one relationship between detail to master can be clustered and there are multiple referential relationships to support. Broad network data structures are extremely demanding of disk I/O accesses. The physical implications of an ERD model are much easier to ascertain if the entities are consistently drawn in relation to each other, rather than by following possible labyrinthine relationship lines between entities and then ascertaining via the crows foot which is the master and which is the detail entity. A quick glance at figure 2.5 shows instantly that it is a "bad news" logical data model.

Incidentally, if this simple consistency rule is followed the crows foot is not necessary. The recording of the crows foot is in fact an explicit recognition of poor standards of drawing a logical data model. The author has never found any difficulty in over a decade of drawing logical data models in positioning the detail entity below the master entity.

Another diagramming approach the author always uses is that the entities are positioned in a "regimental" fashion like soldiers on parade with a total absence of crossing relationship lines, as in figure 3.39. Patient "manoeuvering" of the entities usually provides a solution. Where it is not

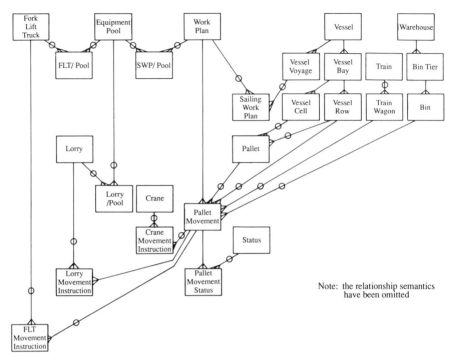

Figure 3.39   Representative port logical data model

possible to avoid crossing lines a stub relationship line is drawn with the entity reference at the end of the stub line, as represented in figure 3.40.

The author is a firm believer in the tidiness of deliverables. If a deliverable does not look professional it has no chance of being professional. A tidy diagram not only provides a sense of professionalism but also aids understanding. The user implicitly appreciates a diagramming standard and thereby more easily understands the information contained in the diagram. Cluttered deliverables, as represented by crossing lines, crows feet pointing upwards and downwards and different components of a deliverable being intermingled, does not make for tidiness. It might be complete, diagrammatically watertight and syntactically correct and yet the receiver of the deliverable will have a feeling of disappointment.

Another tidying up trick occasionally used is where there is a large number of relationships to an entity. A large data model for an oil exploration system had a large number of detail entities to the well entity. The data structure was much simplified without losing any accuracy by merging the relationship lines, as illustrated on figure 3.41.

Define the inter-attribute semantics. Information Engineering defines the inter-entity semantics but not the second type. Inter-attribute semantics are more associated with expert systems and are described in section 5.2.4.7.

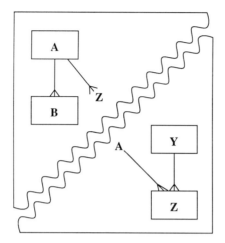

Figure 3.40   Avoid crossing relationship lines

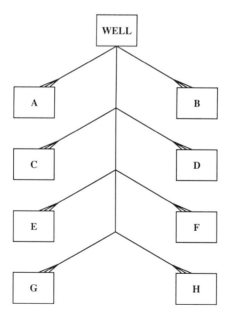

Figure 3.41   Entity modelling drawing optimisation

3.2.9.2 Dataflow diagrams

As part of the tidiness theme the author always draws DFDs in a three ringed manner—see figure 3.42—with no crossing lines. The datastores, processes and external entities are, as in data modelling, regimentally drawn. Examples of this regimentation are illustrated in figures 3.20 to 3.23. Data stores that are accessed by multiple processes are drawn as if they are internal data stores to the higher level process. The advantage of this approach is not only tidiness but also that a neat rectangular boundary line can be drawn around the process boxes, with only external entities outside the boundary. When drawing levels 1 and 2 DFDs the system boundary lines are important to illustrate to the user the scope of the application being designed.

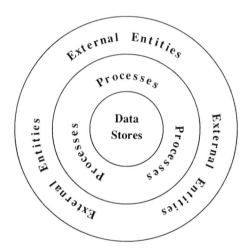

Data flows cross the ring boundaries

Figure 3.42   DFD "rings"

3.2.9.3 Transaction access path analysis

This technique is called process logic/data usage analysis in IEM and data access modelling in Navigator. A general title of data navigation is also used. The technique has already been discussed in part when reviewing "tricks of the trade" to rectify the conceptual weaknesses of Information Engineering. Further points require to be addressed as regards the systematic weaknesses.

Consider the ERD model in figure 3.43. For a sample business requirement "For a specified customer list all unpaid invoices for a specified
product" there are three possible entry points to consider—customer,
product and status. It is necessary to find which entry point provides the
optimum logical access path. This is the same requirement as for testing the
ERD model and transaction access paths for efficiency. New techniques to
do this are described in section 3.1.1.

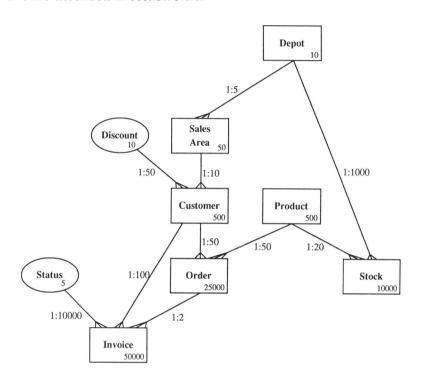

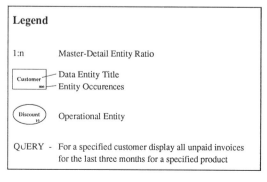

Figure 3.43   ERD data model

Representative access paths for the three entry point possibilities are detailed in figures 3.44–3.46, 3.44 entering on customer, 3.45 on product and 3.46 on invoice status. The logical access paths are drawn pictographically in process logic diagrams and the matching access logic documented in action diagrams in IEM. In Navigator the access path is initially recorded in a procedure access matrix and the matching access logic documented in action diagram as in IEM.

SYSTEM: EXAMPLE 1

AUTHOR: J. HARES   DATE: 1990   PAGE: 1   CONT. PAGE NO: 1

FUNCTION NO: FUNCTION NAME   TRANS ID

ENTITY NAME	ACC TYPE	READ PATH	ACCESS VIA	NO. ACC.	DATA ITEMS	
Customer	R	DIR	—	1	⋮	
Invoice	R	MAST	Customer	100	⋮	Read entire set. Retrieve those with invoice status value of unpaid. Assume 10% hit ratio - therefore 10 invoices retrieved.
Order	R	DIR	—	10	⋮	For access only. Assume 1 invoice matches desired product.
Product	R	DIR	—	1	⋮	
				112		

ACCESS TYPE
I - INSERT   L+ - ADD TO LINK PATH
M - MODIFY   L- - REMOVE
R - READ
D - DELETE

READ PATH
DIR   - DIRECT
SEQ   - SEQUENTIAL
DET   - VIA DETAIL
MAST - VIA MASTER

Figure 3.44   Logical access map: 1

The following details require to be recorded against a transaction path:

• transaction reference/business requirement identification;

• name/number of the entity being accessed;

SYSTEM: EXAMPLE 2						
AUTHOR: J. HARES	DATE: 1990		PAGE: 1		CONT. PAGE NO: 1	
FUNCTION NO:	FUNCTION NAME			TRANS ID		
ENTITY NAME	ACC TYPE	READ PATH	ACCESS VIA	NO. ACC.	DATA ITEMS	
Product	R	D	—	1	⋮	
Order	R	MAST	Product	50		Read entire set. For access only.
Invoice	R	MAST	Order	100		Read entire set. Retrieve those with invoice status value of unpaid and Customer No. specified in Query. Assume 1 invoice matches unpaid, Cust. No. and Product Code specified in Query.
Customer	R	DIR	—	1	⋮	
				152		

ACCESS TYPE		READ PATH	
I - INSERT	L+ - ADD TO LINK PATH	DIR	- DIRECT
M - MODIFY	L- - REMOVE	SEQ	- SEQUENTIAL
R - READ		DET	- VIA DETAIL
D - DELETE		MAST	- VIA MASTER

Figure 3.45   Logical access map: 2

- type of access to the entity—read, write, update, delete and whether relationship links to entities are being established or broken. Increasingly the relational set constructs of select, union, difference, intersect and very occasionally divide require to be specified when accessing/joining multiple entities;
- data item(s) used for selecting the entity occurrences;
- access path—to identify whether the entity is being accessed from a master or detail entity or directly as an entry point;
- access via master or detail—to identify from which master or detail entity previously accessed the current entity is being accessed from. This is only necessary if there are multiple master and detail entity relationships to access via;

SYSTEM: EXAMPLE 3						
AUTHOR: J. HARES	DATE: 1990		PAGE: 1		CONT. PAGE NO: 1	
FUNCTION NO:	FUNCTION NAME				TRANS ID	
ENTITY NAME	ACC TYPE	READ PATH	ACCESS VIA	NO. ACC.	DATA ITEMS	
Invoice Status	R	DIR	—	1	⋮	Status of unpaid. Assume 70% of invoices are unpaid.
Invoices	R	MAST	Invoice Status	8750	⋮	Read set reverse and retrieve on Customer No. specified in Query and date. Assume invoices in time sequence and stored one year. Therefore read 1/4 set. Assume 0.2% hit rate.
Order	R	DIR	—	18		Search on Product No. specified in Query. Assume 1 invoice relates to Product and Customer.
Product	R	DIR	—	1	⋮	
Customer	R	DIR	—	1	⋮	
					35073	

ACCESS TYPE		READ PATH	
I - INSERT	L+ - ADD TO LINK PATH	DIR	- DIRECT
M - MODIFY	L- - REMOVE	SEQ	- SEQUENTIAL
R - READ		DET	- VIA DETAIL
D - DELETE		MAST	- VIA MASTER

Figure 3.46 Logical access map: 3

- number of accesses to the entity for each execution of this transaction;
- the data item(s) in the entity to be accessed. It may be that no data items are to be accessed as the entity is only being accessed as a "bridge" to another entity. In this case identify in the comments column that the entity is for "access only";

- probability of execution of the access operation. The author records this information in the comments column;

- data items used for ordering the entity occurrences accessed. The author records this information in the comments column;

- the assumed storage sequence in which the data in the logical data model is held. If it assumed that an entity is stored in a particular sequence, for example customer is in the sequence of customer number, if the business requirement requires to retrieve customers in customer number order, then access to the customer can be logical sequential and not sorted. This would indicate that indexed access to customer for a relational file handler would be a valid database solution for this transaction. Clearly the transaction is but part of a total summary access path map picture, but it is indicative, particularly if the transaction is high volume and other transactions also require similar access, of the need for a particular storage sequence;

- once the assumed storage sequence of the entities is known then the forward or backward scrolling of a set occurrences of an entity can be ascertained. This information is particularly important if the implemented design uses pointer chain technology to link record types together;

- Comments. This column should be well annotated with a full explanation of the access logic as detailed in the above columns. For example, the document may record that 50 orders are to be accessed for one access to a customer entity. This does not explain that the 50 accesses represent accessing the entire set of orders for each customer accessed. In fact what is meant is that the transaction reads the entire customer/order set until no more orders are obtained. It so happens that the set contains on average 50 orders.

  The comments column can also be used as a "dump" for those items of information that are less frequently filled in, such as sort order and probability of execution.

Additional points of detail that need to be considered are:

- whether the entry point type is direct, logical sequential (when the sequence of key is important) or physical sequential (when the sequence of key is not important);

- whether access to the table is purely for access only or as part of an access path to another table. Too many such "for access only" accesses indicate an inefficient access path, such that either the ERD model or the transaction access path needs modification;

- whether the entire set requires to be accessed or whether it is to be searched on a combination of keys in either a forward or backward direction;

- the recording of referential integrity constraints. Full use of link calls inserting or deleting relationships between tables must be made. The fact that certain file handler types implicitly support some referential integrity constraints (IMS automatically ensures integrity on inserts to one master entity) should not be used as an excuse not to define referential integrity logically. The overheads of referential integrity are still there and must be measured in database design.

While Navigator discusses most of the points concerning data access that the author considers necessary IEM is noticeably less detailed. The points that need to be considered are therefore presented in full.

A set of example transaction access path maps is now described. They illustrate the degree of access detail the author has found necessary to record. The examples also show how the transaction access path maps can be interpreted as to their impact on subsequent database design.

Figure 3.44 illustrates, when accessing invoices from customer, the concept of hit rate—a variation of transaction cardinalities. It is assumed that only one in ten invoices accessed is relevant to the query. Navigator identifies this as probability of execution. IEM does not address the issue.

Consider figure 3.45. When accessing order from the product master entity the entire set of orders for the product needs to be specified as being accessed. To say that 50 orders are being accessed without putting any description about the access would indicate to the uninformed application programmer to issue 50 read order commands and then stop, whereas the given product which is accessed may actually contain n orders from 0 to infinity. An additional point to make is that the access to the orders is for access purposes only, to provide an access path to invoices. The data within the entity is actually not required.

The description relating to invoices illustrates another point. The logical data model indicates that the database cardinality of orders to invoices is on average two. In fact for this transaction, the transaction cardinality is assumed to be one. There is therefore the concept of transaction cardinalities, which Navigator identifies as relative average cardinality. IEM does not recognise transaction cardinality.

Figure 3.46 illustrates yet another point. The query is to retrieve invoices received during the last three months and which are unpaid. Invoices are assumed to be stored in date sequence and are stored for one year in the database. The access path chosen is therefore to read the invoice set from invoice status in reverse time sequence. This means that the file handler needs to be able to support reading a table of information in a reverse sequence according to the relationship to its master entity, in this case invoice status. Only part of the set needs to be accessed. A relational file handler would have some difficulty with this type of access by not providing pointer chain technology to link table rows within a table together. If the query had been to retrieve the last unpaid invoice then a relational file handler would have even more difficulty because the last invoice is not known. With the earlier and much verbally abused pointer chain technology type file handlers this kind of access would, of course, be easy to achieve.

Full and precise specification of the access requirements to each entity type must be specified in the transaction access path maps and in the action diagrams where the access paths are converted into access calls. Only by such attention to detail can the mechanisms which the file handler requires to use to support the logical data accesses be ascertained. Problem areas can be identified to the database designer.

If the file handler has data access limitations these have to be overcome in the application programs. Processing solutions to file handler problems can be included in the action diagrams to pre-warn application programmers. Given the moves towards using action diagrams as the basis of program code generation such explicitly coded solutions to file handler warnings of problems might not come amiss.

3.2.9.4 Performance assessment

The IEM and Navigator manuals describe the features that a database administrator should consider when reviewing the performance of the database and the transactions. Unlike many other leading structured design methods a database optimisation document and supporting explanatory description is provided. However, no worked examples or descriptions of how the technique of database optimisation should be applied is detailed. This is a shame as it is the final place at which the database design is set to match the performance objectives to be met.

Information Engineering identifies most but not all of the elements that should go into transaction resource utilisation timings. Information Engineering correctly identifies that the two main elements as processor and disk I/O time. The processor time elements the method identifies are application program overhead, file handler access calls (these are the logical I/O data accesses to the buffer pool), teleprocessing monitor/operating system overheads (these are both interrupt handlers and with some database vendors are in fact combined as a single facility), a general 20% overhead for the operating system/teleprocessing monitor and disk I/O. The disk I/O are physical accesses to the database data, the indexes and the journal file. The processor elements that the Information Engineering manuals do not identify are the overheads that are incurred if a multi-processor is being used, if the processors are split into client/server architectures and the disk I/O overheads that will be incurred through referential integrity support. Neither does the method show how the processor loadings can be calculated using the transaction resource utilisation timings. Each element omitted is considered below.

It is essential to include the processing and disk I/O overheads incurred in maintaining referential integrity. Consider figure 2.5. When a rate is inserted disk I/O is incurred in checking that all the related master entities/table rows exist. Rate was clustered on disk via City Pair. It was assumed that some half of the rates for each City Pair were in the same page as the related City Pair, so that 50% of the time there was only logical I/O to the buffer pool for the referential integrity access to City Pair. Disk I/O was incurred to all the other tables to which rates was related. The disk I/O incurred to support referential integrity was greater than all the disk I/Os incurred in the rest of the application and was the reason why the performance of this application caused the company unsatisfactory response times when the application went live.

It should be noted that the transaction timing described above requires to know processor size in terms of processor main memory. How much main memory is available for the operating system, teleprocessing monitor, application programs, buffer pools, the file handlers, query languages etc. affects the amount of disk I/O for data and software. Clearly if there is sufficient main memory for a large buffer pool then the volume of data disk I/O will be reduced. Equally if a large area of main memory can be set aside for control and application software the volume of disk I/O incurred through virtual paging is also reduced.

Paper timing exercises to calculate transaction resource utilisation and response times as advocated by Information Engineering has the over-whelming advantage of being a proactive database design philosophy that enables the designer not only to identify those transactions which do not perform satisfactorily but also to identify where a performance problem within a transaction is to be found.

If the performance problem exists there are three and only three areas where optimisation can take place. These areas are:

• the processor;

• the transaction;

• the database.

Some guide-lines as to where a solution can be found are:

• if the bulk of the transactions have a poor performance and no design errors in the transactions (e.g. poor access paths within the database because no entry point is available) are found then the processor is likely to be of insufficient power;

- if a transaction has a poor performance on a "standalone" basis then it is likely the transaction requires re-design;

- If the bulk of the transactions consistently have a poor performance on a particular record type/table then the database design is likely to be flawed in that area.

Once the design is optimised the processor loadings can be calculated. By taking the processor overhead of each transaction, multiplying it by the number of times the transaction runs during a processor time slot, for example an 8 hour processing day, summating the processor overheads of all the transactions and dividing the summated figure by the processor time slot, an average processor loading is calculated. Clearly the loading figures can be optimised to reflect the peaks and troughs of transactions throughputs. The author has used this technique many times to advise clients as to the likely processor speed requirements.

These transaction and processor performance measurements are crucially dependent on accurate path length instruction figures for each file handler function from the database vendors.

4

ADDITIONAL DATA PROCESSING ENVIRONMENTS FOR INFORMATION ENGINEERING—DISTRIBUTED, REALTIME AND CONVERSATIONAL

Information Engineering has been designed to support batch and online processing in a centralised environment. This is but one of six environments considered in this book, the others being distributed, realtime, expert system, conversational and object oriented. These environments were described in section 1.2.

The components of batch and online processing, such as data structure, data access and data process, are relevant to all data processing environments. The design techniques of Information Engineering appropriate to the components are therefore more widely applicable than perhaps initially appreciated—*Information Engineering is generic.* All that requires to be done is to enhance the existing techniques to support the additional features of the other environments, such as the concepts of location and synchronised multi-site updating for distributed database, the concepts of event recognition and synchronisation for realtime processing, the concept of knowledge for expert systems, the concept of continuous dialogue for conversational processing and the concept of logic normalisation for object oriented systems. Information Engineering is an excellent grounding for all these environments.

Each of these environments is considered in this and the next chapter, and the enhancements to the Information Engineering techniques and the addition of new techniques are identified and described.

4.1 DISTRIBUTED SYSTEMS

The transmission of data between locations is becoming increasingly important, for commercial, technical, competitive and performance reasons. Two types of companies are emerging, the megabig, multi-site international companies offering a range of products and services, and the small, usually single site, focus/niche companies concentrating on a single product or service, often in only a single sector of the market. An example of the former type is the major international airlines with numerous offices in multiple sites and countries and offering passengers an integrated set of products (flights) and ancillary services (hotel bookings, car hire and holiday arrangements). Each site has its own data requirements. Typical focus/niche companies are those specialising in information technology training, and in a particular structured design and development method, such as Information Engineering.

There is an increasing speed and complexity of trade. Given the efficiency of modern communications the length of time to conduct business over long distances is decreasing. Customers are able to place a product order at site 1, have the stock allocated against the order from sites 2 and 3 and have the product packaged at site 3 as a single continuous function, for a total delivery time of, say, half a day.

The megasized companies also need to control their multifarious activities. High speed and great complexity demand dynamic and synchronised control. The wide geographical multi-site spread of these large companies means that the dynamic and synchronised control of a company's data across sites can often only be provided by distributed systems.

The dynamic nature of distributed systems also enables these large companies to be competitive with the focus/niche companies. The small specialised companies can often offer a fast and personalised service to customers and thereby gain a competitive edge over their big rivals. By dynamically linking their often widespread activities in a distributed database the large companies can at least offer integrated and fast if not personalised service.

The removal of trade barriers in 1992 within the European Community is forcing these large companies to reposition themselves vis-à-vis each other. This is being achieved by a shifting balance of business alliances, takeovers and mergers. The computer systems of previously distinct companies need to be integrated, preferably dynamically,—hence distributed database.

A number of technical advancements are also encouraging the moves towards distributed systems. There is changing cost profile for processor hardware. For example, IBM is moving towards three different processor architectures—enterprise systems (ES) based on the S370 type processors, application systems (AS) based on the new AS400 type processors and the personal systems (PS) based on the PS/2 type processors. The costs ratio of these processors is currently on average some 10, 2 and 0.2. This illustrates the tremendous reduction in costs per unit of processing power with smaller processors.

Using the cost ratio as a basis, many smaller distributed but interlinked processors could be a cheaper architecture than a single centralised mainframe type processor. The widespread adoption of intelligent workstation/PS client-server processors reflects this cost ratio. Some relational database products are now supporting co-operative processing with front-end, typically application development software, running on a number of low cost workstations, and back-end, typically application support software, running on a reduced sized host processor.

There is little doubt that distributed database is not yet widely adopted, partly because it is currently a financially costly strategy, partly because the technology is recent and not fully developed and partly because there are cheaper and proven low risk alternative technical solutions. The slow speed and high cost of data transmission on wide area networks has also proved a barrier. Distributed database has therefore not achieved "critical mass" as regards sales.

Two trends are reducing some of these impediments. IBM and DEC, the two big players in information technology, are developing distributed database software and, as their technology is developed, will eventually "anoint" the subject. IBM have a particular incentive to develop distributed database software. Much of their software is not portable between their three processor architectures. For example, their DB2 relational database and VMS operating system run on the ES type processors but not on the AS and PS type processors. IBM are thus not able to move the software to the data—they must therefore move the data to the software. The solution to this problem is distributed database.

The other trend is the popular adoption of much faster and cheaper local area networks for distributed systems that are not so geographically dispersed, typically within a building or between buildings a few miles apart.

The final technical reason for adopting this technology is the demand for high performance through distributed and co-operative processing and the other forms of distributed system. This is addressed in the next section.

4.1.1 Distributed database concepts

The two special features of a distributed system—location transparency and update and recovery synchronisation—are the basis of the two concepts that distinguish distributed systems from traditional database processing at a single site—location transparency and multi-site synhcronisation. The user must not be aware that the system is distributed—the overall idea of a "single image" system. Equally, whenever data is updated at multiple sites the update must complete successfully at all the sites, or not at all. Note: the terms site, location and node are used interchangeably and in the context of the usual terminology when discussing the different components of distributed database. For example, people talk about location transparency and multi-site synchronisation.

Many applications function across multiple locations and transmit data between the locations as required. However, the data transmission has been simplistic—through off-line transfer, possibly by tape, or through bulk transmission down a fixed topology telecommunication line, mostly at fixed and predefined times and with the location to which the data is to be transmitted known in advance. The data processing at each location has been localised and not dynamically synchronised with other locations. Such offline distributed processing is the hallmark of decentralised systems. The concepts of location transparency and update synchronisation are therefore not relevant.

Distributed systems are different. A distributed system is one where data and programs used by an application are stored on more than one processor in different locations and the processors are dynamically linked in a synchronised manner and the data and programs function together as a synchronised whole. Furthermore, the data transmission between sites is ad hoc, the messages of data between locations are unformatted and the location of data storage and program execution is not known in advance. The concepts of distribution are therefore highly pertinent.

4.1.2 Distributed vs co-operative vs heterogeneous processing

There are a number of ways in which the technology for distributed systems can be viewed:

- Distributed database

  Distributed databases are concerned with the transmission of data between multiple file handlers of the same type at locations that are geographically widely dispersed. A system could have some of its data in Frankfurt, some of its data in Paris and some of its data in London, all using, let's say, the ORACLE relational file handler.

  Distributed database incorporates the technology that supports the two concepts underlying distributed systems. It is the "all singing all dancing "approach for data distribution. All the other approaches that are used to support the distribution of data and processing require to "do it yourself" to support the concepts. However, the author is not aware of any of the vendors of distributed database software providing all the facilities that are required.

Distributed database (with distributed processing) is illustrated in figure 4.1. The left hand side shows distributed database and the right hand side distributed processing. There are multiple databases at multiple locations, the location databases together forming the corporate database. The two features that distinguish distributed database come into play. Firstly location. The data is potentially spread like "grass seed" across locations, yet the locations need to be hidden from the users of the distributed system. The distributed database software must therefore not only support the location of the data but also have facilities for finding the data automatically. Secondly synchronisation. The location databases are linked dynamically, such that multi-site updates and software and hardware recovery must be synchronised.

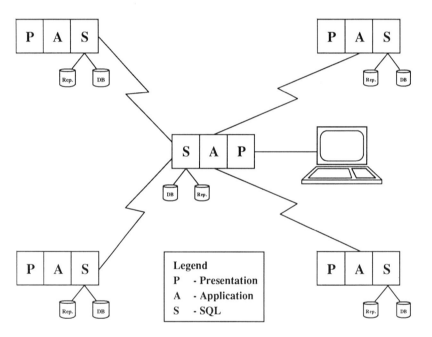

Figure 4.1   Distributed database (with distributed processing)

Distributed databases provide these two facilities via the distributed database manager, as represented by SQL. The manager sits above the local file handler controlling data searching and update synchronisation across locations, with the local file handler then being invoked to access the "now ascertained to be local" data. The important point is that the distribution and synchronisation of data is handled by file handler technology. It is not a case of "do it yourself".

- Co-operative systems

    Figure 4.2 shows co-operative processing. Another term increasingly used is client–server processing. This technology has been developed to support the explosive growth of intelligent workstations (IWS) and the ability to place application software optimally on the IWS or a host processor. A client is a requestor of a service and the server is the provider of a service. There can be a hierarchy of such facilities, so that a client processor can also simultaneously be a server processor.

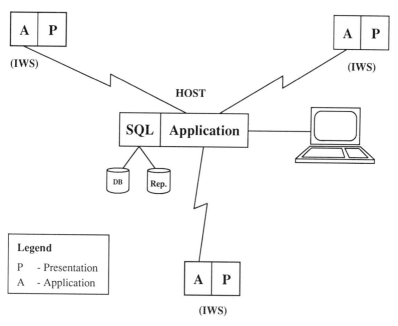

Figure 4.2   Co-operative (client-server) processing

Co-operative processing is very similar to distributed processing. Both send messages to application processes on different processors, as can be seen by comparing figures 4.1 and 4.2. The reason for the separation is that there is file handler technology specifically developed to support it, with specialised calls between the client and the server processors, whereas distributed processing has long been used before client–server architecture was available and required procedure calls between application programs or parts of application programs that happen to be resident on different processors.

   The technology does not support the two concepts of distributed systems. The author regards co-operative processing as the "poor man's" distributed database. Yet, of the different technology classifications for distributed systems in this section, it is the one that is becoming most widely used. Several of the relational database vendors have rewritten the file handler software to support client–server facilities, such as Ingres Inc and Software AG. Sybase produced their SYBASE database product from the outset as being client–server.

There are three major components to the software. The presentation component typically provides screen formatting, data editing built-in functions and help facilities. The application program component can be split in any combination between the client IWS and the server host processor. The IWS client application component would typically include application bespoke data editing facilities and utility functions, often with package software, such as spreadsheets and word processing. The application component on the host processor would typically include database handling, bulk data messaging and management reports. The access component to the corporate database on the server processor would be via a file handler, usually relational with SQL on the host processor. The file handler would be a local file handler without any capability to support distributed database, that is being able to find the data and synchronise updates across locations. Any communication between the front-end and the back-end processors is invoked and controlled in the application program by the application programmer.

Note that there is only one corporate database in co-operative processing. The IWS may contain personal databases, but they are not synchronised with the corporate database. Equally there are only two location types—the IWS and the host. If the data is not on the IWS it must be on the host processor and vice versa. The location of the data is therefore implicit. Co-operative processing therefore does not require to support either location transparency or update synchronization. It facilitates distributed data access rather than distributed data. There is therefore no technical overlap between co-operative and distributed systems.

There is one other difference between co-operative and distributed database. With distributed database all sites are regarded as equal, each fulfilling the same role—there is no concept of a master site. Such is not the case with co-operative processing. In figure 4.2 the host processor has different functions to fulfil from the IWS.

- Distributed processing
  Distributed database is only concerned with the distribution of data. However, the transmission of data between locations is costly, with the processing overheads being up to 100 times the cost of accessing data from the local disk. If there is much data to be transmitted between

locations in support of a business requirement then it may be more efficient to process the data at the remote location(s) and, instead of transmitting the raw data back to the requesting location, to transmit merely the result, the "reply". This approach is often referred to as request or transaction shipping. There would then be correlation and any final processing of the returned result(s) at the requesting location before output presentation.

There is no support for the two concepts of distributed systems. The local process can facilitate the searching for the location of the remote data by accessing the global dictionary that indicates the location of the remote tables of data, but that is the only readily available "help" that is obtained from distributed database if it is installed.

With distributed processing it is "do it yourself" in the application program software regarding the two features of distributed database. The communication between the processes is via a normal transaction code (with any associated parameters and data). That is why the figure shows communication between the sites is via the application component, not the file handler. As will be seen later in this chapter distributed processing can provide higher performance than distributed database, such that the cost and effort of distributed "do it yourself" may be justified.

Distributed processing occurs where program-to-program communication (PTOPC) is used. Consider figure 4.3.

The process at the triggering client site is the master process and sends a data request as a normal teleprocessing type transaction message (that is a transaction code and call parameters) to the remote teleprocessing monitor, which in turn invokes the appropriate slave process, not a file handler, at the remote site(s). The master and slave processes invoke their local file handlers to retrieve the appropriate local data. Each process then processes its local data. The remote slave process(es) transmit a processed reply, not the raw data as in distributed database and remote database access, back to the master program at the triggering location.

The example in figure 4.3 assumes the business requirement is "For all salesmen calculate their sales bonus for the last six months and add it to their current monthly payroll cheque". The master process at the head office triggering site invokes the file handler at the head office to access the salesman's pay information. At the same time the master process also sends data requests to a slave process at the regional office(s), which in turn invokes the local file handler to access the salesman's order information. Each slave process then processes all the orders and calculates the bonuses. The bonus and not the raw data in the orders is transmitted as the reply to the master process. When the master process has received the responses from all the slave processes the individual bonuses can be added to the salesman's basic pay, the appropriate tax and other deductions can be computed and the pay roll cheque issued.

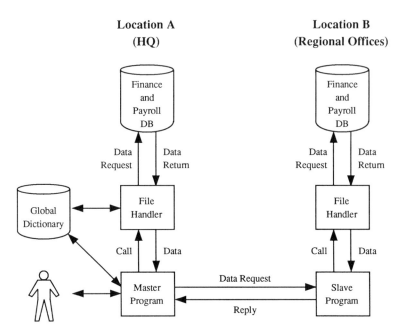

Figure 4.3   Distributed processing

The advantage of PTOPC processing is that:

— data communication is reduced, with processed rather than raw data being transmitted;
— because it is the transaction that is shipped, the slave process(es) are not restricted to the same file handler as the triggering site. The local and the remote file handlers can be different.

The disadvantage is that the programmer requires to understand the concept of location, either by accessing the global dictionary to find the location of the data or through some multi-site searching technique, and the requirement to synchronise the responses from the remote slave processes. If the processing is to be distributed in order to reduce data communication overheads then the distribution and synchronisation of the data has to be supported in the process rather than in the database software.

• Remote database access
  Remote database access (RDBA) is an example of distributed data but without the distributed database manager software being used. Consider figure 4.4. It shows an application program issuing a request to a local client file handler for information about a salesman, and to a named

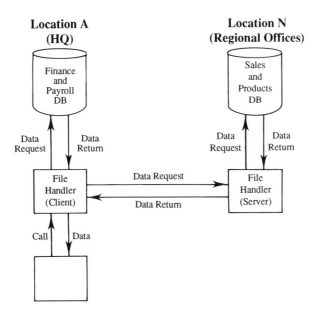

Figure 4.4   Remote database access

remote server file handler supporting a database with the information required about orders won by the salesman. Apart from the Connect call the access to the remote file handler is the same as to the local file handler. The DML commands are the same.

The significant points here are:

— The application program is responsible for issuing a connect statement to the named remote file handler, so there is no location transparency or automatic update synchronisation as far as the application programmer is concerned. This must be taken care of by the application programmer. In the example the business requirement is a retrieval so synchronisation is not required, but it could be that there is a need to update several locations, in which case it would be.

— the data communications will be high. The remote file handler returns the raw data requested, that is all the orders won. There is no local processing of the remote data at the remote location.

• Heterogeneous systems (gateways)

The author has found that there is considerable confusion between a distributed database and a heterogeneous system. Both after all are concerned with sending data between multiple file handlers.

Heterogeneous systems are concerned with the transmission of data between multiple file handlers of different types. For example, some of the data could be stored and accessed using IBM's IMS file handler, some of the data could be stored and accessed using DEC's Codasyl DBMS-32 file handler and some of the data could be stored using Ingres Inc's relational file handler INGRES. These file handler types have different data storage, access mechanisms and access languages. Gateway software mapping the different database data structure and access facilities of the file handler types is required before data communications between the file handlers can be achieved. It is the responsibility of the gateway software to make the data in one file handler type of compatible format to that in the other file handler type.

A particular concern not often appreciated is that, with multiple file handlers involved, it is, like distributed database, necessary to ensure update synchronisation across the file handler types. The facility for this is what is called a two phase commit procedure. Even though both of the file handler types may have their own two phase commit facilities it is unlikely that they are compatible. The gateway software is therefore also responsible for update synchronisation.

4.1.3 Information Engineering and distributed systems

Both versions of Information Engineering record the location of where data is to be stored and the processes are to be triggered. Unfortunately it does not include techniques that fully ascertain the significance of the distribution of the data and logic of an application system across locations. Fortunately, of all the data processing environments which Information Engineering does not support, the distributed environment is the one to which the method can be most easily upgraded. The reason for this happy state of affairs is because of the policy followed by all the suppliers of distributed database software. The policy has been to preserve *without change* the existing database technology for processing in a centralised environment and to "add on" extra software to support data distribution.

The policy results in a number of significants benefits. *All investment in existing database technology and structured design techniques is wholly preserved—one need unlearn nothing.* Database technology and the techniques used in structured design and development methods, such as Information Engineering, require enhancement by addition rather than modification. A further result of this policy, one that is incidental to this book, is that distributed database is a partnership between equal and independent but co- operating centralised systems using current technology, with the triggering site responsible, as far as possible, for finding the location of the distributed data and synchronising multi-site processing.

The enhancements to Information Engineering to support distributed systems are considered from two aspects—the physical technology and the logical and physical design and development techniques. The physical technology is considered first. Although this may appear to be "putting the cart before the horse", it is necessary to understand the technology in order to appreciate the requirements for and implications of data distribution in the techniques and their deliverables.

The enhancements to the Information Engineering logical and physical design techniques to support location transparency and multi-site update synchronisation are described, along with worked examples. The examples are based on two major distributed applications the author has been involved with.

4.1.4 Distributed database technology

All the facilities, bar one, for distributed database are to be found in database software for batch and online processing at a single centralised site. All the facilities relate to data handling. *Distributed database is concerned with the distribution of data, not logic.* As indicated earlier, distributed processing is nothing more than centralised processing with "do it yourself" enhancements to handle the searching of data across multiple locations plus multi-site database update and recovery synchronisation. The facilities are:

- set level processing;

- concurrency control;

- dynamic transaction rollback;

- system rollforward;

- transaction utilisation monitor;

- query optimisation;

- directory maintenance;

- location transparency.

It is location that is the driving feature of distributed systems. If there were not multiple locations then location transparency and multi-site synchronisation would not be required.

4.1.4.1 Set level processing

Set level processing is a *sine qua non* for distributed database software. The basic additional overhead in distributed systems is remote I/O, the sending of messages between sites. The area of greatest processing overhead in any computer system generally is I/O. In centralised processing there are two kinds of I/O—disk I/O and terminal I/O. Distributed database adds a third type of I/O—remote I/O.

In an IBM mainframe processor environment a typical disk I/O to read a table row is some 5,000 path length instructions (PLI). A typical terminal I/O under the CICS teleprocessing monitor software (assuming that the CICS software is in the processor main memory) is some 50,000 PLI for an average message pair (assumed to be 100 characters input and 500 characters output). Advice the author has received is that a remote I/O message on a wide area network can cost up to 500,000 PLI, depending on the telecommunication network design. A remote I/O on a local area network is apparently some one third the overhead.

It can be seen that remote I/O is extremely expensive in processor resources—up to 100 times greater than local disk I/O—and therefore requires to be kept to an absolute minimum. (Note:- The support for remote I/O is largely offloaded from the main processor with front-end processors dedicated to handling data communications.) It is therefore essential to support set level processing as found in a relational file handler, where data is sent as a single remote I/O stream of information rather than n record-at-a-time remote I/Os to be found in pointer chain technology file handlers, such as in IDMS and IMS.

The advantage of set level processing is that, irrespective of whether one is retrieving a specific table row (display customer number 12345) or multiple rows (display all customers with red hair), the data is transmitted between sites as a single remote I/O data message. With record-at-a-time processing each table row will be transmitted as separate remote I/O messages.

Thus if the retrieved set incurs 1,000 rows (i.e. there are 1,000 customers with red hair) then the overhead is 1,000 x 500,000 PLI record-at-a-time messages rather than 1 x 500,000 PLI set message. It is not surprising that earlier attempts at distributed database with record-at-a-time file handlers have not proved successful.

4.1.4.2 Concurrency control

Concurrency control of database data in a multi-user environment is as necessary in distributed as it is for centralised processing. Distributed concurrency control is however only necessary where data is distributed horizontally. Horizontal data distribution is discussed in section 4.1.4.8.

There are two basic distributed concurrency control mechanisms— multi-phase locking and timestamping. The mechanisms are not mutually exclusive and n variations of distributed concurrency control are possible by combining certain features of each.

Locking places a "hold" on the table row to be accessed, the type of hold being appropriate to the type of access. Locking can lead to a deadlock situation. Timestamping does not incur a deadlock possibility, as all transactions are executed only in timestamp order. Timestamping is a crude mechanism as transactions are executed in the sequence they are triggered, rather than in priority order. Both mechanisms require a degree of message passing between sites, the locking mechanism for maintaining the wait-for graphs and the timestamping mechanism for cross-checking and maintaining the timestamp of the last access to the database records.

In centralised processing locking rather than timestamping is universally used. Given the policy followed by the distributed database vendors, most products appear to have adopted distributed locking. The author is not aware of any of the leading non-research/commercially available distributed database products using timestamping. Much research is under way regarding distributed timestamp mechanism. The debate of the relative merits of these two concurrency control mechanisms in a distributed database is still open.

There are two main kinds of lock levels—the "S" lock and the "X" lock. An "S" share lock prevents an update to the data object (usually table row but can be at page or table level) from occurring until the lock is released, but allows other read transactions to access the data object. The "X" exclusive lock prevents any other transactions accessing the data object occurrences until the "X" lock is released, either through an explicit application program COMMIT call or through an implicit lock release at the end of processing. Transactions wishing to access an X locked data object are simply held in abeyance until the X lock is released. Such a procedure as described above will always be correct. (Note: there is a third kind of lock, a "U" lock that prepares an "S" lock for upgrading to an "X" lock. The "U" type lock is not found in relational technology. It is appropriate to the earlier pointer chain technology file handler types.)

In a distributed system where a transaction requires to read a data object an "S" share lock is required on at least one occurrence of the object in the system. Where a transaction requires to update a data object an "X" update lock is required on *every single occurrence copy* of the data object, even when the data object occurrences are stored at multiple sites. An X lock requires to take into account data distribution, an S lock does not. Within a distributed system these locks are maintained in a "wait-for graph" at each site. The graphs show "who is waiting for whom". Each graph is a matrix relating the type of lock with the transaction ID, table ID and row ID.

In a distributed system (and for that matter a heterogeneous system) multiple file handlers are used, one at each site. Should a data object occurrence be stored by more than one file handler, it is essential that, where locking is used, the locks of the data object occurrences are synchronised and occur against all occurrences of the data object at all sites or not at all.

The locks therefore require to be shipped around the distributed network to the site wait-for graphs. The wait-for graphs are stored and accessed as standard data tables. It is therefore necessary to synchronise updates with a multi-phase concurrency control procedure similar to that later described for the two-phase commit procedure.

Where such X locking is used deadlock can occur. In centralised processing this deadlock is called "deadly embrace", and occurs where two application programs require to access each other's "X locked" data object in order to continue processing. In such a situation a deadlock has been achieved. In a centralised environment, the procedure is to back out temporarily one of the transactions and to continue normal processing. The backed out transaction is then restarted. In a distributed environment the deadlocked programs may be residing in different processors at different sites. Such a situation occurs where transaction T1 holds B at site 1 and requests A at site 2, while transaction T2 holds A at site 2 and requests B at site 1. A global deadlock resolution procedure taking into account site distribution is therefore required.

The multi-phase locking overhead is particularly severe as up to $5n$ (where n is the number of sites) messages between sites can occur. In reality only $4n$ messages occur as the fifth message is concatenated with the fourth. This all involves remote I/O, which, as we have seen, is expensive. When a global deadlock is detected the wait-for graphs usually have to be merged in order to ascertain the total distributed deadlock situation. This merging involves yet further remote I/O.

It has been argued that multi-phase locking is an additional two-phase commit procedure for multi-site locking prior to the two-phase commit procedure for multi-site database updating. The author has strong doubts on this. The more he delves into this subject the more he is convinced that the locking for concurrency control is actually part of the two-phase commit procedure—see later in section 4.1.4.3. Enquiries against a number of vendors of distributed database software have failed to identify whether the two-phase distributed concurrency procedure is incorporated in or is distinct from the two-phase commit procedure for distributed database update. The clinching evidence has not yet been obtained. Although probably incorrect this book assumes that the two procedures are distinct.

A problem that multi-phase locking must resolve is the recognition when a message response to a message call is not being received, because of either a hardware/software failure or poor response performance at the remote locations. This must be handled by a timeout mechanism, which recognises that if a response message is not received after a specified period of time then a deadlock must be assumed and the locking procedure must be reversed and restarted.

If, as the author believes, multi-phase locking is another term for the two-phase commit procedure timeout can be a standalone mechanism by which a global deadlock across multiple sites can be resolved. The principle is simple—if the transaction timeout is exceeded assume a deadlock has occurred and begin the normal distributed back out procedure. Two transactions are in deadlock and hence waiting potentially indefinitely for each other to release the lock. The timeout time will eventually be exceeded. Each site recognises this and rolls back and restarts its own transaction. The expense of maintaining and merging the distributed wait-for graphs can be avoided. Concurrency control remains a local function. The SUPRA product from CINCOM has adopted this approach.

The danger of this simplistic approach to concurrency control is that a deadlock may not have occurred, the delay merely being part of a transaction performing badly. More rollbacks than are justified is the potential adverse result. Many distributed database vendors consider the saving on distributed communications worth the small risk of unnecessary rollback.

Timestamping has an advantage in that no distributed "S" and "X" locks are set and the remote I/O of locking and deadlock detection are avoided. Deadlock cannot occur. Shipping wait-for information around the network and testing for timeouts is therefore not required. Transaction backouts and restarts are also not required. Although local "X" locks are still required to ensure correct local concurrency control of the database, the global deadlock resolution software does not use them. Instead every transaction is assigned a globally unique timestamp.

Because transactions can occur simultaneously at multiple sites, a timestamp composed solely of a system time clock is inadequate. In order to make timestamping globally unique, the location ID also requires to be added to the clock time as a minor key. Each data object in the database requires to store a unique timestamp for the last read and update transaction that accessed the data object. When any transactions are in conflict, the younger transaction with a later timestamp value is backed out. Where the timestamps are of equal value the choice of a transaction to back out is usually made on transaction or location priority.

There are many degrees of sophistication in the various timestamping mechanisms. One such mechanism is conservative timestamping.

Conservative timestamping eliminates conflicts by not performing a transaction where a transaction conflict could occur. A transaction waits until all older transactions (i.e. those transactions with a lower timestamp value) have completed processing. Where a conflict could occur timestamping requires to send messages for each transaction to all the remote participant sites to ascertain the "age" of other processing transactions. This is clearly an expensive approach in processing resources because of extensive and expensive remote I/O messaging, and inevitably concurrency is also reduced. It also means that all transactions originating at a site, and not just those in a conflict, must execute COMMIT statements in timestamp order, irrespective of their priority, and even though transaction T2 may reach a COMMIT point before transaction T1, which started processing first. Unless this expensive approach is adopted an update request for a transaction with a "younger" timestamp could be received and processed by a remote site before an update request for a transaction with an "older" timestamp. The older request would have to be rejected and restarted later.

This heavy inter-site communication of multi-phase locking and time-stamping needs to be reduced. Two optimisation mechanisms are available—transaction classes and conflict graph analysis. Transaction classes recognise those transactions where conflicts cannot occur and hence applies the multi-phase locking or timestamping concurrency control procedures only where conflicts can occur. In order to identify the possibility of conflict, each transaction requires to be allocated to a transaction class. As part of system design each transaction access path requires a specification of the tables, rows and columns that it reads and changes. Transactions are then assigned to one or more transaction classes, which contain a definition of what can be accessed as a readset or writeset. The transaction class is rather like the user view facility of a relational file handler.

A representative specification of transaction classes is given in figure 4.5, where it can be seen that the read and writesets of transaction classes TC1 and TC2 do not conflict, but that the TC3 readset is in conflict with the TC2 and TC4 writeset and TC4 writeset is in conflict with the TC2 writeset and TC3 readset. Only where a writeset of one transaction class intersects with a read- or writeset of another transaction class can conflict occur.

In order to minimise the possibility of conflict it is important that the distributed database designer define the transaction classes as tightly as possible. The benefit is that inter-site communication for synchronising locking and timestamping in transaction classes where there is no conflict or the conflict is readset to readset is not required. The net effect is to reduce inter-site messaging and increase concurrency.

The ability to pre-define transaction classes is fine where the update business/transactions are known in advance and specified in the logical design. But what about ad hoc updates, which by their nature cannot be predefined? In order to provide the ultimate safety net for this type of situation a global class also needs to be defined. The global class needs to be defined as being able to access the entire database on both the read and writeset.

The global class mechanism, of course, nullifies the very advantage of transaction classes, because all other transactions will be in a conflict of some kind. Ad hoc unpredefined updates need to be strongly discouraged in a distributed system. The database administrator of a distributed system needs to be able to define very precise security mechanisms in order to prevent ad hoc unauthorised updates to a distributed database.

TC1 Readset:	Select * from Person Where name = "Smith"
TC1 Writeset:	Select * from Person Where name = "Smith"
TC2 Readset:	Empty
TC2 Writeset:	Select * from Person Where name = "Morris"
TC3 Readset:	Select * from Person Where name between "Harris" and "Thomas"
TC3 Writeset:	Empty
TC4 Readset:	Empty
TC4 Writeset:	Select * from Person Where name between "King" and "Roberts"

Figure 4.5   Transaction classes

Conflict graph analysis is a further refinement to transaction classes, such that concurrency is further increased. The graphs identify possible read and writeset conflicts across transaction classes and identify if it is possible to have transactions interleaved rather than synchronised. A conflict graph is drawn in figure 4.6. The conflicts are the horizontal and diagonal lines. These indicate that synchronisation may be required. If there are no horizontal or diagonal lines connecting classes then no transaction synchronisation is required.

The objective of conflict graph analysis is to decide for every pair of transaction classes where conflicting transactions require synchronisation and, if so, what level of synchronisation is required. If the conflict is on two "X" locks then different concurrency control is required than if the conflict is between a "S" and a "X" lock. With the former transaction synchronisation

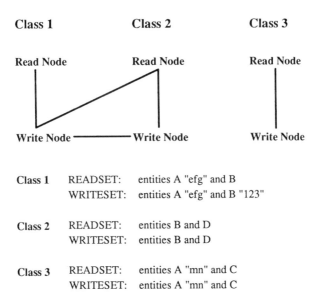

Figure 4.6   Conflict graph analysis

is achieved by backing out one transaction and restarting it. With the latter, the two transactions can be interleaved. Both transactions run more slowly but no transaction back out occurs.

Transaction interleaving in order to increase performance is not a feature unique to distributed database. It is to be found in normal centralised processing and is described in C Date's excellent book "An Introduction to Database Systems" Volume 2. The point that must be understood is that conflicting transactions triggered at different sites can still be interleaved rather than backed out.

4.1.4.3 Distributed transaction rollback

Transaction rollback is the recovery of a failed running application program. In a centralised system transaction rollback is achieved through reading the before image log in reverse time order to the last commit/checkpoint record for the transaction. The problem in a distributed environment is that the transaction may wish to update the same data record at multiple sites. In such a situation the transaction must execute successfully at all the sites or not at all. This requires a mechanism whereby the transaction at the triggering site checks all the remote participant sites that it is ok to update before executing the updates. Obviously a routine of message passing between the triggering and participant sites is therefore required.

The policy followed in distributed database is that the triggering site controls the execution of the message passing. A site in a distributed system is a "master" site *for the duration of a transaction only*, thus preserving as much as possible the concept that all sites in a distributed system are equal. Each message pair (a "call" from the triggering site to the remote participant sites and an "echo" message in response) is called a phase. Distributed transaction rollback is achieved through a "two-phase commit" procedure, as two sets of message pairs between the triggering and participant sites are required.

A single phase commit procedure is inadequate for distributed transaction rollback. As illustrated in figure 4.7, a triggering transaction at site 2 could fail as it is receiving "ok to update" echo messages from the participant sites involved in the multi-site synchronised updating. The figure illustrates that the triggering site has recorded that some of the participant sites have committed their database updates because successful echo messages have been received, but have not recorded that all the participant sites have committed because of a failure during the message receiving phase. Triggering site 2 has received an ok message from site 1 but not from site 3, because of its own failure. The distributed database is therefore not synchronised. All three sites may have committed but site 2 does not yet know that site 3 has achieved a successful commit, in this case because of failed communications between sites 2 and 3. A multi-phase commit procedure is required.

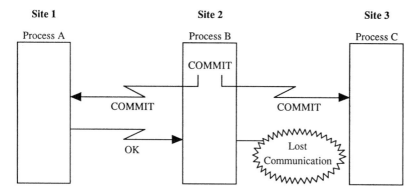

Figure 4.7   Distributed transaction rollback (single phase commit)

A two-phase procedure has been universally adopted and is illustrated in figure 4.8. In this procedure the triggering site broadcasts a "prepare to update" call message to the participant sites, which "agree" to commit a table row, record the fact in their log file with all relevant information

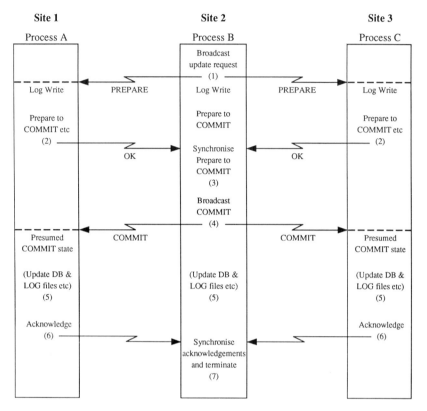

Figure 4.8   Distributed transaction rollback (two phase commit)

about the database table row, and then reply by issuing an "ok to update" echo message back to the triggering site. The triggering and participating sites are now synchronised at the point of commit. Any failure at this point will be sensed by the triggering site and a rollback command immediately issued to the participant sites for local recovery from the log file.

Assuming all is well the triggering site synchronises all the "ok to update" messages, and when it has received a message from all the participant sites broadcasts a "commit" call message to the participant sites. All the sites update their logs and databases in that order and issue commit calls to release the database X lock/timestamp previously established by the concurrency control mechanisms described earlier. The only possible time that a failure can now cause a problem is during the small time window when the participant sites are doing their commit processing. One site could fail, such that the commits are not executed at all the sites. On completion of a commit each participant site then transmits a commit "acknowledgement" echo message back to the triggering site, which synchronises all the acknowledgments and then terminates.

A two-phase commit procedure is inherently more stable, because should the triggering site fail after issuing the commit call message at the beginning of the second phase of the commit procedure then the log records are available at each site for the normal dynamic transaction rollback procedures found in centralised processing. The distributed software will send messages to all the participant sites to indicate a failure has occurred and normal local dynamic transaction rollback is then undertaken and the local locks/timestamps on the table rows are released.

As indicated earlier, distributed systems are not totally robust. There is a period of risk between the time the co-ordinating transaction at the triggering site issues the prepare to update and commit messages and the participant sites respond with their ok to update and acknowledgement messages and vice versa. This period of risk cannot be totally eliminated, for the simple reason that the processors executing the transactions are faster than the telecommunication lines transmitting the messages. It can only be reduced through issuing even more levels of commit procedure, such as three-phase commits and four-phase commits. This inevitably increases the remote I/O processing overheads. The system could then be spending more processor time servicing the message passing than supporting the business requirement.

Any distributed locking procedure requires a timeout mechanism to test for the possibility of failure or excessively poor distributed performance. A triggering site sending an update message to a remote site waits in expectation of a response. The remote site(s) can fail at any time without the triggering site being aware. The triggering site continues to wait for a potentially indefinite period of time. Such a situation cannot be tolerated for long, for obvious response time reasons. A timeout needs to be specified. When the timeout is exceeded, the triggering site re-transmits the call messages as many times as necessary, at a frequency to be specified, to ensure that the messages eventually reach their intended remote sites. Clearly after a further period of time elapses the triggering site assumes a failure and conducts a local recovery procedure, as well as instructing the participating sites to rollback.

In addition if a site failure occurs at any point during the two-phase commit procedure (either at the triggering or participant sites) the recovery procedure at the failing site must communicate with the other sites (what message status are you in?) to ascertain what must be done to ensure that the commit procedure is completed successfully. When the communication is sent every site examines its log to see if it has any record of the transaction in question. If the message is that they have received messages from the coordinating site, then the failed site continues to issue messages to the coordinating site on the assumption that it (the coordinating site) is continuing to function. If the message is that they have not received messages from the coordinating site, then the failed site must assume that the coordinating site has also failed and conducts a local rollback. The other sites will come to the same conclusion when the time-out end point has been reached.

4.1.4.4 Distributed transaction rollforward

System rollforward is required to recover lost data. The data can be lost either through an unscheduled processor shutdown or through a disk crash. With centralised processing the rollforward is achieved by copying the last database dump copy to disk and reading the after image log records accumulated since the last dump in a forward time order direction. An enhancement to this simple procedure is required for distributed systems.

Most vendors of database software provide for lost data by dynamically duplicating the database. When data is lost in the master database, processing is switched to the database copy until the master database is recovered. This is a perfectly acceptable solution, but has the obvious overhead of doubling local database processing overheads.

A finessed approach is illustrated in figure 4.9, whereby during the period of time that a site is unavailable the remaining running sites update a local pending file of all distributed update transactions for the failed site during its unavailability. The entire transaction is stopped. All sorts of co-ordination difficulties arise if the local updates are allowed to proceed, along with the updates to the other running remote sites, without waiting for the failed site to recover. Continued application processing at the running sites with n further updates would mean the failed site getting further and further out of step with the remainder of the system. Synchronised recovery would be impossible.

When the failed site is available it sends a restart message to the running sites, which flush the failed site pending updates to the now recovered site. The recovered site becomes responsible for the rollforward recovery. It timestamp co-ordinates the pending file updates from the running sites and updates the dump/rollforward recovered database and the various remote databases of the running sites which created the pending files with the pending updates using the normal two-phase commit procedure. A temporary pending file is maintained at the recovered site during the recovery process for dynamic updates to the database that occur during the pending update process. The temporary pending file is then progressively updated to the database when the failed site pending files updates have been completed.

No database product currently provides this facility, although developments are under way.

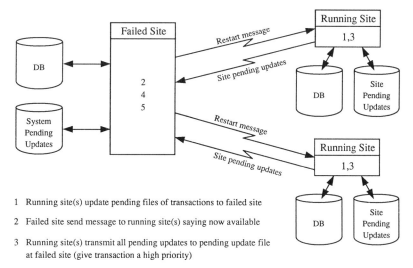

1 Running site(s) update pending files of transactions to failed site

2 Failed site send message to running site(s) saying now available

3 Running site(s) transmit all pending updates to pending update file
   at failed site (give transaction a high priority)

4 Failed site timestamp co-ordinates pending file(s)

5 Failed site update database as a standard process and keep trail of remote
   updates during restarts and applies

Figure 4.9 Distributed system rollforward

4.1.4.5 Distributed query optimisation

Relational file handlers have query optimisers that dynamically ascertain
the optimum access path to the database data. The degree of sophistication
varies considerably from relational product to relational product. The best
optimisers work on the basis of database cardinality lists, which are statistics
that record the set cardinality of related tables based on a common key. For
example, the table customer has a set cardinality with the table orders, in
that a customer can relate to *n* orders. Some products, such as INGRES,
ADABAS and DB2, keep a count of the cardinality between each table row
of customer and the related table rows of order based on the common key
of customer code. Other products, such as Tandem's NonStop SQL, keep
an average count of the cardinality between the tables. Some products,
such as the current (1991) version 6 of ORACLE, keep no set cardinality
count. Most products run an offline statistics utility program that counts
the set cardinality between the tables on any specified key. ADABAS keeps
a dynamic count in the ISN lists. It is the only product to do so. By keeping
these set cardinalities the optimiser can rapidly ascertain the number of
table rows in each table to be accessed for a given set of search keys.

  The sending of data between sites incurs expensive remote I/O overhead. Furthermore, given the slowness of the telecommunication line data

transmission speeds, in particular wide area telecommunication lines, the transmission of large data volumes needs to be minimised. It is therefore a sound policy to send minimum data to maximum data. This can only be achieved if the local cardinality lists are accessed to ascertain the number of table rows requiring access in a distributed transaction.

Currently there are four basic strategies of varying degrees of sophistication that can be used to send data between sites. Beginning with the simplest they are:

• ship remote accessed table data unmerged to the triggering site;

• merge the remote accessed data and ship to the triggering site;

• ship minimum remote merged table data to maximum remote merged data in ascending size of merged tables, before shipping to the triggering site;

• the triggering site to calculate at the total "picture" of alternative remote access and data transmission strategies between sites before instructing execution.

Only the second and third distributed query optimiser strategies have been adopted by the current database products claiming to support distributed database. The second strategy is the most widely used approach. The third strategy is more in line with the policy of shipping minimum data to maximum data. It may involve shipping data around the network before shipping it to the triggering site.

The first two strategies do not require to use the database set cardinality lists. Note that the only criterion of measurement is the number of table rows to be transmitted. Other issues not currently considered are the length of the data stream to be transmitted (i.e. number of table rows × row data length), telecommunication line speed between sites, telecommunication network layout, whether the local data should be included in the distributed query optimisation algorithm and the number of remote I/Os.

A worked example of each strategy shows the different performance implications. Assume the scenario in figure 4.10. The distributed request is triggered at site 3 and requires to access all information concerning certain values of tables A and B at site 1, 2 and 4. The number of table rows to be accessed in each table and the merged results are indicated against the hashed portion of each table.

The first strategy would involve the triggering site issuing access requests to the remote sites, which return 270 table rows, 40 from site 1, 80 from site 2 and 150 from site 4. Six remote I/Os are incurred, 3 to request the data at the remote sites and 3 to send it back. The second strategy merges the

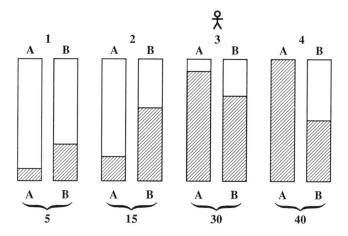

1. Ship 270 rows to Site 3 + 6 remote I/Os

2. Ship 60 rows to Site 3 + 6 remote I/Os

3. Ship 5 rows from Site 1 to Site 2
   Ship 4 rows (say) from Site 2 to Site 4 } 39 rows + 12 remote I/Os
   Ship 30 rows (say) from Site 4 to Site 3

4. Less than 39 rows + 12 remote I/Os

Figure 4.10   Distributed query optimiser strategies

remote accessed tables at their local sites. Thus tables A and B at site 1 produce a merged result of 5 rows, a similar merging at site 2 a merged result of 15 rows and at site 4 a merged result of 40 rows. The merged data of 60 rows is sent to site 3. There would be 6 remote I/Os, 3 to request the data and 3 to send it back.

The third strategy would be for the triggering site to read the remote set cardinality lists first and ascertain the amount of data to be accessed and send the smallest merged table to the next largest merged table and so on until sending the final result to the triggering site for final merging. In the example in figure 4.10 this would entail shipping the merged tables of site 1 (5 rows) to site 2, sending the combined merged result (say 4 rows) to site 4 and sending the combined merged result (say 30 rows) to site 3. This access strategy would involve sending 39 rows between the sites and 12 remote I/Os, three to request the remote cardinality data, three to send the cardinality statistics back to the triggering site, three to send transmission instructions to the remote sites and three to transmit the data from the remote sites to the triggering site.

It is an astonishing fact that the only distributed database product that undertakes this level of optimisation is INGRES. The trouble with this strategy is that the size of the merged table sent from site 2 to site 4 and eventually from site 4 to site 3 is not calculated in advance at the triggering site. With hindsight (which can be calculated with the fourth strategy by combining the separate location cardinality statistics to calculate the size of the transmitted merged tables), it may be that sending the merged table of 40 rows would produce a better, i.e. smaller, merged result than sending it to site 2 with its merged table of 15 rows. The fourth strategy would thus transmit less than 39 rows between the sites, but still incur 12 remote I/Os.

There is thus a balance shift—the greater the sophistication of the distributed query optimiser the fewer the table rows to be transmitted between sites and, once cardinality lists are used, a doubling of the number of remote I/Os. So long as the telecommunication line speeds are slow the emphasis must be on reducing the length of the data stream transmitted between locations. This clearly favours the more sophisticated optimisers. If the line speed increases dramatically (as perhaps on local area networks) without a commensurate decrease in the remote I/O processing overheads then the less sophisticated optimisers come into their own. Distributed database designers must ascertain the distributed query optimisation mechanisms, as it can significantly affect processor and telecommunication overheads and thereby transaction resource utilisation and response times.

4.1.4.6 Distributed transaction utilisation monitor

Relational file handlers have many advantages, one of which is easy data access specification through command and menu driven query languages. SQL is a command driven query language and is the de facto industry standard for relational file handlers. Each relational database vendor has also developed their own menu driven query languages. Users are therefore able to pose ad hoc questions. Many of the ad hoc access requirements may be to retrieve data in bulk. Without realising it users may easily issue requests for a large volume of data and thereby "clog up" the processor and degrade performance. Given the overheads of remote I/O and slow data transmission speeds, such a situation in a distributed system could well be catastrophic.

It is necessary to provide a "governor" facility that can dynamically prevent users unwittingly issuing excessively resource hungry requests for data. Such a governor should measure the processor, disk and terminal I/O resource utilisation overheads of a request. Currently the governor facilities provided, as for example by INGRES and DB2, only measure processor time. If a system is distributed it may well be that the data the user is requesting is spread across the locations like "grass seed". The governor should therefore also measure the remote I/O and telecommunication overheads incurred. IBM provide a distributed governor, which is presumably an extension of their Resource Limit Facility product local governor for DB2. The author has not been able to obtain any details. One would assume that the distributed governor reads the remote cardinality list of the local query optimisers, ascertains the number of remote table rows required to be accessed and thereby calculates, at a minimum, remote I/O and, hopefully, telecommunication overheads.

4.1.4.7 Distributed dictionary

Each site in a distributed system is equal to all the other sites. No site should be considered a master site. However, a distributed transaction must be co-ordinated. Co-ordination requires control. The policy that has been followed is that the site that triggers the transaction acts as the controlling site, but only for the duration of the transaction. Co-ordination is therefore at the transaction and not at the system level.

Given this principle of equal sites there should be no master dictionary recording the distribution of data across sites. What is required is that each dictionary at each site records fully the distribution of data, screen formats, report formats, application programs etc. for all sites. Thus each local dictionary should also be a global dictionary. Currently most products define local information in local dictionaries and contain only a reference to the tables of data in other locations in a distributed network. There are major adverse performance implications of this approach, for example the dynamic parsing of every ad hoc SQL query requires access to remote dictionaries if remote data access is required. This increases transaction overheads and lowers performance.

Clearly where the local dictionaries are also global there is a need to synchronise the updates of the dictionaries across multiple sites. Given that a dictionary is nothing more than standard data stored in standard tables the normal mechanism of the two-phase commit procedure is appropriate and sufficient for online updates.

As an insurance of global distributed dictionary integrity and consistency distributed software should ensure dictionary synchronisation is part of the start-up procedures. For this to occur one site is designated a master site. This is the only occasion that the concept of master site is used at the system level.

4.1.4.8 Location transparency

Users should not be aware that the system they are using is distributed. They should not have to know the distribution of data between sites.

The mechanisms required to support distributed data location transparency are crucially dependent on how the data is distributed across locations. Data can be distributed either vertically or horizontally, as illustrated in figure 4.11. With vertical distribution there is a one-for-one match between an entity and its location. A location can store many entities (physically stored in the form of tables); an entity can be stored at one location only. The great advantage of vertical distribution is that the location of an entity can be identified as an attribute of the entity in the schema description within the global dictionaries at each location. The software merely has to access the global dictionary and the location of the entity and its occurrences can be ascertained. This means that complicated software to search for the location of an entity and its occurrences is not required. If the retrieval request is "For a specified occurrence of C display all related Bs and Ds" then the local global dictionary would indicate that tables C and D are to be found at location 2 and table B at location 1. The recording of the location of an entity in the global dictionaries is simple and provides highly efficient support for finding the location of data. Vertically distributed systems have this efficiency and simplicity.

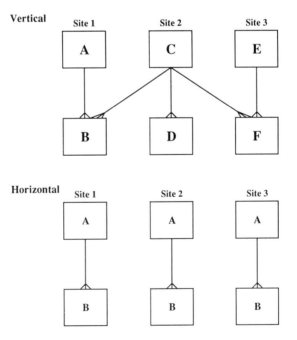

Figure 4.11   Data distribution

Unfortunately the bulk of distributed applications distribute data in a horizontal manner. With horizontal data distribution there is no longer a one-for-one match between a location and an entity type. The problem is the entity occurrences. If it were possible to store the location of each entity occurrence in the global dictionaries, the disk storage requirements and above all the maintenance of the entity occurrence location identifier would be prohibitive. Dictionaries only define entities at the entity type, not the entity occurrence level. The global dictionaries cannot therefore be used to identify the location of horizontally distributed data.

An alternative mechanism is required. The mechanisms are:

• Fragmentation within entities

The entity is fragmented such that specified table columns (vertical fragmentation) or table rows based on a specified value range of the key data item(s) (horizontal fragmentation) relate to specified locations. Such fragmentation vertically structures in a physical design an entity that is horizontally distributed in a logical design. Fragmentation can be specified in the global dictionaries with all the advantages thereby provided.

The trouble is that such fragmentation is of little practical value. The real world does not usually work in an entity fragmented manner. For example vertical fragmentation makes little sense. It is not a real world situation to store the columns containing the order delivery information in Tokyo, the columns containing delivery contact person information in New York and columns containing the order product information in London. The only relevance of vertical fragmentation identified by the author was in a manufacturing environment where certain columns of a product table were appropriate to drilling, certain columns appropriate to lathe machining and certain columns appropriate to robotic processing. The columns of data would be distributed to the processors built into the drill, lathe and robot.

Horizontal fragmentation is also of equally limited practicality in normal commercial environments. It has relevance if one is accessing the table on the key column which is used to provide the value for horizontal fragmentation, for example orders number 1 to 99 to be stored in Tokyo, orders 100 to 199 to be stored in New York and orders 200 to 299 to be stored in London. This is fine so long as one wants to access a specific order on order number. However the real world is that one usually requires to access an order on other than order number. One usually wishes to access orders on a specific customer or product. (There is a little "trick of the design trade" to get round this. Put the secondary index on customer number and product code on top of the primary key on order number. IBM's VSAM keyed sequential data set and Tandem's NonStop SQL file handlers provide this facility.)

- Partitioning between entities
  Where a logical data model indicates that data is distributed horizontally, a solution can be to "bend" the physical design to be at variance to the logical design by stipulating that an entity, which logically is found at multiple locations, is to be stored physically at a single location. One is converting the logically horizontal distribution of data to be physically distributed vertically, again with all the benefits of global dictionary access provided.

- Multi-site searching
  Multi-site searching is the only mechanism that fully provides real world support for location transparency where data is distributed horizontally. Any product claiming to support location transparency in all environments (vertical and horizontal data distribution) must provide a minimum of one multi-site searching mechanism. There are four such mechanisms—broadcast; "round robin"; replicated index; replicated database:

— With broadcast searching a data access request is shipped from the triggering site to all the sites. The advantage of broadcast searching is that the data request response times can be uniform, in that the request is shipped simultaneously to all sites and, if each site processes the transaction immediately, the response times will be made more or less uniform. This, of course, is an ideal situation, as the database and processor circumstances at each of the remote sites will not be identical. A disadvantage is that the distributed data retrieval access overheads are high as all sites are accessed, even though they may contain no data relevant to the request.

— "Round robin" searching involves a progressive walk round each site in turn until the requisite data is found. An advantage of round robin is that only half the sites within the distributed system require to be accessed on average, such that the distributed data retrieval access overheads are only half those of the broadcast mechanism. A disadvantage is that the data access response time is not uniform and varies depending on the number of sites accessed.

— Replicated index replicates all or selected indexes of each site at all the sites. A data access request therefore accesses the local site indexes, all of which except the indexes of the triggering site are replications, to ascertain which site index points to the requisite data. The site pointed to is accessed. An advantage of replicated index is that multi-site searching is not required on data retrieval transactions. A disadvantage is that the replicated indexes require expensive multi-site updating.

— Replicated database replicates all or selected user data tables and indexes at all the sites. The advantage is that all data retrieval requests to the replicated data are local. The obvious disadvantage is that any data or index changes require to be replicated at all the sites.

There is clearly a balance shift in the data retrieval to data maintenance overheads from broadcast to replicated databases, with the degree of balance shift depending on the number of sites within the distributed system. With broadcast the data retrieval overheads are greatest, as all sites require to be accessed. Because no track of where the data is to be stored is maintained, the data maintenance overheads are the lowest. At the other extreme is replicated database, where data retrieval access is minimal as it can be entirely local to the replicated data, while the data maintenance overheads are maximised because of the replication of user data and indexes. It should be borne in mind that updates in a distributed system require, at a minimum, two message pairs between the co-ordinating and participating sites for each set of table rows and supporting log updated as well as possibly distributed concurrency control overheads. The number of databases and log files in the set equals the number of sites in the distributed system.

4.1.5 Enhancements to Information Engineering

One of the two special features of distributed systems is controlled by the distributed database software. Synchronised multi-site databases updating and hardware/software recovery is handled by the distributed concurrency control, the two-phase commit and pending files procedures. Information Engineering does not therefore require to be concerned with the synchronisation aspect of data distribution during logical design, only during physical design.

The policy followed by the vendors of distributed database has been to "add on" the requirements of data distribution to the existing facilities for centralised database processing, the overriding necessity being the preservation of existing investments (financial, technical and human) in information technology. The great benefit of this policy is that what has been used and learned previously is preserved unchanged. What is true of the technology is true for the techniques. *Information Engineering is wholly preserved for distributed systems.* The only enhancements required are that the concept of location needs to be "added on" to the logical design techniques and supporting documentation and the concepts of synchronisation and location needs to be "added on" to the physical design and development techniques and supporting documentation.

The enhancements to Information Engineering will be described using two distributed applications the author was involved with. In both cases information engineering based design and development techniques were used. The enhancements about to be described were applied and proved successful.

The first was a government system that required to issue public documents on demand. Any government requires to support this function and the locations used in this case study are purely illustrative and chosen at random. There were five regional offices, London, Derby, Edinburgh, Manchester and Cambridge. London also had head office functions, such as accounting. Manchester, Edinburgh and Cambridge each had the same volume of business, with Derby being substantially less. Once the documents had been issued to the public a central reference repository was maintained at another location.

There were thus 6 locations but only 3 location types. There were 4 regional offices of the location type regional office and one location each for the location types of head office and central repository. The business at each location type is the same, only the data and business requirement volumes vary.

The concept of location type is important to distributed systems. One of the major problems of analysing distributed systems is that if the business varies across locations then there is a need to undertake a full logical analysis and produce a full logical design for each of the locations. The design effort is substantially increased, and the author's experience is that it is invariably underestimated. Given the business is the same within a location type the scope for reduced analysis and design effort is considerable, particularly if there are many locations per location type. The only information that will vary is the volumes and cardinality ratios of the entities and the volumes of the business requirements.

What can often occur is that there is not a clear dividing line between a location and a location type. It can be that some of the business requirements are the same across locations and some are different across location types. This was the case of the main cargo port and the smaller ports, where the only significant difference in the business was that there were not fork life trucks at the small ports. They were of the same location types but were not totally homogeneous. This has to be watched out for. The degree of business difference between location types can be from small to totally different. A location can belong to only one location type; a location type can have 1−n locations.

The second distributed system was an island port authority, which handled general as well as passenger traffic. The case study was only concerned with monitoring, in realtime, the planning and control of general cargo between the four islands, the mainland of Britain and Continental Europe.

There were differences in the way the business of the ports were run. Only the main port on the largest island contained a warehouse for the storage of the general cargo. All the small ports loaded and unloaded the cargo direct from and onto the lorries, so there was no need for fork lift trucks and the more sophisticated business of planning the loading and movement of the cargo pallets. The movement management function was to be found only at the main port.

The head office was located on the main island and, as far as the case study was concerned, monitored the general cargo movements on a summarised daily basis.

The port authority had five locations, with three location types.

The logical design techniques to be reviewed are those which Information Engineering based structured methods use and include enhancements suggested as necessary in chapter 3. It is assumed the reader is familiar with the suggestions.

4.1.5.1 Process decomposition/dataflow diagrams

As explained in section 2.4.1 the process dependency diagrams do not contain any information that is not already contained in the dataflow diagrams. From the point of this book what is written about the dataflow diagrams and their support for location is also true for the process dependency diagrams.

As explained in section 1.4.2 the dataflow diagrams are built on the data maintenance business requirements. The first thing that requires to be ascertained therefore is the location at which the data maintenance business requirements are triggered. Given that the main design principle of distributed systems is to store the data at the location where it is most frequently accessed, so as to keep remote I/O to a minimum, the location at which the transactions are triggered is clearly essential information. Once the data maintenance business requirements have been identified and catalogued by location within location type the design and construction of the dataflow diagrams can be undertaken as normal, with a set of dataflow diagrams per location type.

Do not expect the dataflow diagrams to be always uniform across location types. Variations within the "common" location type model can occur. For the government system all the regional offices conducted their document support business in an identical manner. For this location type the dataflow diagrams were identical and there was no need for n dataflow diagrams for n locations. The head office included an accounting function so that additional external entities, dataflows, datastores and processes were included onto the "common" dataflow diagrams for the regional offices. The reference centre had a totally different dataflow diagram.

The port company dataflow diagrams varied between the main port and the smaller ports in that the medieval port was not concerned with fork lift trucks. A much simplified diagram of the event level processes for the general cargo function for both the main and the small ports is illustrated in figure 4.12. The small port is missing the processes relating to fork lift

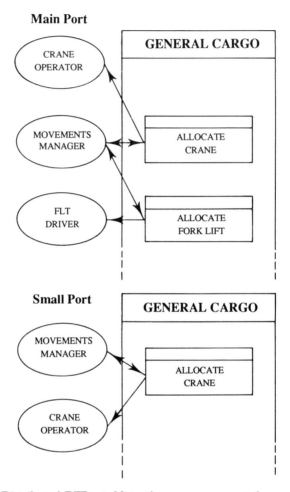

Figure 4.12   Distributed DFDs: 1. Note: the processes are at the event level

trucks. Variations in the dataflow diagrams continued to the next level of decomposition, the problems-to-solve. The main port contained many bays at which vessels could be moored for loading and unloading. The small ports contained only one bay. Therefore the problem-to-solve of ascertaining a bay for a vessel to moor at was not necessary. The different dataflow diagrams can be seen in figure 4.13.

4.1.5.2 Process dependency diagrams

As explained in section 2.4.1 the process dependency diagrams contain no information that is not already contained in the entity life histories, so again

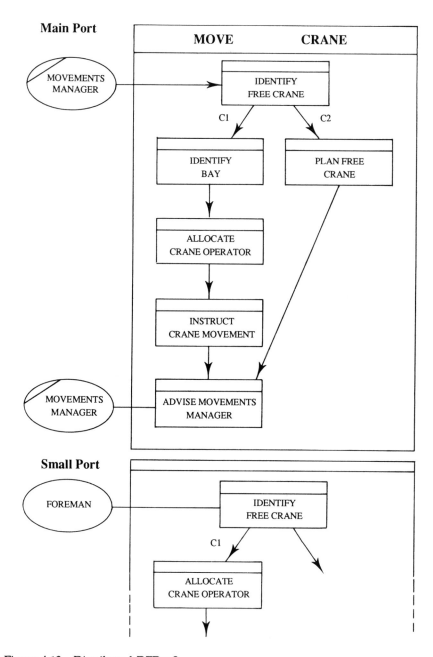

Figure 4.13 Distributed DFDs: 2

what is true of the entity life histories is also true for the process dependency diagrams.

In the movement of cargo pallets at the main port between the loading and unloading of pallets onto and from vessels there was a general sequence of using the crane to load and unload the pallets, the fork lift trucks to move the pallets between the cranes and to a movements planning area and the lorries to "shuffle" the pallets in the yard planning area as required. A similar sequence was followed at the small ports, but without the aid of the fork lift trucks moving the pallets between the vessels and the movements planning area. The sequence dependency at both ports is illustrated in figure 4.14a and 4.14b. In 4.14b there is no process for pallet movement by the fork lift trucks.

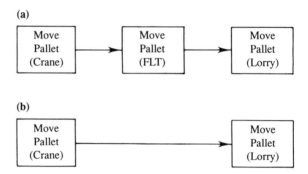

Figure 4.14   Distributed process dependency diagrams: (a) container port; (b) medieval port

4.1.5.3 Entity relationship diagram

As explained in concept nine the physical database and its logical precursor the ERD model should be built from the data retrieval business requirements. As with dataflow diagrams the first thing that requires to be ascertained is the location at which the business requirements are triggered. Once the requirements have been identified and catalogued by location within location type the design and construction of the ERD by location type can proceed as normal.

The ERD varied by location type for the two case study applications in exactly the same way as for the dataflow diagrams. The main port company data model is illustrated in figure 4.15. The data models for the main and small ports are identical except that the small port model contains no entities relating to fork lift trucks. The head office model is entirely different. The

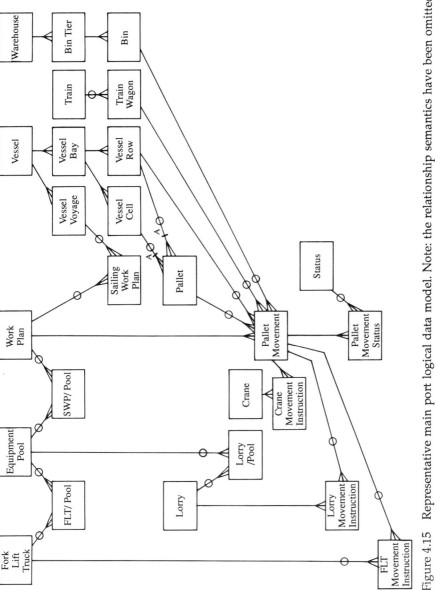

Figure 4.15   Representative main port logical data model. Note: the relationship semantics have been omitted

part that is relevant to the book relates to the fact that the head office required to monitor the daily movements of cargo pallets from a number of viewpoints and not by individual pallet, as illustrated in figure 4.16. The head office data model was therefore radically different from the data models for the other ports. Furthermore the head office had two data models, one for the main port and one for the small ports, and again the model for the small ports excluded the fork lift trucks. This has been the only occasion the author has required to produce two data models for one location type.

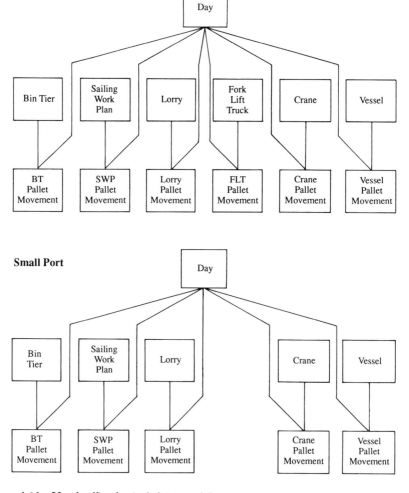

Figure 4.16   Head office logical data models

What can, and usually does, vary by location type and even location are the by-products of the ERD—the data items in the entities (usually little variation) and the entity volumes, lives and set cardinalities (almost always vary). Consider figures 4.17 to 4.19. The examples are based on the government system. Figure 4.17 represents part of the ERD and figures 4.18 and 4.19 the supporting documentation. In figure 4.17a it was ascertained that at the regional offices the volume of grade did not vary by location type, with 18 grades per location, that the grade rate (a figure for the calculation of salaries etc.) and skill set cardinalities also did not vary by location type, whereas the set cardinality of grade to staff did vary by location type. This can be seen in figure 4.18. It was ascertained that there were two grade rates per grade at all the location types and four skills per grade at all the location types. It was found that the head office at London had some seven persons per grade on average, the office at Derby had four per grade and the other regional offices throughout the United Kingdom had eight staff per grade. Here the variation was at the specific location, not location type.

Figure 4.17b with 4.19 illustrates some additional points. They show that a member of staff would be allocated to a printer for the printing of the public documents. While the member of staff was at the printer he/she would process a number of documents. Unlike the previous example the

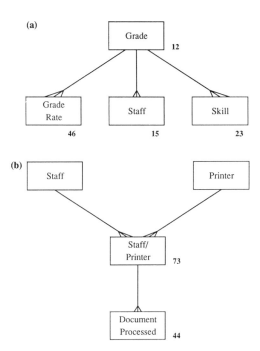

Figure 4.17   Distributed volumes

232

SYSTEM: DATA GROUP NO: 12   NAME: GRADE

ATTRIBUTES

CODE NAME	PK(/) FK(*)	USER NAME	TYPE/ SIZE	COMMENTS/EXAMPLES
	/	Grade code	X2	
		Description	X20	
		....		

OCCURRENCES

ACTIVE	ADD P/M	GTH P/M	LIFE (M)	DEL/ARC P/M
18			As req'd	

DEPENDENT DATA GROUP RATIOS

	GROUP NO.	MIN	MAX	MEAN	WORK AVE	RATIO COMMENTS
STAFF:	15(LDN)	0	60	6	7	10% have zero
	15(DY)	0	8	1	4	70% have zero
	15(OTH)	0	60	6	8	10% have zero
GRADE RATE:	46	0	5	2	2	
SKILL:	23	1	15	4	4	

Figure 4.18   Data group contents/volumes/set ratios

SYSTEM:			DATA GROUP NO: 73		NAME: STAFF/PRINTER				
ATTRIBUTES					**OCCURRENCES**				
CODE NAME	PK(/) FK(*)	USER NAME	TYPE/ SIZE	COMMENTS/EXAMPLES	ACTIVE	ADD P/M	GTH P/M	LIFE (M)	DEL/ARC P/M
	/	Printer No.	N2		LDN-20			1 day	
	/	Staff reference no	X10		DER-8				
	/	Task code	X2		OTH-30				
	/	Work date	N6	YYMMDD					
	/	Start time	N4	YYMMDD					
	/	End time	N4	HHMM log on time					
		.....		HHMM log on time					

DEPENDENT DATA GROUP RATIOS

GROUP NO.	MIN	MAX	MEAN	WORK AVE	RATIO COMMENTS
(LDN) 44	0	400	70	70	0% have zero
(DER) 44	0	400	6	7	0% have zero
(OTH) 44	0	400	85	85	0% have zero

Figure 4.19 Data group contents/volumes/set ratios

volumes of the entity, in this case staff/printer, do vary by location with London having some twenty, Derby some eight and the remaining offices some thirty. The set cardinality of the documents processed per staff/printer also varied as illustrated.

4.1.5.4 Relational data analysis

The technique is unchanged. The practitioner must be aware that the same data may not be found at all locations and also check that the meaning of the data items is the same across location types. If it is not then the relations will vary by location type.

4.1.5.5 Entity life histories

The technique is unchanged but must be applied to all the entities for each logical data model at all the locations. Again the practitioner must be aware that the events that update the entities can vary by location type. Clearly where they do not the same ELH for an entity is valid for all location types. The potentially mammoth task of applying the technique on n data models for n locations can thereby be significantly reduced.

For the government ministry application the ELHs did not vary by location type. Each entity had exactly the same life at all the locations. There were, however, subtle variations in the life of some of the entities in the port authority application. Simplified but representative ELHs are shown in figure 4.20. As with the process dependency diagrams it illustrates that the pallets at the small port were not moved by a fork lift truck. However the life of the pallet at the head office had a radically different life—see figure 4.21.

4.1.5.6 Data navigation/transaction access path analysis

Once again the technique as described in sections 3.1.1 and 3.2.9.4 is unchanged, but the practitioner must be aware of the possibilities of variations by location type, not only in the access path to the entities (different entry points and different access paths between entities) but also in the access volumes.

It was found at the main port that the entry points to the data model for a given business requirement can vary by location. Consider figure 4.22. The business requirement was "For a specified sailing work plan display all pallet movements for a specified pallet". The entry point possibilities were sailing work plan and pallet. At the main port access via pallet would

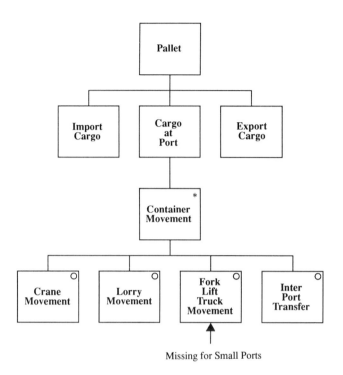

Figure 4.20   Pallet life at main and small ports

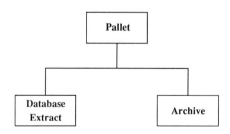

Same Life for all Head Office entities

Figure 4.21   Pallet life at head office

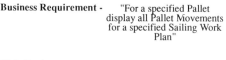

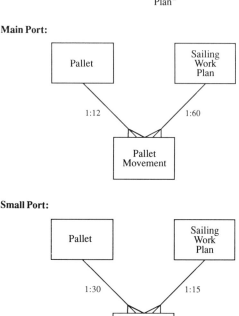

Figure 4.22   Different entry points by location

yield a better access path than via sailing work plan, solely because the set cardinality of pallet to pallet movement was less than via sailing work plan. The reason for this ratio was that at the main port, which had more space, better efficiency could be obtained. A sailing work plan could be a much larger set of tasks for moving pallets and a pallet would require much fewer movements between entering and leaving the port.

At the small ports, with the constraints of geography and space, the sailing work plan was a limited set of tasks for moving pallets, the pallets would have a slower turnaround time and require more movements and "shuffling" around the port before being ready to be loaded onto a vessel. The cardinalities of sailing work plan and pallet to pallet movement were the reverse of the main port, such that the optimum entry point in this case was via sailing work plan.

The access paths illustrated in figures 4.23 to 4.26 have been pasteurised in that the data group names have been converted to numbers. These numbers are not significant as regards the point being made. The access

FUNCTION NO:			FUNCTION NAME: DERBY CASH RECONCILIATION			
DATA GROUP	ACC TYPE	READ PATH	ACCESS VIA	NO. ACC.	DATA ITEMS	CONDITIONS & COMMENTS
1	R	D		2		
8	R	P	1	8		
17	R	P	8	440		
39	R	P	17	462		
				912		

ACCESS TYPE		READ PATH	
I - insert	L+ - add to optional link path	D - direct	
M - modify	L- - remove from optional link path	PS - physical sequential	
R - read		LS - logical sequential	
D - delete		C - via child	
		P - via parent	

Figure 4.23 Distributed transaction access path: 1

FUNCTION NO:			FUNCTION NAME: UK LOCATIONS (excl. London) CASH REC'N			
DATA GROUP	ACC TYPE	READ PATH	ACCESS VIA	NO. ACC.	DATA ITEMS	CONDITIONS & COMMENTS
1	R	D	—	2		
8	R	P	1	33		
17	R	P	8	1815		
39	R	P	17	1906		
				3756		

ACCESS TYPE		READ PATH	
I - insert	L+ - add to optional link path	D - direct	
M - modify	L- - remove from optional link path	PS - physical sequential	
R - read		LS - logical sequential	
D - delete		C - via child	
		P - via parent	

Figure 4.24 Distributed transaction access path: 2

FUNCTION NO:			FUNCTION NAME: LONDON CASH RECONCILIATION			
DATA GROUP	ACC TYPE	READ PATH	ACCESS VIA	NO. ACC.	DATA ITEMS	CONDITIONS & COMMENTS
1	R	D	—	2		
8	R	P	1	53		
17	R	P	8	2915		
39	R	P	17	3060		
				6030		

ACCESS TYPE		READ PATH	
I - insert	L+ - add to optional link path	D - direct	
M - modify	L- - remove from optional link path	PS - physical sequential	
R - read		LS - logical sequential	
D - delete		C - via child	
		P - via parent	

Figure 4.25   Distributed transaction access path: 3

paths are based on the government system. The business requirement Cash Reconciliation has the same access path across all locations, but the access volumes for the entities varied considerably. If all the transactions in the application had the same variations of access overhead the processing power at the London head office would need to be some six times the power of the Derby office.

However the access volumes do not have to vary for a given transaction. The business requirement Receive Application was exactly the same at all the offices concerned with processing the public documents. An application is an application is an application!

There is no rule as to whether the transaction access volumes vary by location or not. It has to be ascertained on a transaction basis.

It was also found that the volume of transactions varied by location type. This is illustrated in figure 4.27. This document, along with the individual transaction access path maps, was crucial to producing summary access path maps per location type.

4.1.5.7 Load matrices/summary access path maps

Summary access path maps are crucial to the successful design of a distributed database, particularly where the data is distributed horizontally across locations.

Location common access path

FUNCTION NO:			FUNCTION NAME: RECEIVE APPLICATION				
DATA GROUP	ACC TYPE	READ PATH	ACCESS VIA	NO. ACC.	DATA ITEMS	CONDITIONS & COMMENTS
22	I	D	-	1		
14	L+	C	22	1		Create link
37	L+	C	22	1		Create link
16	I	P	22	1		
22	L+	C	16	1		Create link
15	L+	C	16	1		Create link
10	R	D	-	1		For access only
6	R	P	10	1		Read reverse until attendance hit. Assume last. For access only.
53	R	P	6	1		Read reverse for hours type. Assume last.
7	M	P	53	1		
4	I	P	7	1		

ACCESS TYPE
I - insert   L+ - add to optional link path
M - modify   L- - remove from optional link path
R - read
D - delete

READ PATH
D   - direct
PS - physical sequential
LS - logical sequential
C   - via child
P   - via parent

Figure 4.26 Distributed transaction access path: 4

Without the summary access path maps the design of the distributed database will be left to the old fashioned "seat of the pants" approach of design practised before the adoption of structured methods. Remember, where the data is distributed horizontally the database dictionary cannot be used to ascertain the location of data and an expensive multi-site searching mechanism for the data across locations is required. The greater the number of sites, the greater the expense of searching.

The purpose of the summary maps is to enable the designer to ascertain objectively whether:

• it is possible to convert the horizontally distributed logical design into a vertically distributed physical design and thereby take advantage of the benefits of access to the global dictionary to ascertain the location of data;

Type: Online

Function No.	Function Name	Function Description	Frequency		Location
1	Print document	Print a document of a specified application	Peak 2250 450 6200	Off Peak (x day) 440 45 1450	 London Derby Manchester
2	Close application	Close specified applications	Peak 25 12 75	Off Peak (x day) 4 - 14	 London Derby Manchester
3	Withdraw application	Withdraw specified applications	Peak 29 7 16	Off Peak (x day) 4 - 17	 London Derby Manchester

Figure 4.27   Distributed update function catalogue

• the balance of data access is data retrieval or data maintenance. If the balance is data retrieval then the "broadcast" multi-site searching mechanism is the most expensive. If the balance is data maintenance then the replicated database mechanism is the most expensive.

The summary access path maps crucial to distributed database design are the data maintenance and data retrieval summary maps by location or location type as appropriate. Summary maps by location are needed where the data access requirements are unique to a particular location; summary maps by location type are needed where the data access requirements are common across a number of locations. Figures 4.28 and 4.29 illustrate how these summary maps can be used to provide answers to both of the above issues.

The figures are not case study based, are somewhat unrealistic and are for teaching purposes only to show how the maps can be used. The maps assume that all the data accesses are distributed. Figure 4.28a has all data maintenance accesses at one location and all the data retrieval accesses at the other locations. The figure illustrates an extreme situation of moving all of a location's data to another location—in this case moving the data of locations 1 and 2 to location 3. The reason for this is that 90% of all data access is at location 3. The overhead of this strategy would be remote I/O from locations 1 and 2 to location 3 to access "their" data, but the overhead would be small as the data retrieval access costs are only some 10% of the data maintenance access costs.

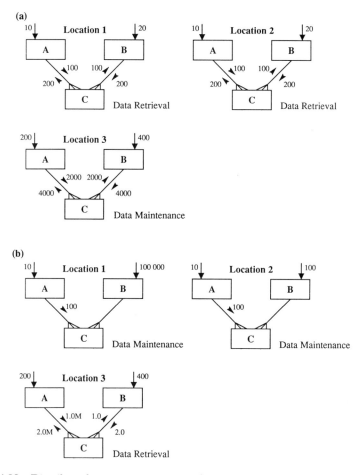

Figure 4.28   Distributed summary access path maps: 1

Figure 4.28b shows that distributed database design can be at the table level—that an individual table can be moved to another location. There are many data maintenance accesses on table B at location 1, very few data maintenance accesses at location 2 and very high data retrieval accesses on tables A and C at location 3. The message here is to put tables A and C at location 3 because 99% of all data access is there, put table B at location 1 for the same reason and to store no data at location 2.

Figure 4.29 is a further enhanced and more realistic example showing, inter alia, which tables and indexes to replicate and at what locations. It shows:

• Do not store table D at location 1, as it never occurs there.

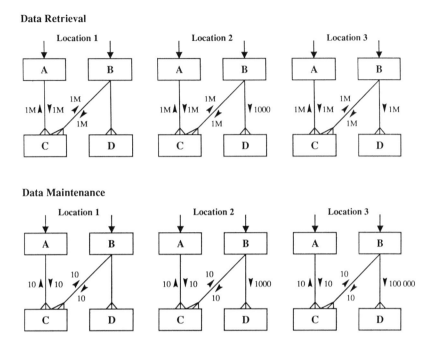

Figure 4.29   Distributed summary access path maps: 2

- Replicate tables A, B and C at locations 1, 2 and 3, because there are low data maintenance and high data retrieval accesses.

- Replicate indexes on table D at location 2 and hold table D at location 3. This is because table D is accessed only a little at location 2 and a large amount at location 3.

What is being achieved in these three examples is the "bending" of the horizontally distributed logical data design to make it vertically distributed in the physical database design, with all the benefits of using the global dictionary to record the location of the data tables. The expensive multi-site searching access mechanisms will not be necessary.

If the "bending" could not be achieved then the summary maps could be used to indicate which multi-site searching strategy should be used. For example figure 4.29 shows that the bulk of the accesses are data retrieval on tables A, B and C. Choose replication.

In addition to producing the summary access path described above it is also necessary to produce summary maps showing the amount of remote data access between locations. One might have a distributed system but the important question is: how much of a distributed system, between which locations is the distribution and is one location more distributed than another? It is a totally different ballgame if 90% of data access is remote than if only 10% is remote. The degree of remote access as a percentage of total data access can vary from location to location.

The location summary access path maps showed for the government system that for day to day issuing of public documents each regional office was self contained and merely required to pass information about documents issued to the location holding the central reference repository. At the end of each week each regional office passed to the head office summarised accounting information. The volume of remote access was therefore low as a proportion of the total and varied by location to location. Access from the regional offices to the head office was solely data maintenance and from the regional offices to the central repository location split more or less equally between data retrieval and data maintenance. Remote accesses were only some 5% of total accesses. This system was certainly distributed, but not much. The system was also distributed vertically as regards all distributed data. Maximum use of the global dictionary could be made and the system was highly efficient.

At the port company the system was distributed vertically as regards the main and small ports in relation to the head office and horizontally between the main and small ports apart from fork lift. However, this horizontal data distribution was of no concern. The fact that there were only two port locations meant that if data was not at one port location it must be at the other. There was no cause therefore to worry about multi-site searching mechanisms.

If the entity is logically distributed vertically then all access to an entity will be either all local or all remote, and hence easy to calculate. If the entity is logically distributed horizontally then some of the accesses to the entity might be local and some remote—it has to be calculated for each entity for each remote location split by data retrieval and data maintenance accesses. A large, tedious but necessary task.

Figures 4.30 and 4.31 show the summary access path maps at the main and small ports and figures 4.32 to 4.34 the volume of distributed remote access between them. The data being transmitted between the ports is information about pallet movements being or planned to be shipped between them. Figure 4.32 shows transactions being raised at the main port to send data to the requisite small port concerning pallet movements to be expected shortly. Figure 4.33 shows transactions raised at a small port to enquire on the main port about planned pallet movements. Figure 4.34 is the reverse of figure 4.32 and is the small port informing the main port about pallet movements to expect. Other inter-site summary maps were produced, for example between the main and small ports and the head office.

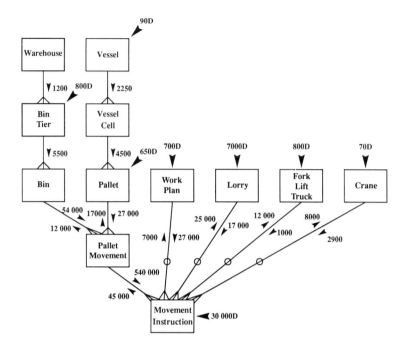

Figure 4.30   Main port summary access path map

A number of points arise from interpreting just these three maps:

• The system was only distributed to some 0.5% of all its data accesses.

• Only some of the entities required remote access.

• The distributed transactions were of the type that could wait for a response time of up to one hour.

Given these findings the enormous cost of a distributed system could not be justified. Data was therefore transmitted between sites on the basis of periodic snapshots in the implemented system.

4.1.5.8 Calculating logical data communication volumes

This is a simple but very productive task. The remote I/O is now known from the various summary access path maps showing inter-site accesses. If all the data in the entities is to be transmitted then multiply the number of logical accesses to the entities by the length of the entity. If only some the data in the entity is to be transmitted take a percentage figure as

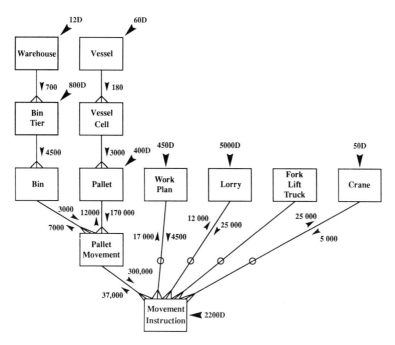

Figure 4.31   Small port summary access path map

appropriate. Endless permutations of "shuffling" the communication lines between the processors around the locations can now be made.

Figure 4.35 shows how the logical telecommunication overheads were rapidly computed for the government system depending upon the design decisions taken. Three of the regional offices had exactly the same volume of business. The number of data accesses between locations was known from the summary access path maps, as was the fact all data in an entity was transmitted when remotely accessed. The total access to an entity was multiplied by the data length of the entity and divided by the line speed to give average line loading. Peak periods could be identified and the loadings easily calculated by taking the relevant portion of data transmitted during the peak period. A 2400 bit stream line was assumed.

The "complete" strategy assumed that each site has its own processor. The "partial" strategy assumed that Derby could be serviced from Manchester and London from Cambridge. All data access—local and remote in the complete strategy—at these two regional offices became remote access and their accesses to the central reference repository had to be added to their respective "host's" accesses. It was a simple case of adding remote accesses together depending on the distribution of processing power in the offices. Endless permutations were tried and easily calculated. In the partial

(Data Maintenance)

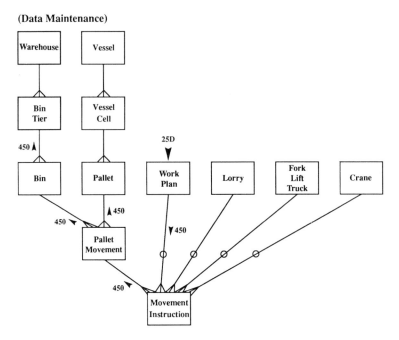

Figure 4.32   Data transfer—main port to small port

strategy it is clear that a higher speed telecommunications line is required between Cambridge and London.

4.1.5.9 Dialogue flow diagramming

No change is required to the technique other than to be aware of possible variations in local requirements. Using the SSADM version 3 notation for screen design it can be seen in figure 4.36 that the contents of the input and output screens can vary by location.

4.1.5.10 Physical design

Given the concept of logical design = physical design the physical design has already been produced, with the one proviso of breaking this "law" (the only time it is advised) when the data is distributed horizontally across many sites. Furthermore, given that distributed systems are nothing more than co-operating centralised systems the techniques of preliminary data

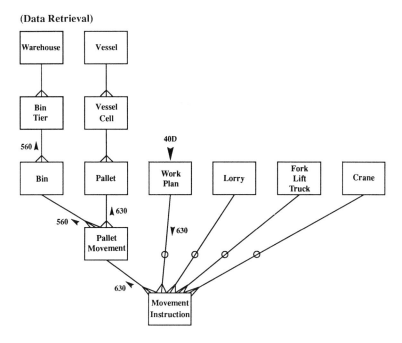

Figure 4.33   Data transfer—main port to small port

structure design, performance assessment, procedure design and software structure design are unchanged.

Notwithstanding the comforting statements about the preservation of skills and learning curves the physical designer of distributed systems must take into account extra facilities, such as:

- the extra remote I/O and local processing overhead of multiple message pairs between locations for distributed locking/timestamping and database updates;

- the implications of remote I/O and data transmission overheads generated by the simplest (send all the remote data unmerged to the triggering location) to the most sophisticated (pre-calculate data transmission and send minimum data to maximum data) distributed query optimisers;

- whether to use distributed database access or optimise with such alternative approaches as distributed process-to-process communication and remote data access;

- the data transmission overheads between sites on hardware recovery;

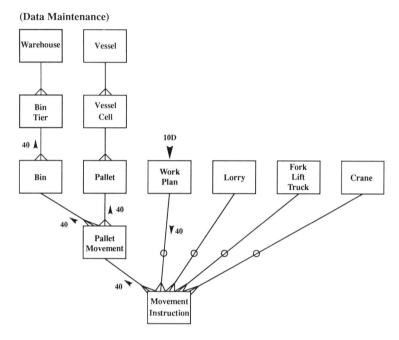

Figure 4.34   Data transfer—small port to main port

- whether application program "deadly embrace" is supported by time-stamping or multi-phase lock messaging with timeout. For either approach consider how to use transaction classes and conflict graph analysis to minimise the possibility of conflict and optimise it where it occurs;

- whether the global dictionary is repeated in full at each site or whether the local dictionaries only have references to the remote sites as regards the data tables held there. If it is the latter consider the ad hoc SQL parsing overheads to access remote data;

- how to minimise horizontal data distribution in the physical design;

- how to limit the potential runaway overheads of ad hoc distributed queries.

4.1.6 Redefining the logical design

As described in section 2.2.1.1 the concept of logical design = physical design is valid for all data processing environments from the strategic down to lines of application program code *except* for distributed database.

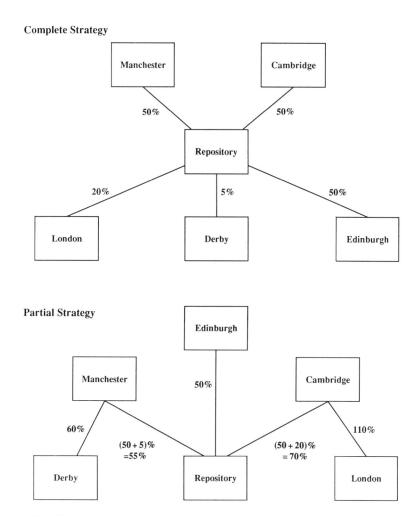

Figure 4.35   Data communications

The problem occurs in distributed systems where the data is horizontally distributed. Horizontal data distribution has been shown to have a major adverse impact on performance on concurrency control and, above all, on finding the location of data. Although the logical design might show that part or all of a distributed system is horizontally distributed the logical design specification cannot be used as the basis of code generation as in the other data processing environments as performance disaster would ensue. The logical design has to be "re-interpreted" as described in this chapter, particularly as in sections 4.1.4.8 and 4.1.5.7 and *modified logically* before physical design. This requirement is unique.

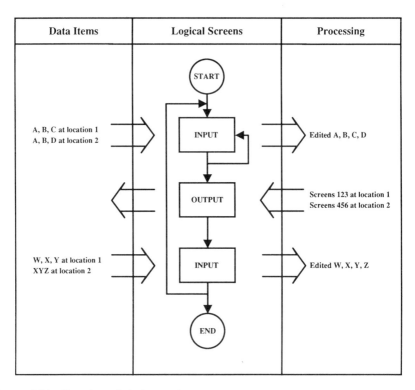

Figure 4.36   Distributed dialogue design

4.2 REALTIME PROCESSING

Ed Yourdon defined realtime systems as being "immediate output of current input". This delightfully succinct definition is delightfully accurate, as it clearly identifies the difference of realtime from online processing. Online processing matches the above definition as regards output—a rapid immediate output response is made to a trigger on the computer system. It does not, however, match the above definition as regards current input. The online output display is based on accessing the database for data, data that will have been inserted at a prior point in time, possibly days, weeks and months previously.

Notwithstanding these differences there is much that is similar between realtime and batch and online processing. Realtime systems deal with data, which must be structured and accessed. Realtime systems therefore require the techniques of entity relationship modelling, relation data analysis and entity life cycle analysis. The accessed data is displayed on screens— dialogue flow diagramming and visual layout design techniques are therefore used. Data requires manipulation and therefore action diagrams must be specified. *All of Information Engineering is relevant to realtime processing.* As with distributed database one need unlearn nothing.

Realtime systems have a number of additional unique features—continuous data flows, event recognition, causally related events and event synchronisation. Techniques to support these features are necessary. Two widely used structured design methods with which the author is familiar have been developed specifically for realtime processing—the Yourdon and JSD methods. There are, of course, other such methods, such as MASCOT. Given, for obvious reasons, that Information Engineering does not provide techniques or guidelines for these unique realtime features, it has been a question of which of these two methods to integrate into Information Engineering when undertaking realtime projects. The JSD method proved incompatible. The method does not produce dataflow diagrams, a generic technique which is widely understood. The specification of logic is based on entity life history like structures, but there is an inconsistency. Data maintenance events that update the database are grouped by entity, such that the resultant application programs are entity based. Data retrieval events that are queries on the database are not so grouped, with the query application programs being event based. However the main problem is that not all the characteristics unique to realtime systems are explicitly recognised. No advice, for example, is provided for handling continuous dataflows and event recognition.

The Yourdon method, by contrast, provides a near perfect match for Information Engineering. Extensive use of enhanced dataflow diagrams is made, with the other techniques for realtime processing adding value to the information implicit in a dataflow diagram. The method could therefore be easily integrated into Information Engineering. The Yourdon use of the Chen diagramming notation for data modelling was discarded, to be replaced by the Information Engineering ERD notation. No conflicts between the two methods therefore occurred. Techniques to support continuous dataflows, event causation and synchronisation, were added to Information Engineering, the second as enhancements to the dataflow diagram technique and the latter on a Yourdon technique fully compatible with dataflow diagrams.

The final selling point for integrating Yourdon into Information Engineering is its conceptual soundness. It explicitly recognises realtime features and separates them from conventional data processing. The control mechanisms necessary to support realtime are separated from the data processing mechanisms of batch and online processing. There is therefore no confusion between the different but dynamically interwoven environments of control processing and data processing.

The only area where the Yourdon method fails is that no technique to handle the problem of event recognition is provided.

4.2.1 Realtime concepts

There are a number of significant differences between realtime and batch and online processing. These differences are based on differing concepts. Those relating to batch and online processing are described in section 2.2. Those specific to realtime are:

4.2.1.1 Events can be causally related

The identification of events is more problematical in realtime systems than in batch and online processing because they can be causally related. Event A can trigger event B, both functioning together as a continuous process. Events are therefore less distinct from each other.

Assume the following scenario, where realtime software is embedded within the equipment it controls. A warship is sailing the high seas and comes under a missile attack. The attack is recognised (event 1) by the warship's radar control program (program A) which triggers program B (magazine control program) to issue ammunition automatically from the warship's magazine and downdate the database record of ammunition in stock (event 2). Program B now triggers program C (gun control program) which loads the gun with the ammunition and updates the status of the gun to loaded (event 3). Program C triggers program D (warship fire control program) to aim and fire the gun and update the status of the gun to fired (event 4).

These events are causally related in that event 1 triggers event 2 *et seq.* They also occur logically at the same point in time and it is only the slowness in the operation of the equipment that physically separates them. This causal relationship poses the question: what is a realtime event? Given that they all occur logically at the same point in time, events 1–4 could be grouped together as one event.

4.2.1.2 Events can occur asynchronously

The above is somewhat simplified in that it ignores the fact that many missile attacks could be occurring simultaneously in a non-predictable manner. Indeed, attacks of other kinds, such as aircraft and submarine attacks, could also be occurring at the same time. The causally related events described above could therefore be triggered by multiple events of different types occurring simultaneously but in a totally asynchronous manner. Control logic to handle synchronous sequencing of causally related asynchronous events is therefore required. This control logic is unique to realtime systems.

4.2.1.3 Events may not be recognised

The warship comes under attack. The question is: is it a missile, an aircraft, another warship, a submarine or a group attack of any combination of the above? In batch and online processing a transaction code is always appended to data being input, so the operating system/teleprocessing monitor can recognise the event for what it is. For realtime events such luxuries do not exist. An event recognition mechanism is required.

4.2.1.4 Information flows may not be discrete

A realtime system often requires to monitor flows of information that are continuous. For example, the system is monitoring temperature gauges and switches equipment off or on as the temperature rises or falls across a threshold. The flow of temperature data is continuous. With batch and online systems all dataflows are discrete and time distinct from one another. They are clearly recognisable and do not require a threshold boundary mechanism to act as a trigger. Discrete dataflows implicitly represent both the content of the data and the occurrence trigger of the flow at a specified point in time, to which a computer system must make a response. Continuous dataflows do not have a built-in triggering mechanism. These require to be designed into the realtime system, as well as a mechanism to have a continuously running program to support the continuous dataflows.

All the above concepts are to do with processing. Of the three logical components of a computer system—data structure, data access and data process—it is the data process component that requires enhancement to support realtime systems. The data structure and data access components remain unchanged from batch and online processing.

4.2.2 The impact of realtime concepts

4.2.2.1 Separation of control from data

It is noticeable that the Yourdon method recognises that application programs are event based. To preserve this concept the method has skilfully separated the "control" access and process logic for event synchronisation from the "data" access and process logic processing the data about the event. Once the control logic has completed synchronisation the control program calls the data process program(s).

The normal coding of application program processing data at the event level, as in Information Engineering, is wholly preserved. Their realtime causal relationships and synchronisation are handled by separate control programs. Information Engineering is therefore entirely appropriate, without change, to support the data processing component of a realtime system.

This control mechanism requires to be able to receive multiple control messages over time for multiple asynchronous events, possibly for multiple entities. It therefore requires to be able to:

- hold itself in a wait condition until the critical event happens (which may be the last event in an unordered sequence of non-critical events);

- switch the application programs processing the realtime event on, off or into a wait condition;

- monitor the state of all its dependent control and data programs;

- pass control data to the dependent control and data programs.

At no time should the control program be accessing or processing user data associated with the realtime events. That is the function of the data programs called by the control program.

The state of a control program reflects the condition the program is at at an instant in time when synchronising realtime events that together affect an entity occurrence. Using the port authority as an example the program synchronising the events affecting a lorry could be in a Lorry Available state. When a certain event or set of events occurs the state could change to Lorry not Available. When another event or set of events occurs the state could revert to Lorry Available.

Control programs, unlike data programs, "talk" to each other dynamically. There is another control program for Lorry Machine Instruction. This control program is dependent on the Lorry control program. The piece of equipment being monitored in realtime is the lorry. The lorry is represented as an entity in the logical data model for the main port—see figure 4.15. The lorry machine instruction is issued for a lorry under certain conditions. The entity lorry machine instruction is a detail entity, and dependent on, lorry. The matching control program can therefore be dependent on the control program for the master lorry entity. When the lorry is matched with a fork lift then, because both entities are always processed together for this business requirement, the lorry machine instruction control program is invoked by the lorry control program. Unlike online processing realtime programs can call each other.

Various techniques are available to monitor the control program state. Yourdon uses state transition diagrams (STD), optionally supported by state transition tables/finite state machines.

4.2.2.2 Pitching of control and data programs

A question which any realtime method requires to answer is: at what level do you pitch the control program?

Clearly it cannot be pitched at the event level as in batch and online processing, because it can be controlling multiple events simultaneously. Furthermore, these events can be totally unpredictable as to their sequence one with another or indeed whether they will occur or not.

Yourdon once again offers a hint when describing realtime software controlling individual items of equipment. A typical example could be a radar antenna which is part of an air traffic control system. The realtime software is part of and embedded in the equipment supporting the radar antenna. The machinery is recorded as an entity in the logical data model. It is therefore a natural consequence that realtime control programs should be at the entity level, synchronising the asynchronous events that the entity, such as the radar antenna, has to cater for.

Pitching the control program at the entity level when undertaking logical design has proved to be very successful on projects undertaken by the author. For the port authority case study there was a control program for the lorry, fork lift truck and crane entities, as the movement of these pieces of equipment was being monitored in realtime. Indeed there was, conceptually, a control program controlling the realtime events for each occurrence of lorry, fork lift truck and crane. The state of each lorry, fork lift and crane regarding container movements needed to be monitored, with asynchronous events affecting each occurrence in an unpredictable manner. While the logic for each control program was common for each entity type, i.e. the logic for controlling the fork lift truck was the same for all fork lift trucks, the requirement was to control the asynchronous events for each individual fork lift truck.

By having a control program as described above there is the sweet situation where the realtime events affecting an entity occurrence are synchronised as a separate task before the actual data processing of the event. Once the realtime events are synchronised the control program calls the data program accessing the entity for conventional application processing.

A clear distinction can therefore be made between realtime and online programs based on their role and mechanisms used. *Realtime control programs should be entity based and fulfil the one function of synchronising a set of asynchronous events that, when brought together in a rational order, update the entity.* Because the events are unpredictable and can simultaneously occur over a period of time, control programs require to be able to switch themselves and each other on, off or into a wait condition. They therefore require to monitor their own states. Additionally, because the events can be causally related and affect many entities, control programs can talk to control programs.

By contrast, traditional online data programs should be event based. Since events are standalone application data programs do not talk to each other. Events normally occur in a predictable sequence or within known limits. Being standalone they also occur discretely at an instance in time. Application programs do not therefore require on/off or wait condition switching mechanisms or the concept of program state.

The question of realtime events is answered. The attack event involved four pieces of equipment: the radar, the magazine, the gun loading mechanism and the gun firing mechanism. *Realtime events* are not just triggers as in conventional online systems, they *are triggers at the entity level.*

4.2.3 Integrating the Yourdon method

This section will not re-describe the Yourdon method. Rather it will detail how it was integrated into Information Engineering.

4.2.3.1 Dataflow diagrams

The Yourdon data flow diagram uses different symbols (for example data processes are circles rather than rectangles) and additional symbols (control processes). The additional symbols reflect the realtime component. Both types of symbols were converted to Information Engineering format. The symbol set is:

- Control stores
    These stores contain data about an event that has occurred or control commands (program stop, start, wait on an event etc.) between control processes and between control processes and data processes.

- Event flows
    Event flows report an event or give a command at a discrete point in time and have no data content. An event flow is an interrupt "pulse" type message between control processes, data processes and control stores. There are three types of event flows: a signal, an activation and a deactivation. A signal merely reports that an event has occurred. An activation is a command to start a process. A deactivation is a command to stop a process. Activations and deactivations contain no data.

- Dataflows
    Dataflows can be discrete or continuous. Discrete dataflows are associated with a variable or set of variables that is defined at discrete

points in time. A discrete dataflow corresponds exactly with a dataflow in Information Engineering dataflow diagrams. Continuous dataflows record the flow of a data value or set of values that flow continuously over time, for example a temperature gauge. The flow occurs between an external entity, data process or data store.

- Control process

  This is a process that accepts only event flows as input and produces only event flows as output. Input event flows may only be signals; output event flows may be any type: signals, activations and deactivations. It is the control process that contains the control logic to handle the sequencing of causally related asynchronous events. Control processes activate and deactivate data processes. A deactivated data process abandons any work in progress and restarts rather than resumes its function when next activated.

- Data process

  This is the standard process for batch and online processing, as recognised by Information Engineering. It can receive signals, discrete and continuous dataflows and activation and deactivation commands. It cannot issue activations and deactivations. It can issue signals to either a control process, control store or datastore and discrete dataflows to a datastore or external entity. Note that this last sentence states that there is no flow relationship to other data processes. This is totally in line with the concepts of event level processing and standalone events, such that data processes and resultant application programs do not talk to each other.

- Datastore

  This is the standard data store, as recognised by Information Engineering.

The usual ring approach described earlier in section 3.2.9.2 was followed in the drawing of realtime dataflow diagrams, as illustrated in figure 4.37. An example of a realtime dataflow diagram based on the port company application is illustrated in figure 4.38. The example reflects directly the ring structure and thereby adds clarity to interpretation. Note that the control processes and control stores are distinct from the data processes and data stores around them. The control processes are concerned with recognising an event and with synchronising an event with other events that are simultaneously but asynchronously occurring against an entity. An example is the control process Control Lorry. Various events are affecting the lorry—that the lorry is unavailable, the lorry is parked and a fork lift truck is related to the lorry.

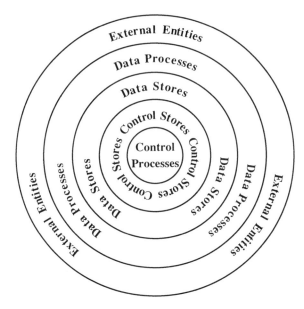

Figure 4.37   Realtime DFD rings

When the synchronisation has been accomplished by the control pro-
cess(es) then the appropriate data process(es) can be triggered for traditional
data processing. Control Lorry triggers Pallet MI, which undertakes the
appropriate data processing, in this case creating a machine instruction for
a fork lift truck to move a pallet. Note also the new "C" type control stores,
and the control flows only between control processes.

Continuous dataflows are not represented as they were not relevant to
the port company.

The dataflow diagram illustrates certain features of realtime systems not
found in traditional batch and online processing:

- A control process supports a particular equipment type, for example a
  fork lift truck.

- Control processes talk to control processes for the same equipment type
  and to control processes supporting related equipment types. For example
  the entity pallet machine instruction is related to lorry.

- Control processes can trigger data processes.

- Control processes are only triggered by other data or control processes.

- Data processes can trigger control processes.

- Data processes can update "C" control stores but not read from them.

- A control process must trigger a relevant data process, i.e. a data process that modifies the entity type the control process supports.

- External entities cannot trigger control processes.

- Control processes cannot access "D" type data stores.

- The control stores act as message repositories between data and control processes. As part of their event synchronisation task, control processes may require to "wait on" another event before proceeding. The messages about previously occurring events require to be stored temporarily until the "wait on" event occurs. For example, the Control Lorry control program requires to wait on for the event Lorry Arrive when the Lorry state is Not Available—see figure 4.39. Only then can the "wait on" Lorry Available message be deleted

4.2.3.2 The specification of control processes

The specification of the access and process logic of the control processes was undertaken by the use of state transition diagrams (STDs). Representative STDs for the control processes Control Lorry and Control Pallet Picking List on the realtime dataflow diagram in figure 4.38 are given in figures 4.39 and 4.41.

Figure 4.39 shows that a lorry alternates between being available, being parked, being busy and being not available. This is reflected in the supporting control program. The initial start point is that the lorry is available. A condition/event Lorry/FLT Related occurs, with three actions/effects—the data process Issue Pallet MI is triggered, the Control Pallet Picking List process is called with a PMI Issued message and the state of the lorry is changed from available to being used. The lorry could also change from being available to being used when the event Lorry Arrive occurs. In this case the action is to "wait on" another event of Lorry Parked. The lorry changes from being used to not available when the event Lorry Leave occurs. The lorry then reverts back to being available when the event Lorry Arrive occurs and the action is to "wait" on Lorry Available. In both cases where the action is to wait on the only affect is to change the state of the control program.

4.2.3.3 Continuous dataflow sampling

This is not difficult. All that is required is additional logic in the action diagrams. Sampling can easily be handled by using a timed sampling mechanism to test whether a threshold has been crossed or not. If a heating

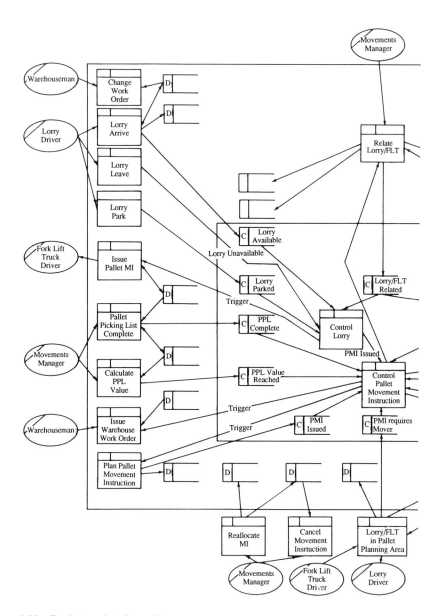

Figure 4.38   Realtime dataflow diagram

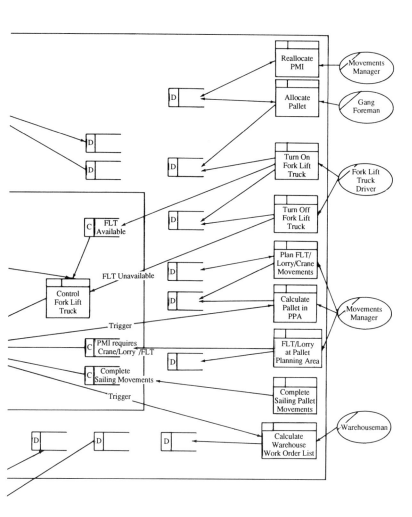

Figure 4.38   Realtime dataflow diagram

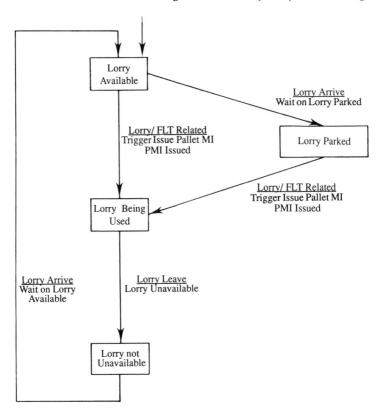

Figure 4.39   Control Lorry state transition diagram

radiator is being monitored to maintain a constant room temperature then the realtime application program re-triggers itself, by issuing its own transaction code to the message queue every *n* seconds, to sample the room temperature. If the threshold is crossing on an upwards temperature path then the logic is to switch the radiator off. If the threshold is crossing on a downward temperature path then the logic is to turn the radiator on.

4.2.3.4 Event recognition

Event recognition was the one problem area, because the Yourdon method, as described in the Ward and Mellor book "Structured Development for Real Time Systems" and confirmed by consultants at Yourdon UK Limited, does not contain an event recognition technique.

   Event recognition is a task for the control processes. Given that control processes are entity based it occurred to the author to use the entity life

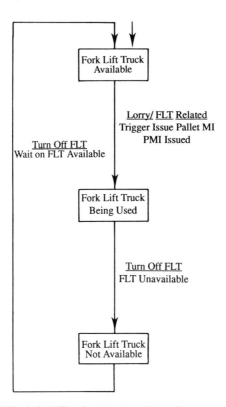

Figure 4.40   Control Fork Lift Truck state transition diagram

history technique (ELH), also entity based, as it used to be used in the SSADM structured design method.

In its previous incarnation ELHs used the posit, quit and admit facility. An event occurs which is not initially recognised for what it is. A posit assumption is made that an event updating the entity is recognised. Using the warship example the position is that the entity warship is under an attack event that is not initially recognised. It is therefore posited as a guided missile attack (the state of the warship control program is updated to missile attack). Processing continues as normal on this assumption. A set of causally related events are triggered on the missile attack assumption—an anti-missile missile is loaded (another event updating the state of the warship control program) and trained (another event updating the state of the warship control program). At this point a quit occurs as the originally posited event is now recognised as a civilian aircraft, the events that occurred since and dependent on the posit must be undone (detrain and unload the guided missile launcher) and an admit be made to proceed on the correctly recognised event.

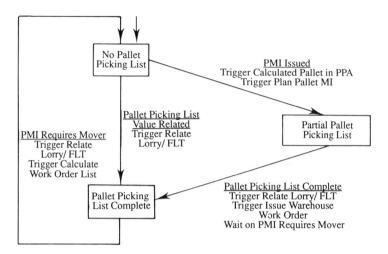

Figure 4.41 Pallet Movement Instruction state transition diagram

The quit could occur anywhere between the events recognise attack and train launcher. A record of any pre and post states of the database changes must be made from the time a posit is made, with the database table rows locked with an exclusive "X" lock, until the posit is confirmed or rejected. If the posit is quitted then the database must be returned to its pre-posit state condition. All changes made to the database from the time that the posit is assumed and the recognition that the posit is valid or wrong must be treated as a single logical unit of work, by being front-ended with a BEGIN statement and back-ended with a COMMIT statement. This ensures that the posited actions are either all successful if the posit is true or all backtracked if the posit is false. When all the pre-posit state changes have been restored the X locks can be released and the recognised event be executed as part of normal processing.

A representative ELH in figure 4.42 using posit, quits and admits illustrates this trail of near disaster. Note the use of parallel lives to handle asynchronous events.

Having drawn the warship event recognition structure the effects of the event (say train launcher) were added to the matching state transition diagram for the warship control program as actions for the corresponding condition event (trigger data process Train Launcher and change control program state) and recorded as a new program state (launcher loaded to launcher trained).

4.2.3.5 Combining the control processes

The control processes linked by control flows require to be combined to generate a single control application program. The link is the control flow

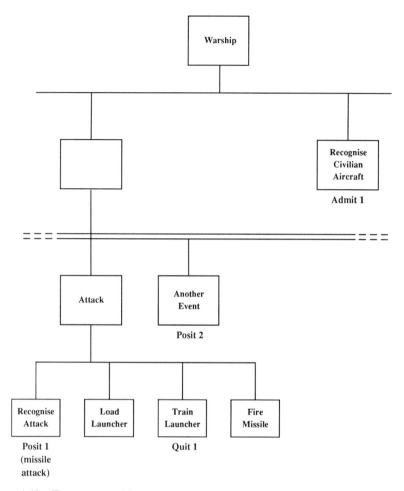

Figure 4.42 Event recognition

between two control processes. This means that the related STDs per control process also require to be combined. Since control processes are entity based at least two entities (master–detail) are involved. As described earlier such related entities are, for example, lorry and lorry movement instruction. The three control processes Control Lorry, Control Fork Lift Truck and Control Pallet Movement Instruction need to be combined as whenever Control Lorry or Control Fork Lift Truck are triggered they in turn trigger Pallet Movement Instruction. The action Trigger Issue Pallet Movement Instruction in the Control Lorry process from the event Lorry/Fork Lift Truck Related links Control Fork Lift Truck and Control Lorry to Control Pallet Movement Instruction. This can be seen in the combined STD in figure 4.43.

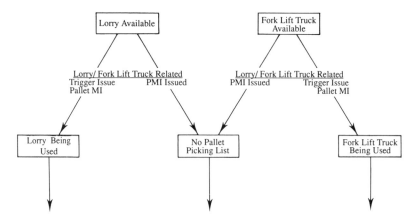

Figure 4.43   Combined state transition diagram

4.2.3.6 *The remaining techniques*

The remaining logical design techniques of Information Engineering, such as entity relationship modelling, relational data analysis, dialogue flow diagramming, visual layout design and action diagrams, were untouched.

PHYSICAL DESIGN TECHNIQUES

The Information Engineering techniques of preliminary data structure design, performance assessment, procedure design and software structure design were untouched. The program design techniques, of course, require to support the data processes as represented in the figure 4.38 dataflow diagram and the database design to the "D" type data stores.

The realtime component was added by:

- using the combined STDs as the basis of specifying the logic of the realtime control programs and converting the combined STD into action diagram code. If it was necessary to split a control program across processors then the technique described in the Yourdon method was used;

- defining the control stores as standard data tables;

- removing concurrency from the STDs. The STDs pay no attention to the concurrency of processes and assume multiple processes can run simultaneously. Unfortunately this is not always true. A processor can only execute a single program "task" at a time. Tasks can be truly concurrent with each other if they run on different processors or on a multi-processor capable of running several tasks simultaneously. The state changes in an STD (which may be a combined equipment type level STD from several entity level STDs) must be converted into a sequence. In figures 4.39–4.41 the three entity level STDs are already sequenced. The combined STD in figure 4.43 is not. The event Lorry/Fork Lift Truck Related triggers two processes simultaneously—trigger Issue Pallet Movement Instruction and PMI Issued, the former a control process and the latter a data process. The technique for removing concurrency is described in the Ward and Mellor book.

4.3 CONVERSATIONAL PROCESSING

Although facilities for conversational online dialogue have long been available they have not often been used. The author has only come across a few applications where it has been necessary to have a conversation with the computer.

Conversational processing is different from online processing. With online processing the screen must remain on for the duration of the dialogue. If the screen is cleared or turned off the information on the screen is lost. With conversational processing it is possible to clear or turn off the screen and have the software automatically store the relevant data on the screen in temporary data stores in processor main memory or on disk and to redisplay the information when the online transaction is restarted and/or to use the screen itself as a data store of previous screen displays.

The and/or indicates two types of conversations—discontinuous and continuous. Discontinuous conversational processing occurs where the screen can be cleared/turned off and the dialogue be interrupted for an indefinite period of time. The information relevant to continuing the conversation is stored in main memory or on disk to be recalled on conversation restart. There is nothing sophisticated in this. Discontinuous conversational dialogue is merely an extension of online dialogue. Continuous conversation reflects the latest technology in the use of X-windows/overlay screens. The conversation begins with a full screen display and then, as further data requests are made, a set of sub-screens are overlaid on each other. The previous screens are redisplayed as the conversation is reversed.

Conversational processing is nothing more than a "sexy" form of online dialogue and introduces nothing fundamentally new to online processing. Information Engineering is therefore an entirely appropriate method to use, requiring only minor enhancement to cater for this enhanced form of the man/machine interface to a computer.

4.3.1 Discontinuous conversations

The technology for this has long been available. IBM's IMS/DC and CICS teleprocessing monitors have been able to support discontinuous conversations for over a decade, IMS/DC with its scratch pad facility and CICS with its temporary work area facility. It is therefore surprising that discontinuous conversations have not been recognised as an integral part of online systems, particularly as it is so easy to recognise, define and support.

The port company once again provides an example. Lorries loaded with the general cargo regularly brought loaded pallets into and out of the ports. The requirement was that the pallets be inspected to ensure they contained what was detailed in the custom manifest for the lorry. There were often numerous lorries. The inspection process was therefore a major task. Several inspectors would work from various start points along the queue of lorries and work in opposite directions towards each other. The start point of inspection for each inspector was to identify the pallets to be inspected and already inspected and the direction of working along the lorries. Each inspector made a note of where the inspection process had progressed to. This information was loaded into the company database.

Inevitably such a major task incurred many hours of work. Not only were natural breaks necessary but the inspection process could well span several shifts. Whenever an interruption occurred for whatever reason the inspector would record the last inspection point against a pallet with all relevant supporting information, to be stored in a scratch pad, prior to switching off the terminal. At a later point in time the original inspector or a replacement would return. The original inspector may well have forgotten what progress had been made and certainly the replacement inspector would require to obtain all source information regarding progress made by the predecessor. It was therefore necessary to have redisplayed the information relevant to the continuing conversation as at the point when it was switched off. The information stored in the scratch pad would be retrieved automatically and displayed on the terminal. The inspection process would continue as normal. By this mechanism it was able to support an inspection process that could incur n interruptions through natural breaks and shift changes.

4.3.2 Continuous conversations

The port company movements planner required to pass an integrated series of questions about the function of yard planning. A set of screens regarding the layout of the general cargo planning area, the cell layout of a vessel, the pallets to be loaded and unloaded onto/from the vessel, planned pallet movements etc., was required. Each screen required to be displayed in overlay form on a large high resolution graphics screen on an intelligent workstation. The overlays could be displayed and related to each other in any order against a master screen of the layout of a vessel and/or the container terminal area. The layout screen could be split to show both layouts in either reduced-to-fit mode or in partial layout with select-and-zoom mode.

It was also necessary, because the yard planning function was a major task (the planning for the loading of a vessel could take several days), to make the continuous conversation discontinuous as well—the screen could be switched off, typically at the end of an evening shift, for full information recall in the morning. No problem was found.

4.3.3 Enhancements to Information Engineering

The logical design techniques were enhanced as follows:

4.3.3.1 Dataflow diagrams

The business requirement that required an online conversation was treated as normal but with the lettering CONV in the heading alongside the process reference number. The conversational process required to access a new type of data store, namely a "C" type conversational store. An example of the dataflow diagram for the conversational processes for inspecting pallets of cargo on the lorries is illustrated in figure 4.44. It shows that a conversational process can access both conversational and data stores and be dynamically related to a realtime process. The control process could send trigger signal messages to the Check Lorry processes, which were treated as far as the control process was concerned as normal data processes. The conversational process could send signal messages to the control process.

4.3.3.2 Composite entity relationship diagram

Data definitions are undertaken against the ERD model. The ERD is therefore the correct place to record the data requirements of the conversations at their interrupt points. Although the ERD data model itself does not require modification the definition of the conversational data to be recorded in the scratch pad needs to be defined. The information required in the port example included pallet number of the last pallet inspected, status of inspection, any comments, direction of inspection, type of last inspection and previous inspector number and name. The conversational attributes were defined in exactly the same way as data attributes in an entity.

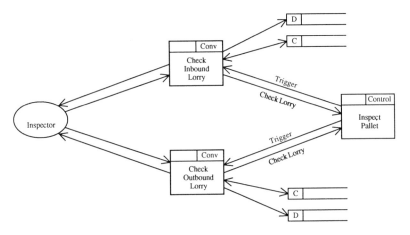

Figure 4.44   Discontinuous conversation

It was also necessary to record the number of conversations that could be outstanding at any one point in time. The maximum number of lorries that could be inspected simultaneously was 4 and it was assumed that up to 6 inspectors could be inspecting a given queue of lorries. It was assumed that the inspection process would continue without interruption for two hours at a time and that the period of time that the conversation would be closed for any interruption would be some 30 minutes. At any one time there could be up to 24 inspectors working. The interruptions to inspection could occur at any time, thus one quarter of the inspectors would not be working. This one quarter would require a conversational record to be stored in the scratch pad. It was necessary to allow for an average 6 conversational records, with a doubling to cater for peak conversations. Each conversation record was some 85 bytes in size. The scratch pad area needed to be about 1K in size. The total scratch pad area for the port as a whole was set at 3K to cater for other conversations.

4.3.3.3 Action diagrams

The action diagram document did not require any modification. All that needed to be taken into account was that when beginning the specification of logic the first access to the message queue is to the scratch pad to retrieve the conversational data. If the scratch pad for the transaction ID is empty then no conversation has occurred and the next access to the message queue is to retrieve the screen display information. When the online transaction is closing down, because a closure of the conversation is required, the last message to the message queue is to record the relevant conversational details of the screen data contents for input to the scratch pad. If it is a normal end of online processing then the scratch pad does not require to be updated with a conversational record.

4.3.3.4 Database optimisation

If the teleprocessing monitor software is able to support conversational processing then all that needs to be specified on disk is a scratch pad area to act as a repository of all conversational records. If the teleprocessing monitor does not support conversational processing and conversations are a requirement of the application then it is a case of "do it yourself". This is not difficult. Treat the conversational scratch pad records as standard data tables, one table per conversation. The table is populated with temporary records of conversations in a state of interrupt. When the conversation is interrupted a conversational record is inserted into the conversational table; when the conversation is resumed the conversational record is retrieved so as to be displayed and then deleted from the scratch pad.

Each conversational record requires a key. In the case of the port authority it was the inspection job number. The first call any conversational application program made was to access the relevant conversational table for the specified inspection job number. This access occurred before any other accesses to the terminal message queue and database table rows. The last access call on a conversational interrupt was to insert a conversational record with the same job number into the appropriate conversational table.

The user of the database optimisation technique required to make no modifications other than to take into account the extra resource utilisation overheads on the processor and I/Os incurred when accessing the conversational tables.

4.3.3.5 Screen design

No change was necessary to support discontinuous conversations.

The mechanism the author has used to support the adoption of X-windows/overlay screens used in continuous conversations is a modified entity life history diagram. An example of this is illustrated in figure 4.45. The same ELH drawing conventions are used. The business requirement replaces the entity and the boxes at the bottom of the structure represent screens supporting the business requirement. In a continuous conversation some of the screens may not be overlaid and are represented as the first level boxes below the business requirement box. Such screens are screens 1, 2 and 3. If a screen can be overlaid then these are treated in exactly the same way as event clusters. The overlays can occur in sequence or in any order. The former type consists of CC1 screens 1–4, this last screen being

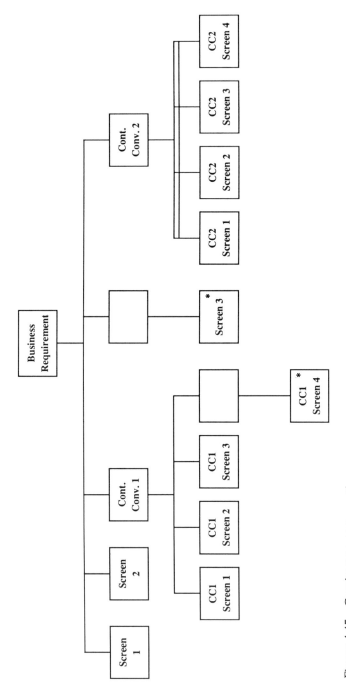

Figure 4.45   Continuous conversation

able to iterate within the conversation. The latter type are CC2 screens 1–4. The lack of sequence is handled by parallel lives. The logic implicit in the modified ELH diagram was coded in the action diagram.

It was implicitly assumed that if the overlay screens were in sequence then any screen cancellation incurred would be by reversing the continuous conversation. If the overlays were not in sequence then the cancellation of a continuous conversation could also be in any order.

The only other enhancement to the technique was to record whether the overlay screens would be in a fixed or floating position, their size, and their icon representation if they were minimised. The position of a floating screen would depend on current screen display conditions, which merely require to be detailed in the system processing column of the dialogue design form.

5

ADDITIONAL DATA PROCESSING ENVIRONMENTS FOR INFORMATION ENGINEERING—EXPERT SYSTEMS AND OBJECT ORIENTED DESIGN

5.1 THE COMMON LINK

Object oriented and knowledge based expert systems are data processing environments that will have an increasing impact on application design and development. Many leading industry thinkers believe that object oriented design is the next "leap forward" for the 1990s as relational technology was for the 1980s.

The author is convinced that the future of object orientation will be more significant and much more beneficial than relational database. For various reasons, the details of which are not relevant to this book, the author has little time for the claims made for relational technology, particularly as regards non-procedural data access. The need to know in SQL the tables in which the data attributes are held and the relationships between the tables when undertaking a join is not non-procedural access. Much is claimed and little is delivered. Such is not the situation as regards object orientation.

As regards expert systems the author was a considerable sceptic but, as a result of studying the subject and supporting technology, is now a total convert to the practical benefits of the technology to both users and system developers.

Much marketing hype is made about a number of database trends. One hears different marketing people talking about object oriented databases, semantic/knowledge based databases, active databases and databases that can handle complex objects. This is particularly the case with object oriented and expert systems technology.

The technical facilities and their relationships to the trends are illustrated below. It shows that there are many facilities that are common to both types of technology, although expert systems uses only a subset of that used by object oriented technology. The facilities listed will be described as you read this chapter.

The reasons why these apparently distinct trends (certainly distinct and certainly trends if one accepts the marketing hype) are considered jointly is because they use much common technology. Indeed, it has been said that an expert system is an object oriented system without procedures/methods and that an object oriented system is an expert system without a knowledge inference mechanism. A product called GOLDWORKS from Goldhill Computers Inc. contains facilities for both expert and object oriented systems, and is therefore real life physical proof of the high degree of technical overlap of these currently distinct data processing environments. The technical facilities and their relationships to the trend are:

Object Orientation				Expert System
OO Database	OO Programs			
X	X	•	Semantic nets/class object model	X
		•	Rules	X
X		•	Frames	X
X	X	•	Procedures/methods	
X	X	•	Daemons	X
X		•	Conflict resolution	X
X	X	•	Property inheritance	X
	X	•	Late binding	
	X	•	Encapsulation	
	X	•	Message passing	
	X	•	Polymorphism	
	X	•	Genericity	

The facilities that have been marked as being used by these new data processing environments are those that are specific to supporting the underlying concepts on which the environments are based.

Both expert and object oriented systems make use of facilities more usually associated with the other. Expert systems make use of the facility of procedures/methods (a facility very necessary for object orientation) within frames, because it has been found useful to use methods under certain circumstances. However, methods are not necessary to support the concept underpinning expert systems. In reverse, object based systems make use of the rule facility, something very much associated with expert systems, but rules are not necessary to support the concept underlying object orientation.

The technology of expert systems and object orientation will be described separately, each followed by an assessment of their potential impact on Information Engineering. Expert systems are considered first as they have been established for a longer time and the technology has "bedded down". There are also several established structured design methods, so that the design techniques are perhaps better understood.

The author does not consider that this assessment of these two technologies is exhaustive. The subjects of expert systems and object oriented design are still in their infancy, notwithstanding all the work that has already been done. The physical technology is new and only now gaining appreciation and acceptance of its potential. As usual, and not unexpectedly, the logical design techniques are some way behind the physical technology. Structured methods for both trends are either in development (GEMINI) or new release (KADS and STAGES for expert systems and HOOD for object orientation) with frequent and major upgrade versions being issued.

This chapter is designed, following a description of the technologies, for the author to add his "two pennies worth" of suggested enhancements to Information Engineering. The suggestions are in line with the policy stated at the beginning to chapter 3. No attempt is made to detail how the enhancements could be incorporated into Information Engineering where worked case study examples to prove the enhancements are not available.

5.2 EXPERT SYSTEMS

5.2.1 Expert system concept

Expert systems have the unique ability to store and access knowledge as well as data. This means that they can represent expertise regarding a particular application domain, for example how to service a car or how to diagnose an illness. Expert systems can therefore be relevant to different types of computer applications from those which have traditionally been developed. Expert systems are particularly suited to those applications that require expertise to solve problems. Traditionally data processing has been for those applications where dumb data is presented to users for them, as homo sapiens, to interpret. Expert systems, by contrast, store knowledge and can therefore offer advice as well as present data. This is their unique feature. *It is the concept of knowledge and resultant advice provision that separates expert system processing from traditional batch and online processing.* They can therefore "assist" and "advise" in such tasks as diagnosis, planning, design and interpretation.

Notwithstanding the many, sometimes esoteric, definitions of knowledge defined by the intellectual community, in an IT environment the definition is much simpler. *Knowledge is a meaningful association of two or more facts or of a fact(s) and a command(s).*

A fact is composed of three elements, a subject, a relationship and a property. These three elements are known as a triple. A triple example could be "Today (subject) is (relationship) Friday (property)". The subject and property, which could either be data or logic, are dumb information when considered in a standalone context. In the triple example today and Friday are dumb data. It is only when the dumb information is brought together as a triple that it becomes a meaningful fact.

Another fact could be that Friday is a pay day. The property of the first fact is the subject of the second fact. These two facts can therefore be combined to create some knowledge, that one gets paid today because today is Friday. Other dumb data could be the days of Monday and Tuesday. It is not until Monday and Tuesday are triple linked with a total of seven different days and associated to form the concept of a week that the individual facts become more meaningful. When related together these facts become knowledge—there is a thing called a week, it is composed of seven days and one gets paid once a week.

Clearly the facts have relevance to a specific application, in this case the domain of time in a western context, whereby a week begins on Monday and ends on Sunday. In a different cultural context a week can begin on a different day and even be of a different timespan.

The technical term used by some expert system products to describe a fact is an assertion.

The facts can be related meaningfully together to form knowledge via either rules or semantic nets. The rules are usually in the form of "If condition A then conclusion B". The rule could be "If today is Monday (one fact) then tomorrow is Tuesday" (another fact) or "If today is sunny (a fact) then go sunbathing" (a command), the meaningful association between the facts and command being the "if ... then ... clause".

There can be multiple conditions and conclusions to a rule. The conditions can be connected by ANDs and/or ORs, but the conclusions can only be connected by ANDs. There could thus be a rule that states "If condition A and B or A and C then conclusion D and E". An interpretation of the rule states that if either the conditions A and B are true or A and C are true then the conclusions D and E can be drawn.

It is also possible to record facts as semantic descriptions—"employee is a person" (one fact) and "person is a mammal" (another fact)— the meaningful association between the two facts being a common subject/property symbol, in this case person. A complete network of such descriptions can be created.

Rule facts are the knowledge representation mechanism that enable expert systems to provide advice. *Rule facts are the active component and can be regarded as knowledge logic. Semantic facts are the passive component, play a supporting role to the rules, and can be regarded as knowledge data.* Note that the classical physical division of a computer system into data and logic, as illustrated in figure 2.3, is still preserved.

Both types of facts can be used in a standalone manner to provide knowledge. The knowledge is ascertained by the inference software. More usually the two types of facts are used to support each other. The inference software enables the knowledge logic to access the knowledge data to infer yet further knowledge.

With the wide range of facilities now available the term logic has acquired several meanings. In the context of this book there are two major classifications—procedural logic and declarative logic.

Procedural logic is that which has been used since the beginning of computing and is conventionally associated with the code in application programs. The logic is positional and composed of individual statements of action. It is positional in that the statements of action only have relevance in the context of their position to other statements of action that precede and succeed them. Furthermore, the logic has to be complete and in the correct order for it to work. The statment of action has no value in its own right.

There is also a sub-division into access logic and process logic. The access logic is the commands that are used to access the information-base. Here again there is a sub-division into record-at-a-time (Read, Write, Update and Delete) of the pre-relational file handlers and the set access (such as Select, Union and Difference) of the relational file handlers. The process logic is for the pre and post massaging of the database accessed data. The commands are sequence, selection, iteration and branching.

Declarative logic is composed of non-positional statements of truth in the form of rules. As the rules are statements of truth they have value and can therefore be used in a standalone context. The rules are non-positional because they are related implicitly together by symbolic matching, with the conclusion suffix of one rule matching the condition prefix of another rule. The software can thereby search for the next rule in the chain of logic no matter where the rule is located. Thus the code can be entered in any order.

Declarative code does not have to be complete. There can be gaps in the logic and the inference software that processes the rules will attempt to "file the gap." The GENERIS example in section 5.2.9.1 of declarative logic includes such a gap and yet produces a full and complete information output result. Clearly the greater the gap the greater the imprecision of the result. The code also includes access and process logic constructs. It thus means that only one construct need be used for the writing of logic instead of the 13 or more required for procedural logic.

An example of the other representation of knowledge (relationship of a fact(s) to a command(s)) can best be illustrated by an example of a rule. The command component has to be in the conclusion of the rule. The rule is "If the date is 31 and the month is January, then issue monthly salary payment." The command is the instruction to issue a payment.

So we have a situation where knowledge can be:

- if a fact(s) is(are) true then some more fact(s);
- if a fact(s) is(are) true then do something;

Knowledge can be pitched at any level of detail. For example, it could be either universally applicable or specific to an application domain. Universal knowledge is a meaningful association of facts that are known to be always true. For example (income + assets) − (expenditure + liabilities) = wealth. Such knowledge is universal. A piece of knowledge specific to an application domain could be that overtime pay = standard pay × 1.25.

Expert systems are able to support new types of questions. By accessing dumb data in a database traditional computer systems have been able to answer such questions as "How much have I spent?" It is up to *homo sapiens* to ascertain the significance of the information presented. The storage of knowledge could be, for example, in the form of a rule that states "If known monthly outgoings are less than £1,000 and the month day is less than 10 and monthly income is greater than £3,000 then likely to have money in the bank", purely because one is at the beginning of the monthly pay cycle. One could therefore pose the question "Should I spend?" Certainly is the advice, if the three conditions to the rule are satisfied. By being able to store data and knowledge one can pose a much more sophisticated question such as "Should I spend money and how much?" The response to this query will be advisory. If the three conditions are satisfied the advice could further be "Yes, you can and you have this much in the bank and these are your bills outstanding and these are your standing orders still to be paid. The remaining monies are *£nnn*".

5.2.2 Knowledge acquisition and construction

There are two complementary ways in which knowledge can be acquired. First, topics must be studied formally, as in a school or when one attends lectures and reads textbooks. As a result of such study knowledge is grouped as perspective and general laws. Successful students emerge from courses in accounting or mathematics with a firm grasp of the terms and laws that constitute the formal theories and accepted principles of their discipline. Principles and laws are useful in explaining and justifying why a solution succeeds or fails, but they are often of little help in finding a solution in the first place. General laws usually fail to indicate exactly how one should proceed when faced with a specific problem.

Knowledge can also be acquired by means of experience or by learning from a mentor. In this case the results are different. Domain/application specific facts are learnt first. Experience, or a mentor, usually teaches the students to rely on rules-of-thumb to perform tasks or solve problems. Students also acquire competence by learning domain/application specific theories. Thus, accountants who learn from a mentor behave as if they know accountancy theory even though they may not. Knowledge acquired from experience results in heuristics. Heuristics are rules-of-thumb that prune the thought process to a manageable size. They tend to focus the attention *on a few key patterns*. Compiled heuristic knowledge is well organised and indexed. It gives an edge when requiring to solve numerous daily problems.

The sequence of learning usually starts at school and from reading books. This baseline is then applied in a real world and is enriched with the rules-of-thumb that are obtained from mentors and experience. The prescriptive knowledge laws are then gradually converted into heuristic knowledge rules.

There are two methods of expert system knowledge construction. The deductive, or more correctly knowledge elicitation, method requires a knowledge engineer skilled in the use of an expert system product and an expert user skilled in the application domain to build the knowledgebase about the application domain incrementally, knowledge piece by knowledge piece. Knowledge elicitation systems require human creation of the knowledgebase. The inductive method, by contrast, can use software to generate knowledge rules based on database examples. The basic principle is that the software generalises from the particular. For example an algorithm could be written that if 95% of 1,000 records read show that managers managing departments with departmental turnover greater than £250,000 have a status of senior, then one can conclude and generate a knowledge rule that states "if manager manages department and department has turnover greater than £250,000 then status is senior."

Clearly, while inductive rule generation is a great labour saving device, there is a risk in such a mechanistic approach, as it may not take account of exceptions that often occur in an application. An exception could be that a senior manager has been appointed to rejuvenate a department in distress, with a turnover of only £100,000. It is usually therefore found that inductive software is a front-end to generate a set of rules, which can then be vetted by the knowledge engineer and expert user.

5.2.3 Expert system components

The basic software architecture of an expert system is illustrated in figure 5.1. There are three main components—the knowledgebase, the inference engine and the man/machine interface. The knowledgebase stores the various ways of defining knowledge, such as rule facts and semantic facts and the dumb data traditionally associated with user data stored in the database. The data component of the knowledgebase could well be stored in a separate file handler, typically relational, with the definitions of knowledge held separately in specialised expert system software.

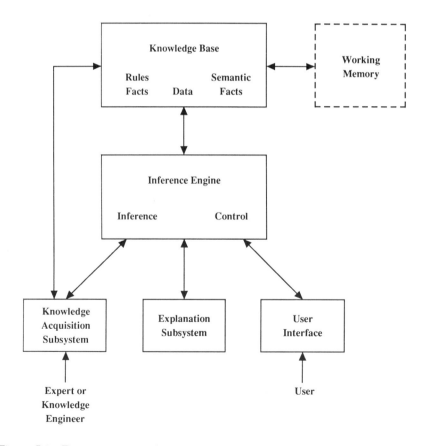

Figure 5.1   Expert system architecture

The inference engine is the software that executes against the knowledgebase. The engine has two prime functions, inference and control. Inference is primarily composed of three main tasks, rule processing, usually by a technique called *modus ponens*, reasoning with uncertainty and conflict resolution. As the reasoning is being executed during a consultation process with a user further facts/assertions are constructed and held as temporary working storage in the processor main memory or disk.

Modus ponens states that when A is known to be true and if a rule states "If A then B" it is valid to conclude that B is also true. Stated differently, when we discover that the conditions of a rule are true we are entitled to believe the conclusions. An example of *modus ponens* could be if you know "If today is Monday then tomorrow is Tuesday" and today is Monday then you can conclude tomorrow is Tuesday.

A second implication of *modus ponens* (and many knowledge based systems depend entirely on this rule) is that certain implications that are valid cannot be drawn. For example, another rule of knowledge states that if B is known to be false, and if there is a rule "If A then B", then it is valid to conclude A is false. This rule is called *modus tollens*. An example of *modus tollens* could be "If Joe Bloggs has a tattoo with a romantic message, then Joe Bloggs has a girlfriend." However, a given fact in the database data of the knowledgebase is that Joe Bloggs has no girlfriend. There is therefore a new fact, by implication, that Joe Bloggs does not actually have a tattoo. This conclusion, as seems obvious to *homo sapiens*, cannot be reached by most expert systems. The common mechanism, therefore, for deriving new rule facts and semantic facts is *modus ponens*. It is a simple intuitively appealing way to conduct reasoning.

In conventional programming we expect that all required information is provided before computation can take place. It makes no sense to try and balance an account with missing numbers. In knowledge programming this is not necessarily the case. It is believed that some of the financial transactions are not accurate or even lost. An inference engine must therefore be able to handle incomplete or unknown or erroneous information.

Incomplete information can sometimes be handled by uncertainty factors. Unknown information is handled by allowing rules to fail when information necessary to evaluate the conditions of these rules is simply unavailable. The results, of course, depend on the exact nature of the conditions. If the conditions are connected to each other by AND then all must be evaluated as true before the rule conclusion can succeed. In this case if the user or knowledgebase answers "unknowing" to any part of the conditions the rule fails. If, however, the conditions are connected by OR then one piece of unknown information need not preclude the rule from succeeding. In the second case the rule may succeed even though the user or knowledgebase answered "unknowing" to a question related to only one condition of the rule. Furthermore a condition could be satisfied even though it is less than certain, for example, the condition that Joe Bloggs has a girlfriend is only 80% certain. This condition uncertainty would propagate to the conclusion. The final inference process is conflict resolution. As a user builds a knowledgebase, using whatever knowledge representation mechanism is appropriate, so the user may, perhaps wittingly, make statements that are or appear to be contradictory. For example, there could be a rule defined by a civil servant that states, based on a law passed by parliament, that persons above 80 years of age are not allowed to buy a car. But at the same time another rule defined by a sales director states that anybody over 18 years of age can buy a car. Such conflicts need to be resolved.

The control function of the inference engine is concerned with rule processing (either forward or backward chaining) and ascertaining the rule access mechanism (usually depth first or breadth first) with monotonic or non-monotonic reasoning. The rule access and chaining mechanisms are described later in this session, with worked examples.

Inference engines can be distinguished as to whether they support monotonic or non-monotonic reasoning. In a monotonic reasoning system all values concluded for a property (property is an expert system buzzword meaning an attribute/data item) remain true for the duration of a consultation session with the user/knowledgebase. Facts that become true remain true and the amount of true information in the system grows steadily or monotonically. These temporary facts (or assertions as they are sometimes called) are stored in the working memory component of the expert system software.

In a non-monotonic reasoning system facts that are true at one time may be retracted later. Planning is a good example of this problem type that demands non-monotonic reasoning. In the early stages of a planning problem it makes sense to make an assumption to go a certain way. Later as information continues to come in it may turn out that an early decision was wrong. The subsequent decisions and consequences need to be retracted (shades of the event recognition problem in a realtime system). Changing the value of a single attribute to retract a conclusion is not difficult. Tracking down all the implications that are based on an initial assumption is difficult and can be a resource hungry process.

Most expert systems marketed today support monotonic reasoning, but allow only carefully controlled types of non-monotonic reasoning.

The third main component in expert system software is the man/machine interface, for the construction of the knowledgebase through knowledge acquisition and for user query/consultation facilities for which advice will ultimately be offered. In knowledge acquisition the expert user describes the expertise appropriate to an application and the knowledge engineer records this as rule and semantic facts as appropriate.

The querying of an expert system is different from traditional processing. With traditional processing a query is raised and a reply made and that is the end of it. In expert systems there is a conversation-like consultation with typically a query and answer session. This is because of the underlying technology. At the end of the consultation chain of rule condition based queries and answers (which may be invisibly undertaken automatically by the inference engine obtaining the answers for the rule conditions from the database component of the knowledgebase) advice is offered.

5.2.4 The knowledgebase

The knowledgebase is composed of two kinds of information—the dumb data as entered by users and stored in a database, and factual knowledge entered by the expert user and knowledge engineer. The data and knowledge are usually stored and accessed by a conventional, typically relational, file handler.

There are three main ways in which knowledge is currently defined— rules, semantic nets and frames. All three are structured as triples. These three facilities are described below.

5.2.4.1 Rules

The most widely used mechanism of the first generation type expert systems, such as CRYSTAL, is to represent knowledge in the form of rules. Rules are the basic execution instructions for the inference engine. The rule structure is usually in the form of "If condition(s) then conclusion(s)". A typical rule could be "If today is Monday then tomorrow is Tuesday". The structure is sometimes reversed. "Tomorrow is Tuesday if today is Monday".

Each rule is a declarative statement of some universal or application domain truth. Each rule therefore has value in its own right. A rule can therefore be standalone. A rule can also be linked with other rules relevant to an application domain to form a ruleset. A ruleset is a group of rules for a particular application domain task (a problem-to-solve process in centralised data processing) for which domain relevant advice is sought. A domain could be how to service a car. Domains can be decomposed into many tasks and sub-tasks and hence rulesets within rulesets. Car servicing tasks could be how to change a tyre, check the oil and maintain the electrics, each requiring expertise and advice.

In order to ascertain if the condition(s) or conclusion(s) is true, the inference engine will access the knowledgebase first and if the answer cannot be ascertained there then usually the condition(s) or sometimes the conclusion(s) is posed as a question to the user. If the user cannot provide the answer a default value is used, that is a rule without a condition.

5.2.4.2 Rule types

There can be four types of rules—inference rules, action rules, daemon rules and truth maintenance rules.

An inference rule is a query against the knowledgebase and makes no changes to the knowledgebase. They are therefore passive, merely imparting knowledge "if condition fact(s) then conclusions fact(s)". A worked example of a set of inference rules is given in section 5.2.9.

An action rule is a rule where the conclusion is an executive statement to do something. The form of the rule is therefore "If condition(s) facts then conclusion command." For example an action rule could be "If the date is 31 and the month is January, then issue monthly salary payment". This conclusion command could well be a procedure call to a conventional application program, which in this case not only issues the monthly salary payment but also updates the database to record the event. Inference rules and action rules can be grouped into rulesets.

Daemon rules are like "gremlins" continuously running (in a virtual context) in the background waiting for something to happen. A daemon rule is similar to a database trigger found in more modern relational file handlers. They are an expensive form of knowledge execution, for they are tested as to whether they should be "fired" on every fact evaluation of the knowledgebase. They are free standing rules and do not relate to any ruleset. They are globally applicable to all the application domains. Their prime role is to interrupt a domain ruleset access sequence in order to undertake some action.

Daemon rules are identified with a slightly different syntax. The IF precursor to an inference or action rule is typically replaced by a WHEN precursor. For example, "When weather is sunny then display sunny weather options screen". Any inference or action rule that has a conclusion that the weather is sunny would automatically invoke the daemon rule, which would be fired and display the sunny weather option screen. The remainder of the ruleset is then processed, if appropriate.

Truth maintenance can also be supported by using the rule facility and, again, the rules are free standing and continuously running, but this time passively. No changes to the knowledgebase and no interrupt to the ruleset processing are made. A typical truth rule could be "When there are no clouds and it is daytime then the sun is shining". It is obvious that such a rule is universally recognised to be true. Like daemon rules truth rules are usually applicable to an entire enterprise application.

Daemon and truth rules are controlled entirely by the inference engine and, unlike the inference and action rules, require no human intervention.

5.2.4.3 Ruleset access strategies

There is one ruleset for each goal/task for which advice is sought. Each ruleset will have one to n rules. The rules in the ruleset can be mapped as a hierarchical structure as illustrated in figure 5.2. Starting at the top it shows that the condition(s) of rule A point to the conclusion(s) of rules B and C, whose conclusion(s) separately point back to rule A. The condition(s) of rule C points to the conclusion(s) of rules B and F. The conclusion(s) of rule C points back to the condition(s) of rules F, A and B.

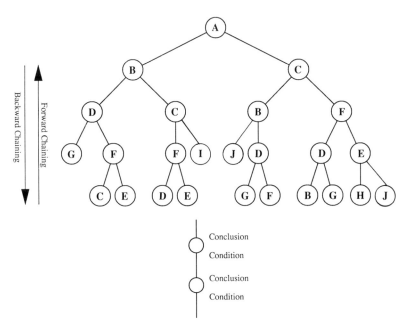

Figure 5.2   Ruleset structure

Backward chaining is down the structure from the single goal rule (the rule with the conclusion matching the goal) and forward chaining is up the structure beginning from any rule with conditions matching the initial set of assertions/facts. It is therefore evident that, although backward chaining has the advantage of starting from a single entry point, in this case rule A, there is the disadvantage that multiple "dead end" rule paths may be accessed before the proper advice is presented. It may be that the rule paths that contain the advice appropriate to the consultation with the expert system is A, C, F, D, G but the rules to the left of the path in the diagram have to be accessed first. Forward chaining has the disadvantage of multiple rule entry points, up to one per initial assertion, but the strong advantage of fixed and efficient access paths towards the goal once the entry point(s) has been established. There is no chance of "dead ends".

Note that the hierarchical structure does not preclude the rules within a ruleset being a network. For example, rule F is related to "higher" rules C and D as well as to "lower" rules C, E and D.

What the hierarchical structure of the rulesets also shows is the access overheads in the ruleset, for both forward and backward chaining. Beginning with backward chaining the conclusion(s) of rule A points to the condition(s) of rules B and C. Rule C points to rules B and F and so on. It also shows that forward chaining can begin on any of the rules C, E, D, G, F, B, H and J. If the entry point was solely to rule H then the rule chain would only be E, F, C and A. If, however, the entry point was E the two rule access path options would be E, F, C, B, A and E, F, D, B, A.

There are a number of search strategies, such as breadth first, depth first, hill climbing and best first. The two most widely used are breadth first and depth first. If the search strategy is breadth first access starts at the first rule appropriate to the goal and then access to the remaining rules is by searching all the rules at the next level down in the ruleset hierarchy before proceeding to the rules in the next lower level in the hierarchy. Depth first, by contrast, accesses the first rule as above but then proceeds down the leftmost rule path and progressively migrates to the rightmost rule path. In breadth first access the sequence would be A-B-C-D-C-B-F-G etc. With depth first access the sequence would be A-B-D-G-F-C-E-C-F etc. Both access strategies are illustrated in figure 5.3.

The most commonly used access strategy is depth first with backward chaining.

5.2.4.4 Ruleset access mechanisms

A ruleset defines knowledge as rule facts for a particular task in an application domain. For example, there could be n rulesets each of n rules to describe the knowledge and expertise required for the tasks of servicing a car. There could be any number of rulesets within the application, for example how to change a tyre, how to diagnose an electrical fault, how to tune the carburettor. A complete hierarchy of rulesets can be obtained. Wherever advice is required in an application domain there must be at least one ruleset.

Within the ruleset access strategy as defined above rules can be chained in a forward and backward direction. The basic mechanism is that rules in a ruleset are chained together via symbolic values with the conclusion(s) *pattern matching* the condition(s) of another rule. Using this symbolic pointer principle rules can be chained in a ruleset in a forward and/or backward

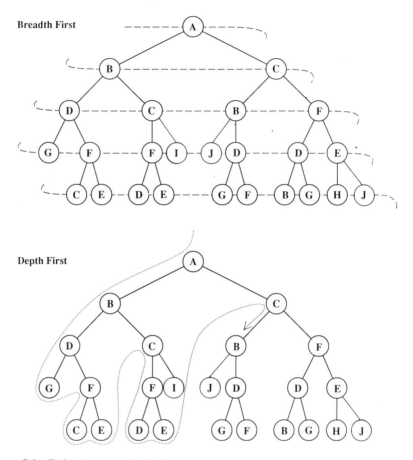

Figure 5.3   Ruleset access strategies

direction with equal facility. If the goal conclusion is known in advance
(I want to buy a computer) for which condition based advice is required
(do so if conditions A + B + C are satisfied) then conclusion based backward chaining rule access is used. When the end of the chain of rules in
the ruleset is reached advice is provided. Backward chaining systems are
sometimes called goal directed systems. If the goal conclusion is not known
in advance and requires to be constructed based on a set of conditions (I
have a temperature, sore eyes, runny nose and headache, what illness do I
have?) then condition based forward chaining rule access is used. Forward
chaining systems are sometimes called data driven systems.

In a forward chaining system the condition(s) of the rules in a ruleset are
examined to see whether they are true or not, given the information available. If they are true then the conclusions are added as temporary assertion

facts to the initial set of facts known to be true (temperature, sore eyes, runny nose and headache), and the system examines the rules again. As the facts are evaluated they are cancelled from the list of outstanding facts. When the end of the chain of rules in the ruleset is reached any outstanding assertion facts (i.e. outstanding conclusions) are displayed as advice. Based on the initial temperature, sore eyes, runny nose and headache facts you have flu.

The basic mechanism used by expert systems in forward chaining is by posing questions based on an initial set of condition(s). If the answer to the condition(s) is yes (assuming the conditions are linked by AND or to a condition if the conditions are linked by OR), the condition(s) is true, and the rule matching all or part of the condition(s) rule is "fired" and the conclusion(s) is drawn. The conclusion(s) is then used to search for any other rules in the ruleset where the condition(s) matches the conclusion(s) of the rule just processed. To ascertain the answer of the condition based questions, the expert system software will first access the knowledgebase to the application domain. If the knowledgebase can answer the question by providing relevant information (for example, yes customer 12345 does have outstanding orders) then the rule is fired and the conclusion is successfully drawn. If the knowledgebase cannot answer the question then the condition(s) is posed as a question to the user. If the user cannot provide an answer a default rule value is used, that is a rule composed only of a conclusion. Depending on the reply given the condition(s) is found to be true or false and the rule is fired or not fired. When the end of the chain of the rules in the ruleset is reached the goal/objective of the ruleset is achieved and appropriate conclusion based advice is offered.

The same basic mechanism is used with backward chaining, but the questions posed are conclusion based. There is also no need to build temporary assertions. The initial question posed is the goal for which advice is required. The inference engine matches the goal to the conclusion of the rules in the ruleset, and then tries to match the conditions of these rules to the knowledgebase or to the conclusions of other rules in the ruleset. Variations of this basic mechanism exist from expert system product to expert system product.

It is possible to switch from forward chaining to backward chaining and vica versa. An example of this will be seen shortly.

An example of rule forward chain firing in a ruleset is illustrated in figure 5.4. The first rule in a ruleset is used to access the knowledgebase to ascertain whether its condition(s) (with forward chaining from an initial set of facts) is true. If the knowledgebase cannot provide the answer the condition(s) is displayed as a question to the user. The first question would be "Is it a sunny day?" If the answer is yes the condition of rule 1 is true, the rule is fired and its conclusion drawn to go sunbathing. This conclusion is then matched against the other rules in the ruleset to see if another rule has its condition matching the conclusion. In the first ruleset the answer is no, so the original conclusion is true and conclusion based advice is displayed to go sunbathing. In the second ruleset, it can be seen that a second rule matches the conclusion of the first rule. If the condition to the second rule is not found in the knowledgebase a second condition based question would therefore be displayed on the screen, which would be "Do you intend to go sunbathing?" If the answer is yes then the next rule would be accessed. Because this second rule is the end of the ruleset chain, the conclusion advice would be displayed to put on sun cream.

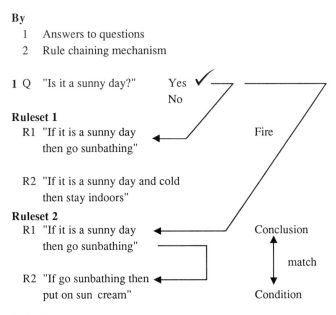

By
  1   Answers to questions
  2   Rule chaining mechanism

1 Q   "Is it a sunny day?"   Yes ✓
                                No

Ruleset 1
  R1 "If it is a sunny day
      then go sunbathing"   Fire

  R2 "If it is a sunny day and cold
      then stay indoors"
Ruleset 2
  R1 "If it is a sunny day   Conclusion
      then go sunbathing"
                                               match
  R2 "If go sunbathing then
      put on sun cream"   Condition

Figure 5.4   Rule firing

Rules in a ruleset can be standalone and not symbolically chained to the other rules, i.e. the logic may not be complete. Where this occurs the inference engine creates a temporary "agenda" list of rules relevant to the task being processed and then tries to match them symbolically by progressively grouping the conditions and conclusions and using the semantic net and knowledgebase. Worked examples of this agenda matching are described when considering the GENERIS and GOLDWORKS products.

Rules are stored on disk as variable length records. This means that they can be treated as normal data. *Rule logic is stored and accessed like data.* To store a rule in free form in full on disk would involve a large amount of disk storage. Rules are therefore usually compressed or tokenised, that is they are given a set of meaningfully coded numbers. Separate tables containing the code descriptions are required to convert the rules to meaningful form when being displayed in question or advice form to the user.

It is important to appreciate that the chaining of rules does not have to be single path, where rule A points to rule B points to rule C. A given rule can point to many other rules, each of which can be in different rulesets. A ruleset can therefore provide multiple pieces of advice, one per rule path. Given that many if not all the rules in a ruleset are accessed when the goal/objective is queried it is important that appropriate rules in the ruleset are clustered on disk in order to optimise performance. However, within the ruleset cluster, the order/sequence in which the rules are stored is completely immaterial as far as the execution of logic is concerned. Given that the rules are linked by symbolic values and are standalone statements of some truth, the rules can be "shuffled" in any order and, unlike the procedural logic of traditional application programs with their flow of control, the declarative logic of rules will still execute correctly.

The rule access mechanisms function within the rule access strategies.

5.2.4.5 Rule storage and access

It will clearly improve efficiency on disk if the rules are stored in the sequence they are accessed on disk within a ruleset and clustered on disk as a ruleset. If the rules are only chained together by the matching of symbolic values each access to a rule will require scanning of the ruleset. This could well lead to considerable inefficiency, particularly if the ruleset occupies a large number of disk pages. It is therefore necessary to be able to chain the rules in a ruleset using a direct pointing mechanism. This can be done by using direct address pointers between rules or by indexing the rule condition(s) and or conclusion(s).

In order to gain initial entry access to a ruleset it is important that the "first/last" rule in the ruleset (depending on the ruleset access strategies and mechanisms) is indexed. Backward chaining is initiated from a goal, so that the only single entry point value (Should I buy a computer with a printer?) need be searched for, usually from a single goal based index pointing to the conclusion(s). By contrast forward chaining can begin from an initial set of facts which may, probably will, vary from consultation to consultation and therefore may or may not be indexed. For example, patients pose a set of ailments to the doctor. The ailments vary from patient to patient and the expert system may not have been designed for all possible ailments. The entry point set of condition facts to the ruleset (in this case the facts are the ailments described earlier by the patient, such as headache and sore eyes) may not be indexed at all, in which case the entire ruleset requires scanning, or only some of the ailments may be indexed, in which case all the rules to the indexed ailments will require to be accessed as a start point to access those ailments not indexed. If the non-indexed ailments cannot be found from the indexed ailments then scanning of the ruleset will be required. Forward chaining systems are therefore more difficult to predict when producing a design. Performance could be adversely be affected.

Rules can thus be chained either using the symbolic mechanism of conclusion(s) matching condition(s) or linking the conclusion(s) and condition(s) through indexes or direct address pointers. One can see that the access mechanisms to the ruleset are exactly the same as to data with relational file handler mechanisms, with the rulesets being tables of data and the rules in the rulesets being table rows.

The initial start point of the chaining mechanism will be the goal (backward chaining) or initial set of facts for which a goal is to be constructed (forward chaining). If the initial entry point(s) is not indexed then the ruleset requires scanning to find the initial rule. A worked example of backward rule chaining is illustrated in figure 5.5. The example illustrates backward chaining to obtain advice regarding the purchase of a computer with a printer. This goal would be phrased as a question to the user "Do you wish to purchase a computer with a printer?" Assume the answer is yes. If the goal is indexed the index would act as the entry point to the ruleset. As the example uses backward chaining the index would point to the rule with its conclusion matching the goal. If the ruleset is not indexed then, of course, the ruleset requires to be scanned.

Goal Statement

Purchase a computer with a printer

Rule 1

If a manager's personal assistant
Then conducting management meetings

Rule 2

If conducting management meetings,
Then writing management memos necessary

Rule 3

If writing management memos necessary
Then producing reports is a requirement

Rule 4

If producing reports is a requirement
Then purchase a computer with a printer

Figure 5.5   Rule chaining (backwards)

It can be seen that the conclusion of rule 4 matches the goal. The index would therefore point to rule 4. Assuming the knowledgebase does not contain the answer to the condition of rule 3 the condition is then posed as a question to the user "Is producing reports a requirement?" If the answer is yes then the condition is used to search the remaining rules in the ruleset to see if another rule has its conclusion matching the condition of rule 4. Depending on the access mechanism the ruleset requires either to be scanned again or accessed by indexes or direct address pointers pointing from the condition of rule 4. It can be seen that the conclusion of rule 3 matches the condition of rule 4. Assuming the knowledgebase does not contain the answer the condition of rule 3 is posed to the user "Is writing management memos necessary?" The cycle of rule matching is completed when the end of the chain of rules in the ruleset is obtained. If the answer to all the condition based questions (after the initial goal based question) is yes then condition based advice is offered "Purchase a computer with a printer if producing reports is necessary, if writing management memos is necessary, if conducting management meetings and if a manager's personal assistant". This advice is obtained by running in a forward direction from the end of the backward chain those rules that were used in the backward chain.

As indicated, one of the attractive features of the declarative code of rules is that the logic does not have to be complete in order for it to work. For example, if rule 1 in the above example was omitted the processing would still continue but the advice will not include purchasing a micro-computer if manager's personal assistant. Equally the order in which the rules are specified is completely immaterial to their ability to execute. If the order of the rules was 4,3,2,1 or 2,1 3, 4 the logic would still execute. The sequence of the code matters not.

The structure of a ruleset using the indexing and direct address pointing mechanisms is illustrated in figure 5.6. The index in this example is used purely for the initial entry point to the ruleset. The index value could be for the goal for backward chaining or set of factual conditions for forward chaining. In this example once the index entry to the ruleset has been obtained the rules are chained using direct address pointers. Indexes could be used just as easily. From the goals/conditions there will be a pointer value pointing to the rule in the ruleset matching the goal value(s) or condition value(s) as appropriate. The index goal pointer will point to a rule, the conclusion(s) of which match the goal value(s). The index condition(s) pointer (there may be multiple indexes each supporting a single condition—thus, in the example there could be three indexes pointing to the conditions D, E, and F, which point to a rule, the condition(s) of which matches part or all of the initial set of condition facts. The pointing procedure then follows the normal mechanism of pattern matching the conclusion(s) of one rule to the condition(s) of another rule or vice versa until the end of the chain of rules in the ruleset is reached.

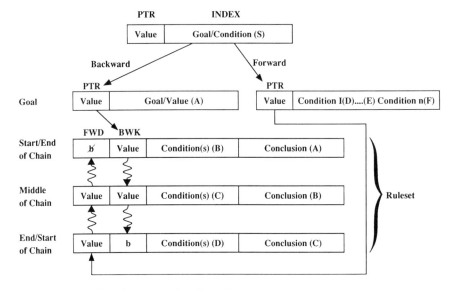

Backward Chaining from Goal Value to Rule Conclusion
Forward Chaining from Condition Value(s) to Rule Condition(s)

Figure 5.6   Rule chaining and indexing

5.2.4.6 Rule I/O

Give that rules are stored as variable length records rule access obviously
involves I/O. As with normal data records logical I/O occurs when the
rules are accessed in the processor main memory buffer pool and physical
I/O when it is necessary, because the rules are not in the buffer pool, to
access the disk. The amount of I/O is easy to calculate, as it is exactly the
same as for calculating normal access to user data stored in table rows in a
database.

Assume that a ruleset has ten rules and each rule takes half a kilobyte
of data. The ruleset is also not indexed, so that scanned access is required.
Assume further that the page size is one kilobyte, so that on average two
rules can be stored per page. The ruleset therefore occupies five pages.
The initial scanned access to pull the ruleset from disk into the buffer pool
requires five pages, hence five physical I/Os. Subsequent scans are only
against half the ruleset on average but, with the ruleset in the buffer pool,
the I/Os are logical. Each rule in the ruleset requires a scan. Since a scan
involves accessing half the ruleset and hence 2.5 logical I/Os, the total
scanning overhead for the ten rules is 25 logical I/Os.

To access a ruleset using an indexing strategy, with the index pointing
from the goal to achieve the start point for backward chaining or set of

initial condition facts for forward chaining (and assuming that there are indexes to each fact in the initial set of facts), would generate on average one physical I/O to read the index to main memory (assume the index upper layers are already in the buffer pool), some five physical I/Os to read the ruleset in physical order into main memory and subsequently two logical I/Os (one to access the index, one to access the rule pointed to) for each access to the ten rules.

In this worked example the scanning approach requires 5 physical I/Os and 25 logical I/Os and the indexing strategy requires 6 physical I/Os and 20 logical I/Os. This ratio between the two access mechanisms will obviously vary depending on the access strategy and access mechanisms in each ruleset and the access requirements of the initial query. A basic rule-of-thumb is that the greater the number of rules per page and the narrower the ratio of one rule to another (usually one to one) the greater the advantage of ruleset scanning—the reverse is true for pointing/indexing.

5.2.4.7 Semantic nets

Another significant mechanism of representing knowledge is the semantic net facility. Semantics is a buzzword which means nothing more than the description of meaning. Semantics can thus provide a meaningful description of the relationship between the entities in the semantic net.

A semantic net looks like a standard entity model, with entities, the relationships between them and, not found in some structured methods, the semantic description of the relationships. It isn't. It is much more powerful, with additional facilities. It is an entity model and more.

An example of a semantic net (part of a semantic net, as we shall see) is illustrated in figure 5.7.

Some of the additional facilities can be seen. It shows, for example, that Employee has a number of occurrences of itself as database data, whereas Mammal does not. Mammal is just a one occurrence description of a "thing" called Mammal. The relationship arrow between master and detail entity also seems to be the wrong way round—a Company can obviously employ many Persons yet the arrows seems to be indicating that the Company is a detail of Person. In fact the relationship arrow is pointing in the direction of what is called property inheritance—Employee inherits the properties of Person.

The three components of the entities, the relationships and the semantic description of the relationships represent a triple, so a semantic net can represent facts, which, as we have seen, when meaningfully combined, form knowledge data. Semantic nets are therefore an important component in the modelling of knowledge and the building of the knowledgebase.

The direction of the relationship arrow indicates the direction of a triple relationship, not, as in the Information Engineering crows foot, the direction

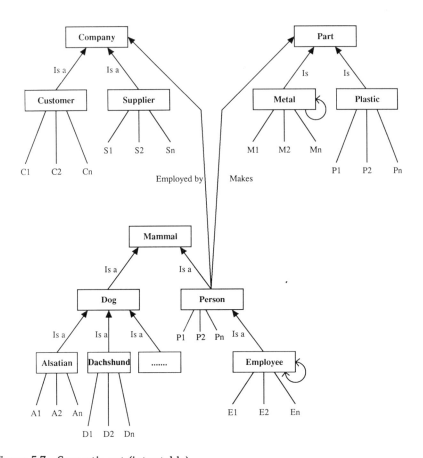

Figure 5.7   Semantic net (inter-table)

of master–detail entities. The entity at the tail of the arrow is the subject and the entity at the head of the arrow is the property, the semantic description being the relationship. An example of a semantic fact in the semantic net example is that a "dog is a mammal."

There are three facilities that are provided by semantic nets that are not in the entity model:

• class entities, and the instances of the class entities;

• property inheritance;

• conflict resolution.

Class entities   The entities/tables in the semantic net can be of two kinds—class and instance. The nearest equivalent in traditional database terminology is that a class table is similar to a record type and an instance of the class table equates to a record occurrence/table row.

What is the class facility? Consider figure 5.32. The figure is used for object oriented technology, but illustrates the class facility well. Only the points pertinent to class will be considered. All the entities in the information structure belong to the class of Mammal, as they are all mammalian. All the entitles below the entity Man belong to the class of man, because Person, Employee and Star Employee belong to the species Man. All the entities below Person belong to the class of Person because ... and so on. The structure of the class information is hierarchical, so one can hear the term class hierarchy models.

Class is thus a means of classifying information according to it's behaviour (another term could be role). All the entities of Mammal to Star Employee have the same mammalian behaviour.

Class is a means by which information is better organised than with traditional logical data modelling. Assume an employee system. There could be an entity of Employee with attributes of Date of Birth and Date of Employment. Relational data analysis would see no incongruity with this and would quite happily normalise both attributes to the key attribute of Employee Number within the Employee entity. "For a given value of Employee Number is there only one possible value for Date of Birth and Date of Employment?" The answer is, of course, yes and both attributes would be placed in the Employee entity.

By contrast, the class facility would point out that Date of Birth has nothing to do with the role of employment, Date of Employment yes but not Date of Birth. Date of Birth is relevant to a "thing" called a Person, and would require an entity for Person to be created. Obviously the employee "is a" kind of person, so that the Employee entity would be a sub-class of the entity Person. The Employee entity would require to inherit the properties of the entity Person so as to obtain the information about the Date of Birth. For each instance of Employee there would be an instance of Person. Property inheritance is therefore a natural corollary, a by-product, of the class facility.

Class data is defined in class entities. Class data is generic data that describes and is relevant to all instances of the class. For example the Man table is a class table. It contains generic data "instantiated" (an expert system buzzword meaning populated with a value) with values that describe all instances of Man, such as number of legs with a value of "2". The Employee table is also a class table containing generic information appropriate to all instances of employees, such as salary of "£10,000 per annum" and "£1 luncheon voucher per day".

This generic class data is a convenient way of expressing facts in semantic form which are recognised as true (all Persons, being of the class of Man, have two legs—a class fact), but to which there may be conflicting exceptions at the instance level (poor Henry has lost a leg—an instance fact). These generic class facts can therefore be used as defaults in deductive reasoning—it is deduced that all persons have two legs.

Class entity data is defined with the generic values in the schema description in a dictionary. The class entity information is defined in the knowledgebase schema in exactly the same way as for a record or table type in a traditional Codasyl or relational database. Each class entity is the "one off" definition of the class entity for *n* instances of the class entity, where *n* can be zero. The class entity Employee, for example, can have *n* instances of employee.

The entities in a semantic net go beyond the facility of the entity in a traditional ERD, such that there can, and usually are, more entities in a semantic net than there are in the entity model. All the entities in an ERD model are still preserved, but there will be additional entities representing a class of something. The data model entity is identified by a key data item, such as Employee Number to identify the Employee entity. Many of the class entities will also have keys, such as Person, with one Person instance for each Employee instance. However there can also be class entities which do not require a key data item. These are entities that are not the "root" entity to *n* instances of the class entities in the knowledgebase.

An obvious example of this is the Mammalian entity. As it is a "one off", being merely a schematic description in the dictionary, it requires no key and is an entity in the semantic net example that would not be found in an ERD model. The same is true for the Dog entity in figure 5.7.

It thus follows that an entity in a semantic net may belong to a class, but need not be an instance.

Recursive relationships in semantic nets can be supported, both one-to-many and many-to-many. Metal illustrates a recursive one-to-many relationship. (Metal) brass consists of (metal) copper consists of (metal) tin. Employee illustrates a recursive many-to-many relationship. (Employee) James is married to (employee) Betty is married to (employee) James.

We shall see through the rest of this chapter that the class facility bestows many other benefits to expert systems and object oriented technology.

Instances of the class entities   The instance data properties are also defined in the dictionary alongside the class data, but are not instantiated with data values in the dictionary. This is because the values to be stored in the instance data properties can vary with each occurrences of the entity instance. Clearly Date of Birth for the Person entity is is not instantiated with a value at the class level because each instance of Person can have a different value. Date Joined Company for the Employee object is similarly not instantiated with a value and for the same reason—each employee could join on a different day.

This latter point illustrates another use of object instances—to overrule class information. Any class values can be overridden at the instance level of the class entity—the instance information is more particular than the general class information and therefore overrides it. Consider the property inheritance model in figure 5.8. At the class level all sub-class entities are instantiated with a value of having two legs from the class attribute Number of Legs within the Man entity, yet poor Henry Smith has the Number of Legs property instantiated with a value of "1". This is because Henry has had a leg amputated. Henry's 1 leg overrides the generic class value of 2 legs. None of the other Employee instances contain a value in the attribute Number of Legs, as they can inherit the value of "2" from the Person class object.

By contrast, with the Date of Employment property there is no need for

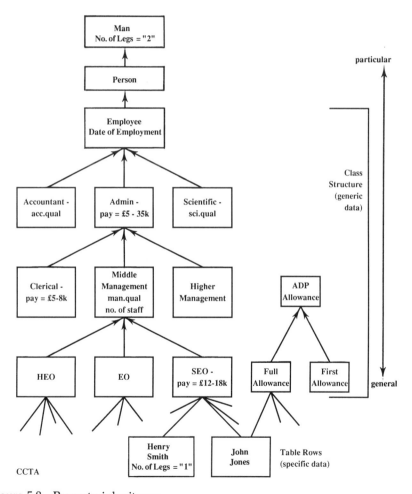

Figure 5.8   Property inheritance

overruling as there is no instantiation of the property at the class level. It is an instance attribute.

Property inheritance (full, partial and multiple)   Property inheritance is a by-product of the class facility. If class is supported there must be inheritance. The Employee entity as a sub-class of Person must be able to inherit the properties of the Person super-class entity.

An often used example of this is the recognition of cars and lorries as special cases of vehicles, inheriting the data properties of vehicle, such as Vehicle Number and Date of Registration, and using their own more specialised attributes, such as Number of Passengers for the car object and Load Carrying Capacity for the lorry object.

Property inheritance is supported with the semantic description of the relationships between the entities in the semantic net. There are, in fact, two types of semantics to describe the relationships—the "is a" inheritance semantics and the free form business semantics. Information Engineering only supports the business semantics. The property inheritance semantics are defined against the relationships between the entities. The business semantics can be defined against the relationship between the entities and between the data properties (expert system terminology for data attributes) within an entity. Business semantics can be inter entity and intra entity.

Each relationship between the entities would normally have a semantic description that describes the relationship. Where the relationship is described as a "is a, is, are, are a" type, a predefined semantic recognised by the expert system software, then the sub-class entity pointing to a super-class entity automatically inherits the properties of the super-class entity. These "is a" type semantics are between entities that are of the same class, entities that have the same behaviour. They are the active descriptions, in that a by-product is provided, namely automatic property inheritance in the direction of the "is a" semantic relationship arrow. Inheritance with the "is a" type semantic description is total. All the properties in the super-class entity are inherited.

The facility of class is the mechanism by which property inheritance is achieved, using the inheritance semantic descriptions. The scope of a class can be ascertained by tracing the "is a" type relationships. There is one class in the semantic net in figure 5.7, the class of Mammal, but with two sub-classes, canine and man. Employee "is a" Person; Person "is a" Man, Man "is a" Mammal, Employee being the sub-class of Person and Person being the sub-class of Man and Man being a sub-class of Mammal. Thus, within the Mammal class group, the Employee is able to inherit the properties of the Person, which in turn is able to inherit the properties of Man, which is able to inherit the properties of Mammal. Person and Employee would inherit, for example, the property of number of legs from Man and warm blooded from Mammal.

Also within the mammalian class group are the entities Dog and the sub-classes of Alsatian, Daschund etc. They, like the Man sub-class, inherit the mammalian property of being warm blooded.

Examples of property inheritance are also illustrated in figure 5.8. Higher management will inherit the pay property of administrators and thus have a salary of between £5,000 and £35,000. The SEOs will override this salary with their own level of £12–18,000 and the clerks a salary of £5–8,000. The more particular information lower down the semantic net overrides the more general information higher up the semantic net. The diagram seems to show that accountants and scientific officers will have no salary.

The "is a" type semantic description is not necessarily appropriate to describe the inheritance relationship between all the entities in the semantic net. It would not be sensible to say, for example, that Person "is a" Company and Person "is a" Part. A Person does not inherit the properties of a Part—there is no common behaviour. A free form business semantic description is used instead, the description appropriate to the business relationship of the entities.

A distinction therefore needs to be made between "semantic net/inheritance semantics" and "database/business semantics". *The former provides inheritance, the latter does not, unless explicitly stated.*

In figure 5.9 a business semantics is defined for the relationship between Customer and Order and an inheritance semantic between Employee and

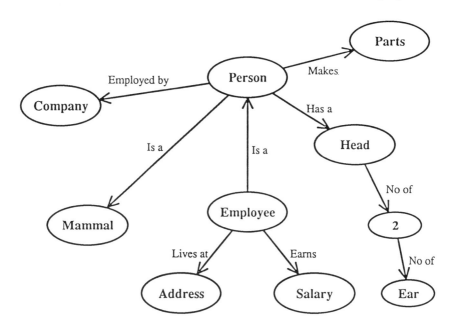

Figure 5.9 Full semantic net

Person. There would be no inheritance between the entities Customer and Order. There is no common class relationship, no common behaviour. There is merely a business semantic describing the purpose of the relationship between the entities. Notice that a Person has three behaviours: as a person, as a customer, and as an employee.

It is the facility of property inheritance that makes semantic nets able to support fully entity sub-types. Relational file handlers, notwithstanding entity sub-type facilities, cannot provide inheritance. They are therefore not able to support actively entity sub-types. Sub-types have to be supported in the logic of the application program. Entity sub-typing was described in sections 3.2.5 and 3.2.6. In figure 3.33 entity sub-type Secured can inherit the properties of entity sub-type Credit Customer, which can inherit the properties of entities Customer and Loan Type. What is being achieved is partial inheritance within entity sub-typing.

In reality what is happening is that the entity sub-type is actually a sub-class entity, Secured and Unsecured being sub-classes of Loan Type. *In order to support partial inheritance the sub-typing of relational technology will be replaced by sub-classing of the semantic net/object class model.* And, as we shall see, sub-classing may be done in the super-class!!

Where a business semantic is used the inheritance of the super-class entity properties will probably be zero, but may be partial.

Partial inheritance occurs where not all the data properties of an entity areappropriate to be used in all circumstances. Partial inheritance is supported through creating sub-class entities, one sub-class entity containing the properties that can be inherited and the other sub-class containing the properties that cannot be inherited, both defined in the schema description with inheritance and business semantics as appropriate.

In figure 5.10a the properties to be inherited from the Company super-class entity for the Person is the company's address and telephone number, but not the company's share value. Person is related to a Company via the "employed by" business semantic description. In the example provided, Person inherits the properties of Company Base Details (defined by a business semantic but with inheritance explicitly stated), because the Person has the same telephone number and address as the company, but not the other data properties of the company. The Person has no interest in the Value of the company. In this example the sub-classing is done in the super-class entity!

Figure 5.10a also shows another, but different, example of partial inheritance. An employee is a sub-class to both Person and Manager. But the relationship of Employee to Manager is not just via an "is a" inheritance type semantic relationship, but also of a free form business type semantic "works for". A more accurate representation is to identify the relationships as in figure 5.10b. The properties that pertain to the Employee as a non-manager, such as hobbies, are stored in the Non-Manager Employee class

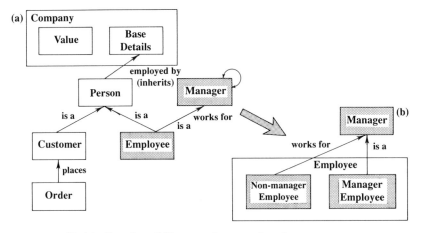

The inheritance is partial because not every employee is a manager

Figure 5.10   Partial inheritance

object and those that are relevant to being a managing employee, such as Budget Allowance, are stored in the Manager Employee class object. The solution in this case is through sub-typing. In this example the sub-classing is done in the sub-class entity.

The inter entity business semantics are those descriptions of the entity relationships found in traditional data modelling techniques, such as in Information Engineering and other structured methods. A typical example could be that a Customer "places" Orders and an Order "is received from" a Customer, the semantic describing the business relationship from master to detail table and vica versa. *The business semantics, like the inheritance semantic, can therefore also create knowledge data* in the form of a triple (Customer (subject) "places" (relationship) Order (property)) and hence be of help in constructing part of the knowledgebase, even though property inheritance is not provided.

Figure 2.12 shows the second type of business semantic relationship, between the attributes within a entity. The semantic description is always between the prime key of the entity and the other non-key attributes. In this case employee "lives at" an address and "earns" a salary. Again the semantic is in the form of a triple, with the relationship being described between the subject, which equates to the prime key of an entity, and the property, which is a non-key attribute of the entity. *The inter-attribute semantic can therefore also act as knowledge data and add to the knowledgebase.* There could be a semantic description between the subject and all the properties of the entity. The example illustrates two such properties and two such semantic descriptions. These inter property semantic descriptions are passive. No inheritance is implied. They are used solely to add meaning to the data.

The author knows of no structured design method which supports inter-attribute relationship semantics.

There can be what is called single inheritance and multiple inheritance. Single inheritance is where an entity inherits from only one super-class entity. An example of this would be Dogs inheriting the class data from Mammal. Multiple inheritance is obtained where there are multiple super-classes from which the class information can be inherited. In figure 5.10a Employee can inherit properties from both Person and Manager. The full scope of multiple inheritance is discussed in section 5.3.4.4.

The author has seen it written that the semantic description "has a" can be used in the same way as the "is a" semantic, with automatic inheritance being obtained. This has to be treated with caution. Surely there is no inheritance in the class model in figure 5.30 where the Broker object "has a" Telephone—the two objects have no common behaviour. But what about the "has a" relationship of the object Valuation and the Company Value. There is a case to be argued that there is a common behaviour, that of financial value. In such a case there should be inheritance—perhaps! Notice that whether inheritance is provided or not is explicitly stated.

Conflict resolution   It is because of the inheritance facility that situations will arise where there is a conflict in the value of the information in the knowledgebase. There can be conflict in the data. There could be a fact that says "a" and another fact in the same class hierarchy that says "b". Different experts have different opinions about something. One expert says the world is round, another says with equal conviction it is square. Inevitably there will exceptions/conflicts to general laws.

The mechanism for solving any conflict between data is the particular overriding the general. The more particular information is always to be found in the entities lower in the semantic net. The lowest and most particular point in the semantic net is the instances of the class entities.

The conflict can be between the instance and the class of an object and between classes of objects. Figure 5.8 shows both types of conflict for data, and the use of the particular versus the general to provide resolution. As regards class to class conflict the sub-type object is more particular than its super-type object. In figure 5.8 the class entity SEO has a salary of between £12,000 and £18,000. This is more particular than the salary level of £5,000 to £35,000 of the Administrator's salary. The SEO class salary level therefore overrides that of Administrators. By contrast Middle Management will inherit the pay property of Administrators and thus have a salary of between £5,000 and £35,000, because they do not have salary levels for their class. As regards the instance of the entity being more particular than the class of the entity assume that Smith has a salary of £22,000. Smith the instance is more particular than SEO the class and Smith gets his/her salary and not that of an SEO.

The full semantic net showing the inter table, inter property and inheritance semantics is illustrated in figure 5.9. It is based on combining figures 2.12 and 5.7.

5.2.4.8 Frames

The third major means of representing knowledge is the frame. Frames are a hybrid of both rules and semantic nets. A frame can contain both knowledge data and knowledge logic properties. The frame is all the information stored in the database about a particular subject. The subject is defined by a key data item. One can thus call these subjects data frames. We shall see the facility of logic based frames when considering object oriented technology.

The "scope" of the subject is based on the principle of foreign keys between instance tables stored in the database and class tables in the dictionary. All the tables containing the key data item are within the scope of the subject.

Frame information is therefore hierarchical in structure. For example, figure 5.13 illustrates that the scope of a frame with a key of "A" can incorporate selected or all the information stored in the table rows of tables A, B, C, F, D and E where the table rows all have the same foreign key of A and the appropriate key value of the frame key value. The scope of the frame can easily be extended by incorporating additional foreign keys in additional tables.

The frames are typically drawn as illustrated in figure 5.11. Each arrow is a slot (slot is yet another buzzword in expert system terminology meaning nothing more than property) and a slot can contain data or logic. This is a major link between expert and object oriented systems. Figure 5.13 shows the structure of the Employee and Father frames with instantiated values in the slots. The career slot contains data and the salary slot contains logic.

Frame Structure

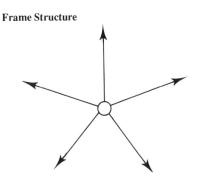

Figure 5.11   Frame structure

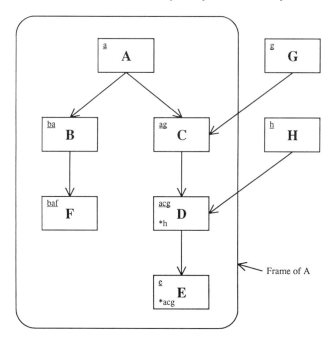

Figure 5.12   Scope of frames

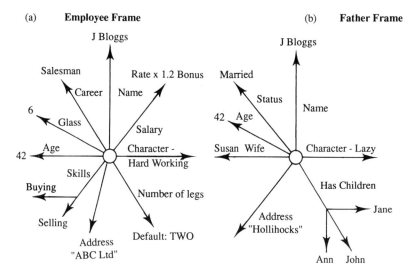

Figure 5.13   Instantiated frame

Figure 5.13 also shows that multiple frames can have the same slots and that a slot can belong to multiple frames. The Employee and the Father frames both have a slot for a name. The relationship between slots and frames is therefore many-to-many. The slots in a frame can be related to *n* tables of data, as in figure 5.13. Using the employee frame in figure 5.13a skill repeats for a given value of the employee frame key and would be represented in the database as a detail table to the employee table.

Once values have been allocated to the slots in a frame the frame is said to be "instantiated". Each frame has a unique key allocated to it, in the example employee number and family/man code, and each frame instance has a key value, in this case J Bloggs. It so happens that both these frames have some common slots, such as name. Note that the value stored in the slots may or may not vary between frames. For example, the employee frame instance J Bloggs has a character of being hard working while at the office, but when J Bloggs is playing the role of father at home he is lazy. A frame can also connect to other frames. For example, the father frame instance Joe Bloggs is married wife to frame instance Mary and child frame instance Jane.

The great advantage of the frame facility is that all database information relating to a specific key/subject class (such as Employees) or key value/subject instance (such as Joe Bloggs) can be ascertained in a single key query. The key might be found in any number of database tables. *There is no concept of table access as in relational file handlers. The major restriction to non-procedural database access is therefore removed.*

The author has heard from practitioners of expert system technology that the scope of a frame can be greater than defined in database and dictionary foreign keys. It could be that the frame subject of A is also to be found in the definition of the rules and in the semantic net tables. Thus, in this case, the frame of A would be wherever A is identified, be it logic or data, and described in the knowledgebase, which includes the database and dictionary. The concept of frames would be much more powerful.

5.2.5 Retraction

One of the problems that can occur in forward chaining, where the advice which is being sought requires to be partially constructed from an initial set of facts, is that an initial assumption(s) made as part of the consultation process is based on the initial facts. The initial facts could be misleading, such that the assumption could prove to be wrong. Any actions taken on the initial assumption(s) require to "undone". A patient complains to a doctor that he/she has a headache, runny nose and sore eyes. In the processing of these initial facts one by one it is initially assumed that the patient has flu. Other facts ascertained from the knowledgebase as part of normal inference processing identify that the patient lives in the countryside, has bee-keeping as a hobby and works part-time driving a tractor at harvest time and generally gets these symptoms from spring to autumn, facts that disprove the initial assumption of flu, to be replaced by the conclusion of hay fever. The flu assumption has to be cancelled and any action taken on the assumption (a bulk anti-flu vaccine order has been raised, the warehouse containing the vaccine is now, having supplied the order, below the minimum stock level, and £100,000 of new vaccine has been authorised to be purchased...!) must be retracted/back-tracked. The retraction and back-tracking is the same problem as event recognition in realtime systems. The back-tracking mechanism is described in section 4.2.3.4.

5.2.6 Uncertainty

The inference mechanism must be able to support the processing of logic and data which may be uncertain.

5.2.6.1 Uncertain logic

Traditional data processing software does not include facilities for handling uncertainty. Data is definitive or null. Expert systems include many ways of supporting uncertainty in knowledge logic, such as classical probability, Bayesian probability, certainty factors and fuzzy logic. All of these use the assignment of a numeric value to a given proposition to indicate its likelihood. The numeric value is a certainty factor (CF). A proposition could be a condition or conclusion of a rule.

Certainty factors lie between 1 and −1 and represent the measure of belief in a given proposition (a positive CF between 0 and 1) and the measure of disbelief in a proposition (a negative CF between 0 and −1). For example a measure of belief or disbelief that it will rain.

In the case of classical probability the propositions are independent and the numeric value will always lie between 0 and 1, 0 indicating impossibility and 1 indicting certainty. The two independent propositions could be the probabilities of it raining and buying a house.

Bayesian probability is an extension to allow the treatment of conditions to the probabilities, the example of the probability rain|sky is red being the probability that it will rain given the condition that the sky is red. The two propositions, sky is red and rain, are not independent of each other.

Certainty factors are designed to cope with accumulation of evidence about a single proposition. For example, two rules happen to draw the same conclusion proposition but with different certainties. Multiple certainty factors for separate occurrences of the same proposition are combined in a way which allows evidence to accumulate gradually on both sides, i.e. rule 1 to rule 2 or rule 2 to rule 1.

Fuzzy logic is used to indicate not so much a probability of a proposition being true or not true but a measure of agreement with an indefinite proposition. An indefinite proposition could be "The car is expensive". This is a relative statement of belief. To a rich person a car of a given price may appear cheap; to a poor person a car of the same price may appear expensive.

1 Classical probability There are many ways by which classical probability can be managed. The propositions are independent as they have no causal relationship. For example, if the independent propositions A and B relate to two throws of the dice, A is the event "A six is thrown on the first throw" and B is the event "An even number is thrown on the second throw", then

$p(A) = 1/6$
$p(B) = 3/6$
$p(A \& B) = 1/12$

Three common ways for the treatment of independent probabilities are:

• Condition(s) to a rule may be less than certain. Uncertain conditions lead to uncertain conclusions. For example, a rule could be "If A (CF 0.5) then B". This will lead to a conclusion that if A is true then B is true with a measure of belief of 0.5.

• Conditions to a rule are evaluated differently, depending on the number and type of clauses and logical connectives they use:

— If uncertain conditions are connected by ORs, take the maximum CF value. For example, a rule could be "If A(CF 0.2) or B(CF 0.8) then C". This will lead to a conclusion that if A or B are true then C is concluded with a measure of belief of 0.8.
— If uncertain conditions are connected by ANDs, take the minimum CF values. For example, a rule could be "If A(CF 0.2) and B(CF0.8) then C". This will lead to a conclusion that if A and B are true then C is concluded with a measure of belief of 0.2.

Where there are uncertain conditions a "threshold of acceptance" should be specified. If the CF factor of a condition is below the threshold then the condition is not accepted as being true. In MYCIN, an early expert system product, rules succeed if the condition(s) certainty value has a threshold value greater than 0.2. The rule succeeds if:

— The condition is a single clause and has a confidence factor (CF) greater than 0.2; or
— The condition contains clauses connected by ORs and the maximum CF value for each of the clauses is greater than 0.2; or

— The condition contains clauses connected by ANDs and the minimum CF values for each of the clauses is greater than 0.2;

- Conclusions of a rule themselves may carry separate certainty factors. Any uncertainty of a rule conclusion is propagated to other rules in the ruleset by multiplying their combined uncertainties together.

An example of rules with uncertain conclusions propagating uncertainty to each other is illustrated in figure 5.14. There are four rules in the ruleset, which if all are fired will produce a combined conclusion certainty of $0.9 \times 0.8 \times 0.9 \times 0.9$ and thereby provide advice to purchase a microcomputer with a printer with an overall certainty factor of 0.57. The system is not massively confident in its own advice!

Goal Statement

Purchase a computer with a printer

Rule 1

If a manager's personal assistant
Then conducting management meetings
Confidence 0.90

Rule 2

If conducting management meetings,
Then writing management memos necessary
Confidence 0.80

Rule 3

If writing management memos necessary
Then producing reports is a requirement
Confidence 0.80

Rule 4

If producing reports is a requirement
Then purchase a computer with a printer
Confidence 0.90

Figure 5.14   Rules with uncertainity

- If both the condition(s) and conclusion of a rule are uncertain then they are multiplied together to produce a rule certainty. For example, "If X(CF 0.5) then Y(CF 0.5)". The conclusion result would be a CF of 0.25.

2 Certainty factors   Facts may be concluded by more than one rule. A combining function blends the certainty factors.

When the inference engine is processing the knowledgebase, a set of common facts/assertions may be concluded by different rules which by themselves each contain degrees of certainty. For example, the value for Joe Blogg's job type may be concluded in one rule as "consultant" with a certainty, a measure of belief, of 0.6 and later concluded again with another rule as "consultant" with a certainty of 0.4. The mechanism to handle this is to combine these less than definite certainties. The revised certainty is then added to another common fact/assertion with a certainty factor, each addition increasing the measure of belief. The algorithm to calculate the addition of multiple common certainties is:

$$mb(A + B) = (mb(A) + mb(B)) - ((mb(A) \times mb(B))$$
$$= (0.4 + 0.6) - 0.24$$
$$= 0.76$$

A and B are the 0.6 and 0.4 values of the common proposition of Joe Bloggs being concluded as a consultant.

The order in which the information is combined does not matter. Combining 0.6 with 0.4 is the same as combining 0.4 with 0.6. As this process of adding revised certainties to other assertions/facts continues, the confidence in the conclusions rises. If a definite conclusion occurs then the combined certainty becomes definite. Indefinite information on the other hand will never accumulate to yield a definite conclusion.

3 Fuzzy logic Fuzzy logic is an example of multi-valued logic: instead of logical propositions being either true or false and independent they have a numeric value, again lying between 0 and 1, and a causal relationship. The difference between fuzzy logic and classical probability lies in the interpretation placed on the numbers and on the way they are combined.

It is usual to combine fuzzy propositions in terms of their values, not their probabilities: $v(A + B) = \min(v(A),v(B))$ as shown in the shaded area of figure 5.15.

This differs from the treatment of ordinary independent probabilities. Here probabilities are used:

$$p(A + B) = p(A)p(B)$$

For an example of fuzzy logic, assume two distinct but related propositions—a car is very expensive (proposition A) and a car costs about £30,000 (proposition B). Figure 5.15 shows a probability curve of A that says that if a car costs about £30,000 then 50% of people regard it as expensive but if it costs more than £40,000 then everybody believes it to be expensive. With a price of about £13,000 then nobody believes the car to be expensive. The proposition of B states that if the car costs £20,000 then nobody thinks it costs about £30,000 (nobody is fooled) but that a car can go up to about £40,000 in the price before nobody can be persuaded that the car is about

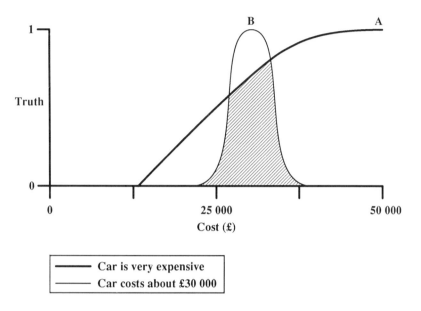

Figure 5.15   Fuzzy logic

£30,000. In between these price ranges a varying percentage of people agree the car can be about £30,000. The shaded area in figure 5.15 is the truth of the combined propositions. Thus if a value is produced within the shaded area any dependent rule conditions is regarded as satisfied.

Note that where the two propositions are being ANDed the minimum result of the propositions A and B is taken, hence the shaded area below the line of the two A and B curves. If the two propositions are ORed then a maximum result is produced.

4 Bayesian probability   Bayesian probability adds conditions to the independent propositions, as represented in the two dice. Consider figure 5.16. Dice are being thrown but, unlike the earlier example of two independent throws of the dice for classical probability, in the context of a condition. The condition is the value of 10. The combination of two figures of 6 + 4, 4 + 6 and 5 + 5 combine to produce 10. These three are equally probable. The probability of throwing 6 on the first throw given the value of 10 is 1/3.

5.2.6.2 Uncertain data

It must also be appreciated that data stored in the database component of a knowledgebase can also contain a certainty factor. For example, it is

$p(\text{6 on first throw} \mid \text{total is 10}) = 1/3$

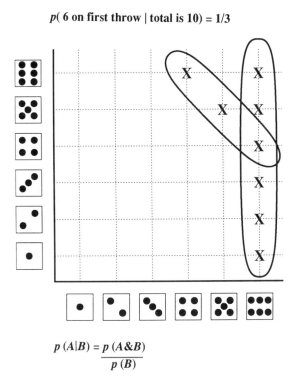

$$p(A|B) = \frac{p(A\&B)}{p(B)}$$

Figure 5.16   Bayesian probability

perfectly legitimate for the expert user to insert data into the database with a degree of certainty less than definite. For example, the user could say that, to the best of his/her knowledge, a person has salary of £10,000 with a certainty factor of 0.8.

5.2.7 Dictionary and database synchronisation

The schema description of the expert system semantic net in the dictionary is more closely integrated with the database data than with normal relational and earlier pointer chain technology type database management systems. Given property inheritance from the database instance tables to the dictionary class tables, when a change is made to a database table all "inherited" tables in the semantic net class hierarchy to the table being changed need to be correspondingly "X" locked for obvious synchronisation reasons. The schema description in the dictionary is therefore treated no differently from user data stored in the database. It is necessary to synchronise locking of the dictionary with the database.

5.2.8 Worked examples

A number of worked examples show how expert systems can be used as intelligent query languages and advice providers. The examples are based on GENERIS from Instrumatic Data Systems Limited and GOLDWORKS from Goldhill Computers Inc. The examples illustrate a variety of features, such as how the components of a knowledgebase are linked together, the criteria on which the access strategy to the rules and the rulesets is based, forward chaining versus backward chaining and the relationship of one ruleset to another ruleset.

5.2.8.1 GENERIS

A worked example of how the GENERIS inference mechanism works and how the individual components of the knowledgebase interrelate now follows. The example is of inference rules.

The GENERIS inference mechanism is based on four components—the database component containing the dumb data, rules, property inheritance through the semantic net facility and local computation. The first three components work in conjunction with each other. The knowledgebase is illustrated in figure 5.17. Note the use of the age property in the database to contain logic, in this case procedural rather than declarative. This is an example of an expert system product taking advantage of technology developed to support the normalisation of logic in object oriented systems. The two rules are inference rules and, in this case, are standalone. They are not chained together, in contrast to the rules in the example in figure 5.5, nor grouped as a ruleset. It will therefore be necessary to build tables of temporary results and hold these in the working memory component of expert system software. The query is that the user wishes to "Display the age and colour of elephants".

In this example GENERIS is being used as an intelligent query language gleaning as much information from the knowledgebase as possible rather than an expert system offering advice. Notwithstanding this prime function GENERIS is quite capable of being used as an expert system.

The inference mechanism begins by parsing the keywords in the query, in this case colour, age and elephant. The knowledgebase is then accessed to find the relevant relationships between the keywords. Colour is in the database as a property of the animal instance table and in the semantic net as a class of colour. The conclusion of both rules 1 and 2 (GENERIS puts the condition after the conclusion) are also both related to colour. There is thus a three way relationship between the three components of the knowledgebase, in this case via colour. Animals also have occupations as defined in the database and the condition of rule 2 has a clause concerned with occupation of circus performer.

Rules

1. Animal has Colour Muddy if Animal Lives in Jungle

2. Animal has Colour Pink if Animal has Occupation Circus Performer

Database

Animal	Birthday	Age (computation)	Occupation	Colour	Location
NELLIE	5/8/89	.... Logic	Circus Performer		
FRED			Circus Performer	Black	
ELEPHANT				Grey	
JUMBO				Dull	Jungle

Semantic Nets

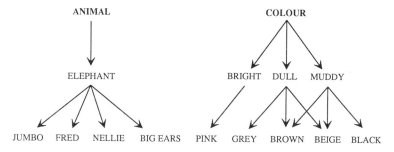

Figure 5.17   GENERIS knowledgebase

The appropriate rules 1 and 2 can now be fired through their conclusion association with colour (backward chaining is being initiated). The sequence is that rule 1 accesses the database to find all animals that live in the jungle and ascertains that it is Jumbo. The result is stored in a temporary working memory table of inferred information—see figure 5.18. Given that the condition of rule 1 is true (that there is an elephant living in the jungle) the conclusion of the rule is true, such that Jumbo must therefore be muddy. Rule 2 accesses the database on the value of circus performer and ascertains that there are two elephants that satisfy that condition and also puts the two elephants, Nellie and Fred, into the temporary working memory table and infers that Nellie and Fred, based on the conclusion of rule 2, are pink. The database information regarding colour is that Jumbo is dull and Fred is black. Combining the inferred and database information produces a conflict on Fred—the inferred information says he is pink and the database information says he is black. The conflict cannot be resolved (both sets of information are at the instance level and there is no priority) and the users

Temp Table			Result		
Elephant	Colour		Elephant	Colour	Age
FRED	Pink	⟶	FRED	Conflict (Pink/Black)	Unknown
	Black				
NELLIE	Pink	⟶	NELLIE	Pink	9
JUMBO	Dull	⟶	JUMBO	Brown Beige	Unknown
	Muddy				
BIG EARS	Grey	⟶	BIG EARS	Grey	Unknown

▨ Information presented by a conventional file handler

Figure 5.18   Temporary and final results

are presented with the conflicting colours for them to resolve. Nellie is pink and Jumbo is muddy (from rule 1) and dull (from the database). To this add the semantic net information. Muddy and dull intersect to state that Jumbo is brown or beige. Using inheritance in the semantic net Big Ears is an elephant and it is known from the database that elephants are grey. Big Ears is therefore grey. Information regarding colour is now complete.

Computation must now be executed to ascertain if any more information can be gathered/computed. The age of the elephants is more difficult to ascertain. The only elephant for which age can be computed is Nellie. For all the other elephants the age is unknown. The output response to the query is illustrated in figure 5.18.

This simple example of using a knowledgebase of rules and semantic net facts as well as data illustrates a number of facilities that relational technology cannot support. It shows that when data is entered into the database by a "standard" user the information may actually be wrong when set against the knowledge of an expert as defined in the knowledgebase. For example, the user says that the elephant Fred is black and a circus performer, the expert, that circus performing elephants are pink. An expert system could automatically correct any database errors on the basis that the expert knows better than the ordinary user. GENERIS happens to leave this example of conflict open.

A relational file handler would have shown little of this information. It would have shown only the colour of Fred as black but without showing the conflict, the colour of Jumbo as dull where actually he is brown and beige and the age of Nellie as a birthday rather than an age. In fact the only accurate information that would have been displayed is the name of the elephants with poor Big Ears totally ignored. All the other information— Jumbo being brown and beige, Fred's colour pink and 9 years of age and Big Ears being grey—would not have been presented with relational technology.

5.2.8.2 GOLDWORKS

GOLDWORKS incorporates facilities for predefining the access algorithms to portions of a knowledgebase and therefore goes some considerable way to providing multiple access mechanisms to the knowledgebase. The structure of the GOLDWORKS inference engine is illustrated in figure 5.19. It is one of the most sophisticated available. The sponsor controls the rule access mechanism in the agenda and controls when rules assigned to the sponsor may or may not fire. Sponsors are used primarily to control the mechanism for the firing of forward chaining rules during the consultation process.

Assertions are dynamic statements of facts that are ascertained to be true during the life of the consultation. The assertions could be initially

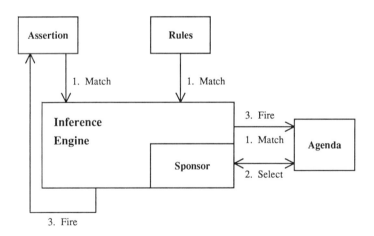

Sponsor - Controls rule selection mechanism in an agenda and groups rules in an application domain

Assertions - Dynamic statements of truth (may have uncertainty)

Rules - Cause and effect logic - antecedents(s) ⟷ consequent(s)

Agenda - Dynamic stack of rules waiting to be fired for query

Figure 5.19 GOLDWORKS inference engine

defined as a set of condition facts when requiring to start a forward chaining consultation. For example, in an illness diagnosis system the assertions could be that the patient has an earache and temperature. Additional assertions may be obtained from the rules and semantic net in the knowledgebase by the inference engine during the consultation process. The consultation will be either to the knowledgebase or, if the assertions cannot be obtained there, with the user. The assertions are held in the working memory component of the expert system software. An agenda is a prioritised queue of rules that are matched on outstanding assertions and waiting to be processed. The rules, of course, are the cause and effect logic statements. They must be allocated to a sponsor and may be allocated to a ruleset. Each sponsor and ruleset is relevant to an application domain task for which advice is sought. The sponsor and ruleset facilities are independent of each other, but can be related explicitly if required.

The sponsor is a mechanism that enables rules to be grouped together into sponsors, with the sponsors related to each other as a hierarchical structure, and executed within the structure in the sequence of top to bottom, left to right, i.e. depth first.

When you define a rule you assign it to a sponsor. Thus you can group rules under a different sponsor according to their purpose and function, i.e. their task in the application domain. This is illustrated in figure 5.20, where an overall sponsor structure is split into six task groupings. The application domain is the servicing of a car, within which there are certain tasks requiring advice relating to electrical, mechanical and other servicing. Within the electrical task there are further sub-tasks relating to servicing the car lighting and heating. Each task and sub-task is supported by a sponsor group.

Sponsors enable the access strategy to the rules within their scope to be accessed in the optimum manner, either breadth first or depth first. If one assumes that the domain expert knows that when a car is serviced the electrical tasks are undertaken before the mechanical tasks, which are undertaken before the other tasks, then it will be best to search the sponsors in that sequence, i.e. depth first. The appropriate access strategy for each sponsor can be predefined in advance, based on an understanding of how the application works. Further refinement would be desirable but is not currently supported. For example, within a sponsor grouping, assume that the most frequent sequencing of rule access to obtain advice in the heating ruleset is between rules 5 to 6 to 15 to 16 to 17, therefore choose breadth first searching, whereas in the lighting ruleset the rule access sequence is usually 7 to 18 to 8 to 19, therefore choose depth first searching. Within the electrical task the rules are accessed in a highly variable manner, so therefore choose the default. It would optimise performance if the rule access strategy could be defined per sponsor.

Example (GOLDWORKS) 1.

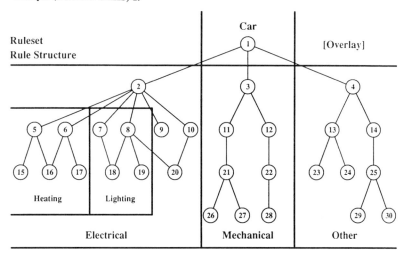

Figure 5.20   Sponsor rule allocation

The agenda is the dynamic list of rules waiting to be fired during the consultation. It is a prioritised queue, onto which agenda items are placed according to their priority, which is determined by the priority of the agenda item rule and the breadth or depth first ordering of the agenda—see figure 5.21. An agenda item is a rule waiting to be fired. An item is actually a pointer to the rule. The ordering of the agenda items that share the same priority is determined by the type of agenda specified when the sponsor itself is defined. The system places agenda items among other agenda items that share the same priority using either a depth first or breadth first ordering. The default ordering is breadth first. In breadth ordering when agenda items are added to the agenda they are placed behind other agenda items sharing the same priority. In depth first ordering the agenda items are placed in front of other agenda items sharing the same priority.

In contrast to the sponsors, rulesets are standalone groupings of rules, with no hierarchical structure and no control mechanisms for their sequences execution. Each ruleset is mutually exclusive. The execution of a ruleset has to be invoked explicitly, typically from an application program. Ruleset firing is therefore intrinsically ad hoc. A ruleset and the individual rules within a ruleset can be invoked from a ruleset—their relationship, if required, is many-to-many. Thus the sequenced processing of the sponsors and the ad hoc processing of the rulesets can be combined to mutual benefit. It could be, for example, that there is a ruleset for providing advice on when and how to rebore a car engine. Under certain conditions

Rule Structure within a Sponsor

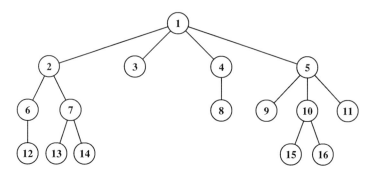

Agenda Sequence (Breadth First : FIFO)

After 1	After 2	After 3	After 4
2 ⟶	3 ⟶	4 ⟶	5 ⟶
3	4	5	6
4	5	6	7 Etc.
5	6	7	8
6	7		

Agenda Sequence (Depth First : LIFO)

After 1	After 7	After 3	Etc.
2	7	4 ⟶	
6	13	8	
12	14	5	
7	3	9	
:	4	10	
:	:	15	
	:	:	

Figure 5.21   Rule firing example (GOLDWORKS)

the mechanical sponsor in figure 5.20 can invoke the rebore ruleset. The sequenced invocation by the sponsor does not compromise the standalone nature of reboring a car engine, which in the normal course of events is not part of car servicing.

Sponsors offer sequential partitioning of the rulebase whereas rulesets offer mutually exclusive partitioning of the rulebase.

The forward chaining mechanism used by GOLDWORKS is that the initial assertions are used to match against the rules which could be fired from the list of agenda items. The rules to be fired are selected from the list of agenda items in the sequence entered onto the agenda. The sequence is set by the rule priority and agenda search specification. Once a rule has been fired from the agenda items, the result of the conclusion is treated as an assertion and added to the list of assertions being dynamically constructed, those assertions which were used to fire the rules are marked as processed and the agenda item pointing to the rule which has just been fired is cancelled. As the rules in the agenda items are fired so the assertions are constructed from the conclusions of the rules and added to the knowledge-base. These assertions can, in turn, cause more agenda items to be created, continuing the forward chain. The assertions are then used to match against the rules and, if a match is found, the rule is fired. The process is repeated for all the agenda items. When all the agenda items are processed the conclusions of the final unprocessed assertions are presented as advice.

Each agenda is controlled by a "sponsor" and each rule is linked to a sponsor and, optionally, to a ruleset. The agenda items that point to the rules can be searched in breadth or depth first manner, as specified in the sponsor. If a conflict exists with multiple rules waiting to be fired the rule chosen is that with the highest priority. Sponsors exist as a hierarchy controlled by a "top sponsor". There is one top sponsor for the overall application. The top sponsor fires its agenda items first and then, if there are further sponsors in the hierarchy, to the next sponsor in the sequence of depth first, left to right order. When all the sponsors have processed their agenda items, control returns to the top sponsor.

A worked example of forward chaining using GOLDWORKS illustrates the inference mechanism processing rules, assertions and agendas. Advice on the choice of wine for a meal is being sought. The rules are defined in figure 5.22 and the sequence of rule firing to ultimate advice provision is illustrated in figure 5.23. Note that the rules cannot be symbolically matched via their conclusions and conditions as they stand. The inference engine software therefore requires to create a temporary table of rules waiting to be processed (the agenda items) and progressively build up the symbolic relationships between the rules during the consultation. The simplistic rule structure in figure 5.2 of a rule nicely pointing to a rule(s) may be broken.

An initial set of assertions/facts are made, possibly the user stating that he/she is about to eat a meal of poultry and the meal has a delicate taste. At point in time 1 these initial assertions match the conditions of rules 1 and

Rules

1. If Meal is Poultry then Wine should be White

2. If Wine should be White and use Light Body Wine then select a Chablis

3. If Meal has a Delicate Taste then use a Light Body Wine

Figure 5.22   GOLDWORKS example rules

322
Expert Systems and Object Oriented Design

P1   Initial Assertion/Facts

- Meal is Poultry
- Meal has a Delicate Taste

Conditions of Rules 1&3 match assertions - therefore put into working memory as agenda items.

Agenda: A   Item #1: Rule 1
            B   Item #2: Rule 3

P2   Rule 1 is fired and conclusion added to assertion and cancelled from Agenda Item List

Assertions:

- Meal is Poultry
- Meal has Delicate Taste } Processed
- Wine should be White

Agenda: B   Item #2: Rule 3

P3   Rule 3 is fired and conclusion added to assertion and cancelled from Agenda Item List

Assertions:

- Meal is Poultry
- Meal has Delicate Taste } Processed
- Wine should be White
- Use a Light Body Wine } Match Rule 2

Last two assertions match Rule 2 conditions so Rule 2 conclusion added to agenda

Agenda: C   Item #3: Rule 2

P4   Rule 3 is fired and conclusion added to assertions and cancelled from Agenda Item List

Assertions:

- Meal is Poultry
- Meal has Delicate Taste
- Wine should be White } Processed
- Use a Light Body Wine
- Select a Chablis

Agenda: Empty

Agenda is empty so unprocessed assertion(s) offered as advice

Figure 5.23   GOLDWORKS example forward chaining

3 and references to rules 1 and 3 are therefore put into working memory as agenda items. At point-in-time 2 the top rule in the agenda items, i.e. rule 1, is fired and its conclusion that the wine should be white is added as an assertion. Rule 1 is cancelled from the agenda item list. The first two assertions have already been processed in order to put rules 1 and 2 onto the agenda item list. The conclusion of rule 1 does not contain sufficient information to point to the condition(s) of another rule, so that no further

additions are made to the agenda item list. At point in time 3 the top item in the agenda item list is ascertained to be rule 3, rule 3 is fired, its conclusion to use a light body wine is added to the assertion list and rule 3 is cancelled from the agenda item list. The two unprocessed assertions—wine should be white and use a light body wine—are matched against the ruleset. The two conditions of rule 2 are found to be a match and rule 2 is added to the agenda item list. At point in time 4 the top item in the agenda item list, that is rule 2, is fired and its conclusion—select a Chablis—is added to the assertion list, and rule 2 is cancelled from the agenda item list. The agenda item list is now empty and the conclusions of the remaining unprocessed assertion(s) is offered as advice—that is select a Chablis.

5.2.9 Enhancements to Information Engineering

The more the author has delved into expert systems technology the more it has become apparent that knowledge is stored and accessed like standard data using a standard file handler, typically of a relational type.
Once the facilities of:

- semantic nets (knowledge data), rules (knowledge logic) and frames (knowledge data and knowledge logic appropriate to a common key) and how they are related together by the inference software

are understood; and it is appreciated that:

- knowledge data is merely a limited extension of a database dictionary/repository;

- knowledge logic is stored and accessed like data;

- knowledge data and logic and database data are related as required to infer yet further knowledge;

the basic facilities of expert systems technology is mastered. Expert systems technology is low risk. What is true of the technology is also true of the design techniques. This low risk is one of the main reasons why expert system products are being widely accepted, in contrast to distributed database.
As with all new trends of information technology, of which knowledge/expert systems is but one, the underlying technology remains very much the same with new layers of software added on top. This is in line with policy followed by the vendors of these new technologies to preserve as far as possible existing technology. This policy was followed, as we have seen, for distributed and realtime systems and is likewise followed for expert systems. The benefits of this approach are that much

of the existing technology and design techniques are preserved. *Thus all of the Information Engineering techniques are relevant to applications requiring knowledge engineering. Once again one need unlearn nothing. The Information Engineering techniques merely require enhancement by addition, in this case for the recognition, representation and processing of knowledge.*

There are few structured methods currently available for the design and development of knowledge based expert systems. The CCTA has funded the GEMINI project to review the feasibility of developing an expert system method standard. When developed, the GEMINI standard will function alongside SSADM. GEMINI will be constructed over the next few years and will be publicly available, as SSADM is now. One of the principal methods available is called STAGES—Structured Techniques for the Analysis and Generation of Expert Systems. STAGES has been developed at Ernst & Young. STAGES also has the advantage that it is designed to be compatible with traditional structured methods, such as Information Engineering. Another method is KADS—Knowledge Acquisition and Documentation System. No method has yet achieved significant market penetration.

Given the newness of expert system methods, the STAGES techniques will be described in some detail. Suggestions as to how Information Engineering can support knowledge engineering and what enhancements are required to its techniques are therefore based on the material from STAGES, as well as the author's own understanding of the underlying expert systems technology.

The following areas need to be addressed in order to use Information Engineering in knowledge based systems:

- Provision of guidelines as to how to select applications requiring knowledge and to identify which areas within the application use knowledge.

- Provision of a set of structural standards regarding the stages, steps and tasks that must be undertaken in an expert system project.

- Provision of a set of procedural standards regarding knowledge engineering techniques, specifically:

  — how to model knowledge logically, as strategic processes, tactical processes, inference and data;

  — how to model knowledge physically in the form of rules, semantic nets and frames, describing when to use which mechanism and how to integrate them and their deliverables;

  — how to decide which knowledge access mechanism to use;

  — how to decide which knowledge access strategy to use;

  — how to design a knowledgebase physically and to calculate and tune its performance;

  — when and how to record knowledge uncertainty and which mechanism to use;

— how to interpret the major role of prototyping in the creation of an expert system design;
— how to validate and verify an expert system prior to release in an operational environment;
— to provide a set of documentary standards;
— how to estimate the costs and benefits of an expert system development;
— to describe the project structure appropriate to an expert system application.

The last four points are not addressed in this book.

5.2.9.1 How to identify expert system applications

There is no hard and fast rule, no fixed mechanism to say this application is suitable for an expert system solution and that application is not. The unique task of expert systems is to offer advice about an application domain based on the knowledge of that domain. The types of application for which advice is most suitable are those involved with diagnosis, interpretation, planning and design. The first task therefore is to classify the purpose of an application and see if it falls within one of these four categories. If it does then one needs to assess whether the application has certain characteristics, such as:

• the problem is recurrent. This means it is more likely to be cost-effective to automate the tasks;

• the problem requires expertise that is both stable and in short supply but available. There should be a shortage of expertise, otherwise there would be no justification for the expert system; however expertise must exist and be available, otherwise the system could not be constructed. The diagnosis of rare deseases would be a typical such application. Certain types of problem are, by contrast, always or often in a state of flux, such as those resulting from scientific research. It is only when the research findings are accepted as valid that the scientific hypotheses can be converted into knowledge;

• the application must be of a manageable size with clear and precise boundaries. Expert systems tend to generate a lot of rules, which in turn proliferate the number of logic paths to be tested. It can soon become impossible to test rigorously all possible combinations.

Once the identification and justification of an expert system has been accomplished one can decompose the application to ascertain which business areas, functions, events and problems-to-solve contain knowledge/expertise from which advice can be offered. The approach adopted by STAGES is to use modified versions of entity modelling (MLDSs) and dataflow diagramming (MDFDs) to identify where knowledge is required and, once identified, to specify the knowledge logic in knowledgebase maps (KBMs) and knowledge data in MLDSs.

The MDFDs are decomposed in the standard manner, preferably as in section 3.2.1. Each process at each level of decomposition is viewed as to whether it is to be implemented in its entirety as an "E" type expert system process, a "D" type data processing process or an "M" type manual process and whether the datastores are "D" type datastores usable by both traditional data processing systems and expert systems or "E" type datastores usable only by expert systems. The process boxes and datastores which indicate a need for knowledge imply a set of knowledge distinct from other processes and datastores. Should there be a need for shared knowledge between expert system processes and datastores the common part of the knowledge should be decomposed into a further process and datastore.

As described earlier the knowledgebase contains dumb user data as well as the other facilities for representing knowledge, such as semantic nets and rules. The database data is a crucial component of the knowledgebase, providing many of the answers to rule conditions from which deductive inferences can be made. It is for this reason that expert systems can access "D" type datastores.

MLDSs are a variant of an entity model designed to show that the structure of data can be dynamic, depending on the context of the data, and supports the concepts of entity classes, entity instances and property inheritance. Consider the modified logical data structure in figure 5.24. The modified data structure model indicates that a company can be either a bank, a retailer or a manufacturer. That these are exclusive possibilities is indicated by the arc. Each possibility gives rise to a different data structure. This structure is dependent on the content of the application as defined in the knowledgebase. A company is a bank if... Many would recognise the retailer, manufacturer and bank as no more than entity sub-types. MLDs does, however, go further in recording the context/business rules that distinguish the entity sub-types as expertise.

Knowledge engineering techniques can now be applied to the areas of the application requiring knowledge.

5.2.9.2 Provide a set of structural standards

This is an aspect on which the author will not comment. The policy followed in this book is that comment will only be made on the basis of practical experience and illustrated with case study support.

Details of how STAGES is structured can be obtained from Ernst & Young.

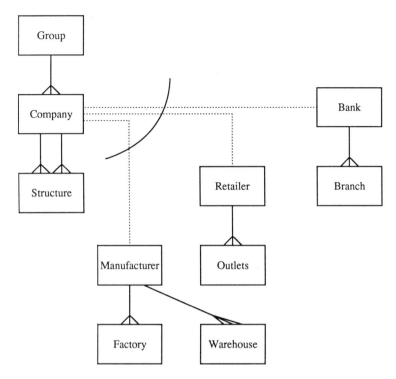

Figure 5.24   Modified data structure diagram

5.2.9.3 *Provide a set of knowledge engineering techniques*

Knowledge engineering techniques represent knowledge in a form which can be computerised. The techniques need to produce two logical design deliverables that are currently used to represent knowledge, namely semantic nets and rules. In STAGES the knowledge data relates to the "E" and "D" type datastores, and is diagrammatically represented in MLDSs and knowledge logic to the "E" type processes in the MDFDs, and is diagrammatically represented in knowledgebase maps (KBMs).

Physically, in many systems, both knowledge data and logic are structured as meaningful groupings of triples. Knowledge data is stored as inter entity and inter attribute semantic descriptions in a semantic net and defined as tables of data in the dictionary schema description. Knowledge logic is defined as rules, which are stored as variable length records, similar to data. Knowledge logic rules can thus also be structured like a data model, rules with relationships to other rules, records with relationships to other records. Such a structure is represented in figure 5.20. These structures can be derived from the KBMs created during analysis.

1 Knowledge data   Knowledge data is nothing more than dictionary table data definitions with extra facilities. The extra facilities are inter entity and inter attribute semantics, class and instance tables, property instantiation and property inheritance. These facilities convert a normal entity model of dumb data into a semantic net of knowledge facts as described in section 5.2.4.7. The table instances show that the dumb database table rows are also part of the knowledgebase and link to the dictionary through property inheritance.

These extra facilities can easily be added onto the normal Information Engineering data modelling techniques. The policy followed by the author is as follows:

• Conduct data modelling using the ERD technique without change.

• Build the semantic net onto the ERD model by identifying the class, adding any new class entities and adding inter entity and inter attribute semantics. The semantic net in figure 5.7 is used as an example. The inter entity semantics can be easily written onto the relationships between the entities. Information Engineering already records relationship descriptions between entities, so users of the method will be familiar with the task. These descriptions within Information Engineering are database semantics, which are defined to "describe" the relationship between entities, not expert system semantics, which are defined to identify property inheritance. For entities in a class group the semantic net description is defined as a "is ", "is", "are", "are a" type description at the detail end of the master to detail relationship. Such a description describes the relationship of person as a detail entity of mammal, with person automatically inheriting the properties of the mammal.

The inter entity component of a semantic net is nothing more than a standard entity model with additional class entities and semantic descriptions showing property inheritance requirements between entities of the same class.

In the semantic net, the relationship arrow between the table points in the direction of the inheritance. There is therefore a conflict with the entity modelling convention in Information Engineering of drawing the crows foot "arrowhead" in the reverse direction pointing towards the detail entity. The description of inheritance by defining the semantic net semantics at the detail end of the relationship overcomes the conflict between the inheritance arrow on the semantic net and the master–detail crows foot arrow on the entity model. The semantic description and not the arrowhead can indicate to the expert system designer that the detail entity is to inherit the properties of the master entity. If no inheritance is required then the detail semantic description can be a free form business semantics but meaningful to the application. Such an example is between person and part. Use the crows foot as standard.

The inter attribute semantic can be easily supported as a comment of the non-key attribute. Remember that the inter attribute semantic can only be between the prime key of the entity and a non-key attribute.

STAGES does not use the inter entity semantic descriptions to show inheritance, instead using different relationship arrow types. Unfortunately the placement of the arrowhead is inconsistent, with the placement of crows feet for other internal entity relationships pointing from detail to master when inheritance is required, and from master to detail when inheritance is not required—somewhat confusing data modelling.

STAGES does not provide inter attribute semantics.

- Define the entities. The entities on the ERD logical data model are implicitly defined at the class level. Some of the entities may also point to instances of the class entity. The class entity data is stored in the dictionary and the instances of the class entity are stored in the database. The entity description form therefore needs two further columns, one to indicate whether the entity itself is class only or can be a class entity with associated instance entities, and the other a property/attribute instantiation column. It could be in the application that there are the Person and the Employee class entities. The application is an employee system that only requires to hold information about employees as instances in the database. The Person entity has been defined purely as a class entity. The only people in the system are employees. Clearly the people are Employees and simultaneously Persons, but are only stored in the database as employees. In reality if it was necessary to also hold information about instances of Person then there is nothing to stop the system holding the instances of persons as well as instances of employees. The only stipulation is that an instance of Employee cannot simultaneously be an instance of Person. The class indicator is there to prevent users putting instances in the database against entities in the application that only serve as class entities.

If the entity is a class entity only then the entity class only indicator needs to be ticked and all the attributes describing the class entity to contain a generic value appropriate to the class in the property instantiation column. Such a class entity in the semantic net example is Mammal, which contains a generic property of number of legs with a value of two. If the entity is also an instance entity it will hold both generic class and instance attributes in its definition. In this case the class/instance indicator needs to be ticked against each individual attribute as appropriate. If the attribute is an instance attribute then it will not contain a value.

The attributes and any class values they contain must be defined in the entity description document.

The upgrading of the ERD logical data model to a semantic net is thus an easy if laborious task.

STAGES goes further in data modelling to identify areas where expertise is required. Data models are drawn of the relationships between attributes where expertise of the understanding of the business context of the attributes is required. An example is given of reference numbers identifying nostro financial deals (banks dealing with banks) and the expertise required for reconciling unmatched deals. "Detective" expertise is applied to whittle away gradually the unmatched deals to identify missing characters, extra characters, wrong characters, transposed characters.... An "attribute" data model showing the relationships between deal reference numbers is drawn.

The author has some reservations about attribute models. Attributes are being treated as objects, just as entities are treated as objects in an entity model, the objects happening to contain one data attribute plus a foreign key attribute. While there is intrinsically nothing wrong with this—an object can be anything you want to make it—the adverse impact on database performance can just be imagined! N single attribute tables! Unfortunately STAGES does not indicate what to do with the attribute models in physical design. Furthermore, the attribute models can only show the valid relationships, but cannot show the business conditions behind the relationships. One still needs to explain the conditions. If the conditions are based on expertise then they should be specified in KBMs, as indeed they are. If one produces KBMs that contain all the information, and more, contained in the attribute models then why produce attribute models?

- Define the frames. Frames are discussed under knowledge data as well as knowledge logic. Being a hybrid of a semantic net and rules, frames fall into both camps. Constructing the frames from the semantic nets needs to be based on all the data retrieval business requirements relating to a common key. "Display all customers with red hair who have taken a holiday in the last two years" could be one such retrieval. The subject here, the subject being the common link to all the information, is customer, the common link being customer number. All retrieval business requirements relevant to customers would identify the scope of customers.

  There seems to be some confusion as to what a frame actually is. In the GOLDWORKS product a frame is nothing more than an entity/table of data. In the GENERIS product a frame has a wider meaning, one that the author prefers, in that the frame is the scope of all the attributes relating to a common key. This is in line with the frame being at the subject level, the subject being the common key.

The real benefit of the GENERIS approach is that the frame is able to get over the deficiencies of relational and command driven and table based query languages, such as SQL. *No matter what the vendors of relational file handlers say SQL is not non-procedural.* The data access component of SQL is based on a standard format SELECT some data FROM certain tables WHERE data values and relationships (if multi table access is required) are true. This means that users of a relational data access language have to know which table contains which data and what are the relationships between the tables. Hardly non-procedural data access! The view facility does not, repeat not, provide an answer. A view is itself a table of data—a virtual table built on a standard SQL query on the base tables. Furthermore a user can have many views and must therefore still understand which data is accessible from which view. Also, for reasons not relevant to this book, views can, under certain conditions, produce invalid results for a query!

An illustrated worked example of a genuinely non-procedural frame based query language using GENERIS is described in section 5.2.8.1. The advantage of the GENERIS approach is that the data in the frame is not restricted to a table and can easily be extended by adding new foreign keys to tables. Thus if a user wants to pose a query on a frame of A (in the GENERIS example A was an elephant) then one only has to include A as a foreign key in a table.

- Record uncertainty. If the data property values at the class or instance level is less than certain record a certainty factor against it.

2 *Knowledge logic* This is defined in the form of rules. No Information Engineering technique as it stands is appropriate for knowledge logic specification.

The first task is to identify which parts of an application require to support knowledge logic. STAGES uses MDFDs as the prime means of this identification. As the processes are decomposed they are progressively identified as requiring to support expertise. Such processes are marked as "E" type processes. Each such process has an implied set of rules, which are recorded in a KBM.

The author suggests making each E type process a ruleset. The rulesets become tables and the rules table rows. One is thus organising knowledge logic as one organises knowledge data. In data storage and access terms there is no difference.

STAGES makes greater use of the dataflow diagramming technique in MDFDs than Information Engineering. Information Engineering does not use dataflow diagrams in such a positive way, but merely as a means of modelling the business structure and grouping the procedures into subsystems and thence into systems. The STAGES differences are:

- The "E" type processes are of two kinds—those that require expertise to "control" the execution of other, possibly lower level, E type processes that contain the "inference" logic more usually associated with the application expertise. Both type of processes require KBMs. The control processes are most easily identified as those with many dataflows to other processes—a somewhat vague definition. Expertise is required to control the execution of the other processes, which themselves may also use expertise. Information Engineering only recognises the need to specify logic for the lowest level processes. STAGES supports multi-level logic.

- Process dependency is identified and by this means the order in which rules/rulesets execute. The author has considerable sympathy with the STAGES approach. As described in section 3.2.1 and illustrated in figure 3.23 problem-to-solve processes are causally related and, although occurring logically at the same point in time as the event to which they relate, do nevertheless have a sequence—process 4.1.1.2 is sequenced after/ is dependent on process 4.1.1.1. In centralised processing this can be used to identify the sequence of program module calling.

  Information Engineering uses process dependency diagrams to show sequence dependency between event level processes but not process sequence dependency within an event. STAGES is therefore at variance with Information Engineering by incorporating the concept of time in dataflow diagramming.

  This use of process dependency is very useful when designing the layout of rulesets and ascertaining the ruleset access strategy. Consider figure 5.20. It could be that the MDFDs identified "E" type processes for heating, lighting, electrical, mechanical and other tasks when undertaking car servicing and, via process dependency, that heating is undertaken before lighting, which is undertaken before electrical ... and that the rules in heating are undertaken in the sequence of 5, 6, 15, 16 and 17. The rule access strategy should therefore be breadth first.

There are some problems with the STAGES' use of MDFDs. As described in section 2.4.2.3 DFDs are not suited to data retrieval business requirements, which are intrinsically standalone and independent. Yet data retrieval business requirements are just as susceptible to requiring expertise as data maintenance requirements. The KBM in figure 5.26 is, for example, for a data retrieval business requirement. In STAGES, data retrieval business requirements are included in MDFDs; advice as to how to prevent the MDFDs becoming unmanageable in size should therefore be given.

The other problem is the use of the E type datastores. STAGES does not identify what data is stored in E type datastores, how the data differs from that in the D type datastores and how the E and D type data is identified and separated. One assumes that knowledge data is included in the E type datastore. Knowledge data is represented as a semantic net. However, a semantic net is nothing more than a standard logical data model with class entities and semantic descriptions between entities and attributes, as described in section 5.2.4.7, to form triples and thereby convert the dumb data in a database into knowledge facts in a knowledgebase. *Knowledge data is essentially dumb data with semantics.* It is the author's opinion that E type datastores are therefore not needed. The data they contain is already existing in the D type datastores. *Knowledge data cannot be separated from dumb data.*

The position of Ernst & Young on this issue is that E type datastores are those which need only be accessed by the E type processes. Identifying these separately is useful because later, in physical design, it may be necessary to identify which datastores should be managed by the expert systems tool and which by the RDBMS.

The inter entity semantics can be recorded on the ERD logical data model and the inter attribute semantics in the standard entity description form.

Once the requirement for expertise is identified a KBM is drawn.

The KBM is the STAGES technique for modelling knowledge logic. Given that knowledge logic is defined in the form of rules and that rules are stored as variable length records it is not surprising that a KBM is a cross between a data structure diagram and a program flow chart. A most elegant solution. The KBMs allow a full representation of the rules in a ruleset and their interactions, and represents all the variables, constants, operators, relations, facts, questions, defaults and actions in the system as illustrated in figure 5.25.

There are certain conventions implicit in the KBM, relating to order and priority:

- Order convention: so as to define uniquely the order in which the rules should be fired or questions be asked, the map should be read left to right and downwards;

- Priority convention: the conditions to a rule need to be satisfied before the rule is fired and the conclusion drawn. The sources of information for the conditions are in the following priorities:

— user data from the database/facts from the semantic net;
— questions to the user;
— further rules in the ruleset;
— defaults.

Symbol	Meaning	Comment
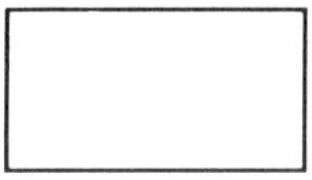 (box)	Variable	Typed identifier
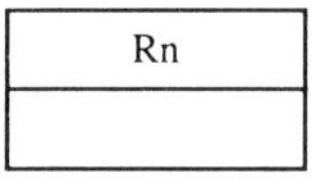 Rn (box)	Rule and principal conclusions	Conditions below Other conditions above
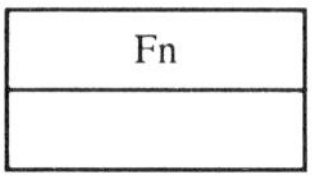 Fn (box)	Fact	Rule without conditions
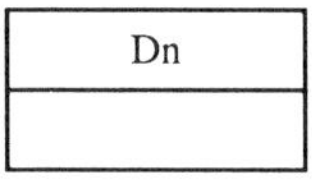 Dn (box)	Default	Rule without conditions
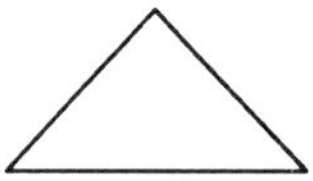 (triangle)	Question	
 (rounded box)	Arithmetic relation or operator	Constants inside box, variable below
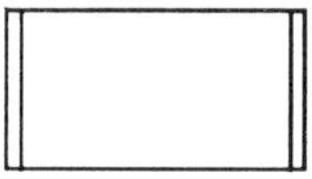 (action box)	Action	Procedure or action
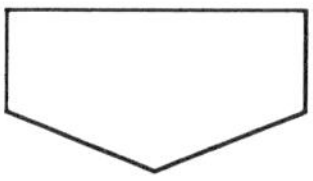 (pentagon)	Continuation	
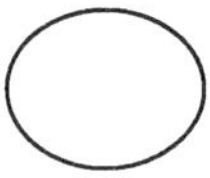 (circle)	Logical Operator	

Figure 5.25   Symbols used in KBMs

Thus, if the user data/semantic net facts return a value of unknown then the appropriate condition is posed in question form to the user and so on down the priority sequence.

- Precision Convention: the top of the KBM should deal with high level, low precision concepts; the lower levels should contain progressively more precise and detailed knowledge. In this way, the declarative nature of the expertise can be maintained and expert users can remain at the top of the map, while non-experts can use an appropriate level of detail and explanation.

• The logical operators used in the conditions and conclusions of a rule may include NOT, AND, OR, XOR (A XOR B = A or B but not both), X(XA = A or NOT A).

The KBMs are of two kinds, the types reflecting the purpose for which expertise is required. STAGES identifies "control" expertise to bring order to the execution of application processes and "inference" expertise for the execution of the application processes.

An example of a KBM—in this case an inference process—is illustrated in figure 5.26. The knowledge map illustrates a ruleset with multiple rule paths. Its structure is exactly that illustrated in figure 5.2 and is therefore the direct basis of drawing the rule structure within a ruleset. It illustrates that, within a ruleset, knowledge can be decomposed into a hierarchical structure, on the lines indicated in figure 5.20 for a particular application.

The purpose of the consultation is to work out the length of the month for the Gregorian calendar and to provide advice as to the number of days within a month. The logic of the knowledge map is that, because by convention one accesses in the sequence of top to bottom, left to right, question one is posed to the user first. Question one on the leftmost rule path asks the month length. If the month length is provided by the user then the consultation is finished. The sequence of the other priorities, such as posing questions to the user, is obviously irrelevant and there are no rules and default values on this rule path.

If the consultation is not finished the second rule path is accessed, in this case to rule one. The bottom of the rule path indicates menu question two, which poses a question regarding month name: is it September, April, June or November? If the knowledgebase provides an answer then the condition of rule one is satisfied, the rule is fired and advice provided that the month length is thirty. There are no other rules and default values in the rule path for testing against the condition of rule one. By-passing the default rule, the third rule path is accessed, that is the rule path beginning with rule two. The answer to menu question two is inspected again to see if the month name is February. If it is then the condition to rule four requires to be tested to ascertain if the year is a leap year. Question three is therefore displayed. If the year is divisible by one hundred or if the year is divisible by four and not by four hundred then the year is a leap year. If the two conditions to rule two are true, that is it is February and not a leap year, the conditions to rule two are satisfied and the conclusion is drawn and advice provided that the month length is twenty eight. Rule three is fired if the conditions to rule two are found not to be true. The fourth rule path, in this case via rule three, is then accessed. Following the knowledge map, the answer to menu question two is inspected yet again for the month name. If it is February then rule four is tested again to find out if it is a leap year.

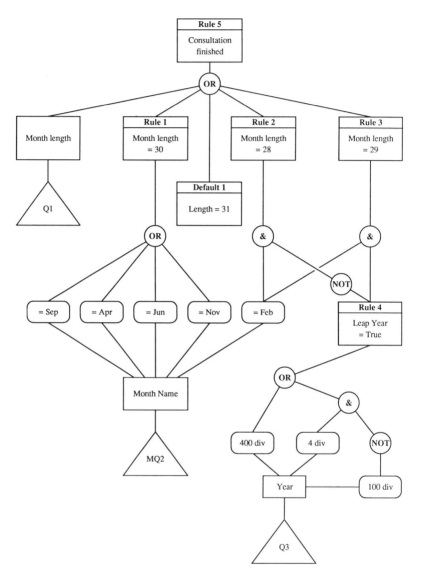

Figure 5.26   Knowledgebase map

The logic for rule four has already been described. If the month name is February and the conditions of rule four are true then the conditions to rule three are satisfied, the rule is fired and the conclusion is drawn, namely that the month length is twenty nine. If rules one to four are not true then the default rule is fired and advice provided that the month length is thirty one.

Using pseudo code the above rules would be defined as:

- *Rule 1*   If month name is September or April or June or November then month length is 30.

- *Rule 2*   If month name is February and not year is leap year then month length is 28.

- *Rule 3*   If month name is February and year is leap year then month length is 29.

- *Rule 4*   If year is divisible by 400 or (divisible by 4 and not divisible by 100) then year is leap year.

- *Default 1*   Month length is 31.

The KBMs contain all information that is necessary for the coding of rules in a ruleset—the sequence in which the rules are to be accessed, the conditions and conclusions of the rules, any uncertainty of whatever type in the conditions and conclusions, the questions to be posed to the users if the answers cannot be obtained from the knowledgebase, and whether there are other rules in the ruleset and if not whether there are any default values as the sources of knowledge.

Given its ability to show the structures of rules in a ruleset and to represent knowledge logic the STAGES KBM facility is an excellent and powerful technique.

Where the conditions and conclusions of a rule contain uncertainty this requires to be recorded as a certainty factor. It is unfortunate that one of the four mechanisms for handling uncertainty described in section 5.2.6 is called by the misnomer of certainty factors. This type of uncertainty should be handled automatically by expert system software, as it is based on a fixed mathematical formula. For classical probability a threshold of acceptance should also be specified for the condition uncertainties. If Bayesian probability is required then a condition(s) requires to be specified against the rule condition(s) in order to create conditional uncertainty (no puns intended here!). If fuzzy logic is required then this can be coded as a set of probability statements. Using the example in section 5.2.6.4 a set of rules could be coded to show the percentage of people believing a car to be very expensive and a car costs about £30,000 to produce the combined result. The KBMs need to be upgraded to show rule iterations about a common test—in this case two propositions and their combined result.

Create one KBM for each E type process and record the rules in the KBM as a ruleset.

3   Knowledge access   Both knowledge data and knowledge logic are stored as table rows. The knowledge data is stored as class tables in the dictionary (one table row per table) and instance tables in the database (*n* table rows per class table). The knowledge logic is stored as variable length records, with the rules being table rows and the rulesets by which action and inference rules grouped as tables. *Knowledge data and logic therefore have the same underlying storage and access mechanisms.*

The considerations in identifying rulesets, ascertaining the ruleset access strategy of breadth first or depth first and whether forward and/or backward chaining is required were identified in sections 5.2.4 to 5.2.7, with an example based on GOLDWORKS.

Some basic principles and task sequences in undertaking knowledge access are:

• Ascertain the application domain for which advice is required. In the GOLDWORKS example the overall application is the servicing of a car, within which there are certain domain tasks requiring advice, such as electrical, mechanical and other servicing. Within the electrical task there are further sub-tasks relating to servicing the car lighting and heating.

• Each task equates to an "E" type process in the MDFDs and each task becomes a ruleset.

• For each ruleset draw the structure of the rules using a KBM.

• From the type of trigger to the KBM decide whether forward and/or backward chaining in the ruleset is required. If the answer (i.e. goal) for which advice is sought is known then adopt backward chaining; if the answer for which advice is sought is not known (i.e. a set of initial conditions is posed) then adopt forward chaining.

The technique for undertaking knowledge access design in STAGES is a version of that described in section 3.2.9.3 and is extremely thorough and elegant. The variation is the explicit identification of the probability of rule firing and rule traverse. (In reality this aspect is nothing more than the probabilities of access to different access paths in a standard data model). The other difference is that the cardinality ratio between the KBM nodes is invariably one to one. Cardinality ratios are therefore not a consideration as they are in conventional transaction access path analysis.

The technique is based on calculating the proportion/weight of accesses to each node of the KBM for each triggering of the KBM transaction. The calculation of weights proceeds as follows:

Step 1 Number each branch of the KBM tree which leads to a node, i.e. to:

• a rule;

• an implied test (e.g if a variable is "unknown");

- a test;

- a logical operator.

Step 2   For each numbered branch calculate recursively PT (the probability of traversing the branch) and PF (the probability that the branch will fire).

PF is calculated as an independent probability and is not conditional on any events except those subsidiary to it in the KBM.

PT is calculated differently depending on the node from which the branch descends. If it is a single node, e.g a rule or a unary operator, PT is defined to be 1. If it is an operator with many arguments, PT is calculated as follows:

- if the operator is AND:
  PT = $\prod$ (PF) (for all preceding branches from the node)
- if the operator is OR:
  PT = $\prod(1\text{-PF})$ (for all preceding branches from the node)

Step 3   The weight, W, of a branch is calculated as:

W = $\sum$WC (for all subsidiary branches) + 1

Step 4   The weight contribution, WC, of a branch is calculated as:

WC = (PT x W)

This is the mathematical formula of what was described in section 3.2.9.3.

Consider figure 5.27. It represents backward chaining knowledge access. The paths with the greatest weighting contribution are those that are accessed most frequently. Using this technique one can quickly ascertain which parts of a KBM are accessed most frequently. In the example it is clear that rules 1, 2 and 4 are the most frequently accessed. It is obvious that the ruleset access strategy should be depth first.

The use of weightings is the opposite of the approach adopted in Information Engineering. Weighting requires their calculation *towards* the entry point. In the example backward chaining is used. The entry point is therefore rule 1. Information Engineering uses a counting of the actual number of accesses *from* the entry point. Both approaches are valid. It is a matter of style.

STAGES only attempts to assess the access to the knowledgebase in database optimisation. This is too late. It should be done as part of the logical design in order to identify potential performance problems before they occur. This is not difficult, and given the concept that logical design = physical design, entirely valid. Just bring the technique forward to an earlier logical design phase of the method.

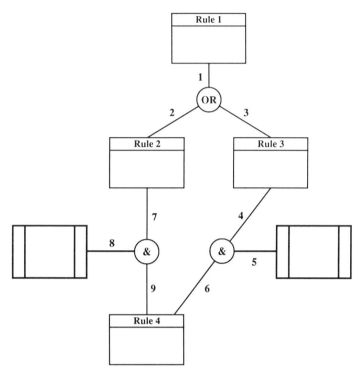

Branch	PF	PT	Weight	Weight Contribution	Subsidiary Branches
1	0.90	1.00	7.76	7.76	2 3
2	0.81	1.00	6.34	6.34	7
3	0.09	0.19	2.19	0.42	4
4	0.09	1.00	1.19	1.19	5 6
5	1.00	0.09	1.09	0.10	6
6	0.09	1.00	0.09	0.09	
7	0.81	1.00	5.34	5.34	8 9
8	1.00	1.81	1.90	3.44	9
9	0.90	1.00	0.90	0.90	

Figure 5.27   Knowledge access

Any linkages of the ruleset to the semantic net/frames structure is usually automatically ascertained by the inference mechanism. This was illustrated using the GENERIS worked example in section 5.2.8.1. Certain products, such as Software AG's NATURAL EXPERT, require explicit linkage.

The calculation of physical I/O overheads in accessing knowledge rule logic in the rulesets was described in section 5.2.4.6. The rules drive access to the knowledge data in the semantic net/frame structures. Each access to the semantic, be it to the class table in the dictionary or to an instance table in the databases is likely to generate disk I/O as well as any overheads in accessing ruleset indexes. Before accessing the knowledge data the rules may require to pose questions to the user. This, of course, generates the standard message I/O to the terminals.

One can calculate the performance of a knowledgebase using the standard practices of database optimisation.

5.3 OBJECT ORIENTED SYSTEMS

5.3.1 The problem

It is inevitable that current technology reflects design decisions made years and possibly decades ago by the developers of information technology. The long gestation period of technology development contrasts to the short period for human thought. It is therefore not surprising that most current technology for the storage and access of data and logic does not reflect the latest thinking. There are now recognised to be a number of deficiencies with the current technology. As always, with the benefit of hindsight, the design decisions taken then can be improved now.

One general problem we face is that there is a physical separation of data in the database and logic in the application programs. This separation is illogical—after all both data and logic are information. This illogicality leads to inefficiency. Because the two are stored separately—the data in the database and the logic in the application program—it is necessary to bring them together before processing can take place.

The policy followed by all developers of information technology has been to move the data to the logic. The data is accessed from disk, brought into the processor main memory buffer pool and from there moved to the application program working storage, all involving expensive logical and physical I/O. It is only when the two are brought together, so that data can be processed and presented to the user according to the logic instructions, that the benefit of a computer system is achieved. The merging of data and logic would eliminate this inefficiency (although at a cost elsewhere, as will be seen—nothing is free of charge), as well as provide many other advantages.

5.3.2 Object oriented concepts

A formal definition of an object is that "it is an entity that exists uniquely and distinctly in time and space, *containing both data and logic about itself within itself"*. While an object can correspond to the entities in a conventional logical data model, there are other object types in an object model for which there is no entity correspondence. There are more objects in a class object model than there are in a conventional data model. *Objects are more than entities.* Objects describe "things" of interest to an application about which data *and/or* logic can be recorded. Entities describes "things" of interest to an application about which data, and only data, can be recorded. *It is the logic component which primarily distinguishes objects from records/tables of database file handlers, which only contain data.* There are other facilities, as will be ascertained in this chapter, but it is the logic that is the prime feature.

The significant point here is that information, be it data or logic, is stored *within* the object to which it logically relates. It is well known that customer name data attribute normalises to the customer entity. Why should not the logic "All customers with red hair receive a lump sum of £100" also not be normalised to the customer entity? The answer is that it can be. The logic, like the data, is normalised.

The first concept of object oriented design is therefore the normalisation of information.

The normalisation of information leads to the second concept, *the creation of application independent information designs*, that is the design of information that is generic to a corporation. To date the only part of information that is corporate is data, hence the creation of corporate databases. The reason for this is that the data has been normalised to the appropriate entity/object and not to a business requirement/event of a functional area of the business. Customer Name is an attribute describing Customer, not a business requirement. It is therefore not specific to an application and its constituent business requirements. The same data objects can be "accessed" by multiple functionally based applications.

The same is true when the logic information is normalised to an object. If the logic is "All Customers with red hair receive a lump sum of £100" then it, like the data, has nothing to do with a particular business requirement/event but with the Customer object, in the same way as Customer Name data. It is therefore normalised to the Customer class object. When logic is normalised like data then it has the same corporate characteristics as data—and in this case the logic can be "re-used" (a word much used by object oriented devotees) by multiple applications.

5.3.3 Object oriented facilities

An object oriented system is a network of intercommunicating objects—each object in itself is totally self contained, but functions as part of a total application system. The object is the basic unit of modularity in system design. The total application system is the total of all the objects and their relationships with each other, plus the application program events, one for each event/business requirement. Many, quite correctly, regard the main procedures as objects.

The objects are stored as traditional tables of information as in a relational database.

By convention people have been talking of object oriented databases and object oriented programming languages. This obviously reflects traditional thinking, but also reflects the fact that they have evolved separately, the object oriented languages long preceding the arrival of object oriented databases, as well as being been developed and marketed by different companies. Notwithstanding this the two subjects are effectively one. If you describe one you in large measure describe the other.

Nevertheless the traditional separation is preserved, as there are certain aspects of object oriented design that a database administrator needs to know that are different from what an application programmer needs to know. The facilities of object orientation are therefore considered under the traditional database and programming headings.

It must be appreciated that although the technical facilities of object oriented systems described in this book are classified as relating to database or programming the facilities are nevertheless relevant to both divisions of object oriented technology. For example, message passing and encapsulation have been classified as being part of object oriented programming, but is also very much part of the data component of object oriented systems.

5.3.4 Object oriented data

Object oriented databases (hereafter this term will be replaced by the more correct term objectbase. It is a new term to become familiar with) are based on four basic features:

- class objects;
- instances of the class objects;
- property inheritance;
- conflict resolution.

Each feature is, by itself, not particularly significant, producing no major upgrade to systems design and development. However, when the facilities of the four features, along with their by-products, such as polymorphism and function name overloading as by-products of inheritance, are combined and related to the facilities of object oriented programming. the full functionality of objectbases is obtained.

5.3.4.1 The object

An object is, in simple terms, composed of two types of information, as illustrated in figure 5.28. The two types are the data and the logic information components. An object does not have to have both types of information simultaneously and can contain data and logic or just logic. The object must contain logic, because, as we shall see, the data component cannot be accessed except via the logic component. The data component is optional. The data component has been described as the attributes and the logic component described as the services provided by the object. Another term for services is methods. This is the term more usually used in this book. The attributes and their values describe the state of the object and the services/methods define what can be done to the attributes.

The data and logic components both describe the object and are defined in the dictionary schema definition of the object. Unlike the standard

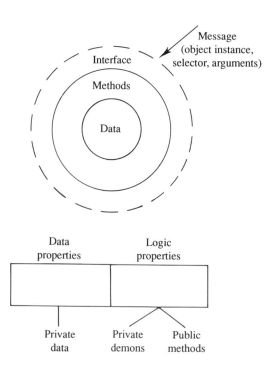

Figure 5.28   Object structure

schema definitions of relational and earlier file handler types, the class object definitions of the properties contain values of information. In the case of the methods the values is the logic. Both components can have many properties (object oriented buzzword for data attributes and methods), which correspond to the fields of a file handler record/table.

There is, in fact, an invisible third component, the interface layer. As part of the facility of encapsulation, object oriented technology does not allow other objects to know what the information is that is stored in an object. Indeed these other objects do not need to know and do not care what the information is. The only thing that the users/other objects need to know is the interface message to send to the object to invoke a named method and the response that will be sent in return. This interface layer is the component that is referenced by the messages that are passed between objects. The interface mechanism is discussed later.

It is now feasible to consider objects as abstract data types, abstract in that the user of the object does not know the data and logic contents of the object.

Objects can, in the same way as the semantic net tables, be stored at the class and instance levels. Classes and instances have the same meaning as in expert systems. Some writers on object oriented technology talk of classes and objects, the objects being the instance of the class. The author prefers the definition of objects at the two levels—class objects and instance objects. After all both class objects and instance objects can store data and method properties and use them in the same way.

The class object contains a definition of all the information about an object that is generic to all the instances of the object. Thus, the class object Employee would contain the attribute definitions and instantiated values and any methods appropriate to all the employees. The instances of the class object are the individual employees in the system. In a traditional database environment the class object would be the record/table and the instance of the class object would be the record occurrence/table row.

As always, class information is stored in the dictionary, instance information in the objectbase. If the data or logic is at the class level it is generic information, relevant to all instances of the class object. Class is a useful way for grouping common information. If the data or logic is at the instance level then it is only relevant to the single instance/occurrence of the object and none other.

5.3.4.2 *The object class model*

The class object model is to object orientation what the logical data model is to relation technology.

The basic structure of a class object model is illustrated in figure 5.29. There are two basic objects groups—the objects that support the application being designed and developed and the objects that support the computer system on which the application will run.

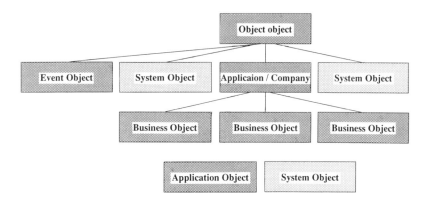

System objects include class libraries, common procedures, windows and menu screens

Business objects include Employee, Broker, Person and Share Allocation

Event objects are the business requirements, such as Calculate Broker Commission

Figure 5.29   Basic structure of a class object model

Within the application group there are what the author calls the Object object, the company object, the business objects and the event objects. The object at the top of the class object model is by convention called the Object object and contains data and logic information that is recognised to be universally true (such as the world is round and if you are in location A then you are not in location B), but is of relevance to the applications. Below the Object object there could be a class object for a company, which contains information that is true at the company level (the company policy is that overtime is standard pay × 1.25). Instead of a company class object there could be an application class object for information generic to an application. There could be some rule that states that invoices received in Manchester have an X% discount whereas those received in Liverpool have a Y% discount. However, given that object orientation is about producing application independent designs such a class object is not to be recommended—and one could argue that the rule is a company rule.

The business objects equate to the entities in a logical data model, but with object orientated facilities included. Certainly all entities remain as class objects in a class object model, but there may well be other business objects "abstracted" as super-classes through class generalisation or as sub-classes through class specialisation of the base entities.

The event objects contain logic that is specific to the business requirements. The event objects are the objects that contain logic that is unique to the events/business requirements of an application, and do not relate to the system or business objects.

Also below the Object object are the system objects. These non-business objects are unfamiliar to those from a traditional data processing background and are not found in a logical data model or semantic net. They are unique to object oriented technology. This, of course, will add further objects to the class object model. They contain the logic supporting system functions, such as data edit routines, print routines and technical processes such as windowing, domain processing and file handling. Many of these system objects can be purchased from specialist vendors.

The event objects contain the logic that links/"glues" the system and business objects together to form in combination the application. The benefits of this are discussed in section 5.3.17.

An example of a class object model is illustrated in figure 5.30. It is for illustrative purposes only. The technical term for such a structure is a class object model. Each rectangle represents a class object and the line between the objects with an arrowhead at one end represents a relationship between two objects, the arrowhead indicating the direction of inheritance and pointing to the super-class object, with the arrowbase pointing from the sub-class object.

The object oriented class object model is similar to the semantic net used by expert systems, in that it also uses the class and property inheritance facilities, but is more powerful, *with additional facilities.* Given that the class object model contains all the information of a semantic net it can also represent knowledge data.

The additional facilities used are:

- the object, with logic properties in the form of methods. The semantic net contains only data properties;

- class objects pitched at any level of information detail or, to use an object oriented term, abstraction. The semantic net supports the class facility and thus can also support entities at higher or lower levels of abstraction than the entity level. *However, the degree of abstraction in a class object model is greater than in a semantic net,* because the scope of software re-use in object orientation is so much greater than for the data in a semantic net. There may well be class objects that contain only logic, this being an information abstraction not found in a semantic net. There is no abstraction for logic in a semantic net, so the need for abstraction is less. *The author believes the semantic net deals only with the business objects, but*

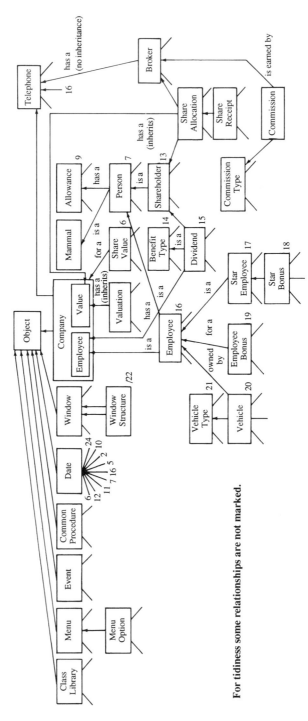

For tidiness some relationships are not marked.

Figure 5.30   Class object model

the class object model contains objects of the other types. There is, however, nothing to stop expert systems using the facilities of object orientation. Products such as GENERIS and GOLDWORKS use both technologies.

This generic class data is a convenient way of expressing facts which are recognised as:

- universally true (the world is round);

- company wide (the company policy is that if invoices have not been paid within 6 months then take out proceedings);

- class object wide (Man has two legs).

The object types in a class object model are:

THE APPLICATION OBJECTS

1 The object object The object at the top of the class object model is called the Object object. The purpose of the Object object is to act as a repository, a sort of "dumping ground", for data and logic that cannot be normalised to any of the other objects in the object model. It typically contains information that is universally true.

2 The company object This is an object new to structured modelling of application information. It contains the information that is more specific, more specialised, than universal truths, but is information that is applied corporately wide.

Examples of universal and company levels of information abstraction have been given in the above section.

3 The business objects The most common object in the class object model is the business object. Users of semantic nets/relational databases would recognise the business object as a standard entity/table of information. The business object almost always contains user data, as in a conventional logical data model. The only business objects with no user data are the key only link objects supporting many-to-many relationships.

A typical business object would be Employee, which contains the data and logic property that is pertinent/normalisable to employee. Examples of this could include the telephone number of the employee for the data component and the calculate annual salary for the logic component.

The entities in a logical data model could undergo abstraction through information generalisation or specialisation, each abstraction creating another business object. The class object model will therefore contain more business objects than a logical data model contains entities. Information abstraction is discussed more fully in section 5.3.4.5.

4 The domain objects   The concept of the domain is the same for object orientation as in a relational file handler. There is no difference. Domains, therefore, also contain information that is universally generic, such as date, or generic to a company, such as the salary range being between £10,000 and £20,000. All the objects that contain the Date and Salary domain objects will inherit all data and logic pertinent to valid values of date and salary.

If both the Object object and the domain object contain information that is universally true then what is the difference in the role of the two object types? The information in the domain objects is normalisable to a specific object type, date being the obvious example. The information in the Object object is more generalised. The domain objects are more specific than the Object object and are therefore sub-classes of the Object object.

5 The man/machine interface objects   Another type of class object is that which supports the man/machine interface, that is the menu screens for the menu selection process and the window screens for the use of windowing technology, the former probably containing screen panel formats and the latter the logic for each of the windowing facilities. The facilities could be defined as sub-classes of the Window object. The man/machine interface class objects are defined as a sub-class of the Object object as they are at the one level below the universal level. If the information about the menu and window screens are universally accepted standards, as is happening with the adoption of the Open Standards, then the information could be defined at the Object object.

The transaction screens properties for the display of business requirement/event information are appropriate to the event and are therefore held within the event object.

6 The common procedure object   The common procedure object is a class object that contains only a logic component, the logic being a common procedure that is application generic and relevant to all the class objects within the application.

In a sense all methods, because they are normalised logic, are common procedures, being common to the sub-class objects of the super-class object in which they, the methods, are placed. A method in, say, the Employee object is common to Star Employee, Employee Bonus and Star Employee.

The common procedures are those that are not normalisable to the business objects because the logic is relevant to many objects. There could, for example, be some logic that is applicable to *n* business objects. There could be some logic that is applicable to Allowance, Person, Shareholder and Dividend, or, indeed of a general nature and not pertinent to any object. A typical example of this is a commonly used access path routine. This procedure would be more sensibly put into the Common Procedure object.

Under these circumstances the author puts the logic into the common procedure object as an instance of the Common Procedure class object rather than as a method property of the class object.

The methods in the Common Procedure class or instance objects are therefore similar to the classical common procedure of conventional application programming. In the class object model the Common Procedure object is a sub-class of the Object object as it is relevant to all the business object in the class object model.

7 The event object   The Event object contains the residue of logic that remains pertinent to the business requirement. It contains the logic for the beginning and the end of the application program. The beginning logic would typically be for the receipt of the input screen information, the initialisation of the variables and the sending of the messages to one or more objects. The end logic would typically be for the synchronisation of the message responses if more than one object is "accessed", any final processing of the returned information and the presentation of the output screen. *It is the only object in the class object model that is pitched at the event level, and effectively plays the role of the main procedure of an application program.*

The placement of the Event object in the class object model has been a matter of some debate. It obviously is not a sub-class of any business or system object. Perhaps the best place to put it from the point of view of information abstraction is as a sub-class of the company object as the events are obviously relevant to the company, but the author has followed the policy of putting it as a sub-class of the Object object. Nobody has ever objected to this.

8 The class library object   The instances of this class object are usually supplied as what are called class libraries. Typical class libraries are objects for system software support, such as bit string handling, array handling, inserting an object, deleting an object, character editing, numeric editing and printing an object. There are a number of vendors of class libraries, both independent third party, such as Glockenspiel, and suppliers of object oriented programming languages, such as AT&T for C++, Interactive Software Environment Inc for EIFFELL and Xerox Parc for SMALLTALK.

These class libraries objects are of a very generic nature, to the extent that they are universal type functions for system processing, and could therefore be stored as methods in the Object object. In the class object model in figure 5.30 the class libraries are drawn as a sub-class of the Object object.

9   The version object   The final type of system object is the object that records the version of objects in the class object model. This object type, which is not shown in the object class model in figure 5.30, can be used in two ways. It can be set up for the maintenance history for some of the class objects or for specified object instances of the class objects. For example, it may be necessary to state that all object instances of the class object Person and its sub-classes created after a specified date are of a different version. Alternatively the object class model as a whole is defined as a new version, with the version object placed as a sub-class of the Object object and as a super-class of the Company object.

Objects can be at two levels—class and instance. As shown in the semantic net the two levels are not mutually exclusive—an object can be a class and an instance simultaneously.

Some of the objects in the example class object model are only at the class level. Such class only objects are Object, Mammal and Date. There are no instances of the class in the objectbase. These objects with no instances contain information that is only relevant to other sub-objects classes, and their instances, that can inherit from it. For example, there is a data property of the Mammal object that shows that all sub-objects which can inherit from it are warm blooded. In the case of the class object model the sub-objects are Man, Person, Shareholder, Employee and Star Employee. The mechanism of inheritance is described as part of the semantic net in section 5.2.4.7.

Some of the objects have a number of lines extending from the bottom of the class object. This indicates that the objects have instances of the class object stored in the objectbase. Window, Shareholder, Share Value, Person, Employee and Star Employee objects are class objects (all objects must have a class) *and* are also defined and stored at the instance level. These objects contain some properties that are not instantiated with a value at the class level. For example the Date of Birth data property in the Person object is unique to each instance of Person. To instantiate at the class level would therefore be meaningless, indeed it would be incorrect, as each instance of Person could have a different birthday. Although defined at the class level in the dictionary the property is instantiated only at the instance level in the objectbase.

Some of the class objects with no instances contain only logic properties, i.e. a method(s). An examples of this is the Telephone object. The Telephone object contains a common procedure for the editing of telephone numbers. All the objects which contain telephone numbers as a data property can inherit the method for editing the telephone number whenever the number is inserted or modified.

An object is anything of interest to the system about which data and supporting logic information is required. Individual properties can be objects—the ultimate "atomic" (a favoured buzzword) level of information normalisation. Clearly the more the objects the greater the access overheads and hence logical and physical I/O. The bulk of data processing is at the conventional table level and the author has tended to follow table based object oriented design. There is nothing to stop "enthusiasts" decomposing to the "atomic" level—objects with a key and optionally a single data property and single method property. This is the approach adopted by the SMALLTALK object oriented programming language. The author would not like to be around to measure performance!

5.3.4.3 Object instances

Unlike the class object there are no sub-divisions of the instances of the class object. All object instances fulfil the same role.

As we have seen object class data is defined with the generic values in the schema description in a dictionary. Each class object is a "one off"—i.e. there is only one instance of the class object in the dictionary schema—the "one off" definition of the class object for n instances of the class object, where n can be zero. The single definition of the class object Person, for example, can have n instances of person.

The instance data properties are also defined in the dictionary alongside the class data, but are not instantiated with data values in the dictionary. This is because the values to be stored in the instance data properties can vary with each occurrence of the object instance. Each person could have a different date of birth. Thus person would have date of birth defined in the schema description but stored with a potentially different value in the objectbase for each employee instance of the class object.

While the object instances are mostly used to contain unique values of the data properties for each occurrence of the class object the object instances can also contain logic. The employee Mary could have a unique way in which her salary is calculated and therefore require a method to be stored at the instance level.

The author is not aware of any system where this level of logic "precision" has been required. There are those of the object oriented fraternity who believe that logic at the instance level is not appropriate, but why can't Mary have a unique method for the calculation of her salary. If Mary can have unique data values why not unique logic values? After all, object orientation normalises and stores logic in the same way as data. The two are no different.

This latter point illustrates another use of object instances—to overrule class information. Any class values can be overridden at the instance level of the class object—the instance information is more particular than the general class information and therefore overrides it. Consider the Employee class object. A method is defined to calculate the basic salary for all employees, who receive a basic salary of £10,000 *unless instantiated otherwise at the instance level.* Mary's method is more particular than the class object's method, so Mary gets her salary and not that of the general employee. Another example is that at the class level all persons are instantiated with a value of having two legs, yet poor Henry has the Number of Legs property instantiated with a value of "1". This is because Henry has had a leg amputated. None of the other Employee instances contain the attribute Number of Legs, as they can inherit the value of "2" from the Man class object. By contrast, with the Date of Employment property there is no need for overruling as there is no instantiation of the property at the class level.

5.3.4.4 Property inheritance

This facility is central to object oriented processing. It forms the basis of the support for software commonality *and* variation. *It is therefore the facility for data and software reuse.* It enables the designer to specify common attributes and methods once, as well as to specialise and extend the attributes and methods in more specific variations of the base case. *It is the mechanism for sharing common, and extending and adding specialised, object information.*

An often used example of this is the recognition of cars and lorries as special cases of vehicles, inheriting the data and logic properties of vehicle, such as Vehicle Number (data) and Pressing Accelerator (method), and using their own more specialised attributes and methods, such as number of passengers for the Car object and load carrying capacity for the Lorry object. *Inheritance is thus a tool for organising, building and using reusable class objects.*

The reuse of existing data and code can generate substantial increases in programmer productivity, without a corresponding increase in the amount of new code that must be maintained in the future. After all, the easiest code to write is no code; and it is also the easiest code to maintain.

When approaching the design of a new system much of the implementation can often be done by simply using the methods provided in the existing class objects containing the methods. Where existing class object methods are not exactly appropriate, inheritance enables new classes to be derived *by adding* the extra data and methods required as object sub-classes to the base super-class. *What we see is ability of object oriented systems to enable an application to be upgraded by the process of addition, rather than the process of modification.*

The author likes to make a distinction between the specialisation of information in the sub-class object or instance of the class object through override and through addition. The example of Henry having only one leg is an example of override in that the instance of the class overrides the Person class object value of two legs. The example of the method Calc_Sal for the sub-classes of Star Bonus and Star Employee is an example of addition, in that the logic in the Calc_Sal method of the sub-class object Star Bonus is added to the logic of the method Calc_Sal in the super-class object Star Employee, which in turn is added to the logic of the method Calc_Sal in the super-class object Employee.

Inheritance is equally relevant to the logic properties. The more specific Calc_Salary method in Star Employee would inherit the more general method of Calc_Salary in the Employee object. The Star Employee would therefore receive the basic salary of Employee as well as the bonus of a Star Employee.

Where there is multiple inheritance with methods there can be situations where ambiguities as to which method should be invoked. Figure 5.31 shows that Seaplane can inherit methods from more than one super-class object. Ship could contain the method Brake and Aircraft could contain the method Park. Which method is invoked depends on whether the seaplane is regarded at an instance in time as a ship or an aircraft. The solution to such a situation can be by specifying the inheritance route to take in the logic of a method in Seaplane by renaming the methods. This is but part of the problem of information conflict that can occur through inheritance— see conflict resolution below for other types of conflict and resolutions mechanisms.

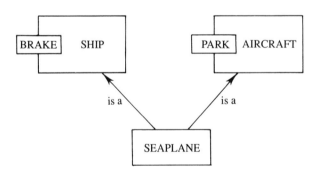

Figure 5.31   Multiple inheritance

5.3.4.5 Information abstraction

Figure 5.32 shows a subset of the object class model with the Mammal object at the top and the Star Employee at the bottom. The objects higher up the class model (and this assumes that the drawing convention followed in a conventional data model of the master entity drawn above the detail entity is also followed in the object class model—in object oriented terminology the super-class above the sub-class) are more general/abstract in the information they contain than the class objects lower down the class model,

Generalisation ←$\xrightarrow{\text{Abstraction}}$→ Specialisation

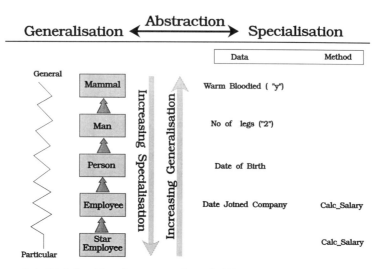

Figure 5.32   Abstraction–specialisation

which are more particular/specialised. For example, the Mammal is a more general case of Species, which is in turn is a more general case of Person, which is in turn a more general case of ... and so on down the class model. All the objects are related by class in that they are all mammalian—they all have a common behaviour. The Mammal object is relevant to all the class objects of the application except the Object object. The Man object is relevant to all the class objects of the application except the Mammal and Object objects. And so on, being progressively more restrictive as one progresses down the class object model.

The Mammal class data property with an instantiated value of "Warm Blooded" is generally applicable to all mammalian species and hence to all instances of the class sub-objects of Man, Person, Shareholder, Employee and Star Employee. The data property of Number of Legs with a class value of "2" is generally applicable to all instances of Persons and to the sub-objects Shareholder, Employee and Star Employee.

The above facilities, being related to data, are the same as those obtained in the semantic net. The logic component also follows the same principle of information abstraction/specialisation. The public method Calc_Salary is relevant at the class level, as all instances of Employees require to have their basic salary calculated. There is also another method by the same name of Calc_Salary for the sub-class Star Employee. The logic in this method follows the principle that it is more specialised than the more general logic in the method of the same name in the super-class Employee object. The more specialised logic would be for the calculation of the Star Employee's bonus, whereas the more general logic would be for the calculation of the Employee's basic salary.

As so far described, the increasing specialisation as one descends the model is only at the class level. However, the specialisation can go further—to the instances of the class. In the case of being warm blooded, all the instances of the class objects that can inherit from Mammal can only be warm blooded—they would die if they were not. An instance of Person would be dead if his/her blood was cold. However total applicability of class information does not have to be relevant to all the class objects. Consider the Person object. Not all instances of Persons will necessarily have two legs. It could be that a particular Person and its sub-classes has lost a leg. The instance (as has been mentioned Henry has lost a leg) would be a specialisation of the class.

The applicability of class information—generic or as appropriate—is entirely context dependent.

John Smart of the Sema Group has pointed out to the author that, based on work by Lalonde and Pugh, the decomposition of objects can be viewed a number of ways. The technical terms are sub-classing and sub-typing. The relationships between the objects is different.

Sub-classing, also called inheritance, is a mechanism for sharing data and logic between objects of the same class. The sub-objects are specialisations of the super-class. The classic example is the object of Person and its sub-classes of, say, Sportsperson and Employee. Both Sportsperson and Employee have attributes/properties describing them and will also inherit the properties of Person. They are specialisations in that each is a particular class of persons. Another example is that the seaplane is a sub-class, a specialisation, of aeroplane. The relationship description for sub-classes is of the "is a" type. An Employee "is a" Person. An object can be decomposed into a set of sub-classes of objects that collectively provide the same functionality as the super-class objects. The sub-classes can be decomposed further to n hierarchical levels of sub-classes as appropriate.

Sub-typing is where an sub-type object can be "substituted" for a super-type object. The example given is that the object Piston is a sub-type of the object Engine. There is no inheritance here.

5.3.4.6 Conflict resolution

It is because of the inheritance facility that situations will arise where there is a conflict in the value of the information in the objectbase. There can be conflict in the data or logic.

The two mechanisms for solving the conflict are the particular overriding the general and priority. The more particular information is always to be found in the objects lower in the object class model. The lowest and most particular point in the model is the instances of an object class. Both of these facilities can be used to resolve conflict for logic. Data conflict is resolved only by the particular overriding the general.

Examples of the resolution of data conflict in the class object model are the same as for the semantic net and have been described in section 5.2.4.7.

Conflict in logic can also be solved by the same principle of the particular overriding the general. The Star Employee object is a sub-object of the Employee object and is therefore more particular. The Star Employee bonus based salary will therefore override the basic salary of the Employee—in this case by adding the bonus amount to the basic salary. The reason for the addition rather than the override is that the method of the same name Calc_Salary is found in both objects, the method in the Star Employee object calculating the additional payment for the bonus rather than recalculating the entire salary and bonus.

This principle may, however, not work in all cases. Consider the following. The Broker object could contain a method that states that brokers are to gain a 30% commission on all deals they win. However, the Commission Type object states in a separate method that commissions of a particular type have a 40% commission. The principle of the particular overriding the general will not work, as the Commission Type and Broker are not related with one object being a sub-type or super-type of the other. Where such a conflict occurs a priority must be allocated to the methods. The Commission Type method requires to have a higher priority than the Broker method, so that when the broker wins a commission of the particular type then the 40% commission rate overrides the 30% commission rate.

Another way to resolve logic conflict is to use the priority mechanism. Assume the following methods "If employee then desk is small" (general because employee is at the class level) and "If employee is Joe Bloggs then desk is large" (particular because employee is at the instance level). The result is that Joe Bloggs will get his large desk. An example of using priority as the resolution mechanism could be "If employee age > 40 then desk is small" (high priority) and "If employee age < 25 then desk is large" (low priority). Inheritance will not solve the conflict because both sets of logic are at the class level. The priority will solve the conflict, such that those over 40 will get a large desk.

There is one further way that conflict resolution can be achieved. Consider the worked example of an expert system query using the GENERIS product as described in section 5.2.8.1. It was explained that Jumbo's colour is muddy and dull, muddy because Jumbo lives in the jungle and dull from the database. The semantic net was then accessed and it was ascertained that muddy and dull intersect to state that Jumbo is actually brown and beige. This can be seen in figure 5.16. Jumbo had in fact been rolling in a pool of water and covered himself with mud and therefore looked dull. The conflict in the two "incorrect" colours was resolved in the semantic net.

5.3.5 Object oriented logic

There are a number of features that are increasingly recognised as being part of the object oriented logic portfolio:

• private methods;

• public methods;

• message passing;

• encapsulation;

• polymorphism;

• function name overloading;

• genericity.

Given that object oriented logic is stored and accessed alongside object oriented data, much that describes object oriented logic has already been discussed in the description of object oriented databases. There are however different aspects to consider. Object oriented programming is a way of writing and packaging software differently from traditional programming. Apart from separating logic from data, traditional programming is written in a form where a program starts with a begin statement and n lines of code later finishes with an end statement. Between these two statements can be logic relating to n objects. The logic is usually anything but object based/normalised.

The main difference of object oriented technology from traditional relational and pre-relational file handlers is the extra component in an object, that is to say the logic component. The logic and the data are both information, the information about the object. Logic is therefore treated, as far as possible, like standard data.

Like the data component the logic is stored in slots. The logic slots are called methods. *The methods are nothing more than a program procedure/module.* The methods are of two types—private or public. Although both types are stored in the same manner, they are accessed differently and play different roles in the life of an object.

5.3.5.1 Private methods

Private methods are system triggered when an object is accessed. They are private because they are not seen and cannot be used by the users. Their prime role is threefold—to edit the data properties in the objects as they are inserted and updated into the objectbase, to prevent improper deleting from the objectbase (you cannot delete an employee if the Date Left Company property is blank) and to provide the usual referential integrity checking facilities. Private methods are therefore really concerned with data maintenance business requirements. For the first two roles many would recognise private methods as database procedures. In the latter role many would recognise private methods as database rules.

As database procedures the private methods can be defined for inserts, updates and deletes. For obvious reasons, they can only be defined at the class level if the task is to edit the data for an object instance insert. For example, it could be that all employees' salaries are within specified value ranges for a given grade. The private method would be specified at the employee class level and be automatically invoked whenever an employee is inserted into the objectbase, so as to ensure that the employee had a valid salary according to their grade.

However, a private method can also be defined at the instance level. This is only pertinent if the object is being updated or deleted, for the simple reason that the object instance must have been loaded beforehand and the private method specified subsequently for the instance. An object instance method would be appropriate if it was necessary to edit in a unique and not a general way the data in an object instance that was being updated or when an object instance was being deleted. For example, for an update private method it could be that the employee instance Mary's salary is the exception to the general rule and that her salary is uniquely outside the value range for her grade. A private method for editing Mary's salary would therefore be defined at the object instance level. Thus, if Mary's salary is being modified to reflect her special condition then the private method would be invoked whenever the salary update was being executed. As regards a delete it could be that at the class level employees cannot be marked as retired if their company pension information is not in order, but the employee instance of Henry has adopted a personal pension plan and opted out of the company's pension scheme. A private method for the Henry object instance would therefore be defined. Both Mary's and Henry's private methods, being instance particular, would override the class general method.

The logic in a private method is triggered automatically whenever the object instance of an object class is accessed as specified in the method. If the method was to be triggered for a delete the method would not be triggered if the object instance access was an update. If the method was to be triggered for an update it would not be triggered if the access to the object instance was for a delete.

The private methods are sometimes known as daemons. The reason for this is that, like the expert system daemon rules, private methods are like gremlins, sitting in the object waiting for something it recognises to happen and only then "jerks" itself into life. All this is unseen by the users, who do not even have to know private methods exist.

5.3.5.2 Public methods

Public methods are unique to object oriented systems. They contain the application logic, the logic that supports a user business requirement, but logic that is normalisable to the natural object. For example the public method Calc_Salary for the calculation of an employer's salary is stored in the Employee object.

The public methods are those that are invoked by the receipt of a message from the event object of an application program or from another object. The message contains the object instance value, a method name, the name typically being a meaningful description of the function being called, such as Calc_Sal for calculating an annual salary, and relevant arguments. The arguments are optional. The method, of course, has been defined by name as a property of the object in the objectbase schema. The schema therefore points the message to the object class specified in the method name, which then accesses the object instance of the object class in the objectbase as required. The public method will execute its logic and process any arguments presented and return a result to the issuer of the message.

Note that there is no concept of knowing in which object (stored as a relational table) the object information is stored. It could be that the method named in the message is contained in an object higher up the class object model than the object instance receiving the message, but this is not important, indeed irrelevant, to the issuer of the message. *One merely has to say, "get me this instance and do this processing on it". You cannot get more non-procedural than that.*

The initial message trigger for a set of public methods appropriate to a business requirement is from an application program event object. If the business requirement requires to access the data in multiple class objects, then there require to be public methods appropriate to the business requirement in each object to be accessed. Each of these public methods requires to be invoked by a message.

For example, when a business requirement requires to access multiple objects, "For a specified customer display all orders for products greater than £10", then co-ordinated messages must be sent to the appropriate Customer, Order and Product objects to trigger the public methods, probably of the same name as the event object name, in the "natural" objects to access the data properties. This can either be from the event object or from other objects previously accessed.

So long as the correct message is sent and a valid result received the format of the data and the execution of the public method logic are irrelevant to the outside world.

The data component in the objects can only be accessed by the public methods. The data in an object is therefore also private and "hidden" from the users. It is the public methods that encapsulate the private data.

Public methods can contain what are called pre and post ambles. The prime purpose of this facility is to enable user specific additions to the public methods. It may be that user Joe Bloggs requires some processing that is unique for him for a certain object(s). It could be that when Joe Bloggs wishes to look at the salary of all the Bloggs' employed in the family firm an additional percentage is to be added onto the basic employee salary. The additional logic can be added as a pre or post amble to the method Calc_Salary depending on whether the increase is calculated before or after the basic salary itself is calculated.

The EIFFEL object oriented programming language uses pre and post ambles for the purpose of checking that the data being input and output is valid. The purpose is therefore more for information integrity than business reasons.

5.3.5.3 Message passing

Whenever an event/business requirement is triggered the event object of the application program sends messages to the other relevant objects containing the information it requires. Objects invoked by the messages can in turn send further messages to other objects as necessary.

The message is not the same thing as a procedure call in conventional application programming. The message is usually of the form the object instances to be accessed, the method to be invoked and an optional set of arguments. The component unique to messages is the specification of the object instances to be accessed.

It must be appreciated that the method being invoked does not have to be in the class of the object the instances of which are being accessed. The method could be anywhere in the class object model inheritance path for the class object instances being accessed. It could be that the business requirement requires to access all information about Star Employees, but that the method being invoked is stored in the Person class object. As Star Employee is a sub-class of Employee, which is a sub-class of Person, the method(s) being invoked in the Person class object can still validly relate to Star Employees and its instances.

This facility of message passing poses some interesting questions. Should all the messages be sent to the other objects entirely from the event object; should only one message be sent from the event object to an object and then from each object to the next object in the chain of objects to be accessed until the object at the end of the chain is reached and from there a message be sent back to the main procedure object; or should message passing be something in between these two extremes. The author likes to call the first approach "round robin" and the second approach "central policeman".

There is no fixed answer. It depends on the application. If the requirement is for the event object to issue a message to an object, which does some self contained processing, to then send a message, possibly with some data, to another object, which does some self contained processing etc. until the final object returns the final processed result then the event object only needs to send the first message and receive the final result. If the requirement is that the event sends the first message, receives the result and then decides whether it is necessary to send another message to another object class or instance, receives the result and then decides etc., then the event object controls the execution of logic for the business requirement and there is no chain of objects messaging each other. There can be any variation between these two extremes.

On balance the author prefers the "central policemen" approach because massage passing and the co-ordination of the responses from the objects is in a single place, that is the event object. Any modifications to the message passing routine can be quickly located without any need to follow a long trail of messages around the various objects.

5.3.5.4 Encapsulation

As already described objects are composed of a data component in the form of attributes and a logic component in the form of methods, and the data component can only be accessed via the logic component. The data component is thus "encapsulated" by the logic component.

The great advantage of this facility is that the user of the object, when sending a message to trigger one of the methods, does not need to know and does not care about the format of the attributes. Objects are therefore excellent implementations of the facility of abstract data types. Abstract data types specifications describe class data structures not as a set of attributes but as a list of services/methods available on the data structures. *The only thing of interest to a user of the object is how the object appears in the interface—that is the message format—and what methods are provided and what is done by the methods to the data attributes held within the object.* The internal processing of the methods is irrelevant to the outside world.

Some examples contrasting the traditional approach to application programming and the object oriented approach can best illustrate encapsulation and the benefits thereby achieved.

Consider the following. A conventional application program requires to read in two real number variables M1 and M2, multiply them together and assign the result to a third number variable M3. Real numbers are usually represented by two integers, the mantissa and the exponent. The program reads two strings S and converts them into mantissa and exponent form. After the multiplication the result is converted back into a string and the string is written out. The code (in the style of an abstract programming language in the form of C++) for such a program could be:

```
Main ()
{
int M1, M2, M3, E1, E2, E3;
string S;
read S
convert S to M1 E1 (this is function 1)
read S
convert S to M2 E2 (this is function 1)
multiply M1 E1 and M2 E2 to get M3 E3 (this is function 2)
convert M3 E3 to S (this is function 3)
write S
}
```

This traditional application program suffers from a number of problems. The major one is that there is no hiding of the data type from the function logic, which has to know the data type and its form. The form of the data in the initialisation and the logic in the functions are visible to each other. The "how it is to be achieved" logic of the functions is intermingled with the data. This can be seen in figure 5.33a, where the format of the data is visible to the three functions.

A more sophisticated approach is to separate the functions, to store them as independent routines and to refer to them by name. Those references are the interfaces. Function 1 is given a reference of s_to_r (string to real), function 2 is given the reference of mult and function 3 is given the reference of r_to_s. The application program merely has to refer to the references, such as s_to_r and mult, and the functions are invoked. The code of such an approach would be:

```
Main ()
{
int M1, M2, M3, E1, E2, E3;
string S;
read S; s_to_r (S,M1,E1);
read S; s_to_r (S, M2,E2);
mult (M1, E1, M2, E2, M3 E3);
```

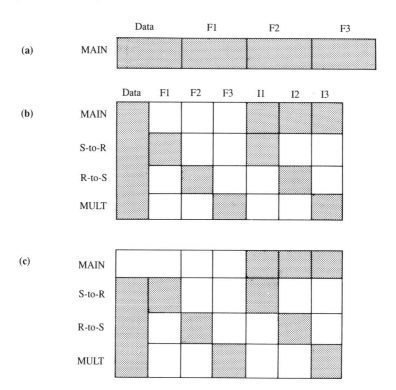

Figure 5.33   Degrees of encapsulation

```
r_to_s (M3, E3, S)
write S;
}
s_to_r (S,M,E) {logic....};
r_to_s (M,E,S) {logic....};
mult (M1, E1, M2, E2, M3, E3) {logic....};
```

The advantage here is that an interface (the references to the functions) has been created for the functions, with the "how" logic of the functions separated from the "what is required" logic of the event component of the application program. However there still is no encapsulation. The interfaces can still see the data (they require to know that the number is a mantissa and an exponent), as do the functions themselves. This is illustrated in figure 5.33b.

The third approach is to create a new abstract data type R for the mantissa and exponent of a real number. The logic of the event component and the functions would be as follows:

```
Main ()
{
```

```
int R1, R2, R3;
string S;
read S; s_to_r (S,R1);
read S; s_to_r (S, R2);
mult (R1, R2, R3);
r_to_s (R3,S)
write S;
}
s_to_r (S,R) {logic....};
r_to_s (R,S) {logic....};
mult (R1, R2, R3) {logic....};
```

The interfaces cannot see the data, as far as they are concerned the data is merely a real number, and it is only the functions (which now become the methods in the objects) that contain the logic to convert the mantissa and exponent to a real number. The interfaces are only able to see the functions in that they make reference to the functions. The only link with the outside world as far as the object is concerned is the interface. Complete encapsulation has now been achieved. The object contains the interface, the data and the functions, which because the technology is object oriented, are stored as methods within the object rather then separately as in the second approach. The full encapsulation can be seen in figure 5.33c, where the interfaces cannot see the format of the data, only the references to the functions. It is the functions, the methods, which then see and access the data. The format of the data is transparent, is abstract, as far as the interface, the message, is concerned. The three component rings of an object described in section 5.3.4.1 have been created.

Encapsulation is therefore the ultimate form of expressing stability in a computer system design. The processing logic and the data in an object can be modified to whatever degree is necessary and it matters not to the outside world. *The impact of change is restricted to the object.* There are no ripple effects to other objects.

It should be appreciated that encapsulation does not assist in software reuse, only in software maintenance. However inheritance, which does provide reuse, could not work if encapsulation was not provided. Encapsulation enables the more specialised sub-objects to be completely decoupled from the super-class object.

Not all object oriented programming languages provide the ability to enforce encapsulation. Smalltalk hides all data values by default but C++ requires the data values to be declared "private" in order to be hidden.

5.3.5.5 *Function Name Overloading, Polymorphism and Genericity*

These three features of object orientation are discussed together as the one leads to the other.

Function Name Overloading occurs where different functions (another term for a method) have the same name. Consider the following:

```
integer A,B;
real X,Y
real total;
Total = A+B+X+Y
```

Both the integer and the real number are variables, but are different types of variable, the one being an integer and the other a real. The + operator is a function, taking two variables and adding them together, to which we will give the name SUM. SUM is therefore invoked three times in the Total line of code to add up different types of variables. When adding up A+B variables the + operator is adding up two variables of the same integer type, but when adding up (A+B)+X is adding up an integer and a real. The + operator function is therefore required to do different things depending on the parameters being passed to it. In fact the SUM function has different "signatures"—SUMII for adding up two integer variables to produce an integer, SUMIR for adding an integer and a real to produce a real and SUMRR for adding up two real to produce a real.

The Total line of code thus looks like:

```
Total = SUMRR(SUMIR(SUMII(A,B),X),Y)
```

In terms of function overloading the function SUM is being invoked three times, but invisibly being invoked in different ways, depending on the variables types being passed. Thus the Total line of code can be re-expressed, using function name overloading, as:

```
Total = SUM(SUM(SUM(A,B),X),Y)
      = A+B+X+Y
```

Function overloading maps the function to be invoked at compile time. The programming language therefore needs to be a strongly typed language, where the compiler recognises what type of data is being processed. The name resolution of the function that is being invoked depends on the type and number of parameters being passed to it. Thus the function SUM would in fact invoke SUMII, SUMRR or SUMIR as appropriate depending on the parameters. What this means is that function with the same "base" name can accept the same number and type of parameters with different messages and know which "overloaded" function to call.

One can see this in the example application program in section 5.3.6, where the method Area invokes different logic depending in whether the object instance being processed is a box (logic is "return length * breadth") or a circle (logic is "return (PI*radiusR2)").

Polymorphism of the method being used, and its natural corollary of dynamic binding, is the ability for a method under the same name to take different forms, depending on the class instance involved. It is a useful addition to the inheritance facility for aiding software reuse. It enables the same software message to refer to many objects instances, each of which can produce a different response depending on the object instance being accessed.

The software component of several objects can each contain a function (method) with the same name and the processing will vary depending on the object instance to which the message has been sent. An example of polymorphism in the case study object class model is the Calc_Sal method to be found in the Employee and Star Employee objects. In Employee the method calculates the basic salary of employee and in the Star Employee the bonus. The message response varies depending on which method is invoked, which in turn depends on whether a Star Employee or an Employee object instance is being accessed.

A more detailed example is given in figure 5.34. There is the class object Employee, with a method Calc_Sal and three instances of the class, Joe, Mary and Fred. There is also a sub-class of Star Employee, with instances of John and Ann and with the another method also called Calc_Sal. If the message is sent to class object Employee because it is known to be the "root" class object to the object instance Joe then the method Calc_Sal in the Employee class object will be invoked, and if the message is sent to the class object Star Employee because it is known to be the "root" class object to the object instance John then the method Calc_Sal in the Star Employee class object will be invoked. (The normal inheritance of the Calc_Sal method from Star Employee to Employee would, of course, be invoked.) This could be a case of static/early binding, in that it is known that the class objects

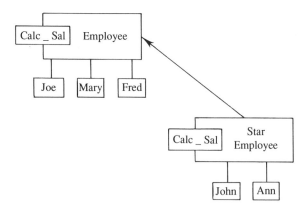

Figure 5.34   Polymorphism: 1

Employee and Star Employee "contain" the object instances required to be "accessed", and the method Calc_Sal can be compiled to the event object for this business requirement. The advantage of early binding is that the appropriate method is identified and bound to at compile time. When the class to which an object instance belongs is known at compile time polymorphism is equivalent to function overloading.

However, assume that the message is sent to the object instance John and Fred. The sender of the message does not know that Fred is an Employee and that John is a Star Employee. A program variable Staff is created, which stores the object instances being processed (see figure 5.35). The sender of the message does not know whether Staff contains an instance of Employee or an instance of Star Employee; it will depend upon which object instance has been most recently assigned to it. For instance either John or Fred may have been assigned to Staff. In order to take advantage of object orientation the software always knows which class object an object instance belongs to. Therefore, when the method Calc_Sal is sent to the variable Staff it automatically invokes the method specified in the class object to which the current occupant of Staff belongs. Thus, if the object instance is John then the method in Star Employee is invoked, with the inheritance to Employee automatically supported, or if the object instance is Fred the method in the Employee class object is invoked. This is a case of polymorphic dynamic binding, in that the method to be invoked is dependent on the position in the class hierarchy of the object instance being accessed, but to which class object the object instance is "attached" is not known in advance.

It is this mechanism that enables object oriented systems to be so easily and safely extended; a new sub-class can be added and all the existing logic that operates on instances of the sub-class's super-classes will continue to work *without modification* and will automatically also work on instances of the new sub-class.

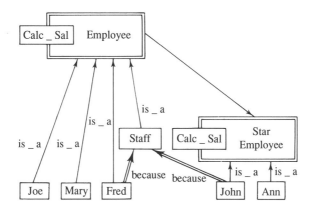

Figure 5.35   Polymorphism: 2

Now let's take polymorphism even further. Figure 5.36 is expanded to include a class object Executive as a sub-class of Employee, with two instances of Bill and Tom. The business requirement is to calculate the entire payroll of all the employees and their sub-classes. Another class object called Payroll List has been created at the more general/abstract level above Employee. It contains a method called Next that reads the instances of the different class object types Star Employee, Employee and Executive. Thus the payroll program consists of the Next method in the Payroll List class object invoking the Calc_Sal method, which in turn is differently invoked depending on which object instance is being used. If the object instance is Ann the Calc_Sal would be from the Star Employee class object, if the instance was Mary the Calc_Sal would be from the class object Employee and so on. There is another polymorphic dynamic execution of the method Calc_Sal.

Genericity is a template for a function/method that will work on any type of data. For example, there could be the class object List, containing three methods, Next that reads a list and returns an instance of the type being read, Is Empty that reads a list to ascertain that it is empty and returns a boolean saying yes or no and Insert that reads a list of data types and returns a boolean saying that an object instance has or has not been

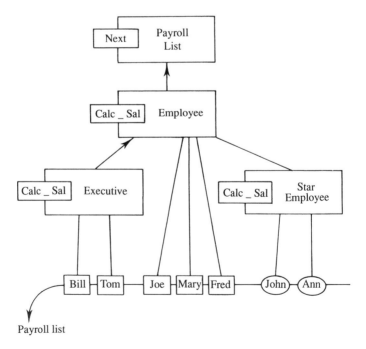

Figure 5.36   Polymorphism: 3

inserted. The methods do not care what the data type is, only that they read in and output some information. The template can be instantiated for specific data types, for example Payroll List for the Employees object class. What has been created is an instance of the object class that operates on the class object once.

5.3.6 The object oriented program

The basic structure of an object oriented program is an event object containing any process logic relevant to the event/business requirement it is supporting and message calls to the other objects to be accessed containing any data and logic pertinent to the business requirement. The event object therefore typically contains logic for the initialisation of the variables to be used, the receiving of input data from a screen if the transaction is online, the sending of the messages to the other objects, the synchronisation of the responses from the objects, any further processing of the data contained in the responses and the sending of output data to the screen if the transaction is online or to a report if the transaction is batch.

Assume two class objects called box and circle.

Using a C++ like syntax (C++ is a superset of the widely used C programming language enhanced to support objects) the box could be defined as

```
Class Box {
        length;
        breadth;
        constructor: Box (l,b) {
        length = l;
        breadth = b;
                }
        method: Area
            return length * breadth;
        method: Perimeter
            return 2*(len + breadth);
}
box instances     box_a box_b box_c
class circle {
        radius;
        constructor: circle (r) {
        radius + r;
                }
        method: Area
            return (PI*radius R2);
        method: Perimeter
            return (2*PI*radius);
}
```

```
*circle instances    circle_x circle_y circle_z

Main()       {
             Box box_a = Box(10,20)
             print("%f",area(box_a));

             Circle circle_x = circle (10)
             print("%f",area(circle_x));
             }
```

The class objects box and circle contain the "how" logic and the main procedure event object contains the "what" logic for the event of printing the areas of the box or circle.

The object oriented approach would say that the main procedure object is the consumer object, the object consuming the responses from the other objects, and the other objects are the supplier objects, supplying the "services" of the methods Area and Perimeter.

Object oriented systems have yet further differences, in this case to relational file handlers. Access to the objects is record-at-a-time, similar to pre-relational file handlers, and not set at a time, so that SQL will not suffice. Another difference is that access between objects is via messages to other methods and not data tables. Data movement is now by explicit message passing between object methods rather than by implicit access by a file handler to the table rows. *Object oriented systems access logic not data.* The invoked method then accesses the data.

It must be appreciated that access logic to tables rows of data is now replaced by messages to objects instances. Transaction access path maps are replaced by message path maps, with the access call being replaced by a message.

Summary access path maps need to be replaced by summary message maps. The same principle of counting the number of messages times the volume of the transactions still applies.

5.3.7 Object oriented programming

Like object oriented objectbases, object oriented programming can be defined in terms of four major facilities—objects, classes, inheritance and message passing. Any programming language supporting these facilities can be said to be object oriented. These facilities are equally relevant to object oriented databases. Other facilities specific to object oriented programming are object states, late versus early binding, class libraries, polymorphism and function name overloading.

5.3.7.1 Object state and behaviour

An object has state and behaviour, i.e. a set of responses to external stimuli (the messages). The state of the object is defined by the data component and the behaviour component is defined by the logic component. Any application has many object instances that are of the same type, with each instance not necessarily being in the same state at a specific point in time. There is an class object called Employee, which contains generic data and logic at the class level appropriate to all Employees instances. Some of the state information can be held in the class object, that is when the data attribute is instantiated at the class level (all Man have two legs), and at the object instance level when the attribute value is unique to the object instance (Henry has one leg). The object behaviour logic can likewise be at the object class or instance level. The method Calc_Sal is at the class level, but Mary could have a method, even of the same name, for the calculation of her personal bonus.

An object which requires some information about the state of another object issues a message to that other object "tell me about your state". The object instance to which this message is sent receives it and then arranges for the appropriate named method from its set of methods to be invoked to service the message request. If the named method is not in the object pointed to inheritance is followed up the object hierarchy diagram until the appropriate method is found.

5.3.7.2 Class libraries

Class libraries are for software and not for data. Class library contain the specification of the data and methods that make up the classes; the data is specified by type and the methods are specified as program logic. These specifications can be compiled into class libraries consisting of templates for the class object. They can be at two levels—those that can be purchased and those that can be developed for the application. There are a number of companies that now provide independently developed class libraries, as well the companies that have developed the various object oriented programming languages. An example of the former is the company Glockenspiel and examples of the latter are C++, Objective C and SMALLTALK, each of which has its own set of class libraries.

The class libraries that can be purchased and are built-in with the programming languages are of the system class object described in section 5.4.3.2, i.e. they contain system functions, such as editing a numeric field and storing an object.

As an application is designed and developed it is necessary to identify class libraries of common operations for the application. If one considers the ELH example in section 5.3.16.4 then the operations that are used in more than one event can be factored out and created as class libraries. Such common operations in figure 5.37 are 3, found in events 2 and 7, and 7, which is a common object delete operation. Both of these common operations could be defined as class libraries as sub-classes of the Object object. The operations for the event 8 could be stored as a method in the business object entity 2 as they are not found in any other entity, and can therefore be normalised to object 2. The same is true for the operations in the objects 3 and 4.

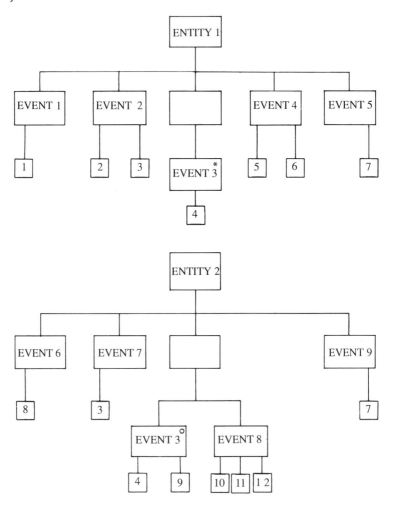

Figure 5.37   Entity life history with operations

The operations in figure 5.37 are the operations for the business requirement/event and do not include the object oriented operations for the sending of messages, screen handling, the synchronisation of the message responses and any final processing before sending the output to a screen/report. All the operations could therefore be normalised to the object entity 2.

Entire methods for the execution of part of a business requirement can also be factored out and stored as class libraries. The best example of this factoring is the common procedure methods, which are exactly the same as the common procedures of conventional application programming. Another approach is that the object instances can be grouped into "classes" of objects, which share the same attributes and behaviour while being able to have different state values for each instance. These common properties can be factored out and be used to make up a base class of software. These base classes of software can be regarded as a special sort of program libraries and reused using the inheritance facility by methods in the more specialised objects "lower" in the object class model. The perfect example of this is data properties belonging to a common domain, such as date.

Thus, when approaching the design of a new system, much of the implementation of software code can be based on existing class libraries of software; where existing classes are not exactly appropriate, new classes can be derived by merely *adding* the specifics required as a new method, even of the same name, in the super-type object, in a new object sub-class.

5.3.7.3 Late vs early binding

With run time/late binding the correspondence between the message and the named method is only established when the message is issued, that is at run time. Run time binding is often called late binding. The advantage of late binding is that new methods can be added to an object after a system is implemented without affecting in any way existing application programs that access the object. Recompilation of the existing methods is not required. It also further decouples the design of a class from that of other classes in the system. Late binding is necessary to support polymorphism, which invokes the appropriate method depending on the parameters passed to the method or the object instances being accessed. The overhead of late binding is the dynamic binding of the software. This will clearly adversely affect transaction response times.

"Early binding", which is identical to conventional systems in that it binds the methods to the messages at compile time, is also possible. It is useful to use if the messages passed to the objects are predictable and will produce predictable results as far as the class methods to be invoked. Clearly there is a performance benefit in that the code is not interpreted at run time.

5.3.8 The "separation of powers"—the consumer and the supplier, the event level "what" from the normalised "how"

An object oriented application program is composed of a set of objects— the event object and a set of other business, common procedure, system, domain and Object object class libraries. As explained in section 5.3.5.4 the event object typically contains messages to the other objects defining what methods are to be invoked for what object instances. The business requirement is "Display all customers with red hair who have placed orders for brown products". Messages need to be sent from the event object to the Customer, Order and Product class and instance objects. The logic is primarily "what" requires to be done, mainly the sending and synchronising the receipt of the messages. The only "how" logic should occur after all the messages have been received from the other objects and when there is further processing prior to the outputting of information to a screen or a report. It is the other objects, the business (in the above example business requirement the Customer, Order and Product objects), the common procedure, the domain, the system and the Object objects that contain the "how" logic.

The role of the event and the other objects are therefore directly opposite—the event object controls the execution of logic for the event/business requirement level processing in that it decides which of the how logic methods requires to be triggered. It therefore issues messages to the appropriate other objects that contain the how logic, the logic that has been normalised/factored out of the event to the other objects, and "consumes" the data information returned. The event object only contains the how logic that is relevant/normalised to the event level, to the business requirement. The factored out how logic in the other object types provides the "service" to the event object.

5.3.9 Objectbase information storage

Object oriented "databases" store objects as tables, just as in a relational file handler. However, they incorporate substantial additional facilities, the central one of which is the ability to store logic alongside the data. To this end a new data type has been created, the data type of procedure. As we have seen, the procedure data type can be a private or public method. An object can contain many slots of information, each of which can contain a data or logic property. An object can contain 0 to N data or logic properties.

Objects are stored and accessed as tables of information. The data component of an object is unchanged from relational file handlers. The logic component is more difficult as it can be of infinite length. The way logic can be stored and accessed with the data can vary. An object based file handler GOLDWORKS stores data and logic as one long variable length record, no matter how many daemons and methods there are for a given object. With this approach all the properties are stored together. The other extreme is to store the method properties separately, each in a variable length record, with a pointer in the "home" object record pointing to the method(s). The POSTGRES file handler adopts a the most flexible approach. POSTGRES is a research project into post relational technology by the University of Berkeley in California under the aegis' of Professors Stonebraker, Rowe and Wong, the founders of Ingres Inc. Ingres Inc developed and market the INGRES relational database file handler. POSTGRES is post-INGRES. Daemons and methods can be defined as a property of an object as a data type of procedure and stored either alongside the data properties or as a separate table with a pointer from the source table row pointing to the separate daemon/method table. Which approach to use for each procedure/method is up to the objectbase designer.

The approach of storing the methods separately has two advantages. The source table row is reduced in size so that the buffer pool is not so rapidly filled. This helps to reduce disk I/O. Secondly, those procedures that are rarely triggered by messages can be stored separately, further reducing wasteful I/O when accessing the "source" object. The frequently used methods are stored alongside the data component in the object. Optimised logic design can thus be practised as part of database design. This is very similar, of course, to the concept of clustering frequently accessed detail table rows in the same page as the corresponding master table row in "standard" databases.

Consider figure 5.38. Assume the format and access in the first class object, where method 1 is accessed whenever the object is accessed, method 2 is accessed 50% of the time the object is accessed and methods 3 and 4 are accessed only 1% of the time. The first approach of storing all data and logic components together would be highly efficient for the methods 1 and 2, because whenever the data is accessed the logic is triggered always for method 1 and frequently for method 2, but not for methods 3 and 4, particularly bearing in mind that they each take 10K of storage (no consideration is made as to whether the code is compiled or in source form). The buffer pool would be very rapidly filled with unused logic with this approach to object storage. It would make good design sense to store methods 3 and 4 as two separate object record instances, with pointers from the "home" object to the method object.

The second approach stores all the methods as separate object records with pointers in the home object pointing to the methods. This approach would be inefficient for methods 1 and 2, as it would incur a disk I/O to access from the home object to the method record. Given the small size of

1 ALL PROPERTIES STORED TOGETHER

DATA PROPERTIES	METHOD 1	METHOD 2	METHOD 3	METHOD 4
1K	1K	1K	10K	10K
	100% ACCESS	50% ACCESS	1% ACCESS	1% ACCESS

◄──────────────────────── 23K ────────────────────────►

INEFFICIENT TO METHODS 3 & 4

2 METHOD PROPERTIES STORED SEPARATELY

DATA PROPERTIES	PTR TO METHOD 1	PTR TO METHOD 2	PTR TO METHOD 3	PTR TO METHOD 4

◄──────────────────── 1K + 4PTRS ────────────────────►

METHOD 1	METHOD 2	METHOD 3	METHOD 4

INEFFICIENT TO METHODS 1 & 2

3 METHODS STORED SEPARATELY
   AS REQUIRED

DATA PROPERTIES	METHOD 1	METHOD 2	PTR TO METHOD 3	PTR TO METHOD 4

◄──────────────────── 3K + 2PTRS ────────────────────►

MOST FLEXIBLE & EFFICIENT

METHOD 3	METHOD 4

Figure 5.38   Object storage approaches

the two methods it would make sense to store them in the home object record and bear the small overhead of buffer pool usage.

The third approach is the most flexible, with methods 3 and 4 being stored as separate object records. The methods are of sufficient size as to justify their being stored separately and thereby not cluttering up the buffer pool for the 99% of the time that they are not being triggered for each message to the object instance.

5.3.10 Object oriented man/machine interface

Although the Oracle relational database product is not object oriented the man/machine interface component of SQL*FORMS is strongly indicative of what an object oriented man/machine interface will look like. SQL*FORMS is a major component of Oracle's 4GL software. It contains the screen painting and application programming components. The great advantage of SQL*FORMS is that it enables logic to be defined as the screen is being painted.

The screen itself is broken into three objects—the screen, the tables of data which may be displayed on the screen and the attributes/properties which may be displayed within the tables. For each of these objects it may be necessary to define logic once the objects have been painted. The mechanism for entering the logic is to move the screen painting cursor to the object, press the appropriate key and a pop-up window appropriate to the object type selected is displayed. The logic can then be entered into the pop-up window for the selected object type. Again, following the principle of inheritance, the logic at the particular level overrides the logic at the general level. For example, if the logic is entered for the object type property then it will override the logic entered for the object type table, which in turn will override the logic for the object type screen. A pictographic representation of the object based entry of logic is illustrated in figure 5.39. In this example the object type is at the column/property level and the logic happens to be an SQL statement.

Note the facility of Post-Change. This is the same as the pre and post ambles facility of object oriented programming, the ORACLE Pre-Change facility being triggered before the database is accessed and the Post-Change being triggered after the database is accessed.

5.3.11 Frames (logic oriented)

This section is about three ways that object oriented information can be constructed, and the differing roles the different construction facilities play and how they function (or should function) together.

There are three ways that the information in an object oriented class model can be related/linked together—the foreign key, the semantic description showing inheritance of both data and logic between sub-object and super-object in the class structure and the facility of the methods in multiple objects being referred to by the same name. The foreign key facility is the mechanism for relating tables of data together as in a relational model and for constructing the data frame facility as described in section 5.2.4.8. The semantic description facility is the mechanism for relating sub-objects to the super-objects for the purposes of data and logic inheritance. The same name for methods in multiple objects is the mechanism for relatingall the logic for a business requirement together and thereby creating the logic frame facility.

The role of the inheritance facility has been explained. It is not often understood that inheritance is only achieved automatically where a message is sent to an object instance of an object class and the object oriented software then accesses up the class object model searching for the method named in the selector component of the message. The "location" of the

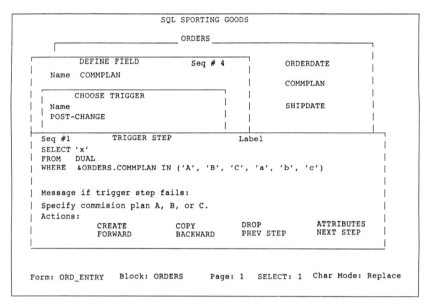

Figure 5.39   Object oriented screen

method is not known by the message, and indeed it doesn't care. But total inheritance for all the logic of a business requirement is not achieved in all circumstances. Consider the Calc_Sal method yet again. The message is sent to the Star Employee object and the method is found in the object pointed to. As far as object oriented technology is concerned that is the end of the matter. Not so. The business requirement also needs to get the component of the Calc_Sal method for calculating the basic salary component of the Star Employee. As far as the author is aware none of the programming languages claiming to support object orientation send messages up the class object model searching for the remaining Calc_Sal methods, for the remaining logic for calculating the Star Employee's salary. They stop at the first "occurrence" of the method. The application programmer is still responsible for sending another message to the super-class object of the object containing the invoked method, until no further methods are found in the inheritance class hierarchy. Inheritance is still a case of "do it yourself". What this means is that the concept of the logic frame is not supported by object oriented technology. Indeed, the author has still to find an object oriented file handler that supports property inheritance.

Let's look at this facility of the logic frame. The logic frame is all the logic, wherever it is to be found in the object class model, for supporting a single business requirement. The great benefit is that the message is sent from the event object to the class object instance lowest in the class object model for the business requirement and inheritance would, in theory, take care of the rest: genuinely non-procedural. (The common procedure objects and class libraries would each require a synonym of the name of the method for the business requirement, or the method would have to send a message itself.)

The "scope" of the data and logic frames, i.e. the class objects containing the common foreign key and the methods of the same name, are therefore different. The data frame facility is the more powerful in that all the data about a subject is supported by the foreign key. The subject is thus at the general level, with all the data relevant to the subject being within the scope. The scope of the logic frame is limited to the scope of the business requirement, which is often a subset of the data frame. There are the usual pros and cons of both approaches. The data frame is all encompassing, but is limited to a hierarchy of information—foreign keys only work up an information model. The logic frame is usually more limited in the scope of the information.

5.3.12 A worked case study

The object class model detailed in figure 5.30 is used as the basis of a worked example of a pure object based system. The details of the business class objects are given in figure 5.40 and of the object instance information in figure 5.41. The full specification of the class and instance objects has not been detailed for the simple reason that it would be a unnecessarily large set of documentation. The specification is the minimum needed to illustrate the facilities and design of an object oriented system.

The application records all the details about certain aspects of a single company—its employees and their remuneration details and the breakdown of the company's value and shareholding.

5.3.12.1 The object class information

The object class model shows certain aspects about information modelling that a conventional data model and relational file handler would not easily or does not support the following features.

- Entity sub-types (or rather object sub-types) in the form of Company and the sub-types Company Employ and Company Value. This can be supported by some relational file handlers, such as DATACOM/DB, by detailing the tables in the SQL data definition language rather than the data manipulation language as initially used. It is a pity that SQL has

(a) Object	Attribute	Len/Format	Class Value	Method (var char) (pre) (post)	Daemon (var char)
Broker	/ Broker Code	5/X		Calc_Comm	Bro_Edit
	Broker Name	15/C		Share_Sale	
	Address	50/X		< user 1 >	
	* Telephone No	11/AN		> user n >	
	Broking %	3/N			
	* Object ID	1/C			
Commission	/ Broker Code	5/X		Method C	Comm_Edit
	/ Date Paid	6/AN			
	Commission Amount	5/N			
	* Commission Type	2/X			
Company(Employ)	/ Co_EmpLSO Indicator	1/C		Method F	CompE_Edit
	Address	50/X	"The ..."		
	Luncheon Vouchers Value	2/N	"£2"		
Company(Value)	/ Co_VaLSO Indicator	1/C		Calc_Dividend	CompV_Edit
	Current Company Value	14/N		Calc_Co_Val	
	Total No of Shares	10/N			
	Current Dividend/Share	5/N			
Dividend	/ Benefit Type Code	3/X		Method H	Div_Edit/
	/ Date Benefit Paid	6/AN			
	/ Company Code	6/X			
	/ Shareholder No	5/AN			
	Total Value	12/N			

Class	Attribute	Format	Default	Method	Method
Person	/ Person ID	9/X		Calc_Dividend	Pers_Edit
	Person Name	15/C			
	No of Legs	1/N	"2"		
	No of Hands	1/N	"2"		
	* Date of Birth	6/AN			
	Personal Assessment	30/C			
	* Allowance Type	1/X			
	* Mammalian Code	3/X			
Share Allocation	/ Allocation No	6/AN		Share_Sale	Alloc_Edit
	No of Shares	6/N		Calc_Dividend	NOS_Edit
	* Shareholder No	5/AN		Calc_Comm	SH_Edit
	Initial Value	9/N			IV_Edit
	* Broker Code	5/X			
	* Company Code	6/X			
	* Purchase Date	6/AN			
	No of Shares Sold	6/N			
	* Date Final Share Sale	6/AN			
	* Co_VaLSO Indicator	1/N			
Shareholder	/ Shareholder No	5/AN		Calc_Dividend	
	* Person ID	9/X			
	* Start Date	6/AN			
Star Employee	/ Employee Code	7/X		Method N	StEmp_Edit
	/ Star Indicator	1/C		Calc_Sal	
	Bonus %	2/N	10%		

Figure 5.40 Object class information

Object	Object Instance	Property Name.	Property Value	Prop' Type
Broker	Broker AB123	⟨post amble 1⟩	"calculate added Bonus on Share-Sale"	Amble
Person	Henry	Person ID	"321"	Data
		Date of Birth	4/6/57	Data
		No of Legs	"1"	Data
		Allowance Type	"A"	Data
		Pers' Assessment	"Hopping along . . ."	Data
Star Employee	Henry	Bonus %	"27"	Data
		⟨pre amble 1⟩	"Add preliminary sum to salary and calculate"	Amble
	Peter	Bonus %	"27"	Data
		"Bonus % + 5000"	Method	
	Susan	Bonus %	"32"	Data
		⟨post able⟩	"Bonus % and calculate additional amount"	Data

Figure 5.41　Object instance information

not been upgraded to support this extra facility. SQL still assumes that the tables sub-types are separate. The correct place to define tables is implicitly in the schema with DDL rather than as explicit DML table joins in the application program. Notwithstanding the DDL upgrades with some relational file handlers the object oriented approach to sub-types is superior. The object oriented solution is inheritance—the object sub-types inheriting the properties of the master super-type object *automatically, implicitly and transparently. There is no concept of object joins.*

- The use of domain objects and the Object object for the storage of data and logic that is generic to the application or universal and therefore not lnormalisable to the business objects.

- The design of system objects in the class object model in the same way as user data.

A number of the class objects have instantiated data properties. The Company (Employ) object sub-type has two properties instantiated with values that are generic to all the instances of the class object. The properties are the Company Address and Luncheon Vouchers Value. *These two properties can be instantiated at the class level because the properties are application generic.* The instantiated class values relate to all the object instances.

The main difference, as to expected, is in the logic component of the objects—the private and public methods. In the case study the private methods have been called by the alternative term of daemons and the public methods as methods. The daemons are for editing the data properties in the data component when the objects instances are being inserted and updated. In most of the business class objects there is a daemon because the constituent data properties requires to be edited. If all the properties can be edited with a common procedure then there is no need for a daemon in the object. There are, of course no daemons in the system objects, as it is not necessary to edit the methods in these objects—it is assumed that the logic in the methods is "bug free".

All the business class objects contain at least one method, for the simple reason that they are needed to provide access to the data properties. Remember the data component in an object is encapsulated by the methods.

The first thing to notice about the methods is that the method is defined in each of the objects that the business requirement requires to access. Consider the business requirement to calculate the broker's commission. The requirement can be specified as "For a specified Broker calculate the commission for the last six months on the basis of the Share Allocations obtained and allocate the Commission according to the Commission Type". There will need to be a method in the Broker and Share Allocation objects, as there is user data in each of these objects the business requirement needs to access.

The application program for this business requirement would be designed something on these lines. The main procedure event object of the application program would issue a message to the Broker object instance specified in the business requirement along with the name of the method to be triggered, in this case Calc_Comm. The method in the Broker object would access the Broker Name and Broking % and send a message to the method of the same name in the Share Allocation class object, along with the search argument for the Share Allocations for the last six months. This method would access all the Share Allocations in the objectbase that had been purchased by the specified broker in the last six months. The method in Share Allocation would first access the Purchase Date and if it was within the last six months then access the No of Shares, the Initial Value and the No of Shares Sold and from this calculate the current value of the share allocation and use this as the basis of calculating the Commission Amount. When this has been done the Commission object can be inserted in the objectbase and a message sent back to the event object to that effect, along with the details about the commission and the broker. The event object can then display the details onto the screen.

This example of an object oriented application program is a relatively simple affair, with no property inheritance, and many programmers would recognise it as not very dissimilar from a conventional application program, the messages being module calls.

A more complicated example would be for the business requirement "Calculate the dividend for all shareholders of a specified company from a specified date". It is assumed that the object oriented product being used supports property inheritance.

The mechanism would be as follows. The event object would send a message to "all instances of Share Allocation for a specified Company and Purchase Date with a greater than value and the name of the method Calc_Dividend. The method in Share Allocation would access the No of Shares minus the No of Shares Sold as appropriate and store the value, lets call it M. It would then send a message to Shareholder for each Shareholder of the accessed Share Allocation, and again the name of the method would be Calc_Dividend (no inheritance here). The Calc_Dividend method in Shareholder obtains the name of the shareholder through inheritance from the Person object instance for each Shareholder instance accessed, and returns the Shareholder Number and Person Name (obviously also the Shareholder Name) to the Share Allocation method. This method also inherits the Current Dividend per Share from the Calc-Dividend method in the Company Value sub-class object of the Company class object (partial inheritance). This inheritance only needs to be done on the first Share Allocation accessed. The inheritance can then be overidden, as there is no need to access the same information for this business requirement. The result M is multiplied by the Dividend per Share to produce the Total Dividend Value. The Dividend can then be inserted for the Shareholder just accessed. A message is then returned to the event object giving the Total Dividend Value, the Person Name and the Shareholder No. The event object then displays this information for each Share Allocation accessed.

5.3.12.2 *The object instance information*

The data and logic components of objects can both be instantiated with values at the instance level. The values at the instance level override the class values, being the most specialised form of information.

Some of the data properties have to be instantiated at the instance level. Such examples are Date of Birth and Personal Assessment. Each person has unique birthdays and personal assessment. There is no general case. Other data properties do not have to be instantiated at the instance level because there is a general case. Such case study data properties are No of Legs and Bonus %. The general case is that all persons have two legs and all Star Employees have a bonus %. The exceptions are the person Henry, who only has one leg, and the employees Henry, Peter and Susan who have unique (to them) bonuses of 27%, 27% and 32%.

5.3.13 Benefits of object oriented design

The deficiences of the 4GL software development technology of the 80s is not sufficient for the 90s. The requirements for the 1990s include the ability:

- to treat all information, be it data or logic, in the same way;
  This is supported by the facility of normalising logic in the same way as data.

- of ensuring that the format and type of information is transparent to the user;
  This is handled by the subject facility using the relational frame and the object oriented class facilities.

- to write logic only once;
  There has long been a set of logical design techniques for normalising data into "clean" data objects as entities in relational form. For example, all the data that is directly relevant to a customer, such as customer name, customer address and customer telephone number, is stored in an object/entity of customer. The data is defined and stored only once. Physical technology to support data object/entities as tables has also long

been available, most particularly with relational file handlers. The benefits of data normalisation, principally in being the basis of entity data access, have long been appreciated. Similar techniques and technology has not been available for the normalisation of logic—until recently. The principal area of logic normalisation is therefore in object oriented programming. The benefit is the same—the logic is written and stored only once.

- to place information to its appropriate level of abstraction. If the information is a universal truth or more limited in its scope or even specific to an instance of something, then to be able to make it so in the design of the computer system;
  This is supported by the class and property inheritance facilities.

- to mix declarative and procedural logic;
  This is supported by the ability of the conclusion of a rule to incorporate a command that calls a procedure (declarative to procedural logic) and a procedure to contain logic that defines the condition or conclusion of a rule. There must be inference software that can recognise the symbolic matching of condition and conclusion logic statements.

- to handle uncertainty;
  The facilities for uncertainty in data and logic are described in section 5.2.6.

- to manage changes to the information, particularly the logic;
  This is handled by information encapsulation in the objects (to prevent a "ripple" effect from the changes to other objects) and by information abstraction through generalisation through the creation of super-class object or specialisation through the creation of sub-class objects of the existing objects in the object class model.

- to manage complexity in the information.
  This is supported by information abstraction.

There are other requirements, such as the need for "intelligent" query languages, but these are not appropriate to software development.

Added to the above functional requirements there are issues of software quality. Application independent designs and correctness, maintainability, robustness, extendibility, reuseability and compatibility of the software code are but some.

Object orientation is about all of these, but particularly software maintainability, extendibility and reuseability. There are other software quality features, such as portability and efficiency, but these are not benefited by the adoption of the object oriented approach.

Object oriented design is about using the mechanism of information normalisation to minimise software maintainability, maximise software reuse and extendibility and obtain the other characteristics of software quality.

Object orientation is already producing benefits. These include:

- *Application independent designs.* One of the major benefits of the normalisation of information is that it facilitates the creation of application independent information designs, that is the design of information that is generic to a corporation, not to a particular business requirement.

  To date the only part of information that has been corporate is data, hence the creation of corporate databases. The reason for this is that the data has been normalised to the appropriate entity/object and not to a business requirement/event of a functional area of the business. Customer Name is an attribute describing Customer, not a business requirement. It is therefore not specific to an application. The same data objects can be "accessed" by multiple functionally based applications.

  The same is true when the logic information is normalised to an object. If the logic is "All Customers with red hair get a lump sum of £100" then it, like the data, has nothing to do with a particular business requirement/event but with the Customer object, in the same way as Customer Name data. It is therefore normalised to the Customer class object. When logic is normalised like data then it has the same corporate characteristics as data—but in this case the logic can be "re-used" by multiple applications.

  The residue of logic from the business requirement will be all that is dependent on the applications. There is some logic that does not normalise to the business or system objects, such as Customers. The logic is relevant to the business requirement. Such logic could be the initialisation of the program variables, the formatting of the input and output data on the screen and the final processing of some data accessed from the information-base, such as the calculation of the bonus of the salesman for this month. This logic is the residue of logic that remains in the conventional application program main procedure, where logic has always been processed at the event, the business requirement, level. And it is the business requirements, by their very nature, that are application dependent.

  The more the logic can be moved away from event level processing and "normalised" to the business objects the greater the independence of the computer system from the application. The designs will be as corporate as possible.

  The benefits of this will be that the information is coded only once, is available for access, under controlled conditions, to multiple applications and users and is much more stable, being subject to change only when the corporation changes its business as a whole and not just a particular business requirement. The need to change the information will be restricted to the application specific parts in the event objects. Estimates have been made that this event logic is only some 20% of all current application program code.

- *The minimisation of code.* Normalised logic is written and stored only one. *Code minimisation is maximised*—there is therefore minimum logic/software maintenance.

- *Easier management of complexity.* By defining logic at the object level the overall complexity of a total application is broken down in a manner that accurately reflects the real world, in that objects are "things" in the real world. Instead of an enormous mass of code that is traditionally pitched at the business requirements/event level, most logic (80%) is now produced at the object level. The only object pitched at the event level is the main procedure event object.

With logic at the business requirement level it is often necessary to access *n* data objects, such that the logic code supporting these *n* objects can potentially be interwoven in an unfathomable sequence of statements. With the object oriented approach the business requirement invokes the appropriate object based logic by sending messages rather than access calls to the appropriate objects, each of which contains the appropriate data and logic. The objects are only accessed via the normalised logic stored in the methods for the data object. It is therefore impossible to interweave logic in an unnormalised manner. One can thus now develop an application incrementally an object at a time. Each object is a standalone and self-contained piece of information. It is the ultimate form of modular system construction.

But this is not the real way in which object orientation handles complexity and software reuse. Object oriented systems take the idea of software reuse much further. An object oriented system is already installed, and there is a need to increase the functionality of the system. This can be often done by the process of enhancing the design by addition through information abstraction and not modification. Assume that there is a need to treat employees differently according to new salary conditions negotiated with the unions. Instead of modifying the current code all that needs to be done is to create sub-classes of the Employee object according to the new salary conditions. For example, there could be sub-classes of employees depending on their engineering skills, each of which receives a different bonus. This is adding to the functionality of the current system by class object specialisation. The more specialised logic in the methods of the sub-class can use the logic in the Employee super-class for the basic salary information and then "finesse" it as appropriate. There could also be a need to create a more general class, as all employees now obtain a common holiday and other entitlements, whereas previously these were negotiated individually.

A general situation of great flexibility therefore exists. A library of business and system class objects might contain a class that has most of the properties needed for the new application. A new sub-class can be derived from the original super-class which has the additional properties required. This entails writing only the code to support the added features of the new sub-class. The rest of the code needed to implement the new class is simply inherited from the super-class definitions.

- *Reliability, ease of change and security.* Traditional procedural programming systems have the data and logic portions of application programs separated. This can lead to a number of problems, especially where more than one programmer is working on the same system. For example, it is relatively easy for one programmer to write a module that relies on side effects generated by code in another module. If this second module is changed, all the modules that relied on the side affect it produced are likely to fail. Change in one module can have an adverse effect on other modules. Change control is much more difficult to manage.

Encapsulation reduces these problems by limiting the information made available to programmers about the internals of an object. In object oriented programming systems the only information available to the programmer about an object is the list of messages to which the object will respond and the responses that such messages will generate. It is not necessary to make assumptions as to how to access an object. All that is required is to issue the message that corresponds to the desired response. One can also change the logic in daemons and methods in an object without any fear of a ripple effect to any daemons and methods on other objects. The interface presented is a common one throughout any program.

Abuse of the data in an object and illegal access is also prevented since it is only possible to access the data through messages.

- *Software Building Blocks.* The way that object oriented technology will evolve is illustrated in figure 5.42. The event objects will act as the "glue" that links the business objects and the system objects.

It has already been established that the system object contain methods that are generic system processes, many of which can be purchased as standard class libraries. The same will happen as regards the business objects. Packaged software is already widely available, but it is at the application level. One can buy an accounting or an inventory control package, because the business procedures for these business applications are recognised to be generic. It is now appreciated that in fact the granularity of the way we go about business operations can be made much smaller than whole applications. Individual steps can, and are,

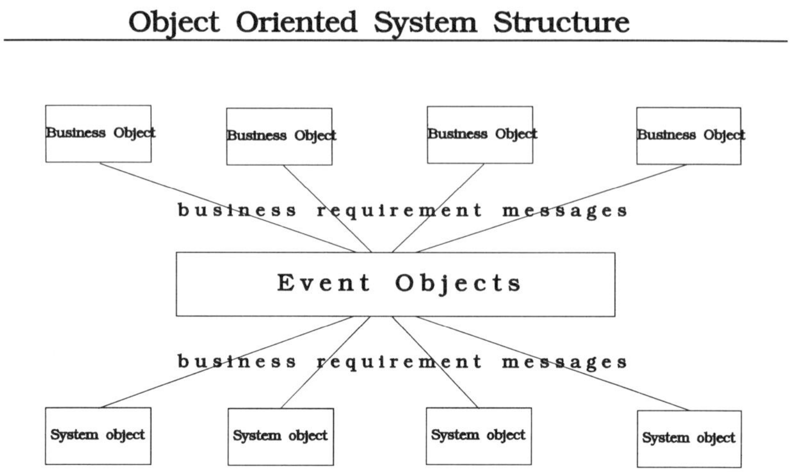

Object Oriented System Structure

Figure 5.42   Object oriented system structure

being written as methods, to be bought as class libraries in the same way as the generic system processes. Such steps could be for individual events, such as Place an Order or Receive Payment, or even more granular than that—add A to B. These generic business processes can also be developed as class libraries.

All that the event objects will require to do is the normal event level logic as already described and the selection of the class libraries appropriate to the business. One will eventually only require to write the logic that is unique to a company's business and the rest will largely be logic for the "cherry picking and glueing" of the business and system class libraries.

- *Natural "English" command based query languages.* Semantics have the benefit that a query language can be made much more user friendly and non-procedural in that the relationships between the objects to be accessed in a query can be specified using the semantics. The query can therefore be more in the form of a natural language and not in the form of a procedural join as in relational query languages. One could say "select the information in the commission earned by broker 123" (the semantic is underlined) rather than "select the information from broker 123 and commission where commission.broker_number = broker.broker_number".

The facilities of object orientation can be achieved with an object oriented programming language, but much requires to be "do it yourself". The message calls between objects have to be made explicit if property inheritance is to be achieved. But the full benefits of the object oriented approach can best be achieved with an object oriented database linked to an object oriented programming language. The language can be specific to the database, such as with GENERIS and its Intelligent Query Language, and ONTOS, which requires one of the traditional languages, such as C++. A number of object oriented databases and programming languages are now available which support object oriented design. One such product has already been identified as GOLDWORKS. GENERIS has been upgraded to support object orientation. Another is from an American company Ontologic with their object database OB2 (formerly called VBASE) and Servio Logic with GEMSTONE. The leading object oriented programming languages are C++, SIMULA (one of the first), EIFFEL and SMALLTALK.

As usual, the technology is ahead of the techniques. None of the leading structured design methods, such as Information Engineering and SSADM, explicitly support the concepts and techniques for object oriented design. However, methods specifically developed for object oriented design are already appearing, the prime example being HOOD (Hierarchical Object Oriented Design) from the European Space Agency. It has been designed specifically for the Ada programming language.

5.3.14 Does object orientation require a new way of thinking?

In discussion with people experienced in implementing object oriented systems the author has been consistently advised that a new way of thinking is required. "You need to throw away much of what you have learnt before about systems design and development and apply new ways of thinking".

The author is not so sure. It was stated in chapter 1 that Information Engineering is generic, because the facilities of the batch and online data processing environment for which it is designed are common to the other and more recent data processing, such as object orientation. Why should object oriented systems be fundamentally different from the generic facilities of centralised processing when the other data processing environments (distributed, realtime, conversational) are nothing more than centralised plus a little bit?

The author has heard conflicting views on this. Based on initial practical experiences a picture of reality as opposed to opinion is emerging. The logical component parts of a computer system are illustrated in figure 2.4. There are two ways in which existing software implementation technology and design techniques can be enhanced—by addition or by modification. The former is much to be preferred if possible, because it preserves the investments in the existing computer systems. *What is becoming clear is that the traditional technologies and techniques for data structure require addition, while those for access and process logic require modification.* But even for the part requiring modification there is a position of comfort. The technique for normalising logic is, as already stated, the same as that for data. We are therefore adding the technique for the design of data to the technique for the design of logic. Even when undertaking message access path analysis against the class object model, which produces a very different access path from that against a traditional logical data model, it is the same technique of access path analysis that is applied.

It is therefore much more a situation of using existing technologies and techniques and enhancing them by addition. The author cannot think of anything that requires a practitioner of relational and other database file handlers to unlearn his/her skills. Apply it differently in some parts, yes, but unlearn no.

However, it does have to be said that, as the author acquires more understanding of object oriented technology and techniques, that his sympathy for the original "throwaway and be reborn again" argument has some merit. It is clear that object orientation is a major subject, with a substantial array of technical facilities to that of traditional processing. The main features that distinguish object oriented design from batch and online processing are property inheritance in the object hierarchy diagram, encapsulation, property instantiation at the class and instance level, polymorphism, function name overloading, logic normalisation and message passing between objects. These facilities have resulted in certain aspects of logical and physical design requiring very different thinking and application, such as:

- much logic is no longer at the event level. With traditional processing it has all been assumed that it is at the event level, the only logic that is appropriate to more than one event being the common procedures.

- the access paths against the logical data model being top down, from the master to the detail entity. This is reversed if there is a need to take advantage of property inheritance.

- a reversion to record-at-a-time processing. The devotees of relational technology will not be too pleased. The author has never be a devotee of relational technology. Of the two features of database technology, data structures and data access, relational file handlers are fine as regards data structure, but flawed as regards data access. Object orientation takes advantage of relational technology on the storage of object, but has abandoned relational set data access.

- the "version" of the method logic to be invoked is automatically taken care of depending on the object instance being processed (by polymorphism) or the argument being passed (by function name overloading).

These are features that are not considered within generic batch and online centralised processing. It is not a case of adding. Certain of these features genuinely require a different approach to logical and physical design. *It seems that, of all the other data processing environments, object orientation does require some modification to the logical and physical techniques of centralised processing.*

It is argued by some (B. Meyer in "Object-oriented Software Construction" Prentice Hall) that object oriented design is the antithesis of the traditional analysis and design structured methods, such as SSADM. These methods typically use the top-down approach of taking a high level process and decomposing it down into its constituent sub-processes. This approach is good at ensuring that the design will meet the initial user requirements, but it does not promote reuseability—the sub-processes may overlap. Reuseable software requires that systems are designed by combining existing elements as much as possible, which is the definition of bottom-up design.

It is quite true that process decomposition is not well suited to assist in software reuse. This is because of the paucity of advice in SSADM as to how to decompose processes properly. This has been rectified in chapter 3. Object orientation merely takes the process one step further. Section 3.2.1 shows that process decomposition should be to the business area, function, event and problem-to-solve level. This is fine for traditional data processing. The additional step for object orientation is that the logic in the processes needs to be normalised to the object to which it sensibly relates. What the author is finding is that it is sensible to decompose processes to the event level and then to apply the rules of normalisation to the logic, so as to place the logic into the object to which it sensibly belongs. Given that the data in object oriented systems remains the same as in traditional processing, this normalisation of logic should be all that is needed in logical design!

The application of the design and development techniques for object oriented systems is detailed below.

5.3.15 Enhancements to Information Engineering

Underlying all the enhancements to the Information Engineering design techniques is the concept of the normalisation of logic and the class facility. Everything concerning information design ultimately hangs from these two features of object orientation.

5.3.15.1 ERD modelling and relational data analysis

The title to this section should be changed to class object modelling and relational information modelling. The class facility is the new feature added for the abstraction of super and sub-class objects from the entities of the logical data model and the rules of data normalisation can be applied to logic. All information, be it data or logic, can be normalised. The structure of data in the logical data model is unchanged. Objects can still be based on keys, relate to each other via foreign keys and contain properties of information. All the entities in a traditional logical data model remain in a class object model. The same is true of the techniques. The enhancement to the existing data modelling techniques to support the concept(s) of the new data processing environment are by the process of addition. The additions are:

- Class. Once the entities are identified in the traditional way the "practised eye" is applied to see if the entities have a common behaviour and therefore belong to a common class object hierarchy. There may be abstraction through generalisation or through specialisation in the form of super-class and sub-class objects to the objects (formerly entities) of the object class model (formerly a logical data model). As described in section 5.3.4.5 the abstraction can go as general as the Company and Object objects and as specialised as necessary. Where there is a class hierarchy the inheritance semantic needs to be applied to the relationship between the objects. With an inheritance semantic there is no need to specify a semantic description of the relationship from super-class to sub-class object and vica versa. Where there is no class hierarchy, business semantics need to be applied in the normal SSADM manner.

  Some practical "tricks of the trade" are emerging to help in the identification of common behaviour between objects.

  Is the property applicable to all "versions" of the class object? If it is not this is indicative of a class object structure, with the attribute requiring to be defined at a lower more specialised level in the class structure. Consider the vehicle object in the class object model in figure 5.30. Assume that as a result of data normalisation it contains the property of Pulled Force. Closer inspection shows that this property is not applicable to the class object Vehicle, being relevant to a class object Trailer. The Trailer needs to be defined as a sub-object to Vehicle. Users of relational file handlers will recognise this facility as nothing more than entity sub-types. The difference with object orientation is that there is now technology to take advantage of the inheritance between the super-type and sub-type class objects.

  Can an inherited data property not apply to an object sub-type? Is property override required? Using the Vehicle example again, it could be that there are other object sub-types to Vehicle, such as Car, Lorry and Van. The Lorry object has in turn object sub-types of Articulated and Standard Lorry. The Number of Passengers property defined in the Vehicle object is relevant to Car and Van but not to the Lorry object and therefore not to Articulated and Standard Lorry. It would be wasteful to define Number of Passengers as a property to the Car and Van objects, as the benefit of inheritance from the Vehicle object would be lost. Yet inheritance of Number of Passengers would not be appropriate to Lorry, but is relevant for other Vehicle attributes. There should therefore be defined in the Lorry object an ability to inherit from the Vehicle object but not for all the properties, that is the attribute of Number of Passengers *switched off*. It may be that there is *partial inheritance* in a class structure. The handling of partial inheritance was described in section 5.2.4.7.

- Class objects with keys. These are class objects which relate to *n* object instances of the class, where n can be zero. The commonly used example for this is the Employee class object. The key is used as the standard facility of uniquely identifying each object instances in the objectbase. The relationship between the class objects in the class object model can be based on the foreign key facility as in relational technology.

- Class objects without keys. There can be class only objects, that is class objects which do not relate to any object instances of the class, the class object Man being the commonly used example of this. Man is a "one off". Such objects do not require keys for their identification. This means that the facility of foreign keys to relate entities objects together will not work. Such class objects can only relate to other class objects through the "is a" type semantic description.

- The possible instantiation of the data properties (formerly attributes) of the class objects. Data normalisation relates to both class data and instance data. There has been no distinction between this in traditional relational analysis. Both levels of data are defined as properties of an object. The rules of data normalisation are therefore relevant to all data properties in an object, irrespective of whether the property is at the class or instance level. The only question to answer is: at what level should the properties be given a value/be instantiated? It is not a case of saying if the same property value can be stored in multiple table rows then the property value is at the class level. The Order Received Date property in the Order class object can contain the same values for many orders, solely on the basis that many orders could have been received on the same date. However, Order Received Date is not a class property. The policy to be followed is that, if the same property value is relevant to *all* instances of the class *except* in explicitly stated exception conditions, then the property is at the class level. In the worked example Henry is the explicitly stated exception of having only one leg, whereas all other persons have two legs. The different property value is the exception, not the other way around.

Once the level of the property is ascertained then it can be recorded in the document describing the properties. An additional column needs to be added to indicate whether the property is at the class or instance level, and if it is at the class level, to be instantiated with a value.

• The semantic descriptions. The upgrades required to the semantics of the relationships between the objects have been described in section 5.2.4.7. It is primarily the description of the "is a" type semantic for the relationship where such a description is sensible (person "is a" man), with inheritance being automatically provided, and free form where such a description is not sensible (person "owns a" car), with the statement as to whether inheritance is required. Some object based products do not use the relationship semantic for this purpose, and define inheritance in the description of the object itself—object B inherits from object A.

• The addition of logic properties to the class objects. These are, of course, the private and public methods. All the class objects must contain at least one public method, as the data properties can only be accessed via the public methods. The instance objects do not require to have a public method, as the class method is the usual way the instance objects are accessed.

• The addition of system objects. These were described in section 5.3.4.2.

• The different placement of the data properties in the class object model from logical data modelling. This is addressed in the next section.

Object orientation makes no use of inter-property semantics.

5.3.15.2 *The normalisation of information*

This term Relational Data Analysis is no longer adequate because it is no longer appropriate to relational technology or to data. It should be replaced by the term Information Normalisation, because the rules of normalisation that have been for so long applicable to data are equally applicable to logic, so that all information, both data and logic, can be normalised.

Database technology is characterised by the separation of data and logic—the data in the databse and the logic in application programs. This is illogical. After all both the data and the logic are nothing more than information.

There are two aspects to consider for the normalisation of information in an object oriented environment:

• the normalisation of logic;

• the introduction of the concept of the role of the information that is being normalised.

The normalisation of data (object oriented)   The rules developed by Dr Codd do not support the concept of the role of the information to be normalised. This is an omission for object orientation. Consider the objects Person and Employee and the data property of Date of Birth. The application is an employee system that records all the instances of employees for a company. But the employees are persons and therefore the class object of Person is abstracted as a more general super-class to Employee. Should the Date of Birth be defined as a data property of Person or the Employee. From the role point of view the data property is relevant to Person and not to Employee— it has nothing to do with employment. With a relational approach to data modelling the Date of Birth could happily reside in the Employee entity and not break the rules of data normalisation—is the data dependent on the key, the whole and nothing but the key?—yes. But with object orientation this is not adequate. Given the abstraction of the Person class object Date of Birth belongs to Person. But there are no instances of Person in the employee system.

There are two choices. Put Date of Birth as a property of Employee and do not take advantage of object orientation or put Date of Birth as a property of Person and make it support instances of Person, one for every employee.

The problem with the object oriented approach is that where there was one table with the relational approach there is now two—and disk I/O is bound to go up.

The normalisation of logic (procedural)   The work of Dr Codd defined the rules for the normalisation of data, and the rules have been widely accepted and applied. *The author believes that the rules for data normalisation are as relevant to logic as they are to data.* Why not—is it just information; just the data? All that needs to be done is to alter the phraseology of the rules to cater for logic.

An example of the normalisation of logic up to first normal form is given in figure 5.40. The rule of first normal form of data is "Take out repeating groups". The test for repetition is "For a given value of the key is there more than one possible value of the data?" Suitably rephrased the wording becomes "For a given value of the key is there more than one version of the logic?"

Figure 5.43 shows the normalisation of the logic for the business requirement of calculating salaries, the logic of which varies depending on whether the object is an Employee, Star Employee, Star Employee Bonus or Employee Bonus. The logic for the business requirement is in the method called Calc_Sal, with the logic "normalised" to the objects the logic is pertinent to. All Employees receive a salary of £10,000; the Star Employees recieve an additional £2,000; the Star Employee Bonus is a further £1,000 and the Employee Bonus is £500 on the basic salary. Thus the logic for calculating the bonus of £1,000 is appropriate to Star Employee Bonus and

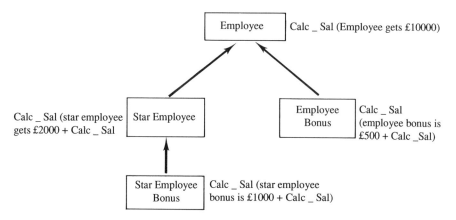

Figure 5.43

is therefore normalised to the Star Employee Bonus class object. It can be seen that the sub-class object contains the logic that is additional to the logic of the method of the super-class. Thus the calculation of the Star Employee Bonus is the combined logic of the Star Employee Bonus (£1,000), Star Employee (£2,000) and Employee (£10,000).

Figure 5.44 shows an example of logic that is normalised to second normal form. The rule of second normal form for data is "Test for part key dependence". The test is "Is the data dependent on the whole key or part of the key?" Again suitably rephrased the test would be "Is the logic dependent on the whole key or part of the key?" The key of the stock object is a compound key of Product Code and Depot Code. The method Calc_Stk_Value is in second normal form in that it is calculating the value of the stock of a product at a depot. The method Increase_Product_Price is not in second normal form in that it is only relevant to product—it is calculating the increase in the price of a product and has nothing to do with the stock at a depot.

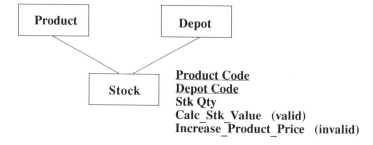

Figure 5.44   The normalisation of logic (2NF at the class level)

The author has not been able to find an example of normalising logic from second to third normal form, but is sure that examples must exist.

What has also proved very appropriate are the two data normalisation tests applied after the relations have been optimised. A suitable rephrasing for logic would be:

- for a given value of the key(s) of an object, is there only one possible version of the logic?

- is the logic in the logic property dependent directly on the key(s)?

This is a perfectly valid way of showing the normalisation of the logic is correct.

The examples given so far are to business objects that one would see in a traditional logical data model. The normalisation of logic is also appropriate to the system objects as well:

- The Object object. The Object object contains logic that is universally applicable. An application that the author is familiar with was a system for the handling of chemicals. If the author knew then what he knows now the chemical formulae would convert into methods that contain logic that is universally recognised to be laws of chemistry and therefore universally true. The logic for these laws would become method properties in the Object object.

- The application object. This class object contains information that is unique to an application, the example given in section 5.3.4.2 being that of the policy for the accounting system whereby proceedings are taken out if invoices have not been paid within 6 months.

- The logic properties to handle domain objects. The best example of a domain object is date, which is to be found as a data property in several objects, for example Date of Birth in Person and Date Joined Company in Employee. The domain values of Date are generic (any domain property is generic) to all types of date and are therefore identified as a separate class object. Since it is applicable application wide, it relates as a sub-class to the Object object. A date's properties could be either a set of valid instantiated date values or a daemon to ascertain valid dates. Another domain object could be X-Windows. With the X-Window object there could be further sub-objects of Scrollable-Windows, Text-Windows and Graphics-Windows.

- The logic contained in the common procedure objects. The procedures could be for a commonly used business process, such as calculating a discount rate. Being generally applicable to the business such common procedure objects are related as sub-classes to the Object object.

- The logic contained in the system objects, typically for system type procedures, such as numeric editing, storing an object and string handling. Being generally applicable the objects would be defined as subclasses to the Object object.

Many would recognise the above object types as class libraries.

- The logic contained in the event objects, that is the logic that is specific to the business requirement. This event level logic by its nature cannot be normalised to a business object, as the logic is not relevant to any key of a business object. Typically the logic would be the issuing of the messages to the other objects, the synchronisation of the message responses received from the objects and any final processing before the information is output and screen formatting.

The normalisation of logic (declarative)   This has caused the author much thought and the answer is still not clear. There is no reason that declarative logic cannot be normalised like procedural logic—it is nothing than another way of representing information. But that reasoning is the simple part. Does one normalise the logic of the rules based on the conditions or the conclusions? Unforetunately the condition is usually about A and the conclusion about B. To which object, A or B, should the rule go? An extreme example could be "If the world is round and Joe Bloggs is big and the President of the United States is on the campaign trail then it is raining and necessary to get your car repaired". Where does one start with that rule?

How about normalising the rules to the query that they are providing advice to? But what if the query itself has components that are to be found in multiple queries? The ruleset in figure 5.5 has the query about purchasing a computer with a printer. There could well be another query about advice for selling a computer with a printer and the rules in figure 5.5 could well be relevant to selling as well as to purchasing.

If declarative logic is to be combined with object oriented design then it requires to be normalised. The author is not aware of any solution to this problem. At the moment people are designing around it.

5.3.15.3 *Process decomposition diagrams/dataflow diagrams*

The techniques are unchanged, the only addition to consider being the decomposition of the processes.

One of the problems of both related techniques is that most of the methods that use them do not provide very good advice as to how to decompose the processes and to what level of decomposition to go to.

Advice such as "Decompose until you get to a satisfactory level of detail" and "Lower level processes contain more detail" is not very helpful. Advice to both of these questions is provided in section 3.2.1.

Object oriented processing provides the answer to one of these questions—the level to which you decompose. *What the author has found most practical is to decompose the processes to the event level, as detailed in section 3.2.1, and then to normalise the logic to the objects to which they appropriately belong.* The normalisation of logic is described in section 5.3.16.2. This approach has the advantage that the traditional approach to decomposition is preserved as far as possible.

The event level logic is normalised to the main procedure/event object and the remaining logic to the other objects as appropriate. Most of the logic is normalised to the business objects the event requires to access. The example of the Calc_Sal being decomposed into four methods of the same name, with one method being normalised to the Employee object and the others being decomposed to the Star Employee, Employee Bonus and Star Bonus objects perfectly represents this. The methods in the Employee and Star Employee objects are to do with the calculation of the basic and star salary and the methods in the Employee Bonus and Star Bonus are to do with the calculation of the bonus of both employee types.

5.3.15.4 ELHs

The entities/objects now contain logic properties as well as data properties. Both property types can be inserted, updated and deleted and therefore both property types have lives. The approach adopted by the author has been to keep the two property types separate—they have very different and separate lives, even though they belong to a single object.

The data properties can have many different events affecting them, they can occur in sequence, can iterate and can be selective, can incur quits and resumes and can occur in parallel, all in a potentially highly complicated manner. The ELH technique is unchanged for the data properties of objects from that described in section 3.2.7. The state variable used to monitor the correct sequencing of the object's data life is tested in the logic of the general purpose attributes editing method of each object containing user data.

The logic properties, by contrast, have simple lives—they are entered, potentially undergo n iterations of code modification and are deleted. Each modification of code in a logic property is the same event, although clearly different lines of code can be affected. The life of the logic properties is therefore in a standard ELH form—an insert, followed by n iterations of updates, followed by a delete.

The final reason for separating the lives of the logic properties from the data properties is that their lives are also independent of each other. The updates to the logic are asynchronous to and in no way affect the lives of the data properties.

To be honest the author has not bothered with constructing an entity life history of the logic properties in an object.

5.3.15.5 Dialogue design

There are two types of screens—menu screens and transactions. The transactions screens support the man/machine interface for a business requirement.

The menu screens are not pitched at the event/business requirement level. The menu screens contain options for/are generic to the selection of many business requirements. The menu selection and screen formatting logic is therefore not normalisable to a natural object in the class object model. They should be normalised to their own class objects.

If the logic for transaction screen handling is generic to many business requirements then the logic should normalisable to a common procedure class object. If the screen logic is unique to a business requirement then it should be normalised to the event object for the business requirement to which it is unique.

5.3.15.6 Transaction access path analysis

It must be appreciated that in the action diagrams access logic to tables of data is now replaced by messages between objects. Transaction access path maps are replaced by message path maps, with the access call being replaced by a message.

It also needs to be remembered that the inheritance facility should provide automatic access between objects, but only when accessing from the sub-object to its super-object. It is therefore necessary that messages are sent to the lowest object(s) in the class model for the business requirement if inheritance is required. This was seen in the second worked example of an object oriented application program. The sequence of message calls to objects in the objectbase is therefore not the same as that for accessing tables in the database.

Summary access path maps need to be replaced by summary message maps. The same principle of counting the number of messages times the volume of the transactions applies. Data movement is now by explicit message passing between object methods rather than by implicit access by a file handler to the table rows. An object can receive and send many message types, the message invoking a method(s)/daemon(s) with an argument, which can be data derived from the other objects already accessed and/or a parameter to undertake some task.

5.3.15.7 Action diagrams

The action diagrams contain the logic of the methods and daemons and
must therefore name the object to which the method/daemon "belongs".
Processing in object oriented systems is still event level triggered. The sending
of messages between the objects to be accessed for the event are all initially
triggered when the event/business requirement occurs. As we have seen
in non-object oriented systems application programs are pitched at the
event level and the constituent modules at the problem-to-solve level. What
is true of traditional batch and online centralised processing is also true
of object oriented processing. Once again it is a case of the facilities of
centralised processing being generic, with the facilities of object orientation
being additions. *Application programs in object oriented systems are also event
based but, instead of being composed of problem-to-solve modules, are composed of
a set of normalised object base methods but one.* As explained in section 5.3.5.3,
the "but one" is the main procedure/event method object, the logic of which
is still pitched at the event level. The succeeding objects are "chained" in
the sequence required to be accessed for the processing to proceed, as in
conventional processing, either under the control of the "central policeman"
or "round robin" policy of message passing.

The approach adopted by the author is still to use the action diagrams
for the specification of methods and daemons, be the logic to the various
class objects in the object class model or to the separate event object. The
logic properties to all the class object needs to be defined as part of the
object description—it is after all just another property that happens to
contain logic rather than data. The event level action diagrams become
the main procedure objects in the application programs and the object class
model object level action diagrams become the daemons or methods in the
appropriate system, domain, common procedure and business class objects.

5.3.15.8 Database design

In line with the concept of logical design = physical design database design
has already been done. At a more specific level it needs to be appreciated
that the design rules of database design have not been updated to reflect
object oriented file handlers. However, the principles of database design
are unchanged, except that the entities in the entity model become objects
and not tables. Clearly the definition of the data properties in the database
schema is unchanged, but the schema also needs to include the definitions
of the daemons and methods, data property instantiation and inheritance
specification.

It was stated earlier that the merging of data and logic would eliminate
the inefficiency found in "conventional" systems of moving the data to

the logic. However, care needs to be taken. Some object oriented systems are proving to be very inefficient, particularly those that are not able to store the logic properties of an object as a separate record, but chained from the "home" object. With logic now being treated as data it is pulled into the buffer pool rather than main memory, as in conventional program processing. Thus the buffer pool can become rapidly "clogged up" with logic, with a consequent rise in disk I/O. This is particularly the case when the logic properties are not stored as separate records, because much of the logic in the buffer pool is unwanted. The inefficiency is therefore avoidable. With object oriented systems there should be no distinction between main memory and the buffer pool. Processor architecture needs to be altered.

5.3.15.9 Program design

The basic mechanism of program identification and batch program sequencing in Information Engineering is unchanged for object oriented design. In a practical world the author has found that module identification in an object oriented design is simple. The processing that is at the event level is within the application program main procedure event object. Typically this logic is concerned with initialisation of program variables, the synchronisation of the message responses, any processing dependent on the synchronised responses and any screen formatting. The "modules" are the normalised logic in the daemons and methods within the other objects. Methods can in turn issue further messages to other methods in the same or other objects, thus creating the classic program structure chart. The format of the messages and their returned information can be defined as in conventional programming.

Program structure charts are perfectly valid in object oriented programming.

INDEX

action diagrams, 19, 21, 40, 44, 45, 46, 50, 62, 63, 71, 72, 73, 81, 82, 88, 89, 94, 104, 114, 116, 172, 175, 176, 184, 189, 251, 259, 266, 270, 404, 405
ADABAS, 117, 215
AT&T, 351

backward chaining, 283, 286, 287, 288, 289, 291, 292, 293, 294, 314, 315, 338, 339
Bayesian probability, 308, 312, 337
Boston Consultancy Group, 97
Boyce/Codd, 166, 167

C++, 351, 364, 366, 371, 373, 393
CACI, 25
canonical synthesis, 20, 86, 111
cardinality, 45, 76, 102, 104, 105, 133, 188, 215, 216, 217, 218, 219, 234, 236
  ratios, 76, 106, 338
  statistics, 105, 217, 218
Central Computing and Telecommunication Agency, 23
centralised processing, 5, 7, 8, 11, 155, 203, 204, 205, 206, 210, 213, 214, 332, 393, 394, 395, 405
certainty factors, 308, 310
Chen, Peter, 251

class
  facility, 297
  object, 298, 299, 343, 345, 346, 347, 349, 350, 351, 352, 353, 354, 356, 358, 361, 362, 368, 370, 371, 373, 379, 380, 385, 395, 396, 397, 401, 405
classical probability, 308, 309, 311, 312, 337
cluster analysis, 23
co-operative systems, 197
Codasyl, 20, 21, 34, 35, 75, 115, 117, 134, 202, 298
Codd, 73, 174, 399
concurrency control, 34, 203, 204, 205, 206, 207, 208, 209, 212, 223, 249
conflict graph analysis, 208, 209, 248
conflict resolution, 282, 283, 296, 304, 343, 355, 357, 358
Constantine, 26
conversational processing, 2, 4, 6, 10, 11, 115, 192, 267, 271
critical success factors, 24, 42, 97, 99
CRYSTAL, 284

D2S2, 25
DAFNE, 27
data redundancy, 125, 130
data views, 20, 69, 90, 115